The Letters of
Dorothy L. Sayers

1899–1936: The Making of a Detective Novelist

Also by Barbara Reynolds

Dorothy L. Sayers: Her Life and Soul
The Passionate Intellect: Dorothy L. Sayers' Encounter with Dante

Translations

La Vita Nuova
Paradiso (with Dorothy L. Sayers)
Orlando Furioso

The Letters of Dorothy L. Sayers

1899–1936: The Making of a Detective Novelist

Chosen and Edited by Barbara Reynolds
with a Preface by P. D. James

Hodder & Stoughton

Introduction and notes Copyright © 1995 by Barbara Reynolds
Preface Copyright © 1995 by P. D. James
Letters Copyright © 1995 by the estate of Dorothy L. Sayers

First published in Great Britain in 1995 by Hodder and Stoughton
A division of Hodder Headline PLC

10 9 8 7 6 5 4 3 2 1

British Library Cataloguing in Publication Data

A CIP catalogue record for this title
is available from the British Library

ISBN 0 340 53623 3

Printed and bound in Great Britain by
Mackays of Chatham PLC, Chatham, Kent

Hodder and Stoughton
A division of Hodder Headline PLC
338 Euston Road
London NW1 3BH

Contents

Acknowledgments

The majority of the letters represented here are in the possession of the Marion E. Wade Center at Wheaton College, Illinois. My first thanks therefore are due to that institution and in particular to the Associate Director of the Wade Center, Mrs Marjorie Lamp Mead, who has done everything possible to facilitate my task. I am grateful also to Mr Tony Dawson for typing onto disc the many hundreds of letters from which I made my choice. I also thank Mr Laurence Harbottle, executor of the estate of Anthony Fleming, for the original commission to proceed with the work and for his skill and patience in negotiating various legal difficulties which delayed progress for several years. Mr Bruce Hunter of David Higham Associates, acting as my literary agent, gave me valuable advice and assistance, for which I am most grateful. Miss Carolyn Caughey of Hodder and Stoughton, Publishers, set firm guide lines and patiently helped and encouraged me to conform to them when the avalanche of material threatened to overwhelm us both. I thank her most warmly. I also thank Mrs Christine Casley who as editorial reader brought consistency to the lay-out and made several helpful suggestions.

For permission to publish seven letters to Wilfrid Scott-Giles and to quote from his book *The Wimsey Family*, I am indebted to Mr Giles Scott-Giles and to his sister Mrs Rosemary Bundy. For the four letters to Donald Tovey, I thank the Reid Music Library, Edinburgh University and Mr Roger Savage who discovered them. I thank Ms Kathryn L. Beam for negotiating permission for me to publish two letters to Maurice Browne belonging to the Volkenburg-Browne Papers, Special Collections Library, University of Michigan. For six letters to Helen Simpson I thank Mrs Clemence Hamilton, her daughter. Mrs Fortuna Fleming kindly allowed me to choose from a third of some eighty letters in her possession written by Dorothy to her parents in the early years of her marriage. I thank her for this concession. For the letter to F. J. H. Jenkinson I thank the Syndics of the Cambridge University Library. For the letter to Arnold Bennett I am indebted to University College London Library (Ms. Ogden 96 / 11 Arnold Bennett Collection). I recall with special gratitude that the late Sir Ashley Clarke first showed me the letters to Harold W. Bell when I was his guest at the British Embassy in Rome in 1962. He later sent me copies and gave me permission to publish them.

Many people have kindly answered questions and helped me with the annotations. I thank first three members of the Dorothy L. Sayers Society: Mr Christopher Dean (Chairman), Mr Philip L. Scowcroft (Research Officer), and Mrs Christine Simpson (Publications Officer). I thank also Miss Pauline Adams, Librarian and Archivist of Somerville College, the Rev. Colin Backhouse, Rector of Bluntisham, and Mrs Ingrid Backhouse, Messrs Samuel French, Miss Livia Gollancz, Professor Detlev Karsten, Professor John M. Kernochan, Mr Andrew Lewis, Mrs Penelope A. Penney, Dr William Radice, Mrs Brigid Somerset, H. E. Mr Adrian Thorpe, and Mrs J. B. Williamson, Clubhouse Librarian of the Royal Automobile Club.

I am most grateful to Baroness James of Holland Park for her Preface and for all her encouragement and enthusiasm about the project from the outset.

To all these people and institutions, and to any I may have inadvertently omitted, I express my gratitude.

Barbara Reynolds

Illustrations

Most of the illustrations are published here for the first time. Mrs Evelyn Bedford (*née* Compline), who knew the Sayers family from girlhood, lent me the photograph reproduced on the jacket. I owe thanks to her also for the information that in the smile and glance of the eyes Dorothy here much resembles her father.

I thank the Godolphin School, Salisbury, in particular the Bursar and Clerk to the Governors, Commander J. Loring, R.N., for finding and allowing me to reproduce part of a staff photograph taken in 1909. I thank the Master and Fellows of Balliol College for the photograph of Maurice Roy Ridley taken at the period when Dorothy L. Sayers recognized him as 'the *perfect* Peter Wimsey'. I thank Mr John Culme for the photograph of Lewis Waller. The photograph of Hugh Allen is reproduced from Cyril Bailey's *Hugh Percy Allen* (Oxford University Press, 1948). Several photographs, hitherto unknown, I owe to Mr Jack Reading, who most kindly made available glass negatives originally in the possession of Muriel St Clare Byrne. I am especially grateful to Mrs Brigid Somerset, the daughter of the Rev. Leonard Hodgson, who supplied the photograph of Dorothy walking in a wood, which may have been taken by him. To the Marion E. Wade Center I express thanks for three photographs of Dorothy as a child, the reproduction of a cartoon by David Low and of the letters it inspired and the 'fake' photograph with Eustace Barton. For the photograph with Helen Simpson, taken at the Detective Club, I thank Mrs Clemence Hamilton.

Preface
by P. D. James

Dorothy L. Sayers, novelist, poet, dramatist, amateur theologian and Christian apologist, is one of the most versatile writers of her generation; she is also one of the most controversial. To her admirers she is the writer who did more than any other of her age to lift the detective story from its status as an inferior puzzle to a respected craft with claims to be taken seriously as popular literature. Her detractors, deploring what they see as her snobbery and elitism, and focussing their dislike on her aristocratic detective, Lord Peter Wimsey, would deny her any claim to be more than an outdated and pretentious entertainer. But the fact that, thirty-eight years after her death, she can still provoke controversy and stimulate argument, and is read with pleasure by a new generation, is a measure of the resilience of her talent, as is the number of biographies and studies published in recent years. Chief among these, of course, is Barbara Reynolds' sensitive and authoritative biography *Dorothy L. Sayers: Her Life and Soul*, for which the biographer drew on Sayers' private letters. Now with this, the first volume of the letters, Dorothy L. Sayers is revealed as a remarkable letter-writer whose correspondence both identifies and explains the woman and sets a private life in the social context of an extraordinary and tumultuous century.

To an extent this first volume is an hors d'oeuvre, a satisfying and substantial pleasure to the taste buds, but one which stimulates our appetite for the second course of letters, written when Dorothy L. Sayers entered her most successful years. Dr Reynolds has wisely followed the logical course of presenting the letters in chronological order so that we have what is in effect an epistolary autobiography covering, in this first volume, Dorothy L. Sayers' childhood and schooldays, her time as an Oxford undergraduate and the difficult years in which she was searching for a career and for emotional satisfaction, followed by marriage, maternity and increasing success. The last section covers the six years from 1930–1936 which Dr Reynolds has entitled 'Celebrated Author and Private Person'.

Barbara Reynolds' footnotes are particularly successful, providing both fact and comment. When in doubt she assumes ignorance on the part of the reader and, although English readers may not need to be told that 'the Bod' is short for the Bodleian Library, and 'Eights Week' is about rowing at Oxford, overseas readers may well be less informed. Nothing is more irritating than collections of letters in which the editor assumes that all readers share her knowledge. Dr Reynolds also consistently relates the events of Dorothy L. Sayers' life to the detective stories, a relationship which is one of the most fascinating aspects of the correspondence.

Personal letters can be the most revealing of all literary forms especially when, as in this case, they were not intended for publication. Dorothy L. Sayers had most of the qualities necessary for a lively and successful correspondent; command of language, honesty, self-confidence, a lively interest in other people, humour, strong opinions and a pugnacious appetite for a fight in a good cause. It is interesting to see how her earlier letters from her father's rectory at Bluntisham, and later from the Godolphin School at Salisbury which she entered as a boarder in January 1909, reveal the essential character of the woman she was to become. In later letters she writes that she hated school, but there is almost no evidence of this in the lively accounts she wrote home, letters full of news about cathedral services, excursions to Old Sarum to see the excavations, visiting drama companies, her own playwriting and acting, and her part in the varied life of the school. The Godolphin seems to have provided an education as liberal and enlightened for the age as it was thorough. But she may well have been unhappy. It couldn't have been easy at fifteen to leave the shelter of the rectory, where she was a precociously intelligent and indulged only child, and be thrown into the competitive and judgemental maelstrom of a girls' boarding-school. But, except in her letters to the only man she loved in her life, she is always reticent about personal unhappiness. She was, too, protective of her parents all her life and as a schoolgirl she may have felt that the confession of real misery could only cause them pain. But it was probably also a matter of pride. To admit to unhappiness might suggest that she was less successful and less popular than she wanted her parents to believe. All her life, the boisterous self-confidence and occasional exhibitionism guarded a heart that was both proud and stoical, and one that was capable of keeping its secrets.

Most of the letters Dorothy L. Sayers wrote from Oxford – she went up in October 1912 as a scholar of Somerville College – are a continuation of the schoolgirl's routine of a weekly letter home and are similar to those from the Godolphin: exuberant, egotistical and uninhibited. We would like to have had some of her parents' replies. Sometimes they must have felt physically battered by these weekly missives from their self-opinionated and forceful daughter.

She was in France when war broke out and had some difficulty in getting home, but the war, its politics, progress and justification, seems to have made little impact on her life. We find none of the self-searching idealism of Winifred Holtby or Vera Brittain, but unlike Vera Brittain she had no lover or brother involved. For families at home with no relative at the Front it was possible to remain virtually immune to the horrors, if not the inconveniences, of the First World War. A letter in May 1915 sets out Dorothy L. Sayers' proposal to take a month's nursing training at any hospital which would have her with a view to nursing in France, but it came to nothing, and it is difficult to imagine her submitting to the hierarchical and draconian discipline of the Army Nursing Service. In a letter dated 27 July 1915 to her friend Muriel Jaeger written from Bluntisham Rectory, she describes how a cousin and uncle, both from the Front, had paid a visit to the rectory. Both men had nervous breakdowns. Dorothy L. Sayers writes:

> Jolly business, war. Both seem uncommonly gloomy over the pros-
> pect, but I don't know how far they can really judge. I'm rather
> glad they've gone because I do so hate everlasting war-talk, and
> I'm always in terror of Mother getting another of her nervous
> attacks.

As might be expected, Dorothy L. Sayers was to be far more involved in the Second World War.

In her letters home from University there is very little mention of happenings at the rectory, but perhaps there was nothing very much happening, or nothing which she felt worth discussing. Her life at Oxford was very full and there are mentions of parties, dresses, singing in the Bach Choir under the celebrated Dr Percy Allen, food and clothes, the men who were attracted to her, and the appropriately-named Mutual Admiration Society of which she was a founder member. The Oxford letters provide an interesting insight into what it was like to be a woman student at Oxford in the early years of the twentieth century. The rigorously enforced separation of the sexes would seem almost unbelievable to a modern undergraduate. There is one risible account of Dorothy L. Sayers clambering over other people's feet in the theatre to explain to the senior student of Somer-ville how she, Dorothy, came to be sitting unchaperoned with a man.

But perhaps this largely segregated life was more conducive to successful scholarship than is today's Oxford, where students are expected to succeed sexually, socially and intellectually and the strain is considerably greater. There is no mention in Dorothy L. Sayers' letters of any student having a nervous breakdown because of the pressure of university life, although this first generation of Oxford women was not universally welcomed by the University.

The letters from 1916 to 1920, when Dorothy L. Sayers had come down from Oxford, are chiefly concerned with her efforts to find a satisfactory job. She disliked school-teaching (a letter gives her salary as £120 per annum, non-resident) and the corresponding letters remind us how little alternative choice there was, in fact, for a highly-educated woman at that time. She was still relying on her parents for support and she shares with them her problems with difficult and rapacious landladies and the trials and satisfactions of finding and furnishing a flat. She was beginning her career as a novelist and a letter of 22 January 1921 makes the first mention of a detective story, later to become *Whose Body?*

'My detective story begins brightly with a fat lady found dead in her bath with nothing on but her pince-nez. Now why did she wear pince-nez in her bath? If you can guess you will be in a position to lay hands upon the murderer, but he is a very cool and cunning fellow.'

It is apparent from all her early letters about her writing that she regarded the detective stories not as novels but as ingenious puzzles written primarily to make money. It is likely that this view continued with her until she wrote *Gaudy Night* and used the genre to explore the themes of the almost sacramental importance of work and of intellectual honesty, and the conflict between the demands of the mind and the emotions. It was a conflict which was to dominate her own life.

Her letters in the early 'Twenties are still chiefly to her parents, but one subject she didn't write about was her infatuation with the writer John Cournos whom she met in 1921. A letter home in July of that year is, however, frank about her unhappiness. 'I can't get the work I want, nor the money I want, nor consequently the clothes I want, nor the holiday I want, nor the man I want.' She could have had the man she wanted if she had been prepared to practise birth control and live with Cournos outside marriage. It was she who ended this unconsummated and frustrating love affair, and the child she subsequently bore in secret, and whose existence she kept a secret all her life, was fathered, not by the man whose children she wanted, but by a largely unemployed motor mechanic whom she took on the rebound. To reject the man she loved because he insisted on birth control, and subsequently to become pregnant by a man she didn't love, betrays an ineptitude in matters of the heart which is perhaps not untypical of a highly intelligent but sexually inexperienced woman who was, in the words of her alter-ego Harriet Vane, 'cursed with both head and heart'.

The letters to John Cournos after he had left England and she was coping with intense private grief, holding down her job as a copy-writer and financially supporting her son, make painful reading, but to no one else did she betray her misery. All her life Dorothy L. Sayers bore her own burdens. John Cournos, who refused to marry her because he didn't believe in marriage and didn't want children, very soon married in America a woman with children. Dorothy L. Sayers depicted her relationship with Cournos with honesty and insight in her novel *Strong Poison* in which Cournos is the murder victim Philip Boyes. So at least she had the satisfaction of killing him off in fiction.

The final section in this first volume, which includes letters written between 1930 and 1936, is the most fascinating for a writer. These were the years of Dorothy L. Sayers' greatest success as a writer of detective fiction, and the letters concerned with her craft and with the writing of the play *Busman's Honeymoon* are fascinating. Her private life was less satisfactory and she achieved fame while coping with an increasingly demanding, envious and ill-tempered husband, support-ing her son, whose existence she never revealed except to the cousin who cared for him, and coping with domestic and servant problems. But by the end of 1936, when this volume ends with a letter to the theatrical producer Maurice Browne about the success of her play *Busman's Honeymoon*, she could look back on half-a-lifetime of cour-ageous living and ultimate achievement. But the work which she herself would undoubtedly have considered the most important was still to come, as was her life as a public figure, and the enjoyment with which I read this first volume of letters is matched only by my happy expectation of pleasure to come.

Introduction

It was Anthony Fleming who first thought of publishing his mother's letters. He spent some time on the project and when he died in 1984, aged sixty, he was planning an edition of eight volumes. The present collection, of which this is the first instalment, is per force less extensive but will be found, it is hoped, sufficiently representative.

In *The Mind of the Maker*, Dorothy L. Sayers writes scornfully of the sentimentality of someone unable to trim holiday snaps so as to make them into well-balanced pictures, piously preserving 'a strip of blank sky or the out-of-focus intrusion of Uncle Bertie's boot'.[1] Some of the letters and parts of letters omitted here are in the category of 'Uncle Bertie's boot'. But not all. It was often painful to have to choose between several interesting and engaging letters. Nevertheless, restraint was required if proportion and balance were to be achieved. There was never any question of censorship. All the letters are devoid of obscenity, malice or libel.

In her Preface P. D. James observes that, presented in chronological order, the letters form 'an epistolary autobiography'. This is true, especially of those covering the early years. The majority, being addressed to her parents or to her cousin Ivy Shrimpton, provide a consistent chronicle. It was in fact the basis of my recent biography, *Dorothy L. Sayers: Her Life and Soul*,[2] in which other letters, not included here, are also quoted. Thus the two books will be found to augment and illuminate each other.

Dorothy L. Sayers began her writing career as a poet. Her first two publications, *Op. 1* and *Catholic Tales and Christian Songs*,[3] were volumes of poems and she continued to write poetry all her life. For some years she was convinced that she could not write prose. Yet her creative, well-constructed letters, from childhood on, show how mistaken she was. It is a short step from their spontaneous style, as lively as speech,

to the personable narration and dialogue of her novels. Quite a few
of her characters have her way of expressing themselves, notably
Lord Peter Wimsey and Harriet Vane and even occasionally Charles
Parker. Many episodes and details of her everyday life, mentioned in
her letters, turn up again in her novels. She denied persistently that
these were autobiographical but, as her letters abundantly demon-
strate, they are shot through with gleams of her personality.

The question arises: to what extent are the letters themselves a
work of fiction? In many of them the creative writer is plainly to be
discerned: in her eye for a significant detail (an umbrella-stand stuck
full of swords in France at the outbreak of World War I), her skill in
bringing an episode to life by casting it in dialogue (Purfield and the
missing pound of bacon), her satisfaction in making the most of a
good tale (the wedding of her cousin Gerald Sayers). People who
feature in her letters are as vivid and memorable as characters in her
novels. Monsieur Roubaud, the theatrical director, who charms the
schoolgirl Dorothy with his courteous French ways, Miss White dealing with amused competence with effusive schoolgirls, the diligent
Miss Prosser showing Godolphin girls round the National Gallery
and getting puffed going up a staircase, talking no less volubly the
while, Basil Blackwell as a young man (a perfect cameo sketch),
Leonard Hodgson making his impetuous proposal of marriage, Uncle
Cecil, thrice married, caught carrying on a clandestine affair in a
potting-shed at night, Aunt Gertrude with her gossipy and interfering
ways – there are a whole range of new Sayers characters who live on in
the imagination. One of my favourites is Miss Hickes, the disillusioned
governess who burns the letters of her unfaithful suitor ('two whole
boxes full', says the observant thirteen-year-old, eyeing the scene with
the detachment of a writer).

What of herself? Is she also a character in her letters? She said
that she dramatised herself as a child, playing the part of the heroine
or more often the hero of books she read. For a long time she was
Athos the musketeer. In some of her letters she looks on at herself,
as when she sets out to charm Herr Jost at her German viva, or flees
from Cousin Eleanor coming out of church; but I find no sustained
persona behind which she hides. For the most part she writes of herself
unfeignedly, revealing more than she conceals. The letters which
puzzle me are the ones to John Cournos. They are published here for
the first time in their entirety, that is to say, all those which have
been preserved. It was important that they should not appear to have
been censored. They show her as deeply unhappy, but they also give
the impression that she was playing a part of being unhappy, or trying
to find the role which would best help her to regain her balance. The
sad little ploy of Troilus and Pandarus, which does not quite ring

true, is perhaps an instance. Her fear that she might easily become promiscuous seems intended to scarify, while her reproaches (however well deserved) would carry more conviction if she affected fewer poses.

The references to her son, on the other hand, are straightforward. There is no play-acting here; in fact she deliberately avoids assuming a maternal role, even when writing to the boy himself. Nor is there any posturising for posterity. When Ivy Shrimpton died, Dorothy asked her son, who was then grown up, to destroy all letters in Ivy's possession, but she took no pains to ensure that he did so. In the event he did not. It is not known whether he intended to publish those concerning himself. He allowed James Brabazon[4] access to all of them, only asking him to conceal the name of his father, who may then have been still alive.

Dorothy L. Sayers knew very well the fuss there would be when news of her son's existence came out after her death. She once told me that she hoped that 'the other Dorothy Sayers' (a singer and entertainer) would die first: 'Everybody would think it was me and I'd be able to read my own obituaries.' How would she have coped, one wonders, with representatives of the tabloid press on her doorstep, scenting a story? (News of her 'adopted son' was published at once when she did die.) A wry comment she made to me shortly before her death suggests that she might have shrugged off the whole hulla-balloo, as perhaps she did the thought of what was bound to happen in the end. After all, there was nothing she could do to stop it. 'Do you remember', she asked, 'all the brou-ha-ha there was when it came out about Wordsworth's illegitimate daughter? Yet it made no difference to his poetry.'

She also said that rummaging around in a writer's life was bound to be disappointing, like going through a waste-paper basket full of discarded carbons and paperclips. As regards her own letters, she was mistaken. If they do nothing else, they show the circumstances in which she wrote her books, what her aims were and how far she considered she had achieved them. As I said in the Foreword to my biography, 'the more we get to know and understand her, the more we will appreciate and comprehend her works'. She would not have agreed,[5] but it is true none the less.

Barbara Reynolds

[1] Methuen, 1941, p. 107, n.
[2] Hodder and Stoughton, 1993.
[3] Basil Blackwell, Oxford, 1916 and 1981.
[4] For his biography, *Dorothy L. Sayers: the Life of a Courageous Woman* (Gollancz, 1981).
[5] Or would she? After all, she bemoaned the lack of personal information about Wilkie Collins, whose biography she set out to write.

1899–1908

Childhood

Dorothy Leigh Sayers was born on 13 June 1893 at 1 Brewer Street, Oxford. Her father, the Reverend Henry Sayers, was then headmaster of Christ Church Choir School and Precentor of the College. When Dorothy was four and a half years old he accepted the living of Bluntisham-cum-Earith, a combined country parish in Huntingdonshire (now Cambridgeshire), East Anglia. Her earliest letters were written to her mother who from time to time returned to Oxford to visit her brother Henry Leigh, Fellow of Corpus Christi, who married Alice Maud Bayliss (Aunt Maud).

1899–1902 (Age: 5–8)

To Her Mother[1] Bluntisham Rectory
February 1899[2]

My darling Mother

How do you like being in Oxford? Have you visited Old Tom[3] yet?

I went to Earith[4] this afternoon, and Mrs Hard[5] gave me an orange, I ran all the way with my hoop. I am going to have a violin practice with Daddy when I have done my letter. I am almost sorry I have got a holiday from dictation. Jacko is quite well and so is Jocko, he, is good but Jacko is still naughty.[6]

Give my best love to Margaret[7] and ask her when she is coming to Bluntisham again, tell her I want her to come.

I am sending you a few snowdrops with my best love.

Now good bye darling Mother from
your loving little
Dorothy

[1] The original spelling and punctuation of the first four letters have been retained.

[2] The date is added in her mother's handwriting.
[3] Tom Tower stands at the gateway to Christ Church, opposite Brewer Street. The 101 strokes of the bell every night at five past nine remained in Dorothy's memory.
[4] About a mile from Bluntisham.
[5] The wife of a farmer and fruit-grower. The name Hard is still known in the vicinity.
[6] Two furry monkeys, Dorothy's favourite toys, about which she invented stories.
[7] Her cousin Margaret Leigh, who, like Dorothy, was later to win a scholarship to Somerville.

To Her Mother   Bluntisham Rectory
No date, but January 1900

My dear old Mummy

I got fifteen and eleven pence half penny in my Missonry box, I think that was very good dont you? Daddy made me a snowman today and, by-the-bye we had a heavy fall of snow this morning which just spoilt the skating. Do you know the little animals confessed to me that they *steal Polly out of the kitchen and ride him*!!![1] We snow-balled the dogs to-day, and that coward Bruce ran home for his very life and was *afraid of a bit of snow*. Grannie[2] has begun your cushion, and it is prospering, but if Elliston[3] would give you a few bits she would like to have them but she won't take them if you have to pay for them. Now good-bye

with love from all I remain
your loving daughter
Dossie[4]

P.S. Tell Uncle Harry I have got to the verb Possum[5] in my Latin.

[1] An example of Dorothy's habit of inventing stories about her toys.
[2] Grandmother Sayers, her father's mother, who lived at the rectory.
[3] The name of a draper's shop in Oxford.
[4] 'Dossie' was her first attempt at pronouncing her name. Her parents called her this for some time.
[5] The first person singular, present indicative of the verb *potere*, to be able to. Her father began teaching her Latin when she was six.

To Her Mother   Bluntisham Rectory
No date, but February 1900

My dear Mother

I hope you are enjoying yourself in spite of the weather. Yesterday I gave Granny a piece of Butter Scotch. She put one half in her mouth and then seeing (I can't write this nicely because Granny is interrupting) something of interest in the paper, began to read it, with the result that she swallowed it whole or rather it stuck in her

throat. Aunt Mab[1] suggested a dose of cold water to wash it down which did no good, afterwards doses of hot to melt it which finally got it down. This evening I won a penny for saying the future simple of 'Malo' 'I prefer' at the first guess.[2] I was very glad to hear the good news from the front[3] and would you beleive it I read the whole of the leading article to Grannie and Mab.
Now good bye

> best love from
> Dorothy Sayers

P.S. Love from all

[1] Aunt Mabel Leigh, her mother's sister, who also lived at the rectory.
[2] *malo* is the first person singular, present indicative of *malle*, to prefer (a shortened form of *magis velle*, to wish more). It is an irregular verb, of which the future simple is: *malam, males, malet, malemus, maletis, malent.*
[3] It was the period of the Boer War. Ladysmith was relieved on 28 February 1900.

To Her Mother   Bluntisham Rectory
No date, but 1901

My dear Mother
    My cold is almost well now so you must not fret about me. The Concert will be to-morrow, as Miss Feary[1] *will* be able to come then. I *was* able to go to Miss Tebbutts[2] after all, and spent a very pleasant evening. I enclose an aster (dried) which I dried some time ago, also a dried stock and dhalia. Guy[3] and I have been given some cardboard, and are fashioning armour for ourselves, and I have made myself a coat-of-arms out of some blue paper, cut in the shape of a shield, with a golden heart upon it, and the motto, 'To Glory or to Death'. I give a representation of it on the first page. Chapman[4] is making a bed on the other side of the drive to match the first, I think they will look very pretty.

> With love from all,
> your
> loving
> daughter
> Dorothy

[1] Dorothy's violin teacher, who took over from her father.
[2] Two families named Tebbutt lived in Bluntisham. They were not related. D.L.S. used the name in *The Nine Tailors*.
[3] Guy Cooke, the younger brother of one of Henry Sayers' pupils at the Choir School in Oxford, was a boarder at the rectory and shared lessons with Dorothy. He was to die in World War I. (See also letter to Ivy Shrimpton, dated 10 December 1928.)
[4] The gardener, whose son Bob later became gardener at the rectory in Christchurch, Cambridgeshire, when Dorothy's parents moved there in 1917.

Ivy Shrimpton, Dorothy's first cousin, was the daughter of Amy Leigh and Henry Shrimpton. Eight years older than Dorothy, she was born in California and later educated at a convent school in Oxford run by Anglican nuns. She frequently stayed at the rectory in Bluntisham and played an important part in Dorothy's creative and emotional development. When Henry Shrimpton died, Ivy and her mother made a living by fostering children. In this capacity Ivy was later to be of great assistance to her cousin.

1906–1908 (Age: 13–15)

To Ivy Shrimpton   Bluntisham Rectory
No date, but 1906

Dearest Ivy

How are you getting along? I hope you are feeling better than you did when you were here.

We get along very well this term, indeed; Betty[1] is nowhere near such a nuisance as I was afraid she would be, and there have been no ructions at all to speak of. Miss Hickes[2] is very nice, I like her awfully, but she is not half as clever as Miss Matthews, and does not *really* know quite enough for the post. Still, she is an immense improvement on Old Pearse. She has taken over the editorship of our magazine, *Something New*, and we publish a big number monthly, instead of a little one weekly. . . .

We are going to do a little play at the end of this term. It is an awfully good one, called 'Such is Fame'.[3] It is for four people. Miss Hickes is going to act. It is about a very young authoress (your humble servant), who has just written a successful book. She is talking at first to her cockney servant and confidential adviser, Jane. This part is most amusing. Miss Jessica Whynbush (that's me) has, rather imprudently, drawn one of the characters in her book from a combined portrait of her two aunts (Miss Hickes and Betty Osborne) whose names, by the way are 'Miss Agatha Prynne' and 'Miss Rebecca Sidway'. . . .

Please give my love to Aunt Amy and Uncle Henry.

Good-bye,
from your ever-loving cousin Dorothy

---

[1] Betty Osborne, who shared lessons with Dorothy at the rectory. Her parents lived in the vicinity.
[2] The new governess.
[3] Written by Dorothy, perhaps with help from her governess.

To Ivy Shrimpton   Bluntisham Rectory
27 January 1907

Fair Coz (as people say in Shakespe[a]re's plays), . . .

You remember my telling you about Miss Hickes and her medical
student and the letters of 32 pages, etc, etc? Well, you will be much
amused to hear that after all this grand talk, and writing, and fuss
generally, they are 'off'!! Pretty quick work, I call it.
Summer holidays: Saw him for 1st time. Talked and walked with him
– also danced with him.
Xmas Term: Wrote letters. Called him 'Dear Tom', and 'Dear Sin-
ner', and talked (to me) of going out to India with him as Mrs Butt.
Xmas Holidays: Off!! Letters burnt. (Two whole boxes full.)
Easter Term: 'Tom' stigmatised as a 'liar'. Miss Hickes very bitter
and cynical, when love or men are in question!
'Vanity of vanities, saith the preacher, all is vanity'. . . .

We have had some lovely skating the last few days. The ice is quite
black and as smooth as proverbial glass. It was awfully funny to
watch Mademoiselle[1] struggling along. Ho! ho!

Do you remember a talk we once had in the garden? I said people
– poor people – ought to be enlightened about the creation, and not
think the earth was made in a week, etc, etc. Well, to-day (Septua-
gesima Sunday) Daddy preached a very nice sermon, on that very
point, showing them how to reconcile science with the Bible. Most of
them listened with great attention, but one or two looked as if they'd
got a new idea, and it had staggered them a wee bit. Not that they'll
think another word about it after to-day – at least, I shouldn't think
they would. . . .

[1] The French au pair girl, with whom Dorothy spoke French.

To Ivy Shrimpton   Bragelonne[1]
No date

Belle cousine –

Many thanks for your letter. I was in bed with a slight wound
('wound' sounds much better than cold and is more fitting for a
musketeer) when I received it, hence my delay in answering. My
wound is now completely healed but d'Artagnan[2] has got a bad one.

My enclosure is a piece of paper that was used at the post-office
to wrap up some sweets we bought. I send it, as I think it may interest
you to see what drivel some magazines can print. I'm sure I could
do better if I tried but, *belle cousine*, the fact is, I lack the gumption
to begin. I don't know somehow how to set about tackling an editor.

I think, next time you come, we must really set about trying in real good earnest. By myself, I somehow don't seem to have the energy to sit down and send off half-a-dozen MSS to half-a-dozen editors of half-a-dozen papers but perhaps if we *both* set about it. . . .

I am writing upstairs in my quarters. My little room *is* so nice now. His Eminence[3] the other day presented me with a rug and a cushion. I have brought my devils from my room and have hung them over the writing table. I use them, for the nonce, as a rest for my quill-pens, to show to whom I have dedicated my writings!! I have covered the walls with musketeers of my own drawing, all on horse-back, of course, except a big head of Athos, of which, to confess the truth, I am rather proud. I have been doing a lot of drawing lately. The wall is further embellished by a group of musketeers' hats and swords and things that I did in lesson-time, and a portrait of my violin.

Porthos[4] and I have been frightfully busy lately. We are going to try and give a concert near Xmas, and invite Mrs Osborne etc. Not the Coopers, needless to say. Do you remember, when you were here, our once acting a scene out of *Les Femmes Savantes*,[5] up here in my quarters? We are going to do that in costume. Porthos and I are the men in costumes of the musketeer period, and Miss Hamilton and Aramis[6] take the women's parts. We have been hard at work making a curly wig for Porthos, as, of course, his hair is too long; it was a job, but it is done at last. It is made of jute. I, of course, wear my own hair, curled at the ends. Miss Hamilton is in black, with a big lace ruff, standing out behind. My genius invented the ruff, or rather collar. It is on a cardboard foundation and is a great success. It should, of course be wired, but that was too much trouble. Then we did her hair up in long ringlets, like Henrietta Maria,[7] with Mrs Chapman's goffering-irons, the same that we used for my moustache. Miss Hamilton does look so nice – quite pretty, though she is not really so. . . .

> Your devoted cousin
> Athos

[1] By now Dorothy had begun to read Alexandre Dumas' *The Three Musketeers* in French. She became enamoured of it and allotted the parts of all the characters to family and friends. The rectory was called the Château de Bragelonne, her father was Louis XIII, her mother was Cardinal Richelieu. She dramatised herself as Athos and Ivy was the Duchesse de Chevreuse, his beloved. Succeeding governesses and au pair girls played other roles. The American novelist Willa Cather (1873–1947) likewise regarded the musketeers as real ('her three best friends').

[2] The part played by the new governess, Miss Hamilton.

[3] Cardinal Richelieu, i.e. her mother.

[4] Played by the French au pair girl.

⁵ Comedy by Molière (1622–73), first produced in 1672.
⁶ Played by Betty Osborne.
⁷ The sister of Louis XIII and wife of Charles I.

To Ivy Shrimpton   Bragelonne
3 September 1907

This letter is all about the famous Dull Red,¹ so don't expect anything else.

My love
I am so excited I can hardly lay pen to paper! I have got Dull-Reditis! I have been steeped in Dull Red ever since you left! He leaves alas! to-morrow, but my acquaintance with him has progressed so much during this last day or two that I feel I can rest on my laurels. For it was nearly all my own cleverness. I have just been spending the whole morning in his company, in *earnest conversation* (?) !!! And how I *do* wish you were here to talk about it and laugh at it all. . . .

You would never believe how clever I have been! You will be astonished when I tell you that on Monday I rode from Earith to Needingworth with him, and again nearly from St Ives to Bluntisham! On Tuesday I didn't see him, but yesterday his mother came to tea here, and I tackled her and I've got all their 'ghosts' – yes, *his* ghost! and they've got a photo (signed) of me in Musketeer dress! and then I rode up here with him, and talked to him all morning, and he told me his other Christian names – he is Arthur Cyril William – and he told me the devil's telephone number, and finally I decorated him with – what? – you'll never guess – what do you think – try – try again – three times! – give it up? – well, then, with a Dull Red Rose!!!! We found it on the road and I stuck it in his button-hole. Isn't it shocking!?!?! He just stuck outside our front gate talking for hours – really, without exaggeration – and people kept on passing . . . By the bye, before I forget, I must explain about the telephone number. If you want to call up the devil on the telephone, his number is

7734

turn the page upside down and you'll see why.² . . . I think he was nicer than I've ever known him. He told me a lot about himself. I can't tell you everything, it would take too long. I told him he had frightfully bad manners – and he cheerfully agreed with me. What *are* you to do with a person like that? I contradicted him as much as ever – I always do – but we never actually quarrel. . . .

I have studied the matter, and can tell you positively: – his eyes are brown. They are darker than Marthe's and truer and look more steadily at you, except when he is laughing, but they are not so dark, not nearly so dark as yours. They are nice eyes – his best feature I

think. He says that he is always taken for a foreigner, usually a
Spaniard or an Italian. . . .

I think that by now you will have had enough of Dull Red, I cannot
of course expect you to take the same interest in him that I do. This
letter is entirely about him. I do wish you were here, darling Duchess,
to talk to.

> Ever your devoted
> Athos

[1] A young man named Arthur Cyril William Hutchinson, who visited Bluntisham with
his parents during the summer. He was nicknamed 'Dull Red' by Dorothy and Ivy after
the colour of the ball he played with on the rectory croquet lawn.
[2] The hand-written numbers turned upside down form the letters HELL.

To Ivy Shrimpton   Bragelonne
23 February 1908

Chère cousine! . . .

I am at present engaged on rather a long and difficult piece called
'The Prisoner of War', the last of the 'Songs of the Crown'. It is
supposed to describe the feelings of a prisoner of war confined in a
dark and dismal dungeon. . . . He begins hopefully and cheerfully.
He next relapses into despair with suicidal tendencies – abandoning
these gloomy ideas after a while he decides to wait for his release.
That is as far as I have got at present; he is going on to become
feverish and delirious in confinement. Then will follow, in prose, a
short conversation between his gaolers. Then, in the last part, he is
led away to execution, in joy and triumph at thus obtaining his freedom. It sounds rather bald just said like this, but it is all right in
verse. Sir Roland has not got on much since you went. I am going
to take him up as soon as I have got rid of some of my more pressing
work. It is so difficult to find original adventures for 7 young men to
take part in.

There was such a nice concert at Somersham on the 17th. They
asked me to go and play the fiddle, and as I played rather a difficult
piece, Miss Beale came over to play for me. She came by the 5.30
and stayed the night. The concert was at 8 o'clock, and we all went
– The King, Miss Beale and the Three Musketeers and d'Artagnan.
We had to have two traps to take us – it was tremendous fun. When
we got there we were shown into a little room – no, it was really
rather a big one – behind the stage, to take our things off. Miss Beale
and I had to be tidy to make our appearance on the stage, and there
was no looking-glass! *Ma chère*, I had literally one inch of cracked
glass in the handle of a fan, *voilà tout*!!!! However, it was all right, and

we managed to put ourselves fairly decent. It was a lovely concert. They had got a splendid tenor rejoicing in the name of d'Arcy de Ferrars – down from London – he sang most beautifully. He was a stout, grey-haired, middle-aged person, with a seal-ring and a seraphic smile. Then there was an enormously fat lady, with an endless double chin, vanishing away into her neck. She sang a sentimental song about the swallows. I liked the look of her, though, because she looked so pleasant and good-natured, and she had such a sweet smile. . . . Then there was also a girl of about 16, I should think. *She* was very fat too, and she had on a very full white skirt which, being short, stood out *miles* all round. Down her back cascaded a long, light-brown pig-tail, garnished with two big white bows. She had a most extraordinary voice – a very high soprano, and it sounded just as though she were singing through a key. Mr Turner[1] was there, and simply surpassed himself. He was *so* funny, and he quite convulsed us all. He knocked down my music-stand once, and you should have seen his face as he picked it up and apologised to it, and asked it if it were hurt! The audience roared. There was a Mrs King, too, who sang charmingly, she was rather nice-looking, and very graceful, and I liked her very much. She had a long enough neck to give points even to me!!![2] I think those were about all, except your humble servant. I played twice – in all, three pieces and an encore – for they encored me – they did indeed! But oh! You never saw such a platform! It was (apparently) composed of long thin planks, with trestles at each end, and (I should say) absolutely unsupported in the middle. I had a tremendously loud, noisy piece to play, and all the time, at every stroke of the bow, the platform shook, and danced, and swung, and sprang, and jumped, and rolled, and tossed like a ship at sea. . . .

I was much interested to hear about your cousin, Freda. I daresay she will, as you say, change her opinion. If she does, I expect you will have to be very careful about what you say. Converts are usually very sensitive, and it is difficult to avoid offending them. . . . So, if your cousin *should* become a R.C., I should humbly advise you, if I may (I speak as a fool) to accept the position with a good grace and not to make a fuss or to make her feel uncomfortable. And, above all, don't try to argue. It never does any good, except to sharpen the tongue and the temper. . . .

And now that I am writing about this, it seems to be an opportunity for me to say something that has been in my mind for some time, and which I have never liked to say for fear of offending you. It is dreadfully difficult for me to say these things, because I am so much younger than you are, and yet when I notice things, I feel that I ought to tell you of them, especially of this particular thing, because,

I think, if you aren't careful, it will spoil your life for you very much. It is difficult to say. Perhaps it will be easier to write it. I think, old girl, that you are just a bit inclined to form a harsh judgement – or perhaps I ought rather to say, a hard judgement of other people. You are just a little inclined not to consider that some people may have quite peculiar temptations to put up with, which do not particularly assail you, and that some things which are easy for you are an awful fight for some others. I think this arises from the fact that you have rather a high moral standard, and if people don't keep up to it, you are a bit apt to condemn them, without considering that they may have had great excuses for what they did wrong. I observed this first, I think, when we were reading the Musketeers, and my attention being turned to it, I have noticed it several times, since. I think you are a little apt to say, in effect: 'What this man did was an offence against morality, it was therefore wrong and inexcusable. I do not care what excuse this person had. He did wrong; therefore he is a wicked person, and there is an end of it.' Dear old girl, get out of the way of thinking that. It is terribly closely allied to Pharisaism, which, you know, is the one thing Our Lord was always so down upon. And I think that this attitude towards other people will make you have fewer friends, because they will be afraid of you. I shouldn't like to feel, Ivy, that supposing some time I sinned a great sin, that I should be afraid to come to you for help, only, unless you would try to make allowances for me, I'm afraid I should.[3] St Paul says, as you heard this morning, 'Though I speak with the tongues of men and of angels and have not charity, I am become as sounding brass or as a tinkling cymbal,' and I think one phase of charity is making allowances for other people's mistakes.

I have written all this in fear and trembling, and even now, I dare hardly look back at what I have written. Don't be angry. Try not. It's very difficult to say these things. If you see a person walking along on the extreme verge of a precipice, and if you screw up your courage to go and warn him off, ten to one he turns round and snaps at you: 'Don't be officious.' Besides, upbraiding other people for Pharisaism, looks so unpleasantly like the same sin in one's self that it is rather like jumping into a bottomless ditch to pull another person out. I rather wish I hadn't mentioned the subject. Shall I tear up the letter? No, I think not, only, don't be angry, please, because I don't want to lose my best friend for that. Write as soon as you can, please, to tell me whether I have or not. My motives are irreproachable, I feel it, but people's motives and people's words are not always the same thing.

There! it's done! I've said it, and hated saying it, if that's any satisfaction to you. And now, dear brethren, we will have a hymn after the sermon for those of you who have not gone out in disgust half-way through the address.

[1] A chemist of St Ives, who was also an amateur comedian and ventriloquist.
[2] Dorothy was nicknamed 'Swanny' at school because of her long neck.
[3] It is a strange coincidence that sixteen years later D.L.S. did have need to turn to Ivy for help.

On 28 June 1908 Dorothy wrote to tell Ivy that she was going away to school. She broke the news in Musketeer style: 'I am leaving the Court and going far away. I am going to School! Out and alas! for our noble company. The grand bond will be broken for ever after Christmas! for ever and ever. And now, no more shall the Four Musketeers walk side by side in the garden, or fight together for the King.' On 26 October 1908 she struck a more prosaic note: 'Preparations for school have begun – blouses are being made and under-clothing stocked; a trunk has been looked up and the train itself looked out.' Ivy spent a few days at Bluntisham after Christmas to say good-bye. In the meantime her parents had taken her to London to see Shakespeare's Henry V.

To Ivy Shrimpton   Château de Bragelonne
No date, but November 1908   par Blois
                                         Orléanois

My own dear love
Your sweet letter filled me with rapturous joy. A thousand times did I press it to my beating heart; a million times did my devoted eyes re-read its gracious words, while my exulting tongue called down unnumbered blessings upon my beloved Marie. Oh woman! How solely does man's happiness rest upon thee! A word, a look, a smile are sufficient to change the whole aspect of the world. To see you again! To hear your voice once more! Oh! my love, I am filled with a joy that is almost sorrow, so deep and anxious is it. Love! Should aught happen to prevent your coming! I tremble when I think from what slender threads depends the life and fortune of man. Day and night I hope and wish and pray that nought may occur to place a barrier betwixt us. Love doth not always cast out fear – it sometimes engenders it.

My real reason for writing is to send you the following lines, humbly and lovingly addressed to you. How I welcome each falling leaf! It is a grain of sand in the hour-glass, and each leaf, each grain, brings nearer by one little span our moment of meeting.

Rondeau

When the leaves have left the tree,
When the summer days are past,
Then the Spring will bloom for me;
When the leaves have left the tree,
When thro' land and sky and sea
Howling sweeps the northern blast,
When the leaves have left the tree,
When the summer days are passed.

Over all the woods and lea
Autumn leaves are falling fast,
Bright in gold and cramoisie,
Over all the woods and lea.
'Neath my darling's footsteps – see!
Is their rustling carpet cast;
Over all the woods and lea
Autumn leaves are falling fast.

When the leaves have left the tree
Comes my love, at last! at last!
Wintry gales before her flee,
When the leaves have left the tree,
Lo! the violets suddenly
Burst in bloom where she is passed;
When the leaves have left the tree
Comes my love, at last! at last!

How strange 'twill seem, dear, for we shall be quite alone together.
The French girl is going at the end of the term, and there will only
be you and I – only you and I! What long talks we shall have together
in the red firelight, with the chestnuts crackling on the grate; long,
long talks, with nobody to be bored by our conversation or to have
the lamp brought in early. You in the big arm-chair, I seated at your
feet, before a glowing coal-fire, with the shutters closed, and the long
shadows leaping on the wall. I have made some new songs to sing to
you, and we will have all the old ones as well (provided I do not
catch a cold), for songs sound best in the semi-darkness. And while
the snow falls and the wind blows I will sing to you of summer and
love and noble knights, and we will 'go riding, riding' together into
the land where legends live and the hills are gay with gold.

And then we will play chess by the fire-side – and we will tell
ghost-stories and tales of long ago, and we will laugh at all our old

jokes which never grow stale and we will empty a bottle of my wine
to our love and to my success at Salisbury.

Oh! we shall be happy!

I am too glad to be able to tell you anything. When you come you
shall hear all that your loving

> Athos
>   can tell you

To Ivy Shrimpton   Bluntisham Rectory
26 December 1908

My dear girl

Just a line to tell you that I have fallen madly, hopelessly, desperately in love with the splendidest, handsomest, loveliest, most magnificent man in England. He has the most delicious voice you ever
heard, and the most wonderful and glorious eyes ever seen!!! And his
smile!!!!!!!!! *Adorable! Ravishing!! Exquisite!!!* I have four photographs
of him in my bedroom and I kiss them every night!

Unfortunately I fear that my passion is totally unrequited. Indeed,
I doubt whether he has ever seen me!! What complicates matters
further is the fact that the gentleman is already married!!! Sounds
bad, doesn't it? Do you know who he is? He's the most charming,
handsome and magnificent man in London. His Christian name
begins with an L and his other initial is nearer Z than A. Do you
guess? Give it up? You shall know his name on Wednesday.[1]

> D.L.S

[1] The man in question was the actor Lewis Waller (1860–1915), a handsome matinée
idol, much admired by others besides Dorothy, for there was a 'Keen on Waller Club'.
One of his most celebrated roles, in which Dorothy saw him, was Shakespeare's Henry V.

1909–1911

School

On 17 January 1909 Dorothy, aged fifteen and a half, entered the Godolphin, a girls' boarding-school in Salisbury. The headmistress was Miss Alice Mary Douglas. The two members of staff who had most influence on her were Miss Florence Mildred White, who taught French and German and was for a time her form mistress, and Fräulein Cäcilie Fehmer, from whom she had piano lessons. Dorothy took a lively part in the life of the school, acting in plays, some of which she wrote and produced herself, singing (sometimes solo), playing the violin and the viola in the school orchestra and forming highly charged friendships.

First term January–March 1909 (Age: 15)

To Her Parents   Oakhurst[1]
No date, but 31 January 1909

Dear people[2]

I have such a lot to say that I don't know where to begin. I suppose I had better start by informing you that I have been put into the Lower V. I am not yet quite settled, however, as I seem to have too much work to get in and no time to do it in. I am afraid I may have to give up Latin or something. I had a violin lesson last Thursday. Miss Harding is very nice and I think she will be a very good teacher.... They have really an awfully good Band. Miss Parson plays the violin, and Miss Bagn[a]ll, our form-mistress, the double-bass. There is also a 'cello, but I don't know who plays it, and a lot of violins. We are at present learning a suite by Purcell and a Minuet by Schubert. I play 1st violin. It was great fun yesterday; I enjoyed it thoroughly....

I am simply broken-hearted about Coquelin.[3] How dreadful! Isn't it? Within about 9 months both brothers have left the stage, one for an asylum and the other for the grave. Who will act Cyrano now? and Tartufe? and Mascarille? and Figaro? I was absolutely *horrified* to get the paper-cutting. Poor Coquelin! And I have never seen him – and now I never shall! . . .

I'm afraid you'll have a dreadful bill for things like goloshes and ties and drill-dresses for this term. Everything has to be put down and the account sent in with the other things. I fear you'll find it rather a long one this time, but it won't be so bad after I've got all my things.

I don't seem to have such a lot to say, after all, except that I return to the bosom of my rejoicing family in nine weeks next Wednesday. I shall be extremely glad to return, you may be sure. It will be lovely to get home again. School's all right, but it isn't home.

Everybody is talking and most are grumbling so I must say good-bye before I go quite distracted.

Ever so much love to everybody from your loving
      Dorothy

¹ Like all similar schools, the Godolphin was divided into 'houses'. Dorothy was at first placed in Oakhurst, which then had nine pupils.
² Dorothy's letters from school are intended for both parents and for Aunt Mabel, although they are usually addressed to her mother.
³ Constant Coquelin (1841–1909), a French actor, famed for his interpretation of comic valets in Molière's comedies. He died on 27 January 1909 while rehearsing for Rostand's *Chantecler*. Dorothy's enthusiasm for Molière almost equalled her love for Dumas.

To Her Mother   Oakhurst
7 February 1909

Dearest old Mother

It really is sweet of you to write so often and such lovely long letters, too. I wish I had more time to answer them. I have really a good deal to say, but I don't quite know how to say it all. I had my first game of hockey on Friday and my second yesterday. As a result I am very stiff to-day, though, as I was only playing Back I did not have any hard running to do. . . .

My new form-mistress, Miss White, is very amusing. She teaches French and German, and she has a most marvellous command of language. If one is translating anything, she insists on a most elegant and flowery rendering, and then she gives one a choice of about five eloquent translations of the same phrase. She is rather a good-looking woman, with hair just turning grey, which flies out in an unruly fringe in front.

We h[ave] such a quaint little mathematics mistress in the Lower V, called Miss Hancock. She has a funny little red turned-up nose, and funny little bird-like eyes and funny round owl-like spectacles with black rims, and a funny little cheerful voice. She is said to be a dissenter and a radical, and to consider plays immoral, so she wouldn't come to the mistresses' play, or have anything to do with it. I like Miss Payton very much now. I was rather afraid of her at first; she is sometimes so extremely sarcastic, but I think she is really very jolly. She gives us English lessons – essay and Spenser etc. and Shakespeare *of course*.

Our Latin mistress is awfully jolly. She wears glasses and has beautiful auburn hair, and such a lot of it. Her particular peculiarity is saying 'All right', whenever anybody gives a correct answer. Her name is Miss Taylor, and in the play she took the part of Diana Darcy; she looked simply charming in a *School for Scandal*-period dress, with a big hat and her lovely hair.

Every Monday I am having a French walk with Miss Jeffreys. She teaches French in the Lower V. She has been in France for a long time and speaks beautifully. The funny thing is that she is so awfully like a French person. I really thought at first that she was one. She has just the same little ways as French girls, and she looks as French as French. I was quite astonished to find she was English. I had my first walk with her on Monday. We mourned together over the death of Coquelin. I met a girl the other day who had been to see *Henry V*, so we compared notes on Lewis Waller. I quite enjoyed myself. One benighted girl at Oakhurst – her name is Margaret Bourke – asked me: 'Who *is* Lewis Waller?' I blush for her!

I'm most frightfully pleased to hear that the bachelor's room is ready for a friend, because I'm going to ask if I may bring Violet Christy down with me for a few days at Easter. May I? *Please* say I may! I asked her last night, and she says she'd love to come. She's writing to *her* mother to-day, to know if she may come. She is awfully nice. I'm sure you would like her. She is a nice, quiet girl, not one of your 'loud, robustious women', and she's fond of reading and writing and acting and things like that, and she bicycles etc – *please* say she can come. She lives in Essex, so it won't be very far out of her way to come to us. . . .

I'm so sorry to hear that Margaret[1] doesn't find school come up to her expectations. I was afraid she would find parting with her mother rather a 'pull' as Traddles[2] expresses it. If she can't even eat, I'm afraid she must be in rather a bad way. I may as well assure you, *en passant*, that school has exactly the opposite effect on *me*; I eat enormously and I'm *always* hungry at meal-time. One can have two helpings of everything if one likes – I usually do. . . .

We are going to get up a sort of little play soon. Miss Payton is writing it. It is only a very little one – just the story of Red Riding-Hood,

with a few! variations. It is very short and rather silly, but we have
to get it done before Lent, and haven't much time. I am to be the
wolf, who turns out to be a Prince in disguise. Will you please send
– do I ever write without saying 'will you please send'? I'm *so* sorry!
– but *will* you please send me a few scraps of my cavalier costume?
There's no hurry – any time next week will do. I shall need my
red breeches, my black sash, my yellow stockings and a pair of lace
ruffles. . . .

> Ever your most lovingest
>   Dorothy

[1] Her cousin, Margaret Leigh.
[2] The character in Dickens's *David Copperfield*.

To Her Parents   Oakhurst
No date, but third week in February 1909

Dearest people
   Such a lot of things have happened this week! It has been most
exciting. We shall feel awfully flat in Lent. . . .
   I'm really awfully sorry about Margaret – how simply *horrible* to
have to learn those loathsome collects on Sunday. Which reminds me
to tell you that that sort of thing is very nice here; one is not bothered
a bit about religion etc. etc. We have prayers in the Hall every morning – just a psalm, a hymn, a short piece of gospel and a few prayers,
not in the least long or tiring. We have no collects or anything of that
sort to learn on Sundays. Evening prayers at school are quite short
too, and then, just before we go to bed each house has a short reading
and a prayer said by the house-Mistress – in our case, Miss Payton.
So you see we aren't much bothered. I don't know what it will be
like in Lent, of course, but I shouldn't think it would be very bad,
because the Upper V is going to act some scenes out of *Coriolanus* this
term, and is allowed as a great favour to have it in Lent, so I hope
Lent won't be too extremely strict. . . .
   I am so glad you've got *Orthodoxy*. I am not surprised to hear that
Chesterton[1] is a Christian. I expect though, that he is a very cheerful
one, and rather original in his views, eh? . . .
   I have got a very nice hockey-stick for 7 / 6 – one *can* get them
for 5 / 6[2] but I thought that they would probably not be very
satisfactory at that price. I am appalled at the long bill I seem to be
running up, but I can't help it. I shan't need so many things next
term – at least, I hope not. We don't really *have* to play hockey, only
if I play we shall just be an Oakhurst XI, which is rather exciting.

You see, Oakhurst is not really a proper, separate house yet, but we do as much as we can to make ourselves feel as if we were.

Now for the news of the week – On *Monday* an individual with very much curled-up hair arrived from the hair-dressers and washed our heads. This process will be repeated before the end of term. On Monday evening some of the music mistresses gave a sort of little lecture on the concert we were going to on Wednesday evening. Miss Mixer (consult prospectus) gave the lecture, and Fräulein Fehmer and Miss Atkinson played parts of the programme to us to illustrate the lecture. Fräulein Fehmer is my piano mistress; she is an old dear, I like her awfully. She is very amusing; she is always talking about her old master, Herr Scholtz,[3] and nearly all her music is arranged by him. The lecture was very interesting – Fräulein F. plays beautifully; we enjoyed it very much.

Wednesday evening we were all taken (except the little ones) to hear Ernst Lengyel, the wonderful young pianist.[4] He is 15, I believe. Of course, he plays marvellously. He had such an extraordinary way of bowing, he stood up stiff, and then suddenly doubled up in the middle, as if he were broken in half. . . .

On *Thursday* our wonderful play came off. It really went much better than I expected. I think I told you that it was a new version of 'Red Riding-Hood', invented and written by Miss Payton. I was the wolf, who afterwards turned into a fairy prince. I had a horribly hot costume, composed of a hideously furry head . . . 2 fur rugs and a pair of woolly gloves. . . . Underneath I wore the Prince's costume – red breeches, a drill tunic, a sash and a moustache. It was *so* funny. Everybody roared when I made my appearance. Mary Bourke made a very pretty Little Red Riding-Hood. Violet Christy was *awfully* good as the grandmother, with her hair powdered with flour. There was a great sensation when she jumped out of bed and hid underneath, and the Wolf got into bed in her place. There was also a stir and a great deal of laughter when the wood-cutter (Marjorie Wolley-Dod) came in and knocked off the head of the Wolf, disclosing the fairy prince, who then threw off his skins, sprang (thankfully, it was *so* hot) out of bed, and ended by marrying Red Riding-Hood. . . .

And now, dear people, do believe that I am perfectly well and reasonably jolly, though I'm *awfully* glad that this is such a short term. It'll be glorious to get home again. . . .

Good-bye, dearest people. I send you loads of kisses and hugs all round. Ever your loving
        Dorothy

[1] G. K. Chesterton (1874–1936). *Orthodoxy* was published in September 1908.
[2] Seven shillings and sixpence, five shillings and sixpence (old currency).

³ Bernhard Scholtz (1845–1918), studied with Plaidy, von Bülow and Rheinberger. He taught at the Munich Hochschule für Musik, 1870–5, and later in Dresden. He was an accomplished pianist and fine teacher, and wrote many piano pieces in the fashionable salon style of the day. He also edited the complete Chopin piano works for the Peters Edition. Dorothy could hardly have done better than to study with the pupil of such a distinguished pedagogue. Miss Fehmer became a professional pianist, giving concerts in Milan before taking up a post at the Godolphin. (For Dorothy's musical attainments, see William Phemister, 'Dorothy L. Sayers and Music: *Musicienne Malgré Elle*', SEVEN: *An Anglo-American Literary Review*, Volume X, pp. 59–75.)
⁴ Nothing is known of this young prodigy. From his name he would seem to have been Hungarian.

TO HER FATHER   Oakhurst
No date, but March 1909

To the King[1]
Dear Sire

Pray excuse this paper. I must just tell you about the Latin play we went to last night. It was the story of Romulus and Remus, in 3 scenes. They were written by Miss Taylor, our Latin mistress, the one I told you about, who has such lovely hair; do you remember? It was given in the Hall by IVa and IVb and one or two out of the Lower V. It was great fun. The first scene was the hiding of R and R in a cradle, near the river, by the slave who had been ordered to kill them, and their being found by the wolf. The slave was awfully good. Then came the founding of Rome, and the death of Remus; Remus was my favourite actor in this scene. The last scene was the rape of the Sabine women. It was so funny. One of the Roman citizens tucked his bride right under his arm, and carried her out shrieking and kicking. The whole play was jolly good, and most awfully amusing. It only took a quarter of an hour, so the audience demanded it all over again, and we saw it twice over. We had done the play with Miss Taylor in class just before, so I understood every word of it. I did enjoy myself so much. Violet and I went together from Oakhurst; we were the only two who went. We wouldn't have missed it for the world. It was simply killing. Romulus and Remus had perfectly magnificent brass helmets; I can't say where they got them from.

We have just returned from Cathedral. The Dean didn't preach after all. Bad luck!

Ever yr Majesty's humble servant
Athos

[1] Her father, who took the part of Louis XIII in the Musketeers game.

To Her Parents   Oakhurst
No date, but ? 14 March 1909

Dearest people

I expect Aunt G.[1] is writing you a long account, with many underlinings, of our meeting yesterday. It was simply sweet of her to come, and also of you to arrange for her coming. I'm so afraid, though, that it was my silly letter of a few Sundays ago that made you bother about it. I didn't really mean to bother you to come, or anything like that, you know, though of course it was just lovely having Auntie down. We had a jolly afternoon, we had tea with a Miss Buckle who lives quite close to Oakhurst. She has promised to ask me to tea sometimes. Isn't it nice of her? Curiously enough, Violet and her mother, who is down for the week-end, had invited me out to tea the same day, so, as Aunt G. had to start for her train at 4.25, I joined the Christys after that, and had a second tea with them at the 'Old George'. Mrs C. is very nice indeed. We had lunch with them at the Cathedral Hotel. We happened quite by chance, both to go to the same place. I was very glad, because it was an opportunity for Aunt G. to see Violet. I think she was very pleased with her. By the bye, I'm sorry she couldn't come on Tuesday, but I should have had a lot of bother to get away for such a long time, in fact, I don't know that it would have been allowed.

I'm so awfully sorry to hear about Mrs Ball, also about old Mrs Godfrey. It seems as if everyone had only waited for me to come to school in order to die, beginning with Coquelin and ending with Dicky.[2] It's dreadful. Oh dear! I'm glad the holidays are getting so near. I *do* want to get home, – though of course I'm all right here – but I want to see you all. I say! how absolutely *glorious* to go and see the Musketeers![3] I wonder how long it will run. Till Easter, anyway, I should think – probably longer, it's an awfully popular piece. If it stops at Easter, can we see it on our way home – though it will be Holy Week. My word! How scandalised Miss Fairclough would be at the idea. Have I told you that everybody loathes Miss Fairclough? She is an old donkey, really. Excuse bad language, but really she is a billy! Never mind! one can't like everyone, and most of the mistresses are awfully nice. I pointed out one or two of them to Aunt G. yesterday. She saw the wonderful Miss Westlake, the games mistress. I've told you about her. She's the mistress everybody is so cracked on, the one who acted the Lady High Examiner in the Mistresses' Play. She really is jolly good-looking, and very nice, but the way some of the girls, particularly the Wolley-Dod, go on about her is too absurd.

Last Thursday we had another of those lectures on Wealth and Poverty. I enjoyed it immensely, though perhaps not *quite* so much

as the last. I think I forgot to mention that the lecturer's name is
Marryatt[4] – at least, that is how it is pronounced, I'm not sure about
how it's spelt – it may be Marriott, for all I know.

Nothing else of much importance has happened this week. *Coriolanus*
comes off next Saturday – I must stop writing and study my part –
or rather parts. I am several little oddments in different places – here
a 3rd citizen, there a 2nd servant – in one place a commoner, and in
another a conspirator. We have a jolly good Coriolanus – did I tell
you her name was Marjorie Hardy? She is rather pretty – at least,
she has very nice dark eyes. I do hope the play will go off decently.

I was almost forgetting the most important thing – Please thank
the Queen[5] *awfully* for the lovely chocolates – especially the 'nut'.
They're simply delicious.

Good-bye for now –

Loads of love
Dorothy

[1] Aunt Gertrude Sayers, whose style of letter-writing, with many underlinings, D.L.S.
imitated in the letters of Miss Climpson.
[2] The pet canary at home.
[3] The part of d'Artagnan was being played by Lewis Waller.
[4] J. A. R. Marriott (1859–1945), later Sir John Marriott, also gave a course of lectures
on the Problems of Wealth and Poverty in Buxton Town Hall in 1913. Vera Brittain
attended them and was encouraged by Marriott to try for Oxford. (See *Testament of Youth*,
Gollancz, pp. 60–3.) Educated at Repton and New College, Oxford, Marriott was a
lecturer in Modern History and Fellow of Worcester College from 1885 to 1920. He was
elected Member of Parliament representing Oxford University.
[5] Aunt Mabel Leigh.

To Her Parents   Oakhurst
No date, but end of March 1909

Beloved Mother and revered Cardinal and everybody . . .

This has been an awful week of exams. I do hate them. I have been
trying to do the test-papers, but of course I found them difficult as I
have only had one term's work at them and that my first term. I must
read up some English in the holidays. We had a very nice Spenser
paper. I have one more paper on Monday – French unseen – that
ought not to be very dreadful.

Wasn't it simply glorious Oxford winning the boat-race? It was
most exciting yesterday. All the girls wore their colours. I made myself
a magnificent Oxford badge and wore it proudly all day. Yesterday
was rather exciting altogether, as the final hockey match was played
in the afternoon between School-house and Sarum. It was very close,
but Sarum won the cup by 3–2.

We had a lovely treat on Friday. Fräulein Fehmer (who teaches me the piano; she's an old dear) gave a Chopin Concert in the Hall. It was simply lovely. She plays divinely. I never enjoyed a piano concert so much in my life, I think. She played such awfully pretty things. She is very fond of Chopin, and interprets him splendidly. . . .

Miss White is an awfully decent sort, but she does make me laugh. Violet asked her the other day to write something in her album. The book came back with the following inscription in a large hand all across the page:

'Laodamia' l. 73-78[1]
Wordsworth Mildred White

Miss W. was simply bursting with amusement over her little joke. We were all most frightfully amused. . . .

Till Wednesday
Athos

[1] Be taught, O faithful Consort, to control
Rebellious passion; for the Gods approve
The depth, and not the tumult, of the soul;
A fervent, not ungovernable love.
Thy transports moderate, and meekly mourn,
When I depart, for brief is my sojourn.

Second term June–July 1909 (Age: 16)

To Her Parents   Oakhurst
No date, but beginning of summer term 1909

Dearest family

This term has started really rippingly! Everybody is perfectly amiable and charming, particularly Fanny M.[1] I don't know what's come to them all. Paytie is quite sporting this term, really; I only hope it may last.

Our exeat begins on Friday, June 11th and lasts till Tuesday evening. I hope His Maj. is free then. I say! Do you know, I've discovered that Paytie, who always used to be so sarcastic and superior about Lewis Waller has got a 'crackation' herself! I nearly died when she told me. She is violently enamoured of Forbes-Robertson[2] – ho! ho! She says he's jolly good. We must see him some time. I have heard that Matheson Lang's[3] Hamlet is very good. . . .

The German girl[4] in my room is very nice, I think. She does not speak much English, and of course she feels very strange, but I hope she will feel happier soon. I had such a fright last night at dancing; I was sitting out a dance with Marjorie Gabain when Miss Douglas stalked up, smiling. The following dialogue ensued:–

Miss D. (smiling) How is Anna getting on?
Myself (much embarrassed and not knowing whether to stand up or sit down) I think she seems happier now than she was at first.
Miss D. I am very anxious about her. You will see, won't you, that she gets partners to-night from other houses, not only from Oakhurst.
Myself (overwhelmed by a ghastly sense of responsibility, but a trifle more collected) Yes, Miss Douglas.
Miss D. I do so want her to be happy.
Myself I think she is getting on better now, Miss Douglas.
Miss D. (with terrible amiability) A great deal owing to you, I think.
Myself (crimson and completely annihilated) Oh! no, Miss Douglas.
(Exit Miss D. still smiling)[5]

I forgot to tell you that my English, French and German papers were very good. Fanny M. and Paytie are very pleased. But oh! dear me! the history. We haven't heard the marks for that yet. Ugh! I am trembling. I know I've done rottenly. Fanny M. read me a little lecture on Friday, saying that I'd had wonderful advantages, and must not be too exalted! I disclaimed any feeling of exaltation. She really is awfully sweet, is Fanny M. I think she is quite my favourite. She was very pleased with the little plant I brought, which arrived quite safely. . . .

[1] Fanny M., or Fanny Maud, was the nickname of Miss Florence Mildred White.
[2] The actor, Sir Johnston Forbes-Robertson (1853–1937).
[3] [Alexander] Matheson Lang (1877–1948), actor-manager and dramatist.
[4] Anna Hoffmann, to whom Dorothy continued to be kind and who once stayed at Bluntisham during the holidays. She and Dorothy met again after World War II.
[5] Several of D.L.S.'s letters contain long passages of narrative cast in dialogue.

To Her Mother   Oakhurst
20 June 1909

Darling Mummy
How I wish you had been with us![1] We had the most superlatively glorious time anybody ever had. It was simply splendid. Tree's[2] company is absolutely perfect. There was not a single person in the cast who was not excellent – everyone was magnificent, from Tree to

the unfortunate girl who took the part of Maria and to the excellent
foot-man, whose name in private or rather in public life I forget, but
who was awfully good. The screen scene was killing. We had such a
ripping Joseph Surface (Basil Gill).[3] I have got a jolly photo of him
which I'll show you in the holidays. He is jolly nice looking, and he
plays splendidly. Of course Tree was absolutely glorious. The scene
where he quarrels with Lady Teazle was too charming for words. I
have got a splendid post-card of that, too. Marie Löhr[4] is so pretty
and charming. She is only nineteen. Everybody fell in love with her.
The Queen of Swords minuet! – isn't it perfectly sweet? It was simply
killing. Sir Peter danced with Lady Sneerwell in the centre, and Lady
Teazle with Sir Benjamin Backbite just beside them, and all the time
Lady Teazle kept poking Sir Peter and tweaking his pig-tail and
pulling the skirt of his coat, and he looked round, simply *furious*! It
was so lovely. Raymond was quite delighted; he said, all of his own
accord, that he had never laughed so much before and that it was far
more amusing than any modern play could have been. I think Raymond is really a delightful young man – he is so fresh – not a bit
blasé. He was awfully nice to me in London. He took me to the White
City[5] on Tuesday, and took me all over the best part of it. He is
simply ripping at sitting on the various tradespeople who fly out upon
one at every step and try to wheedle one into buying. It is really not
a place for an unprotected female. It needs a man to get the better
of these people – they are all so horribly plausible. He (Raymond, I
mean) was very nice, though, and let one stop and look at things –
it is so dreadful to have a person always hurrying you along and not
letting you look at things. There is some awfully jolly statuary at the
Exhibition – we enjoyed ourselves awfully there. We finished up with
the Scenic Railway. My dear! You would *die* if you went on. It's
simply awful – we enjoyed it thoroughly. You've absolutely *no idea* of
the terrific speed at which you rush down! I only squealed once, and
that was because my hat nearly blew off. It does give one a funny
feeling in one's inside, though – one really feels as if one were going
to be hurled to destruction. . . .

No time for more.
Dorothy

[1] Her parents had arranged for her cousin Raymond Sayers to escort her to the theatre
to see Sheridan's *The School for Scandal*, in celebration of her sixteenth birthday.
[2] Sir Herbert Beerbohm Tree (1853–1917), actor-manager, famous for his Shakespearean
productions.
[3] Basil Gill (1877–1955), played a wide variety of roles in Shakespeare and romantic
drama.
[4] Marie Löhr (1890–1975), an Australian-born actress, toured with the Kendals between

1902 and 1907. She was acclaimed for her performance as Lady Teazle in Beerbohm Tree's revival of Sheridan's *The School for Scandal*.

[5] A large popular amusement park in London. Built for the Olympic Games in 1908, it was later used for greyhound racing, as alluded to in *Unnatural Death* (chapter 9) and *Murder Must Advertise* (chapter 12).

To Her Mother Oakhurst
No date, but July 1909

Dearest Mother

Holidays begin on the 28th and end on the 16th. I don't mind a bit about how they are arranged, nor, I think does Violet. I thought it wd. be rather nice if she and Raymond were at Bluntisham at the same time, as we cd. go bicycle rides together, but just as you like. Did I tell you – no, I only heard this week, I think – that Raymond is going to come and see me on the 10th. He is going to stay over the week-end. Isn't it awfully nice of him. We are going to hire a bicycle if it's fine and go for a ride on Sunday. I think it'll be awfully jolly. It *was* so funny when I asked Paytie if I might go out on Saturday and Sunday with my cousin. She evidently had doubts as to the propriety of the proceeding, for she said: 'I suppose your parents know about it, Dorothy; it's all right isn't it?' It was rayther [sic] killing, wasn't it?

I'm sorry your visit to Oxford isn't turning out as pleasant as you expected. Of course, it is tiresome not to have one's little solitary jaunts. I wish I were with you.

Nothing has happened at all this week. I think I told you that Miss Fairclough had departed from Oakhurst. It is more peaceful now than it was.

Yesterday afternoon we had an impromptu Fancy-dress Ball, with just what we could get together out of the house. Violet looked splendid as Lady Teazle, in an eider-down and 2 counterpanes. I contrived my old Henry V costume (*not* the armour, though). It was great fun.

Violet and Mary and I are going to try and get up a little play on the 17th. I am sending to Bazin[1] for some of my costumes. We are clubbing together to pay the postage. Of course it will only be a very small concern, just for Paytie and the rest of Oakhurst. So I shall have to stop my correspondence early and start writing the play. And really there is most awfully little to write about to-day. Miss White, about whom you usually hear exciting tales, has been in a vile temper all the week, and blowing the whole form up sky-high. The mistresses had a party last night and high jinks. We could hear them laughing and talking like anything, for the party was held in the house just opposite. They had theatricals and no end of fun, lucky pigs!

Everybody, almost, is in a shocking temper, particularly Margaret, so things are cheerful, as you may imagine. *I* am in a good temper.
Ever looking forward to the holidays

Your loving
   Dorothy

P.S. Please give my love to Aunt Maud.
Please make your own holiday arrangements. You know about servants etc. . . .

[1] One of the grooms to the Musketeers, probably Mrs Chapman.

To Her Mother   Oakhurst
No date, but July 1909

Dear Mother
   Here's a pretty letter for an unfortunate wretch to receive when she's expecting her home letter on Tuesday! No news and a disappointment. I have lost my temper, and with reason. If you were going to object why in heaven's name didn't you do it when I wrote just after half-term and before we had fixed the date? I told you he was coming then. I wish I'd never been such a fool as to tell you that silly nonsense about what Miss Payton said – of course I was exaggerating! Besides, it really is absurd. As if one couldn't go for a bicycle ride with one's cousin! If he could haul me all over London on Tuesday surely he can see me in Salisbury on Sunday. Girls are always having cousins and people to see them. Talk among the girls? No, I think not; I've mentioned the fact to one or two and they seemed to think it the most natural thing in the world, and said how useful it was to have cousins. Paytie seemed to think it perfectly natural, too; she only said what she did because I hadn't heard from home. Of course if you like Violet could come with us on Sunday to play the dragon!!
   I can't possibly write and tell Raymond he can't come now. If anyone is to write, you must. It would be ridiculous for me to make the excuse that I've had enough holidays, because I miss no lessons at all, and I couldn't possibly write and tell him it wasn't proper, could I? Really, you *must* write yourself. I'm very sorry, but really, I never thought there was any harm in going out to lunch with one's cousin – who might be one's brother for anything anybody knew. Anyway, I don't see how I can write to Raymond, so I leave it to you.[1]

   Ever yours, Dorothy

[1] The situation seems to have been resolved, to judge from the happy tone of the following.

To Her Mother   Oakhurst
No date, but July 1909

Dearest Mother

I am simply head over ears in the play – to say nothing of work.
Every spare moment I am writing programmes for all I'm worth.
I am doing simply lovely ones, in exact imitation of real theatre
programmes. The play is written[1] and the costumes have arrived,
but there is still heaps and heaps to be done, and I am simply
overwhelmed with business. You see, of course, I have to stage-
manage as well. Violet helps, but I have most to do in the way
of arranging and writing and painting things, to say nothing of
writing the play, learning my part, etc, etc, etc. It's rather a rush,
and how we're going to get the rehearsals in, heaven only knows, I
don't! . . .

[1] By Dorothy herself.

Third term September–November 1909 (Age: 16)

To Her Parents   Oakhurst
No date, but 26 September 1909

Dearest people

I simply can't write – I'm absolutely *dead*. Last night was simply
terrific! Of course you know it was Commem.[1] I had a most killing
time, and enjoyed myself no end. There was school service at 10.30
– the whole present school was in the gallery and the form-rooms and
the old girls (about 200) in the Hall. It was awfully hot, but not as
bad as it was on Friday night for the mistresses' Play, when the whole
school had to pack into the gallery – 220 of us! It was terrible, but
we enjoyed ourselves so immensely that we didn't mind a bit. It is
such a jolly play – we screamed with laughter the whole time –
the new jokes were perfectly splendid – there were some about Commem: and one about the Budget and a lovely one about Cook and
Peary.[2]

Yesterday was the great day. After service the old girls took their
friends down the town. Everyone cd. do just what she liked. . . .
Immediately after tea which lasted till 7.30 the Hall was cleared
for the dance. It was simply glorious. I had a scrumptious time,
and a most killing dance with Fanny Maud. She had on the most
lovely red dress – at least, not exactly red, but a beautiful sort of
artistic red pink – only, oh dear! She does *not* know how to hold

up a train. At 10.10 we all sang 'Auld Lang Syne' and said good-
night to Miss Douglas – poor beast! She had to give over 500
handshakes! . . .

[1] Commemoration: the annual party given for former pupils of the Godolphin.
[2] Robert Edwin Peary (1856–1920), an American explorer, reached the north pole in
1909. Another explorer, F. A. Cook, claimed to have forestalled him by a year.

To Her Mother   Oakhurst
No date, but 3 October 1909

Dearest Mum
    Many thanks for letters etc. as usual. By the way I quite forgot in
my last to thank his Majesty for the Greek Testament. We tackle it
twice a week. We are at present struggling with aorists and augments
and paradigms. . . .
    Yesterday we went with S. Margaret's[1] to Old Sarum, to see the
excavations.[2] They have uncovered some *lovely* perfect walls, and a
postern gate. It is most fascinating to see the great socket where the
huge beam went across to bar the gate. They have found lots of
Norman and Roman pottery and iron-work. We got hold of some
awfully nice men who took us round and showed us everything. I am
sending Aunt Mabel some relics. I hope they will arrive safely. . . .
    We have just been released from going to Cathedral. We have been
instead to Miss Lucy's[3] service at St Margaret's and in consequence
we are feeling much gooder and happier than if we had had to sit
through a long service. . . .
    I daren't write a long letter this week because I have to make a
speech at Debate on Wednesday. Jean Smith is proposing the motion
'That the study of the Classics is more beneficial than that of modern
languages' and I am opposing the motion. So you see, I must prepare
my speech, especially as Miss White (who is going to speak) has
threatened that if I don't win this debate for her she'll never speak
to me again 'Except in the way of business of course, Dorothy.' So,
good-bye

        Dorothy

[1] One of the Houses at the Godolphin.
[2] The visit inspired her to write a poem, 'Captivo Ignoto' (To an Unknown Prisoner),
which was published in *The Godolphin Gazette*, No. 44, Autumn term, 1910.
[3] Miss Lucy Douglas, the sister of the headmistress.

To Her Parents   Oakhurst
No date, but 10 October 1909

Dearest people

I am again in an extremely weary and sleepy state. Yesterday we
had a perfectly lovely time. St Margaret's and Oakhurst went to Miss
Lucy's 'hut' in the New Forest. It is an absolutely sweet little house
– so tiny, but so complete – with a tiny kitchen range in the sitting-
room, and two bedrooms, and a real weather-*cock* on the roof. Two
little wretches from St Margaret's calmly climbed up onto the roof
after tea and twisted the weather-cock round the wrong way. Miss
Lucy *was* so cross – no wonder! They had only just succeeded in
regulating it. We wandered about the forest all afternoon and found
some most lovely toadstools – pink and red and blue and green and
black. The bracken was just turning and looked beautiful – I brought
back a great bundle to put in the VI. Tell His Majesty that work in
the VI is very much like work anywhere else. Miss Jones is just the
same as usual – yes, Violet and I have French with F.M.[1] Your last
letter shocked me very much indeed – I fear that you are becoming
much too great an admirer of the said lady. You mention her several
times and beg for news of her. I am feeling quite upset about it, and
consider that a 5-minutes' conversation ought not to produce such
an effect upon you. . . .

I have just been reading *The Nebuly Coat*;[2] I like it immensely. I
think it is well written, especially the part about falling off the tower.
I am going to get Violet to read it. I thought at first that Lord
Blandamer was going to be hateful, but at the end I quite liked him.
I can't bear the architect – he's such a self-righteous young man, do
you remember him?

Do you really mean that Valérie Stafford is going to be married?
Well, well! according to that I shall be of marriageable age next year.
You had better begin to keep a sharp eye upon all stray young men
– only now I come to think of it there are none to keep an eye on –
except Dull Red, and perhaps not even he. Terrible place, isn't it? –
Bluntisham, I mean. . . .

    Adieu. Love to all from
        Athos

[1] Fanny Maud, i.e. Miss White.
[2] A novel by John Meade Falkner (1858–1932), first published in 1903. It made a lasting
impression on Dorothy's imagination. 'My own *Nine Tailors*', she later wrote, 'was directly
inspired by that remarkable book.' (Letter to Cyril Lakin, editor of the *Sunday Times*.)

To Her Parents   Oakhurst
No date, but 17 October 1909

Dear people – I'm in such a state of mind I can hardly write – no, it isn't Fanny Maud – or at least, only partly, though I daresay she had a good deal to do with it if one only knew and anyway she told us, and you never saw anybody so bursting over with exuberance in your life! We had the most killing French lesson on it on Friday; she told us the whole story of the play,[1] and we roared with laughter the whole time – she really does read rather rippingly, and she has got a jolly voice – did you notice it? By the way, I haven't told you what it is yet – well! On Thursday – (Church-time: to be continued in our next.)

Well! I was just going to tell you before church about the lovely, glorious, splendid, jolly, gloriousest, splendiferousest piece of news that Fanny gave us on Thursday! On Wednesday next as ever is, a French company – a Paris company (of whom five are from the Odéon[2]) are coming down to Salisbury to act *L'Avare* in the County Hall, specially for our benefit!!!!!!!!!!!!!!!!!!! Isn't that glorious????????? No wonder we are all off our heads! I don't know what to do with myself, I'm in such a state of mind – so is Miss White. It is to start at 7.30, and to last till 10. *So* exciting! Anna heard the news first from Fanny and told me. We then went out to practice la X,[3] and saw F.M. approaching. I pounced upon her like a hawk upon the prey to hear all the details. We simply had a glorious French lesson on Friday – we did nothing at all but sit and listen to Miss White reading and telling about the play. We roared with laughter all the time. And oh dear! just at the end she said (speaking of one of the young *men* and one of the young *women* in the play) 'and so in the end it turns out that Valère and Marianne are *sisters*.' Of course we all became helpless with laughter, and roared and roared and roared! So she looked blankly round upon us, and we roared and roared still more, and she looked more and more puzzled – finally she said in a pathetic voice – 'What *is* it that's so funny? What *are* you all laughing at?' So we became more and more helpless and Natasha was getting purple in the face, so she looked more puzzled still, and murmured 'Valère and Marianne are . . .' and then it dawned upon her, and she got pink all over and oh! she *did* get *so* pink!! – and she roared with laughter and said: 'Brother and sister I meant, of course. I was thinking of the German word *Geschwister*' – It *was* funny. I do believe that woman *thinks* in German. . . .

[1] Molière's *L'Avare*.
[2] A theatre in Paris.
[3] Lacrosse.

To Her Parents   Oakhurst
No date, but 24 October 1909

My dearest people,
    What shall I say about Wednesday evening? That it was glorious?
perfect? ripping? delightful? killing? splendid? beautiful? No adjective
could properly describe the delightfulness of it all. It was too lovely
for words! The only drawback is[1] . . .
    The performance began at 7.30, but she was in the Hall from 6.30,
because the man who arranged things couldn't talk French and the
French people couldn't make him understand so Miss W. came to
the rescue, and when we arrived, there she was chattering voluble
French to a very French little *directeur*, who was completely bowled
over by her fascinations and followed her about like a little dog. She
was thoroughly in her element, grinning and – *rayonnant* – there is no
English word for it. . . .
    The County Hall is not an ideal one for theatrical performance,
but it's not half bad. They did not appear to possess a bell, so apprised
the curtain-*drawer* of their readiness by making a tremendous *fracas*
with a stick. It was delightfully primitive[2] – but the acting! *Mes amis!*
heavenly! so beautifully harmonious! exquisite! and the French! It
did one good to hear such French as that – it was perfect! Cléante
(M. Rollan of the Odéon) was an *angel* – we all fell violently in
love with him – Harpagon was awfully good – Miss Whi— I mean
somebody I know complained that he was too good-looking. I mildly
suggested that the poor man couldn't help his features – 'owever! But
it was *too* glorious!! F.M. was off her head with delight. Lovely! . . .
    Now I must say a word about other things. I am so glad the Harvest
Festival was a success. I wish I had been there – Oh! by the way, a
dreadful thing has occurred – I am left stranded without any needle-
work or crochet to my name – can you supply me with some work to
do – I don't mind what, so long as it doesn't exact a great deal of
thought, because we're read to all the time. . . .
    I return to the bosom of my family on the 21st.[3]

    Till then
    I am
        with love
            yours ever affectly.
                D.

[1] The drawback was that Miss White asked Dorothy to write 'a really racy, amusing
account' of the performance in French for the school magazine, which Dorothy did.
[2] At this age Dorothy did not know that the traditional signal in the French theatre for
the raising of the curtain is a triple thump on the stage with a heavy stick. This is known
as *les trois coups*.

³ i.e. 21 December. This sounds like a reply to an enquiry from her parents, who then arranged to meet her in London on that day and take her to the theatre.

TO HER PARENTS   Oakhurst
14 November 1909

Please excuse pencil – it's *so* much quicker, and I have a lot to say. First of all, many thanks to His Majesty for the P.C.s¹ and for the darling little sketch which has captivated every one. I am going to pin it up in my cubicle. Yes! It's a very short time now to the end of term. It's rather appalling (though of course I want to get home) because we are going to have a play.² That is, if Miss Bagnall approves. It is to be *Aldrovando*³ (with the bad language toned down – Miss B. was much amused when I suggested this) – if on perusal Miss B. thinks it will do. Will you please send it by return of post? It is in the black book with *The Wit*⁴ on the outside, and it is to be found in my quarters in the row of books under the window. I shall probably want some costumes, but I'm not quite sure yet what. I must have the boots I'm afraid – I don't see how I *could* act the part of a bloody villain *without* the boots, do you? I shall want my brigand hats and my swords and dagger – you know my dagger? It's a paper-knife in private life with a hilt of green stone. I shall also need shirts and a doublet and both pairs of breeches and the black robe with the lace collar – also the mauve one and a length of mauve art muslin – what a list! Well, there is loads of time so they can come gradually – besides, the play must first be approved of. . . .

We had such a splendid time yesterday afternoon. There was a performance in the town of ancient dances, such as the Coranto, the Galliard, the Sarabande etc., and ancient music of the 16th and 17th centuries, and old songs. There were songs and a string quartet to accompany the dancing, and Miss Nellie Chaplin, who is the manageress of the company, played several solos on the harpsichord (a beautiful old instrument, dated 1789). The dancing was simply wonderful, and *so* pretty. It was such an interesting performance too – I always wanted to see what some of those old dances were really like. It was most tastefully got up, and the costumes were simply charming. Have you ever heard the harpsichord well played? It is most curious – very pretty, though, tho' it would get monotonous in time, as there is very little variation of tone; though more than I should have expected. Miss Chaplin played really wonderfully. We enjoyed ourselves no end. I had never seen any really good dancing before.

We are looking forward to Cathedral this afternoon. Our dear darling Dean is going to preach on 'Tennyson and Religion', and the Anthem is going to be 'Crossing the Bar'.[5] It ought to be simply lovely. I only hope we shall be able to get decent seats – everybody will be wanting to hear the Dean. I wish you could hear him. . . .

Ever your devoted
   Athos

[1] Postcards.
[2] An interesting example of Dorothy's pleasure in school activities. She later said that she hated school but evidently this was not always so.
[3] A romantic drama in verse, set in Spain, written by Dorothy before she went to the Godolphin.
[4] Another play in verse, a wittily devised comedy. Both MSS are privately owned.
[5] Probably in the setting by (Sir) Joseph Barnby (1839–96), composer and conductor.

To Her Parents   Oakhurst
28 November 1909

Dearest People
   I am desperately and violently and hopelessly in love, and I must go to the theatre in the holidays to get over it – Petruchio!! Oh! I shall dream of him, he was too angelic for *words*. Simply *sweet*! He was *too* delightful. He looked the part simply rippingly and he had *lovely* eyes! He acted magnificently – people who have seen them both say that he is better than Benson[1] in the part. I *am* so jealous, Anna and Violet went last night to see him in *Hamlet* – (Violet's mother is down here.) Anna says he was splendid – he is a perfect darling, really. He showed one so awfully well that Petruchio is only pretending all the time and really loves Kate.[2] The Shrew herself was *magnificent* – I never heard anybody scream as she did – and *so* pretty. I believe she really is his wife. His name is Baliol Holloway,[3] and I have got his portrait, only not as Petruchio – I couldn't get that – but as Hamlet.
   There! it's rather hopeless when I get cracked on an actor, isn't it? Two of the company were ripping – the rest were not awfully good. Baliol Holloway and Emily Leslie (that's his wife) and Weir (who played Biondello) and Victor Wiltshire (Tranio; he was simply *ripping*) and the man who played Grumio – I forget his name for the moment – are ever so much too good for the rest, esp. the first two – they ought to get a move. I'm sure it would do them much more good to have minor parts in some really first-class company, than always playing leading rôles with a whole lot of inferior players. Because they're really *ripping*, both of them, and he is an angel incarnate – though a few superior St Margaret's people did say he was an

awful bounder – he wasn't! I will tell you all about it when I get back
– it's not very long now. Have you asked Ivy yet? . . .

   Yours ever lovingly
   Dorothy

[1] Sir Frank Benson (1858–1939), actor-manager, renowned for his Shakespearean roles
and productions. In 1901 he founded a school of acting.
[2] The adult Dorothy L. Sayers took a more negative view of the play. In *The Mind of the
Maker* she writes: 'It is a falsity . . . that makes both actors and audience uncomfortable
about *The Taming of the Shrew*; whether it is played as burlesque or softened into sentimental
comedy, we are still left protesting that " 'Tis a wonder, by your leave, she will be tamed
so", and nothing will persuade us that characters like those would really subdue themselves
to a plot like that.' (Methuen, 1941, p. 55.)
[3] Baliol Holloway (1883–1967), actor, who played leading parts in Stratford-on-Avon
Festivals. He joined Frank Benson's company in 1907.

*Before going back to school in January 1910 Dorothy went to Oxford to stay
with her Aunt Maud. While there she wrote to her parents: 'We went through
Somerville this morning. It does look a jolly place. We saw the library – so cosy
and nice. I* must *get there.'*

   *In this term Dorothy was confirmed. She later said that this was against her
will but there is no sign of reluctance in her letters from school. On 13 February
1910 she announced laconically: 'I am to be confirmed this year – we go to Canon
Miers' (if that's how he spells himself) Confirmation Classes on Tuesday and
Friday.' Her references to services in Salisbury Cathedral are enthusiastic. In
January she wrote: 'We have just been to Cathedral to hear the Anthem, "In
the beginning God created" . . . It was* lovely! *Canon Morris preached – he
is rather a favourite of ours, so we thoroughly enjoyed ourselves.' In March she
wrote to her cousin Ivy Shrimpton: 'I was just forgetting to tell you – I am to
be confirmed on the Wednesday in Easter week – in the Cathedral – isn't it nice?
I was christened in a Cathedral too' [i.e. Christ Church, Oxford].*

Fourth term January–April 1910 (Age: 16)

To Her Mother   Oakhurst
? January 1910

Darling Mum!

   You are an *angel*! I have just had an interview with Miss Douglas,
and I think it's all right about German. *Angel*!!! She was quite ripping
about it – she said – 'Your mother says you want to work with Miss
White – of course, everyone does –' so it seems as though the goddess

were appreciated. Will you please send my hockey-pads and my
Revised Version of the Bible. The pads are in the cupboard in my
room – I don't know where the other is.

Ever yours joyfully,
  D.

TO HER MOTHER   Oakhurst
20 February 1910

Dearest Cardinal . . .

The everlasting subject of conversation at the present moment is
Rostand's *Chantecler*[1] – we hear of nothing else. I have ordered it from
Hachette, but it won't be published till the end of the month. I say,
if you can come across any reviews of it anywhere, or accounts or
pictures, *do* send them – we've got to write about it for to-morrow
week. Is it possible to get French papers in Oxford? It would be so
nice if you could get a French account of it. I have sent to Porthos[2]
to ask for the *Figaro*, but even if he can get it it will most likely get
delayed in the Channel with this beastly wind. We are translating
Chantecler's Hymn to the Sun this week, and that loathly woman[3]
is going to make me read it aloud next Wednesday in class 'really
dramatically, Dorothy!' Isn't it awful? I do *hate* making a fool of myself
before everybody like that – and it looks so beastly 'sidey' too – I
abominate that sort of 'show-off' – and not content with that the
brute is printing the silly sonnet I translated in the magazine[4] – I
was *furious* and she merely laughed at me – what *is* one to do with a
woman like that?

Never did I see such abominable weather! It's perfectly filthy to-day
– blowing and raining like fury. Yesterday there was a little sun and
it blew without raining – we went a ripping walk up on the downs
with Miss Ralph – it was perfectly glorious!

We had quite an exciting debate on Wednesday – the motion was
'That competition is necessary to progress.' It was carried by 6
votes. . . .

Miss Douglas said we were to tell our people that the caps and
veils for the Confirmation are provided by the school, all alike, unless
our parents want us to wear any particular sort – which I am quite
sure you don't. The service is on the Wednesday in Holy Week, in
the Cathedral – Miss D. says we are to wear something fairly warm,
and that we can put a coat over if it's cold. I should think I had
better have my best white skirt (which is at Bluntisham), and a plain
white blouse, hadn't I? Muslin is so beastly chilly, unless the weather's
boiling hot, which it doesn't look like being, and Miss Douglas said

particularly we were to be warm enough. Of course, there's loads of time yet, but I thought you'd like to know about things beforehand. . . .

I wonder if you could possibly find out for me from Aunt Maud or any bookseller's, particulars as to the price, etc. of a book that Coney recommended in the hols., – *An Essay on Comedy* by George Meredith.[5]

Now I really must stop, as I have to write to the King – and answer a *long pi-jaw* from Aunt Annie.[6]

Ever your loving
   D

[1] Edmond Rostand (1868–1918), French dramatist, author of *Cyrano de Bergerac* (1897) and *L'Aiglon* (1900). In *Chantecler* (published in 1910) all the characters are animals or birds. Miss White was certainly up to date in her teaching.
[2] The Musketeer name of Mlle Plard, who had stayed au pair at the rectory in Bluntisham.
[3] Miss White.
[4] 'The Death of the Sun' (from *La Mort du Soleil* by Leconte de Lisle, 1818–94), published in *The Godolphin Gazette*, no. 45, p. 11.
[5] George Meredith (1828–1909), *On the Idea of Comedy and the Uses of the Comic Spirit*, published in 1877. The recent death of Meredith had probably drawn special attention to his work. Coney was Constance Wollaston, a fellow pupil.
[6] Aunt Annie Sayers lived in Oxford and was to plague Dorothy with a 'pi-jaw' (a long pious talk) when she was at Somerville. (See letter from Oxford, dated March 1914.)

To Her Parents   Oakhurst
13 March 1910

Oh! my dearest people, what a dull term this is! Very nice, but deadly dull in the way of letters. Beyond having the misfortune to lose my fountain pen, which as a matter of fact I did ages ago, nothing has happened. Even the goddess[1] provides but little amusement. Oh! dear! – it is indeed serious if I can find nothing to say about Her. I *am* sorry about Uncle Cecil and Co.![2] What a *beastly* nuisance – it *is* such hard luck. I do hope and pray Ray[3] may be able to stick to the army – can't he exchange into another regiment where one doesn't need so much money? Not that I know anything about these things. I told Maud Turner, whose papa is of the Army – she was most sympathetic and said – 'He ought to exchange into an Indian Cavalry regiment (her father is Colonel or Captain or something in one) – we are all as poor as Church mice there!' adding 'that her father wd. be awfully glad to help him in any way'. (Maud is a jolly nice girl, in spite of being very pretty and connected with the Army) – I said: 'Unfortunately I can hardly write and suggest it, can I?' To which she replied dismally: 'No, that's the worst of it.' – However, all this apart, I suppose he'll probably have to – what on earth does he think of doing, though? It's awful hard luck on Uncle Cecil, having to start work again now.

I am most awfully excited about the bells[4] – I'm just bursting to come and hear them – It *will* be lovely. It will take more than one man to ring them all, won't it? They are going to be chimed, aren't they? Are you going to spring-clean the belfry at the same time? I don't think it would hurt it – eh? I remember getting jolly grimy last time I peregrinated up that staircase. I suppose they will be used for the first time on Easter Day. I wish I were going to be there. Do come down for the Confirmation if you can, but of course the bells must come first, and I shall not be jealous of them – dear things.

What do you think of Oxford's chance for the race? At 'Contemporary' on Thursday, Miss Bagnall said that the Light Blue crew was quicker but that our style was better and our rhythm steadier. I do hope we shall win! *Dear* old Oxford! It's like no other city in the world – I wonder why I love it so – I always feel when I go there as if I were going home – I think it must be the spirit of some old ancestor alive again, because after all, I've never really lived there – *consciously*.

I had an argument with Miss White in class the other day about the immortality of the souls of animals – and I am seeking an opportunity to renew the discussion in private. We are now doing Boileau[5] – he is safe and steady – Descartes[6] was dangerous and interesting – I find Boileau a little dull and bourgeois, with all his excellent character, I'm afraid – the good people of this world are generally rather uninteresting – why is this? . . .

Canon Myers is jolly nice. I went in the other day to tell him about my besetting sins and we ended by discussing Oxford and my future career. Phoebe wondered what on earth I was making such a terrific long confession about. . . .

I've just been reading the life of Helen Faucit,[7] out of the library – it is awfully interesting – Fanny Maud recommended it to me – 'The very thing for you, Dorothy, just your style'. I wish reading these things didn't fill me with such a wild desire to become great – However, I never shall be that. I was pleased to find that she says a lot about the drama and its 'mission' which is just what I tried to say in my article for the *Belfry*[8] – you remember Coney and me arranging about the *Belfry* in the Xmas holidays? I'm afraid Violet is not awfully keen, but Coney and Anna are.

By the way, have you had a communication from Miss Prosser about taking me to the National Gallery – I believe my name has been put down. . . .

[1] Miss White.
[2] For details, see letter to Ivy Shrimpton, 9 April 1910.
[3] Her cousin, Raymond Sayers.

[4] See note to letter dated 23 March 1910.
[5] Nicolas Boileau (1636–1711), French poet and critic. His maxims on poetry, *L'Art Poétique*, had an important influence in the seventeenth century.
[6] René Descartes (1596–1650), French philosopher. His method of reasoning acquired a destructive power in the hands of anti-authoritarian rationalists. This may be what Dorothy means when she says he was 'dangerous'.
[7] Helen (Helena) Faucit, Lady Martin (1820–98), actress, author of *On Some of the Female Characters of Shakespeare*. Her husband, Sir Theodore Martin, published her biography in 1900.
[8] Evidently a successor to the magazine she produced with her governess at Bluntisham, *Something New*.

TO HER PARENTS   Oakhurst
21 March 1910

My dearest people . . .
   We had a most glorious time in town yesterday. Miss Edith Jones took us up – 11 of us – and we met Miss Prosser at Waterloo. We then proceeded by tube to the National Gallery, where Miss Prosser took us through the rooms in chronological order as far as possible, pointing out all the best things that we could look at when we went by ourselves – of course, we were very much rushed for time, but Miss Prosser said what she wanted most was not so much to show us things as to show us what to see for ourselves some time when we had leisure to study the pictures quietly – it was awfully nice. We ate sandwiches in the basement of the National Gallery and felt sacrilegious, especially when a female in a purple hat walked in and started staring at us and the pictures alternately. Then we got a cup of tea (with difficulty, on account of our numbers; we had to be ejected from one full eating-house). We went to Burlington House to see three things in the Diploma Gallery, viz. a tondo by Michael Angelo, a cartoon by Leonardo da Vinci and a contemporary copy of the *Last Supper* of L. da V. Incidentally we saw the original drawings of Flaxman[1] which illustrate your Pope's Homer. We had to climb up miles and miles of winding staircase, and Miss Prosser got very puffed, but talked none the less volubly. Then we went to the British Museum and saw the Elgin marbles and the Egyptian and Assyrian things – oh! it *was* lovely, only we had so little time – I must go again some day, it *is* so ripping there. We saw heaps of lovely old illuminated books, the statuary is just *glorious*! I say! When we come back on the 6th couldn't we stay the day in London and take Anna[2] to the Tate Gallery? Miss Prosser is awfully anxious she should go there, and has promised to make us a list of the things we may legitimately contemplate and admire. . . .

Good-bye – Think of me conducting the singing to-morrow!
Awful . . .

Good-bye till the 6th

Ever your loving
    Dorothy

¹ John Flaxman (1755–1826), sculptor and draughtsman.
² Anna Hoffmann.

TO HER PARENTS   Oakhurst
23 March 1910

My dearest people

The service is just over; we have a whole half-holiday, which is
convenient, as it enables me to have decent time for writing – It was
an awfully nice service, and everything was most beautifully arranged,
so that there was no fuss or muddle – It was a huge affair – about
200 candidates, I should think – the Cathedral was absolutely packed.
We drove down to Cath. – it was a glorious day – I was quite hot in
my muslin frock – we sat on the N. side, in the 3rd row from the
pulpit – I was on the outside of our row. Our veils were most awfully
nice – chiffon – very simple with just a little ruche at the top. I thought
they looked nicer than any others, and people who could see better
than I could say the same – I think nothing is more horrid than a
skimpy little tail of net with a vast bunch or bunches on top – I
suppose one ought not to think about such things, but I *do* like to see
things in really good taste – ours most certainly were that.

We went up to the altar a whole row at a time, and the Bishop¹
moved along and did us in twos, only I was the odd one at the end
of the row, so I was done alone. Then we came down on the N. side
of the Choir, so that there was no jostling or passing each other to
get into our places. . . .

The Bishop's address was quite nice, but not awfully exciting – I
wish our Dean were a Bishop! – only then we shouldn't see him so
often. I had a small talk with Canon Myers last night – he is ripping.

We are all to make our Communion together on Easter Sunday –
the whole (confirmed) School with us – I think, don't you, it would
be nicest to have it then, with the School, and Miss Douglas would
like it, especially as I am in the VI, etc. – I will come on the 17th,
though – I asked Miss Douglas – she said she thought that would be
the best way, if you didn't mind – you see, being at school, one feels
rather out of it if one doesn't do things *with* the school.

I'm so glad the bells seem so satisfactory – I hope they're 'going
up' all right.²

Miss Bagnall has just given me a sweet little picture – Pettie's *Vigil*[3] in memory of to-day – isn't it sweet of her. . . .

I must just write a word to one or two other people now, so good-bye

Ever your very loving daughter
    Dorothy

P.S. I never can write about my *feelings* – that's why I haven't.

---

[1] The Rt Rev. John Wordsworth.
[2] The new bells in Bluntisham Church, a ring of eight, were dedicated on Easter Eve 1910 by the Ven. Gerald F. Vesey, Archdeacon of Huntingdon. During a service of thanksgiving, they were chimed by the Rector for the first time and peals were rung by him and others at the conclusion. Dorothy took a great interest but was unable to be present as she remained at school over Easter for her first communion in Salisbury Cathedral. (See *A Short Account of the Bells of St Mary's Church, Bluntisham-cum-Earith* by the Rev. H. Sayers, M.A., St Ives.)
[3] John Pettie, R.A. (1839–93), a Scottish painter.

To Ivy Shrimpton   Bluntisham Rectory
9 April 1910   St Ives
                                         Hunts

Dearest coz!

Very many thanks for your letter, to which I fear I have nothing very interesting to say in answer. The Lent term is a dull one, and though it was awfully nice this year there is nothing particular to tell. I told you, I think, that I was going to be confirmed. It was a lovely day, and it all went off beautifully. It was a huge ceremony – about 220 candidates, I think – and the Cathedral was simply *packed*. Most of the school went. The great Miss White was there – she was jolly nice to me that morning – I am beginning to think she may be a really nice woman, and not merely fascinating. She has been most wonderfully amiable this last term – quite extraordinarily so – may it long continue. Next term I hope that our French division will give a French play, under her auspices. I have asked her about it, and she seems most awfully keen. Next term Mother is going to come down to Salisbury for the week-end, and we are going to have Miss White out to lunch or tea or something. I hope nothing will happen to prevent it – Isn't it dreadful, the way I yarn on about Fanny Maud? I used to think I never could entertain a violent affection for anybody, but there! one never knows!

I suppose you have heard about Uncle Cecil having lost all his money, through a beastly lawyer who cooked the accounts and then cut his own throat! It is dreadfully bad luck on them. Uncle Cecil is trying to get something to do, but of course, it is very hard for him to get anything, on account of his age – and of course, too, he has never been used to doing any work for himself. Gerald is going into a bank. Raymond hopes to be able to stick to the Army – I believe his half-brother, Johnny Fleming, is going to allow him something – What a blessing he is such a good, steady fellow! It is dreadfully hard luck on him, as all his mother's money, which was to come to him at Uncle Cecil's death, has been bamboozled away too, and he at least has not deserved such hard luck. Of course, Uncle Cecil has been to blame in the matter – I don't know quite how, but he has been careless about it, I think, and *would* put money into unsafe concerns. Mother is always very cross with him, of course, and said she always expected it. . . .

The new bells are up, and sound most beautiful – there are 8 of them – a whole octave – so different from our old 5 – with one cracked! Of course, we can't have them 'rung-up', because the tower is not strong enough to stand it, but still, they sound very sweet chimed, though they are not as loud as if they were rung.

I do not suppose it interests you to know that I am having a new coat and skirt (ready-made at Bryant's[1]) of a vivid pink colour, with a huge burnt-straw hat with black velvet ribbon. The chief point of interest to me about them is that I want to wear them to-morrow, and they have not yet arrived.

I was on the Cardinal's bicycle yesterday when the back tyre went off with a pop and a fizz like a champagne cork – most tyre-some!

Good-bye for the present

Ever your loving
Athos

[1] Name of a draper's shop in St Ives.

Fifth term May–June 1910 (Age: 16–17)

To Her Parents   Oakhurst
22 May 1910

Darling people

No news, absolutely none, except that on Friday we went to a perfectly lovely memorial service[1] in Cathedral. The music was simply glorious – Beethoven's, Chopin's and other Dead Marches and the Dead March in Saul.[2] 'O God our Help'[3] was something too thrilling for words. I do think that is without exception the finest hymn ever written. . . .

I trust I may pass that silly exam. this year. It won't be Miss Hancock's fault if I don't. I spent half yesterday afternoon finding the area and volume of a room of idiotic proportions, and unravelling the speculations of some utter fool who had his money in 4% stock at 90 and also in something else % stock at another price, and sold the whole boiling out, and invested in something totally different – and after all these transactions, the difference in his income was exactly £1 per annum on the wrong side. I am feeling a trifle more hopeful than I did at the beginning of the term. . . .

We had a sermon this morning in St Edmund's in course of which the man, while discussing the doctrine of the Trinity, observed that Arithmetic was the meanest of the sciences. I *was* so pleased. I glanced out of the corner of my eye and caught that of Marjorie Napier, who also suffers from that science, and we enjoyed the joke with a quiet satisfaction. There was a person behind us, saying all the nice damnatory parts of the Athanasian creed with a quite appalling fervour. She seemed positively to enjoy the idea of everlasting fire – she *must* be certain of her own orthodoxy and uprightness of soul! What a peculiarly ugly sort of chant it is sung to, by the way – like a very dreary litany, with, I am really very much ashamed to observe, a certain amount of comic relief. It is very wrong, of course, but I really *do* think it is comic in parts, and the oftener I hear it, the oftener and more forcibly does this strike me.[4] How frightfully shocked Mr What's-his-Name – the High Church individual who came to the concert, I mean – would be if he could read this.

I say, it's time to sing hymns – Good-bye
        D.

[1] In commemoration of King Edward VII, who died on 6 May 1910. The Godolphin School followed the custom of the time and wore mourning, i.e. black ties and black hat-bands.
[2] The march from Handel's oratorio, *Saul*.
[3] The hymn, 'O God, our help in ages past / Our hope for years to come'. (Words by Isaac Watts, tune St Anne, composed by William Croft.)
[4] The adult Dorothy L. Sayers remembered her early feelings about the Athanasian Creed and refers to them in *The Mind of the Maker* (Methuen, 1941, pp. 120–1).

To Her Parents   Oakhurst
29 May 1910

Dearest people
    There is nothing very exciting to write about this week, and it's jolly difficult to write anything, because everybody is arguing about

plays. We can't decide what play to have. I wish we could hurry up and agree about it. People never do agree, you know, until about a week before the time, and then things have to be done in a violent hurry – such is life! This week has been quite pleasant in its way, although not awfully thrilling. I was furious with Miss Jones on Tuesday, because I found out that she had been bullying Fanny Maud about me, and telling her that I spent more time than I ought over my French and slacked over all my other work, so I was angry. The woman! She blows me up about it every Monday – I'm sure I don't care, because it's not true – look at the Maths. I'm doing now! It's all because I won't spend three hours a week over Jonesey's silly history – Miss Jones can go to Jerusalem or further for all I care! But I do draw the line at worrying Miss White! I do! I thought she probably did, but I didn't know for certain till Tuesday, when Fanny was giving me back a prose that she was rather pleased with, and said in a worried sort of way that she hoped I didn't spend more time than I ought over my French. I said I didn't and that I hoped she hadn't been hearing anything of the sort. She said she had – I *was* angry. I told her it wasn't true, and that when I did take a long time over anything I did it out of lesson time. I saw her afterwards in the library and told her all over again, with additions, and I told her one or two other things as well. She was so nice about it. But I am still angry with Miss Jones. . . .

On Friday week the invasion of head-mistresses begins. I suppose I shall see Miss Rice whom I nearly made the closer acquaintance of. (N.B. Never use a preposition to end a sentence with.) By the way, we had such a killing French lesson the other day. Fanny Maud and I disagreed. She said that we needed a disjunctive pronoun in English; I said I didn't see why we wanted one; she said that it was pedantic and absurd to say 'It is I'; I maintained that it was both ugly and incorrect to say 'It's me'; she said that heaps of people were advocating the use of 'It's me'; I said that I had also heard the use of the split infinitive advocated, and didn't think it was any the prettier or more correct for that, and that I didn't intend to use either the split infinitive or the objective for the nominative. She said 'Of course you know that you will be swimming against the stream, Dorothy – the feeling to-day is all the other way. Do you mind that?' I intimated that I didn't care a hang. It was great fun. The whole class joined in. We had a most ripping time. On Friday it was terrible. She put me on to read one of Mme. de Sévigné's[1] most sentimental letters. She had just been making us laugh like anything over the letters before, and we were all feeling frivolous, and when I started, I absolutely collapsed into the most awful fit of weak giggles I have had for a long time. It was hopeless. I couldn't stop myself. I wept copiously.

Everybody joined in. It was Pandemonium. Miss White didn't know what to do with herself. She was shaking with laughter, and every time I looked up and tried to calm myself I caught her eye. She has the most fearfully infectious laugh – smile, rather – I mean that if she smiles you have to laugh because she looks so quaint. It was hopeless. Never before have I had such a fit of the giggles in French lesson.

We had a Debate on Wednesday. The motion was that – 'It is better to be a Jack of All Trades than a Master of One'. It was a very dull discussion. Miss White and I spoke on opposite sides. I supported the motion and she opposed it. I was so delighted at one point, because Miss Jones made a very foolish statement, and I got up and squashed her promptly and witheringly, and everybody agreed with what I said and were pleased with me for having said it. I was *simply* delighted. It was such a treat to be able to squash old Jonesey with the approval of the whole school. That's one reason why I like debates – you meet the mistresses on equal terms – you are all honourable members – and you can argufy with your revered form mistress till all's blue if you like, and pour out your sarcasm upon her with crushing force. The motion was eventually carried. . . .

[1] Marie de Rabutin-Chantal, Marquise de Sévigné (1626–96), French letter-writer. Her letters offer a vivid picture of public and private life in France in the seventeenth century. Those to her daughter, Mme de Grignan, are among the most touching, though in places they appear over-expressive to modern readers.

To Her Mother   Oakhurst
19 June 1910

Darling Mummy

We are just enjoying a most ripping half term and the most gorgeous weather. . . . On Friday we had a lovely time. We drove to a place called Lake; it is somewhere near Stonehenge, I think. We had been invited to tea by some dear little people who live the simple life in a little house on the top of a hill, overlooking the most perfect scenery. The old grandfather, whose name is Mr Lovibond, is most awfully clever, and a perfect old dear. He owns Lake House – a glorious old place, but has let it and built himself this sweet little house on the hill. He actually built it with his own hands, with the help of his gardener, all except the putting on of the roof, which he had to have done for him. He is awfully interested in the village people, and has started up a weaving industry in the village. He took us to see it. It was charming to see a girl sitting spinning at the door, while motorcars whizzed dustily along the road. The old chap then punted us about the river and showed us his lovely big trout in the stream.

Yesterday was perfect! We all went to Miss Lucy's hut in the New

Forest and stayed there for tea and supper. We wandered about the
Forest all afternoon and picked wild foxgloves. It *was* lovely. Really,
though, the most exciting part of it, to me, was that I made the
acquaintance of a kindred spirit. She is one of the new girls at Oakhurst this term – and her name is Molly Edmondson. She, like myself,
is considered a 'weird freak' by the conventional portion of this estab-
lishment. Her great ambition is to go on the stage and she loves poetry
etc. She really seems to be awfully nice. I am so glad I walked with
her. Her father is a clergyman somewhere in the Black Country.[1] I
have asked her to come out to tea with us when you come down here.
Perhaps if we really become friends she might come some time in the
holidays. It would be nice, wouldn't it, as she is really keen on the
same things as I am. We exchanged ideas on the subject of the estab-
lishment of a National Theatre, and the elevation of the drama to its
proper place as a noble and inspiring art etc. We seemed to agree *à
merveille*.[2] . . .

Good-bye – in fact, *au revoir*, till Saturday week

Ever your very loving
Dorothy

[1] Name given to parts of Staffordshire and Warwickshire, blackened by the coal and iron
industries.
[2] Marvellously.

To Her Parents   Oakhurst
17 July 1910

Dearest people
I told you anything there was to say yesterday, which was nothing
at all. Nothing has happened in particular – except that – oh! yes, I
didn't tell you that I have been presented with a Red Girdle for
deportment(!!!) so you see, the Cardinal's[1] 'keeping on' at me has
had good results.

We have just been to St Thomas's, as a great favour and a special
exception, etc., because Miss Douglas doesn't think people ought to
change their church because of the preacher, – to hear the end of the
Dean's sermon. It was awfully fine and a beautiful service.

The play seems to be getting on pretty well. Could you please send
me my dagger paper-knife – I think it is either in the schoolroom or
my quarters or my bedroom. If not, it is probably somewhere else,
but I *must* have it, please, if you can find it, because I have to offer
to stab Jean in my scene. My dress will come to seven and something,[2]
but I want to pay for part of it myself, please, because I said she was

to get plenty of stuff and do it properly, so the expense is my fault, only I can't bear skimpy clothing.

Dear people! I haven't seen Fanny since she got your Eminence's letter – I shan't dare to meet her eye. *Send me her letter. Don't forget!* If she does come, Aunt Maud really must come too – only then the goddess won't be able to have the best bedroom. What shocking treatment for an immortal! However, she probably won't come. Oh! lor'! Everybody is so bad-tempered just at present, except Miss Hancock, who is a little dear . . .

The exams. have been deadly dull, except that there was a misprint in the dictation, and Fanny was in agonies of mind about it. Eventually she told us, and now *hopes* we shan't be disqualified. Weird old bird! . . .

[1] Her mother.
[2] Seven shillings and some pence (in old currency).

TO HER PARENTS   Wellmead[1]
No date, but summer holidays, 1910   Fryerning
                                                   Ingatestone
                                                   Essex

Dear people

Here I am, safe, with my box, my tennis-racquet, my book, my purse and my keys. I had a ripping journey all the way. At Sutton a Miss Marshall got in and we talked. She knew who I was, and said would I come over to tennis some day? I said I should like to very much. She has 7 brothers (!) – one of them (in the army) is at home now.

At Ely I talked to an elderly and communicative person who had come to meet her daughter. From Ely to Cambridge I had a very nice man – he was something to do with the law and had come to Ely to see about an embezzling post-office official, who had appropriated about £300 and been seized with remorse and given himself up. (Persons in post-offices, *please note!*) With him (the nice man, not the embezzler) I talked about the Coronation[2] and how sinful it was to spend so much money on gorging and guzzling (them were not my words but that was my meaning). He quite agreed and made himself variously pleasant. At Cambridge he took his departure after presenting me with *John Bull!*[3]

Between Cambridge and London I had a talkative little old boy in a black silk travelling-cap, who was a great expert on modern, mediaeval and oriental literature, and languages generally. We conversed on education. At Bishop's Stortford a long youth got in and went to sleep in a corner. Later we had a sprightly office-boy carrying a motor-tyre which he put in the rack but, being remonstrated with by the linguistic old gentleman and the guard, he planted it in the corridor. He then started to talk cheerfully, and the motor-tyre naturally led the conversation to large hats and their inconvenience in railway-carriages and trams. Eventually the sleepy youth awoke and the old gentleman made conversation with him, and so to Liverpool Street Station.

Just before we got there a dishevelled and excited female thrust her head in at the door and asked me in frantic tones whether we had passed (!!) Liverpool Street Station – I think this was what aroused the torpid young man. He said it certainly would be alarming if we *had* passed through Livpl. Street and thereafter became, as I have said, conversational. On getting out I left my book on the seat. It was restored by the torpid youth as I wrestled with a porter. I departed from London by the *4.22* (Oh! Daddy!) and got to Fryerning in time for tea. I then played two sets of tennis rather badly. After dinner we mouched round and pretended to do some singing, but neither Mrs C. nor V. have any great idea of time, which makes part-singing highly unsatisfactory. V. is as usual – her manner is self-satisfied and irritates me. However!

Love from D.

¹ Dorothy had gone to stay with Violet Christy.
² Of King George V.
³ A newspaper edited by Horatio Bottomley. It is mentioned by Lord Peter Wimsey in *Unnatural Death* (chapter 3).

Sixth term September–December 1910 (Age: 17)

To Her Parents   School House
25 September 1910

Dearest people

I feel as if there were an awful lot to say, but there's so little time and so much talking. Natasha Harris, the School House Prefect, has not come back yet, so (this will please Daddy) I am having to act as prefect in her place – it *is* a nuisance. We have got a much larger VI this year, but we are not all prefects – I am one, though, and do not enjoy it. I am also the new Editor of the Magazine – another bore! . . .

I am having *seven* German lessons a week – some with Fräulein Seipp, who is awfully nice, and some with F.M. Fräulein Seipp and I have a little lesson all to ourselves on Monday and another on

Thursday, in which we study Faust.[1] The French lessons are not all arranged for yet. . . .

No more mathematics! It *is* gorgeous! Lessons are quite different – The new classics person seems to be very nice, but I have only had one lesson with her as yet. Miss Jones has been amiable so far – I don't know how long it will last. . . .

I have tons of letters to write and things to do, so good-bye

With heaps of love from
    Dorothy

[1] Goethe's *Faust*. The adult Dorothy L. Sayers was to write a drama for Canterbury Cathedral on the subject of Faust, *The Devil to Pay*. See also her article, 'The Faust Legend and the Idea of the Devil' in *The Poetry of Search and the Poetry of Statement* (Gollancz, 1963, pp. 227–41).

TO HER PARENTS   School House
8 October 1910

Dearest people
    There's no news. None. The course of events has been as uneventful this week as it well could be – except that I have got into various odd rows with the goddess. I did not send in my German prose on Wednesday – with dire results. I have never been so blown up but once, by the same person. Rather a mistake on my part, wasn't it? I do German with the Bishop of Ely's[1] cousin, Eleanor Chase. She's an awfully nice girl, and rather a friend of mine. She came to Oakhurst this term. . . .

    I have been talking to all sorts of people lately about my chance of doing anything on the Stage – amongst others, Miss Bagnall and Miss Douglas – Miss D. thinks I should not be any good. Miss Bagnall thinks I might, but both agree that I'd better not do anything about it till I leave college, so there is no fear of anything happening for another four years at least. Miss Douglas rather thinks I should probably be a greater success as a dramatist than as an actor. You don't mind my talking it over with people, do you, dears? Of course, if it were ever so, I'd never go on without your leave. I must show you a newspaper cutting I came across the other day about Tree's[2] school. If ever I tried at all, it would be there. By the way, supposing I could (I don't think I can, though) get another awfully nice girl to come and stay with me in the Xmas holidays, could we manage to put her up at the same time as Mollie? because she is also awfully keen on acting, and we could do some ripping things. I don't expect for a moment she can come, though, but I should like to ask her, if I may.

There really is nothing to tell you, and I'm dead tired after two of the most long and boring services you *ever* attended. I nearly fell asleep in Cath. this afternoon.

Good-bye

Ever your very loving
    Dorothy

[1] The Rt Rev. Frederick Henry Chase.
[2] In 1904 Sir Herbert Beerbohm Tree founded what is now the Royal Academy of Dramatic Art. This is the school to which Dorothy refers.

To Her Parents   School House
16 October 1910

Dearest people . . .
    I must [relate] the event of the week – Shackleton's[1] lecture on Tuesday. It was simply wonderful – I had never seen a hero before, and it was rather a thrilling experience. He is extraordinarily British – very quiet and drawly-voiced and quite absolutely splendid. We are all in love with him, and buying post-cards of him. I was sufficiently excited on Tuesday to indite a sonnet to the gallant explorer – not a bad sonnet either, as my sonnets go. Shall I angle for his signature as I angled for Baliol Holloway's? I might send him the sonnet,[2] to save myself the trouble of writing a letter. . . .
    He told one awfully good story about Professor David,[3] who was on the expedition, and was a *very* polite man. Mawson, one of the explorers, was doing something or other (in the hut, I think) one day, when he heard Prof. D.'s voice calling.

D. Mawson!
M. Yes!
D. Are you busy, Mawson?
M. Yes.
D. *Very* busy, Mawson?
M. Yes (gruffly).
D. *Really* very busy, Mawson?
M. Yes, what do you want?
D. Well, I'm very sorry to trouble you, Mawson, if you're really busy, but I'm down a crevasse, and I can't get out!

Just one more story, and I must leave Shackleton. He was showing some people round the exhibition of the explorers' things one day, and he had shown them the tent and the cooking stove and the various things, and answered a lot of questions, when an old woman, who had followed him round and listened with great interest to all his explanations, planted herself in front of him, and in a loud and penetrating voice, thus addressed him: – 'Young man! You're talking a great deal – have you ever been down there yourself?' . . .

[1] Sir Ernest Shackleton (1874–1922), explorer, who took part in two Antarctic expeditions: 'Discovery' (1901–4) and 'Nimrod' (1907–9). A sledging party, led by Shackleton, reached within 97 mi. of the south pole. He was knighted on his return. His lecture in Salisbury was one of his many fund-raising events.
[2] She did so. It was published in *The Godolphin Gazette*, No. 44, p. 21.
[3] T. W. Edgeworth David, who led a second sledging party and reached the area of the south magnetic pole.

To Her Parents   School House
23 October 1910

Dearest people . . .

I spent yesterday afternoon after games acting *Richard III* with Mollie. Of course, this morning in 'pi-reading'[1] Miss Douglas must needs read: 'The lower animals are for us living object-lessons of various vices – greed, cunning etc. For this we do not blame them, any more than we should want to hang an actor who played Richard III'. Of course I and those who knew were in fits of laughter. . . .

We had Daddy's hymn-tune[2] on Wednesday. It went rippingly and everyone sang up like Trojans. It has been hugely admired. It is known as 'D. Sayers's Tune' – I think people will begin to think I wrote it, so I correct them, so they then call it 'D. Sayers's father's tune', which is longer, but more correct. We had such a dreadful time in St Edmund's this morning – the Decani[3] side of the choir was rent by schism – one faction supporting one rendering of the chant, the other ready to die for an alternative version. I chose a side and backed it valiantly for about 6 verses, with much opposition from the opposite side – at length the opposition gave way, and but for a few spasmodic howls, gave us no more trouble till the end of the psalms. . . .

Ever your loving
Dorothy

[1] Probably morning assembly.
[2] A setting of the hymn beginning 'Bright the vision that delighted / Once the sight of Judah's seer'. It is usually sung to the setting by R. Redhead (1820–1901). Dorothy's father is known to have composed other hymn tunes but none appear to have been published and no MS copies have come to light.
[3] Decani, genitive of Latin *decanus*, dean, the term for the choir stalls on the south side, where the dean of a cathedral sits.

To Her Parents   School House
6 November 1910

Dearest people
    An eventful week. To begin with, on Tuesday I received the
following: . . .

    31 Oct. 1910
    Dear Miss Sayers
        Please forgive me not answering yours before. I have been very
    busy. I quite remember the school of girls.
        I thank you very much for the sonnet only you are too kind to
    us in it.
                    Yours sincerely
                    Ernest Shackleton

So much for audacity! Such nice writing, my dears, but quite illegible!
Sir Ernest Shackleton is a really nice man. Miss White was most
awfully bucked – I told her before I told anybody else except Mollie,
and she told me to tell Miss Douglas, so I did, in fear and trembling,
and, would you believe it? She was quite pleased. She wasn't as nice
as F.M. about it, though – she doesn't know how, you know – she
meant to be awfully nice, but she hasn't got the art of saying a nice
thing nicely. . . .
    Well, the other great event is that the French actors have been.
They came to the school and played *Le Bourgeois Gentilhomme*.[1] It was
simply splendid – only the very nicest man of all wasn't there, M.
Rollan. Of course I didn't talk to the actors at all, but after the
performance I had a nice little chat with their manager, M. Roubaud.
He is absolutely sweet – a perfect dear – I do love French people.
One gets sick of school sometimes and being 'Dorothy' to everyone,
and blown up by everybody, from Miss Douglas to one's Games
Representative. You can't think how pleasant it is to be smiled and
bowed to, and called, 'Mademoiselle', and paid compliments, and be
told that you are '*si charmante*',[2] and that a pleasant and vivacious
little Frenchman is '*ravi d'avoir fait votre connaissance*',[3] and hopes to see
you next year; and to send him to fetch you programmes, and be told
that he will fetch them with '*tout le plaisir du monde*'[4] and to tell him
that he is '*mais trop gentil*'[5] and to thank him '*trente mille fois*',[6] and to
be asked with an accent of polite incredulity whether you are really
English, and told that 'Mademoiselle' speaks French '*à ravir*'.[7] – Miss
Douglas was rather decent, really, because she let me ask Miss White
to ask them for their autographs, and I have got a page of my album
full of scrawly signatures. M. Roubaud got them for me, the dear!

He promised to send me the photos. of all the actors, but I don't know whether he will. I asked after my favourite M. Rollan, and he said he'd been very ill; he had to serve his time in the army, and slept on something damper than usual, and got dreadful rheumatism all down his right side, and his doctor had absolutely forbidden him to play at present. All this with much explanatory bowing and gesticulation. Miss White and I stood by and said '*Quel malheur!*'[8] and hoped that he was coming back soon; he said 'Oh yes! he was coming back, but for the present his doctor '*lui avait absolument défendu de revenir*'.[9] Altogether, I enjoyed myself hugely – the performance itself was simply splendid, M. and Mme. Jourdain and the Maître de Musique being particularly good. . . .

>   Ever your loving
>   D.

[1] Comedy by Molière.
[2] So charming.
[3] Delighted to have made your acquaintance.
[4] All the pleasure in the world.
[5] But too kind.
[6] Thirty thousand times.
[7] Ravishingly.
[8] How unfortunate!
[9] Had absolutely forbidden him to return.

TO HER MOTHER   School House
13 November 1910

Darling Mummy
    There's simply no news, and I've been yarning away to Uncle Percy[1] till I've simply no time left, especially as Mollie and Eleanor Chase came to tea, and I had to entertain them, which wasted a lot of time. Violet Christy wrote the other day, and says she wants me to come at Xmas, so I said I would – I'm only going for a few days, though, because the Xmas hols. are so short, and I want to be at home.
    I'm so glad the new pony seems to be turning out so well – the other one seems to have been a very bad lot – It will be awfully nice having a trap again. One can't always ride a bicycle, at least not with decent clothes on, especially on one of those lovely windy days so common in the fens!
    Do you know, I've quite fallen in love with Fräulein Seipp – she is such a dear – she and I get on awfully well together. I pleased her so much last week by translating a bit out of *Faust* into English verse.

She has sent it to Germany as a specimen of English intelligence. I'm
so bucked. . . .

[1] Her mother's brother, Percival Leigh, who settled in Australia.

TO HER PARENTS   School House
28 November 1910

Darling people

I went to Dr Bardsley yesterday. He says that my headache was
due to my eyes, and that I did the right thing in going. It seems that
though I've got 'beautiful long sight' – in fact, more than the normal,
I have what he calls astigmatism, in one eye particularly, which makes
close work a strain. I haven't felt it up to now, but just lately you see
I have been working a bit harder, and it's just begun to show. The
upshot is, that I am to wear spectacles for reading – not for always,
thank goodness! Of course I could have glasses, but for schoolwork
spectacles, though ugly, are less bother.[1] Dr Bardsley observed that
in this civilised world it was necessary, though my sight would probably have served me excellently in a state of nature. Do let's live the
simple life! Dr B. is a weird old fish, with a husky sepulchral voice
which makes one want to clear one's throat all the time he's talking.
The first thing he told me was that he knew Granny and Grandfather
and Uncle Edward in Willesden. I said 'How curious!' in my politest
manner – He says I ought to go and see him again in about 6 months'
time. – I'm quite all right again myself now, thanks awfully. . . .

Molly and I had rather a good rehearsal of *Richard III* yesterday
afternoon. What a fool one feels spouting villainous heroics in a linen
collar and striped tie. However, when it came to my 'sharp-pointed
sword' being represented by a pen-holder, I struck. . . .

Au revoir – Ever your very loving
    D.

[1] Spectacles were metal-rimmed, with ear-pieces. Glasses were pince-nez, which the adult
D.L.S. often wore. This distinction in terms is out of date.

TO HER PARENTS   School House
11 December 1910

Dearest people

Do you know I really had an awfully funny time in town yesterday.
I won't write a long account, because I shall soon be back and that
sort of thing tells itself better by the living voice, as we say in Paris.[1]
The Frenchman was a perfect little darling, the German not so nice.

The exam.[2] was in the Drapers' Hall in Throgmorton Street – it was all very imposing and grand with its oak panelling, stained glass windows and magnificent chandelier. The rooms were extremely large, and one entered through tall folding doors, and felt very small indeed. I was escorted by an old Godolphin girl who met me in London. I go up for the written work on Tuesday and stay till Friday with Miss Janet Douglas.

Miss Harding is a weird old fish and she burst into the VI the other day and demanded abruptly whether, to oblige her personally, I would like to learn the viola – she would give me a short instruction and lend me a viola and music to practise in the holidays. Would I take a day to think it over. I did so, and said I saw no objection except that of transporting two fiddle cases across London and learning a new clef – however, if it's going to please her, I might just as well learn something new if I can without expense – the viola is a useful thing to be able to play, as very few people learn it. Take anything you can get for nothing – Grab! in short – is a good motto – I have grabbed. She seems pleased – Heaven knows why she is so anxious about it. . . .

I'm simply living for the holidays. I don't think I can stand more than one more term of school, though really in some ways I've enjoyed this term more than any other, almost – People seem to like me better this term and I haven't quarrelled with Miss Jones once!!

I was forgetting to tell you that Sarum House gave a party last night of a most original kind. They had tableaux, each of which represented a well-known advertisement, and you had to guess the advertised article. The tableaux were excellent. After each there was a dance. I had a dance with Miss White, but of course we talked exam. all the time. . . .

[1] *Cela se dit mieux à la voix vivante.*
[2] The Cambridge Higher Local Oral Examination in French and German.

Seventh term January–April 1911 (Age: 17)

To Her Parents   School House
22 January 1911

Dearest people

Term has begun much as usual. The people who usually scowl at me or ignore me received me with open arms and wreathed smiles, the distinguished H. Locals Candidate, and there was the usual fuss at prayers[1] – I'm sickened with it all. Eleanor [Chase] and I are doing French together. You will be delighted (as I was) to hear that I am to take my scholarship in French literature and not in German. I am happy. By the way, F.M. says she'll try and find some nice people in Paris – she said this of herself without being asked. She says she thinks I haven't much chance for a Somerville scholarship, because people of 24 or 25 go in for them from other colleges, and they rather prefer this, whereas Lady M's[2] prefer young girls, if promising.

Miss Harding has revealed the reason of last term's remarkable request. She has an Orchestra in the town and some of us are going down every Tuesday to play in it. She wanted another viola, and chose me – thinking, I suppose, that I was a good-natured sort of brute. This means, I am sorry to say, chucking Special Singing, as they happen at the same time – I explained to Miss Douglas and she said it would be best, and I'm to take Big Singing instead. I know you won't mind – at least, I mean, you'd rather I did the orchestra than the singing, wouldn't you? . . .

I ought to inform you that there is a case of measles at Nelson House . . . but it has gone to the San.[3] and the whole house is in quarantine so it probably won't spread. . . .

[1] The headmistress announced that Dorothy Sayers had come top in all England in the Cambridge Higher Local Examinations, with distinction in French and spoken German.
[2] Lady Margaret Hall.
[3] The school sanatorium.

To Her Mother   School House
28 February 1911

Darling Mummy

Feb. 17th is the anniversary of Molière's death and we're going to celebrate it by giving the 3rd act of *Les Femmes Savantes* to a few select guests. I am stage-managing – it was my idea. Miss D[ouglas] likes it very much. Will you please send me the costumes? So sorry to bother you, but I'm frightfully keen on this . . .

Also, sweetest Mummykin, if you *could* make me a new pair of red sateen breeches, as wide as the yellow pair, I should never be able to thank you enough. I shall want the old red pair as well. Lastly, will you ask Daddy to send the Saint George Suite for 2 violins.[1] There is no hurry, but I'd like to have the things fairly soon and the violin duet at once, so as to be able to write again if anything else is wanted. *So* sorry to bother you – I'm going to act Trissotin.

Much love
    D.

¹ Composed by George Saint George (1841–1924). His music was popular with violin students.

A member of School House caught measles and went off to the Sanatorium. On 29 January Dorothy wrote: 'So far both I and the rest of the "troupe" have escaped. I do hope nothing may happen to prevent the play coming off.' And again on 5 February: 'We have only invited 15 people. I am living in terror lest someone should go and get measles before the day.' Dorothy and a friend went for a walk and talked to the School House patient through the hedge. Perhaps for this reason Dorothy herself caught the disease. Double pneumonia developed and she almost died. Her mother came to help nurse her through the crisis. After convalescing in a nursing home in Salisbury, she returned to Bluntisham. By the end of April she had recovered but she spent the summer term at home. One result of her illness was that her hair fell out and for the first few weeks of the autumn term she was obliged to wear a wig.

To Ivy Shrimpton   Bluntisham Rectory
24 April 1911

Dearest girl

It's nearly post-time, but I must write to you – I've had 9 weeks' arrears of letters to clear off and I'm only just beginning to see my way through them. I must say quickly what I have to say.

1) I'm quite well again.

2) I'm so sorry you've had such dreadful trouble with your house. You *are not* to be house-hunting when I want you to come and stay with me – do you hear? You've got to come.

3) My quarters are so nice now. We've had the window opened (if you remember, only one side of it used to open), and the frame and sill painted white. It makes all the difference to the light and airiness of the room.

4) I've got a whole set of real proper knuckle-bones – a school friend who has been staying here, and I picked them up in the garden. We must have some good matches this summer.

5) We've got a French Professor of Languages (!) coming here next month. I found him in the paper. He is only 24 and Mother doesn't think it's quite proper – There! now you can joke about someone else and leave poor Dull Red alone. . . .

Eighth term October–December 1911 (Age: 18)

To Her Parents   School House
8 October 1911

Dearest people
    Many thanks for letter and parcel. There is no news at all of any
kind, except that the night before last I had to give the whole House
a fearful blowing up on the subject of – what do you think? – untidiness!!! I did feel such a hypocrite!
    No – I'm not doing any teaching – being House Prefect it would
be all unpossible [sic] – I have only too many duties as it is – mostly
unpleasant ones – giving people rows and trying to behave myself. . . .
    [Fanny M and I] quarrel about various things all through our
lessons – last time it was about Browning – she declared that he was
difficult to like and I declared he wasn't and then I said I hated
Wordsworth (whom we are doing with Mr Bodington) and she was
shocked – and then we disagreed about a play of Racine's. . . .
    Our beloved Mr Johns[t]on[1] (the late Bishop's Chaplain) who
preaches such good sermons is still (Heaven be praised!) at
St Edmund's. He preached this morning on the Song of Solomon.
Canon Sowter[2] is preaching in Cathedral. I like him very much, so
that ecclesiastically speaking I am fairly happy. The choir was quite
mad this morning. They always conclude with an ornate, two-fold
Amen, and to-day the boys started the second amen about a bar and
a half before the men, while the organist with his back to them
flourished an ineffectual baton. The curtain which conceals the organist from a too-curious congregation was not completely closed this
morning, and we enjoyed an excellent view of the organ-blower, who
was convulsed with merriment all through the service and talked
incessantly to the organist. . . .

[1] The Rev. Charles Mallam Johnston, of Exeter College, Oxford.
[2] The Rev. F. B. Sowter, Canon Resident of Sarum from 1910.

To Her Parents   School House
22 October 1911

My dears, . . .
    Look here! We are going to do *The Merchant of Venice* for a house-play
. . . and I am to play Shylock (!!!!) – will you please send me Daddy's
beard[1] and 3 pairs of breeches and your little old brown cloak and a

false nose some time before the end of the month – and bag Auntie's Shakespeare with the pictures of Irving and E. Terry[2] and send it at once, *please* – I *must* have a nose – and I *can't* get one here, but if you, either of you happen to be in Cambridge or London – oh! I beg and beseech that you will step into a make-up shop and ask for a Jewish (not a comic red) nose, and instructions how to put it on – I'm simply distracted about my wretched nose – is there anything helpful about Shylock in that Life of Edmund Kean?[3] Darlings, I'm *so* sorry to bother you, but I really must – and oh! could you step into the toyshop – Hill's – in St Ives and get me three-penny worth of *grey* jute for a moustache? . . .

The French players are coming on Saturday. They are going to do *Les Précieuses Ridicules* and *La Poudre aux Yeux*[4] – I don't suppose I shall be able to speak to M. Roubaud this time, as they are coming to a hall in the town. I do hope Rollan will come this time. I shall weep if he doesn't – he *is* so ripping! . . .

Mr George gave me a song last week 'Four by the Clock'.[5] He stopped me after I had sung him the first verse, and said: 'I see you are going to be my prize dictionist – you sing with real musical feeling – you are the only girl I've had who sings '*Four* by the *Clock*' – They all say, '*Four by* the *Clock*' – even the composer's wife does it.' The rest of his lesson was not so complimentary – except that I sang him an exercise, all full of runs, and he said I had such a splendid sense of rhythm – I wish I wasn't so fond of being praised. I won't work for people who don't encourage me!

Miss Etlinger gave a ripping concert yesterday – she sang some topping songs, among others 'Who is Sylvia?' and 'Cupid and my Campaspe'[6] – afterwards somebody asked me 'And what *is* a Campaspe?'

I must stop now, as I've a lot of letters to write – give my love to the GYM[7] – I want to come home more than ever – I am dying to break his celibate heart with a hopeless passion. How lucky I wasn't born beautiful – I should have been an awful flirt.

    Ever your devoted
    Shylock

Don't forget my *nose!*

[1] The false beard her father used to wear in his role as Louis XIII in the Musketeers game.
[2] Sir Henry Irving (1838–1905), and Dame Ellen Terry (1847–1928).
[3] Edmund Kean (1787–1833), reputed one of the greatest English actors, famous for his Shakespearean roles, among them that of Shylock. The biography mentioned may be that by F. W. Hawkins, 1869.
[4] The first play is by Molière. The second is by Eugène Marin Labiche (1815–88), who wrote mainly farces. *La Poudre aux Yeux* (Dust in One's Eyes), 1861, has a moral message.

His best known play is *Un Chapeau de Paille d'Italie* (An Italian Straw Hat), 1851.
[5] Words by Longfellow, set to music by James Albert Mallinson (1870–1946), who composed over 400 songs. His wife, who was Danish, was a professional singer.
[6] A lyric from *Alexander and Campaspe*, a comedy by John Lyly (1554?–1606):

> When Cupid and my Campaspe play'd
> At cards for kisses, Cupid paid.

Campaspe was a beautiful harlot whom Alexander the Great handed on to Apelles, who drew her in the nude.
[7] Good Young Man – her father's pupil who was boarding at the rectory.

To Her Parents   School House
29 October 1911

Dearest people
   I have been too fearfully busy even to send you a post-card, but I expect you deduced from my silence that the things you sent had arrived quite safely and that the beard would do perfectly well – at least I think so. I don't think I shall need a wig, unless I had a nice grey half-bald one; my own hair is rather thick on top[1] for Shylock. . . . The rehearsals are going remarkably well so far – Portia is going to be extremely good and so is Antonio. I don't seem quite to realise Shylock yet, but perhaps that will come with study.
   The French players came last night, and were just as perfectly ripping as usual. There was only one man the same as the last two times – he was absolutely splendid as the doctor in *La Poudre aux Yeux* – Mascarille in *Les Précieuses* was very good now, though perhaps he played the part a trifle more farcically than I had expected. A very amusing little unrehearsed comedy happened afterwards, which left me triumphant, for myself, but with a sad heart for the followers of Thespis. M. Roubaud saw me during the performance, recognised me, and we both bowed and smiled. Smothered fury of Matron and Miss Parson, who sat next me, blocking my exit. After the performance, Roubaud stood by the door – Miss Douglas was some way ahead – I knew I should have to pass the man and that he would speak. I didn't know what to do – I turned to Matron: 'May I speak to M. Roubaud? I know him from last year, and he knows my aunt (Ye powers!)' 'No.' Hopeless. I looked for Miss Douglas – a seething crowd surged between – I was struggling to get to her, but Miss Parson stopped me – 'Go on out at once, Dorothy, hurry up.' 'I have to speak to Miss Douglas, please.' 'Go on now, you must speak to Miss Douglas afterwards.' (Insolent fool! She knew why I wanted to speak, and was determined to prevent it.) – It was no good – I had to pass the man – I had done my best to get leave, but they wouldn't

let me – I determined not to speak first, but I knew it was inevitable. I was passing out of the door when he spoke – there was no help for it – short of absolute rudeness I could not escape the meeting. I had to reply politely. Almost before I could say good-evening Miss Parson was at me, dragging me off – I had hardly time to answer his polite remarks coherently, and Miss Parson was at me the whole time – I had to go – Heaven only knows what he thought of my manners! I caught up Matron, who was waiting for me – I said 'I'm sorry, Matron, he spoke to me first' – She said – 'I should have ignored him' – Dear saints! – I had been simmering, and at that my blood boiled up like a witches' cauldron. Oh! the spirit of scorn and pride – that thinks a couple of shillings can buy free soul and spirit, and that the right to laugh at a man's antics upon the stage confers the privilege of treating him as a dog – insulting his feelings – Do you think that if Roubaud had been a singer or a painter I should have been bidden to ignore him? – Well! well! – the spirit of pride and contempt that buried the great Molière secretly at dead of night, is still alive – How long, O Lord, how long? – But to return to my story.

I came up from the town in a fury. Arrived at School, I went straight to Miss Douglas, and told her all about it – she was *perfectly ripping* and said I had done perfectly right, and Matron and Miss Parson hadn't quite understood, and it was quite right of me to come to her about it. I was awfully glad I had, for that confounded Viper had been before me – Miss D. said: 'Miss Parson said something to me about it, but I explained to her, and I think she understands now.' I hope to Heaven she gave that woman a good dressing down. Pompous, interfering, conceited ass!!!! Excuse strong language – but that woman does *rile* me, and I *hate* having to put up in silence with the insults of a handsome fool, and she *never* by any chance speaks politely to me.

You will think I have made a great fuss over a little thing – but it is not the mere fact of not having been able to speak to Roubaud that makes me so angry – but it's the underlying *spirit* of the thing – thank the pigs I am not a snob! – or is that a snobbish thing to say? – but I really don't think I am. However, I think I really scored off the Viper and Matron in the end – but I hate that Roubaud should think me rude – I only trust his feelings were not hurt.

Well! well! – there's an end of that – I wrote a sonnet[2] and let it all out. . . .

Ever your loving
Athos

[1] This makes it plain that Dorothy's hair had grown since her illness and that by the end of October she was no longer obliged to wear a wig.
[2] Published by James Brabazon in *Dorothy L. Sayers: The Life of a Courageous Woman* (Gollancz, 1981, pp. 40–1).

To Her Parents   School House
29 November 1911

My dearest people

There is nothing to tell you. Nothing at all has happened lately, except that I, being in perfect health, was made to see Dr Kempe on Monday and to take *his* tonic, which, whatever Matron may say, is neither more nor less than Fellowes's syrup.[1] The editing of the magazine is practically finished, for which I sing *Te Deum*[2] – Talking about singing, we must do that carol-singing we were talking about. To-morrow I am going to send you a rather nice carol book that we might choose some out of – King Wenceslas of course and 'Earthly friends may change and falter' and '*Quem Pastores*' – 'Unto us is born a Son' is a topping one – it is the one we had for the singing competition last spring. The 'Three Kings of Orient' aren't in this book, but I am going to get them. When I get home I shall buy a hektograph jelly and copy them out. Mr George was much touched by my thoughtfulness in jellying the *Ave Maria*, and in a burst of enthusiasm told me that he wanted me to sing a solo – think of it! – at the end-of-term concert. I howled, but he persisted. He's quite mad – I think as a matter of fact Miss Douglas has been agitating for soloists, and as there's only one other person who sings besides me and she has no ear, it is rather Hobson's choice[3] with Mr George, poor man! I wish he wouldn't wear such a loud black and white check suit, it gives me a fit every time I see him.

Ah! but there *is* a piece of news though! what do you think it is? – you'll never guess – to the end of her days your daughter will be able to say that she has played the violin in the Albert Hall –!!! – she need not add under what circumstances! The facts are thus – The Godolphin School Orchestra has been invited to play in a huge orchestra of all the London schools, on the occasion of the (I think Miss Harding said) Exhibition of Dolls – but I didn't quite catch what she said. It is rather an honour, since (I think) only two other country orchestras, Oxford and Winchester, have been asked to play. The concert is on December 13th. – so you see I am getting quite a list of public engagements!!!!! The Musical Evening is on Dec. 6th. . . .

I have no idea yet whether we shall be able to have our play; I haven't been able to go to Miss Douglas yet. It won't be till much later anyway – perhaps not till next term – I almost hope we shan't have it this term, as there are so many things happening, and all the actors will be here but one, next term. However, we shall see.

I am writing to Coney to-day, I will suggest the end of the holidays

– which end shall we have the G.Y.M.? Anyhow, I refuse to appear
before him for the first time in a school hat – my chance of fascinating
him would be clean gone for ever. If he is at home when I come home
you must get him out of the way when I arrive. I will burst upon
him in all the glory of a becoming costume!! Dear, dear! what awful
nonsense I'm talking! I think it's a very good idea that Ivy should
come a week before the holidays. She can talk to the G.Y.M. and
they can broaden each other's minds, for from all accounts he is as
narrow in his ideas as she is. I do wish he were not vowed to celibacy
– we might make a match for him. I wish he were going to be there
in the holidays, I could give him lessons – not in Greek and Latin
certainly, but I daresay a little English literature would not injure
him. . . .

[1] A well-known tonic of the period, containing iron.
[2] *Te Deum Laudamus* (We praise Thee, O God), words attributed to St Ambrose, sung at
Mattins.
[3] Hobson's choice: an expression meaning 'this or none'. Tobias Hobson was a carrier
and inn-keeper in Cambridge, who also rented horses. He obliged every customer to take
the horse which stood nearest the stable-door, or go elsewhere.

To Her Parents   School House
6 December 1911   'Stir-up' Sunday[1]

Darlingest people
    How absolutely ripping to be able to put such a date to my letter
– I'm counting the days to the holidays. . . .
    I say, I hope you're not being alarmed by this scarlet-fever scare.
I don't think there's much danger – I wish I did – I'd give my ears
to come home – but really I don't see how I could catch it. It's not
like measles. It is a very slight case. . . .
    Canon Dugmore's[2] been giving us lectures about the Reformation
which would have been very interesting if one could have followed
what he said. But he has his lecture all written out, and reads it and
can't read his own writing, and reads all wrong, and all the wrong
dates, and stammers and corrects himself – and then, having, only
in his last lecture, said a few vague things about the changes made
in the Liturgy, calmly gives us to write as an essay: 'The Origin of
the English Prayer-book.'! Can you please send me your (Mother's,
that is) Roman Missal, which, (like most things) will be found in my
quarters. Miss D. is going to try and get us the prayer-books of
Edward VI. . . .
    How *very* kind of *dear* Mrs Wilde to say I was good-looking!!!! She's
completely mistaken – but that's quite beside the point. It's only that
when I am properly dressed I give a sort of spurious impression of

good looks – it's more a kind of smartness than anything else –
Heigh-ho! I'm longing to put on a trimmed hat again! . . .

[1] The twenty-fifth Sunday after Trinity, so called from the first two words of the collect:
'Stir up, we beseech thee, O Lord, the wills of thy faithful people . . .' It announced to
schoolchildren the near approach of the Christmas holidays.
[2] The Rev. Ernest Edward Dugmore, Canon of Sarum from 1890.

*This is the last extant letter to her parents written from school. At the beginning
of the following term, Miss Douglas announced that Dorothy Sayers had had
to leave on account of illness. She may have caught scarlet fever or shown signs
of coming down with it, but there is no record of this. On 12 November she had
written to say: 'I'm looking forward frightfully to the holidays – how I do
dislike school! and everybody thinks I'm so keen on it!' Her feelings about school
varied. The episode concerning Monsieur Roubaud had occurred in October of
her last term and her resentment concerning this may not have subsided. At the
age of eighteen she was beginning to chafe at restrictions. Nevertheless she was
looking forward to the school concert, to playing with the orchestra in the Royal
Albert Hall and to the production of* The Merchant of Venice *in which she
was cast as Shylock. It is not known whether she took part in any of these events.*

*For whatever reason, after Christmas 1911 she worked at home, continuing
nevertheless to be tutored by Miss White by correspondence. With this help, she
sat for the Gilchrist Scholarship to Somerville College in March 1912 and was
successful. She attended Commemoration in September 1912, when she received
a prize for photography (one of her hobbies) and as a farewell gesture made a
donation to the Old Godolphin Girls' Scholarship Fund.*

1912–1915

Oxford

On 11 October 1912, aged nineteen, Dorothy L. Sayers went up to Oxford as a scholar of Somerville College. Her intention was to take an Honours degree in French but to qualify as a candidate she had to pass certain preliminary examinations in Latin (known as Littlego or Smalls) and in divinity (known as Divvers). She was also required to take oral and written examinations in German.

Her parents had friends in Oxford who invited her to their homes. Her cousin Gerald Sayers was an undergraduate at Christ Church. Aunt Maud Leigh and her daughter Margaret, who was to win a scholarship at Somerville the following year, were another social contact. Several elderly female Sayers relations, whose attentions she did not welcome, also resided in Oxford.

First term October–December 1912 (Age: 19)

To Her Parents　　　　　　　　　　　Somerville College,[1]
27 October 1912　　　　　　　　　　　　Oxford

Dearest people . . .

The week has proceeded in its usual orderly fashion, beginning with Sunday, and ending rather late on Saturday night, with the Fancy Dress affair. The latter was quite a success – some of the costumes were excellent. Mine was much admired. . . .

Gerald came to tea yesterday. He was particularly amiable, and quite laid himself out to be entertaining. I showed him over the Coll. and he was gracious enough to say that everything was much nicer than he had thought it would be.

The other day I came in from Mrs Dixey's.[2] . . . I had an awfully good time. Giles was very nervous and dropped the scones into the ashes and the chocolate cakes on the hearth-rug; otherwise all went well. May Lock was there, and two other men – one from Hertford and the other from New Coll. – well, I came in, and there was Eleanor Sayers' card on the table. I heaved a sigh of relief, and thought I need not return the call for a long time. I had been comfortably settled down for some time with a Vergil, and was just going to dress for dinner, when the wretched woman was announced. Fortunately I was able to tell her that I had only five minutes to spare. She began at once about the Christian Social Union.[3] . . . I would not listen, and got rid of her. I behaved as coldly as I could, so that even she saw it. But she was quite unabashed, and said 'Good-bye – I have so much enjoyed seeing you – more than you have seeing me, I'm sure.' She departed – the next day I received a letter – Law! – It began like this: 'Dear Dorothy – Thank you very much for receiving me so kindly last night. I really mean this,' and then proceeded to develop into a kind of tract, about my mind not being sufficiently awakened to the terrible social and economic evils of the present day – gassing on about the Fatherhood of God and the Brotherhood of Man, and ending somewhat as follows: 'I see that you do not sufficiently realise what all this means to us. Up till now your clever young mind has been too much occupied with other matters to enable you to think of these matters, even if you had wished. I was just the same at your age, before my mind was awakened by my work in the London slums. I hope you will not mind my saying this to you, as I have already grown very fond of you' – etc.

I was so angry that I put the beastly thing into the fire, and sat down to write the very rudest letter I could think of. I poured out the vials of my most scathing sarcasm over her. Was it very awful of me? She is such a fool, she *will* not understand a hint, or a veiled sarcasm, or a polite chilliness – I *will* get rid of her. I have received no answer to the letter, so perhaps she is crushed. I cannot help hoping so.

On Wednesday I went to Dr Allen's[4] Orchestra Concert. It was really very good. I fell most fearfully in love with Debussy's *Après-midi d'un Faune* – I do adore reeds – they are so magnificently impersonal and mysterious. I was also enraptured with the Schubert Symphony in C. The other items were Beethoven's Leonore Overture,[5] which rather disappointed me, and the Liebestod out of *Tristan and Iseult*.

Work goes quietly on. Mr May[6] seems doubtful about it's being a good thing to take the sporting chance,[7] but will tell me more definitely in a week or so.

This afternoon I am going to have tea with Biddy Mee and to call on Mrs Brabant.[8] She left a card on me at the beginning of the week.

I was unfortunately out, but the card informed me she was at home on Sunday afternoons, so I shall tootle round and see. . . .

[1] This is the earliest extant letter of D.L.S.'s first term at Oxford. It was her habit to write home every Sunday. Since she went up on 11 October, it is likely that she wrote on the thirteenth and twentieth of that month, but these letters have not come to hand.

[2] Dr F. A. Dixey, M.D., Fellow of Wadham, and Mrs Dixey were friends of D.L.S.'s parents. They had two sons, Giles and Roger, and a daughter, Maud. Giles, a contemporary of D.L.S., was a poet. During his lifetime he published twenty volumes, of which the last was dated 1971.

[3] Founded in 1899 by Brooke Foss Westcott, Charles Gore and Henry Scott Holland.

[4] Dr (later Sir) Hugh Percy Allen (1869–1946), organist, conductor, and musical administrator, Fellow of New College. During Dorothy's time at Somerville he was the conductor of the Oxford Bach Choir, which she joined. In 1918 he succeeded Sir Hubert Parry as Director of the Royal College of Music and Sir Walter Parratt as Professor of Music at Oxford. A handsome man of vibrant personality, he was the object of adulation to women members of the choir, Dorothy being one of his most ardent admirers. See Cyril Bailey, *Hugh Percy Allen*, (O.U.P., 1948).

[5] *Leonora No. 3.*

[6] Mr Herbert May, who coached her in Latin. D.L.S. described him in later years as follows: 'As soon as I took residence in Oxford, I was sent to a warrior called Mr Herbert May, with instructions that I was to be crammed through Smalls. Mr May lived in a narrow, semi-detached house in the gloomier purlieus of Oxford, in a perpetual atmosphere of snuff. With this he refreshed himself all through his coaching.' (See 'The Teaching of Latin: A New Approach' in *The Journal of the Association for the Reform of Latin Teaching*, vol. XXXVIII, no. 3, October 1952, pp. 69–92.)

[7] i.e. Whether she should take Smalls that term.

[8] Biddy Mee and the Brabants were friends of her parents. At this period the paying of calls was a social duty not to be evaded. Quite a lot of D.L.S.'s time at Oxford was spent in respecting such formalities.

To Her Parents   Somerville College
10 November 1912

My dears!

If this letter is extremely incoherent (I warn you beforehand) it is because I have been suffering untold things. I have just returned from S. Barnabas, whither I had gone thinking to enjoy the service . . . I got there only just in time, and slipped into a seat at the back. We had risen to our feet for the first time (either during the first hymn or the epistle I suppose) when somebody just in front of me dropped first her glasses and then her book. I trembled with foreboding – '*subita gelidus formidine sanguis deriguit*'[1] – it was – it *was* Eleanor Sayers! – Why, having once noticed her, was I quite unable to dismiss her from my thoughts? – Partly, I think, because she fidgeted so. I do dislike to see a person stand on the kneeler while the 'clerk' is giving out the notices and crane forward to see what is going on. Anyhow, after a sermon about 4 minutes long from a very young, fervent and poetical parson, who was just beginning to be really interesting and suggestive when he startled us all by muttering 'In the name of the Father – um, um, um' and skipping neatly out of his stole and down the pulpit-steps – after this, and after service and after the last hymn, I was still undiscovered. But as we stood to wait for the choir to pass out – a rather lengthy process, because they do so much walking about with a cross and candles before they get started – out of the corner of my eye I saw her turn round and stare at me, as I stood, gazing with rapt devotion into the 'incense mists'. Down I sank upon my knees in an ecstasy of silent prayer, waited till the general movement of the congregation obliged her to move, and fled down the other aisle. As I ascended that slummy and objectionable long up-hill street which leads back to Walton St. – Little Clarendon St. to be precise – hastening along, looking neither to right nor to left – I heard a voice 'Dorothy!' I turned – terror lay cold at my heart. It was Margaret![2] – Never in all my life have I been so glad to see her – So that all was well which ended well. But the nervous strain was terrible. And now I shall never have a moment's peace in church. I shall always be afraid of meeting her. . . .

On Friday night I went to a Suffrage meeting to hear Prof. Murray[3] speak. He talks awfully charmingly and was very interesting. What a Shakespe[a]rian forehead he has got, to be sure! . . .

Amphy Middlemore[4] and I have started a society among about 6 of the First-Years, for mutual admiration.[5] We meet every week to read our own works. Our first meeting was last Wednesday. I read 'Earl Ulfric' and 'Peredur'[6] and another girl read two things and Amphy provided the refreshments. It was really quite a success. I hope we shall be able to keep it up. . . .

With best love to all
Yours ever devotedly

Dorothy

I have asked Mrs Dixey to tea on Weds. We are going to feed her on crumpets.

[1] '[my] blood chilled and froze with sudden fear' (Virgil, *Aeneid*, III, 259–60) The reference is to the appearance of the Fury to the Trojans.
[2] Her cousin Margaret Leigh.
[3] Gilbert Murrary (1866–1957), the Classical scholar and translator of Greek drama. He was a member of Somerville College Council.
[4] Amphyllis Middlemore and D.L.S. were at the Godolphin together.
[5] This is the first mention of the Mutual Admiration Society, which, like the Inklings, served to encourage creative work in its members. Election was decided on the merit of an original entry in prose or verse. A motto was adopted: 'The best of what we do and are, just God forgive.' Several of the members remained life-long friends.
[6] Poems written by D.L.S. while she was at Bluntisham.

TO HER PARENTS   Somerville College
1 December 1912

Dear people . . .

Do you know, I've made a grand discovery! There is absolutely *no* objection to smoking, except in Common-Room. Isn't that grand? One better than Girton,[1] eh? I believe I left a box of cigarettes behind me – *do* like an angel send them along to help me through Smalls.

We had a fire-practice the other day – rather exciting. Our corridor was supposed to be cut off from the stair-cases by flames, and we had to descend from the window by sheets. I went first, and breathed a devout prayer of gratitude when I found the knot was firm! It was really awfully thrilling, only if there had been a real fire we should have been burnt alive because we were such a long time getting the sheets ready. . . .

I'm yearning to get home – Only think! if this were school I'd only have done about half a term! Are you all right at home? all of you? . . .

[1] Girton College, Cambridge. It was unusual for women to smoke at this period. (Dorothy's mother also smoked.)

Second term January–April 1913 (Age: 19)

TO HER PARENTS   Somerville College
19 January 1913

Darling people,

There is simply nothing whatever to write to you about, except that I am having a very good time and that it is pouring with rain. The woman who coaches me in German is awfully jolly, though the work is boring. The French person[1] is nice too. I had to bring my notes on Montaigne's Portrait of Himself[2] to the first class, and there hold forth upon it. It was a little awkward, because I hadn't made any notes, but I contrived to invent some in a great hurry, and all passed off quite well.

We had a M.A.S.[3] meeting the other day. Of course only one other person had done any work. I managed to get Caspar Melchior and Balthasar[4] finished in time. I will send them to you when I have made some corrections.

People are being very nice this term. If college were not so jolly, I expect I should do more work. I do feel so lazy. Never mind! . . .

On Feb 14th some man is coming to address us about the Brontës.

It will be rather ripping, I should think. I shall have to read up *Wuthering Heights* again. By the way, I wonder whether it would be troubling you awfully if I asked you to hunt up the *Napoleon of Notting Hill*[5] and copy out a little passage for me. (It is probably in the den.) The passage is the one in about the last chapter but one or two, which begins with Adam Wayne saying: 'Tomorrow we shall have a new experience, fresh as the flowers in May – we are going to be beaten'. I want just that remark, and Turnbull saying, 'What makes you say that?' and Adam's answer.[6] If this is a great bore, never mind. I want to stick it in an essay, but the essay could do quite well without it. . . .

[1] Miss Mildred Pope (1872–1956), her tutor in French, later Professor at Manchester University, a distinguished authority on Anglo-Norman dialect and literature. D.L.S. had a great admiration and affection for her and later portrayed her as Miss Lydgate in *Gaudy Night*.

[2] Michel de Montaigne (1533–92), French essayist. There is no essay entitled 'Portrait of Himself'.

[3] Mutual Admiration Society.

[4] A dialogue between the three Magi. D.L.S. was to write a dialogue between the Magi twice again: in the nativity play, *He That Should Come*, and in *The Man Born to be King*. Charis Frankenburg (Barnett), a member of the Society, said this was her 'most interesting recollection'. See *Not Old, Madam, Vintage* (Lavenham, Suffolk, 1975, pp. 62–3, 66).

[5] A novel by G. K. Chesterton, first published in 1904. See also letter to Mrs Chesterton, dated 15 June 1936.

[6] The passage occurs in Book V, chapter I. Adam's reply is: 'We have been in the most horrible holes before now; but in all those I was perfectly certain that the stars were on our side, and that we ought to get out. Now, I know that we ought not to get out; and that takes away from me everything with which I won.'

To Her Parents   Somerville College
26 January 1913

Dearest people . . .

One of our year gave a most awfully exciting party the night before last. The college is supposed to be haunted by the ghost of a nun, and we got the party together to see the ghost. We worked ourselves up into a most frightfully creepy state with all sorts of grisly stories till eleven o'clock. Then, as the clock struck, we gazed from the window across the lawn, and there – from the west wing, across the lawn by the library – there flitted a shadowy figure in the black and white garb of a nun!! – it was *so* thrilling! – Miss Middlemore was the ghost, and she really did it magnificently – only really it was a jolly dangerous joke to play, and I'm thankful none of the uninitiated saw her. The joke was that she had smothered her face and arms with luminous paint – which she tried to wash off in water – with the result you might have expected! However, I believe it is wearing off now! There is quite a ghost craze going on in college now – wherever one goes to tea, people are telling psychic stories! I am getting quite a collection of new horrors. There's a book of very gruesome grues in the library, called *Ghost-stories of an Antiquary* by James[1] – very nice and nasty!

Miss F. S. Thomson and I went for a bicycle ride this morning; we got to South Hinksey. Isn't it a dear little place? I'd love to live in a village like that, where the houses stand just anyhow, and the road wriggles gently around them. . . .

[1] Montague Rhodes James (1862–1936), a scholar of vast and varied learning, author of *Ghost Stories of an Antiquary* (1904) and *More Ghost Stories of an Antiquary* (1911). D.L.S. was to include one of his stories, 'Martin's Close' in the first volume of her anthology *Great Short Stories of Detection, Mystery and Horror* (Gollancz, 1928).

To Her Parents   Somerville College
2 March 1913

Dearest people

I'm nagging away like anything at those silly old Acts of the Apostles, so I've really awfully little time to write. The exam. is on Wednesday, but we've no idea yet when the Viva will be. Terms ends to-morrow week, and if the Viva isn't over by then, we shall have to stay up for a day or two, and I'm afraid we shall have to turn out. I wonder whether I could possibly ask Mrs Dixey to let me put up for a night or two . . .

I have bought Chesterton's *What's Wrong with the World.*[1] Parts of it are very pleasing. I forget whether you have read it. If not, I will bring it home with me. . . .

My dear good Mummy, nobody could hate Bernard Shaw more than I do – But it isn't 'rot' he writes – it's damnably clever half-truths. I'd like to wring the man's neck!

Having read two Gospels with more attention than I had ever before given to the subject, I came to the conclusion that such a set of stupid, literal, pig-headed people never existed as Christ had to do with, including the disciples.

Good-bye – I'll write later and tell you about when I go down.

With love
    D.

[1] Published in June 1910, in answer to Charles Masterman's *The Condition of England* (1909).

To Catherine Godfrey[1]   Bluntisham Rectory
April 1913   Friday in Easter Week

Dear Tony
    Certainly not!
    Speaking as a baptised and more or less educated member of the
Catholic Church of Christ as in England by law established, certainly
not! The C.U.[2] is no more a *necessary* corollary of Christianity than
the Inquisition. The only *necessary* products of Christianity are those
which Christ appointed. He did not encourage misty theological discussion, but taught by authority and by example. The Early Chris-
tians did the same. They met to pray and to exhort. Thus the Catholic
Church in the Middle Ages. Discussion of beliefs and dogmas came
in, I suppose, with the Renascence,[3] but rested on the authority
of the Bible which had become overlaid with the authority of the
Church.
    The C.U. appears to me more like a product of Darwinism.
    Yes – you must aggressively save souls, but you will never do it by
unprofitable argument.
    I know little about the C.U. but it seems to me from all I hear of
it, to begin from the wrong end. Christianity rests on Faith, not Faith
on Christianity. If you have read *Orthodoxy*[4] you will see what I
mean . . .
    Hear! hear! – I'm simply dead sick of telling people about Oxford,
and how many there are of us at Somerville and how many dons
there are, and why have I got to do an exam. in German when my
subject's French, and do I see much of the Prince of Wales, and do
we have lectures with the men, and is there a tennis-court at Somerville, and what is the name of our Head, and what time are lights
put out at night, and how do we get milk when we make our own
tea, and may we go to the theatre, and have I made any particular
friends, and what sort of people live in my passage, and have I one
room or two and will the new buildings be finished when we get back,
and do the maids wear caps and aprons, and when was the college
founded and are there more women students at Oxford or Cambridge?
I suppose people have to ask questions.[5]
    My friend from Girton[6] has just been staying with me for a few
days. We were all rather annoyed with her, though, because she has
adopted that dreadful 'pose of being natural' which is the posiest pose
I know. You know what I mean. She dresses all anyhow and does
her hair hideously, and sprawls about all loose at the joints in ugly
attitudes and wears no stays.[7] She is also loud in her assertions that
she 'hates' nice clothes and 'can't bear' jewellery and thinks it's 'an
awful bore' to make herself look decent. It is such a pity because she

is a very good-looking girl – and it's all put on, you know. She's just as self-conscious in her ungainliness as the vainest person in her elegance, and talks as persistently about clothes, to abuse them, as other people do to gloat over them. She is also very keen on Socialism and suffrage and eugenics[8] and God knows what – but I have observed that she is enormously taken up with the fact that her cousin the Bishop of Ely has been exalted to the House of Lords, and never ceases talking about it, though with an elaborate affectation of contempt. So much for Socialism! I do wish to goodness people would be sincere about things!

I must stop now, I think, and see if I can discover anything about the characterisation in the *Chanson de Roland*. I have been so dreadfully 'off' work lately. I expect Elsie[9] has been doing five hours a day all the time. What a thing it is to have a well-regulated mind!

With best wishes for your birthday, and much love
Yours *in saecula saeculorum*[10]
    Dorothy L. Sayers

[1] One of D.L.S.'s contemporaries at Somerville. It was a fashion among women students to give one another masculine nicknames. Catherine Godfrey was 'Tony', Muriel Jaeger was 'James' or 'Jim', Florence Barry was 'Jack'. Dorothy Rowe, for some reason, was 'Tiddler'. D.L.S. does not appear to have had a nickname, though she sometimes signed herself 'John Gaunt' after she had played that part in a college production of Stevenson's and Henley's play, *The Admiral Guinea*.
[2] Christian Union.
[3] A then fashionable way of spelling Renaissance.
[4] By G. K. Chesterton; published in 1908. D.L.S. had read it while at school.
[5] Cf. Harriet Vane's comparable irritation in *Gaudy Night* (chapter 13).
[6] Eleanor Chase, who was at the Godolphin.
[7] A predecessor of the 'burn your bras' brigade?
[8] Cf. Miss Schuster-Slatt in *Gaudy Night* (chapter 2).
[9] Elsie Henderson, a contemporary at Somerville.
[10] Latin: for centuries of centuries, forever.

Third term April–July 1913 (Age: 19)

To Her Parents   Somerville College
20 April 1913   Oxford

Dearest people
    I do feel so happy! We are not going to be widowed and left desolate after all.[1] As soon as I got up to College I found a lovely post card, which announced as follows:–

Oxford Bach Choir and Choral Society.

It is proposed to hold a festival of four concerts, devoted exclusively to the works of J. S. Bach, at the beginning of the Summer Term, 1914.

    I. Three Cantatas

    II. Orchestral and Choral Concert to include the Magnificat

    III. Three Motets: 'Be not afraid'
                            'Come, Jesu, come'
                            'Sing to the Lord'

    IV. The Mass in B minor

It is hoped that the Society will realise the seriousness of this undertaking, and that every member will do everything possible to ensure its success. . . .

Everybody has come up fearfully smart in new clothing. Elsie has got a very pretty fawn coat and skirt, with a coat rather like mine, and a new hat of which she is inordinately proud. We have been (all of us, I mean, not only Elsie and I) talking about nothing but clothes all the time – so much for our craze for untidiness! . . .

2 o'clock Back from church. I took Elsie, and our skirts were so tight it took us about 10 minutes to kneel down. Mine is ever so much better now that it is let out. I wore my hat with the pink scarf, having got my hair just right for it and the brim at the right angle, and everybody admires it so much, I shall keep it exactly as it is. So that's also all right. . . .

With love to all (including H.M.![2])
    Dorothy

P.S. I had to call on Mrs Brabant . . . because Elsie wanted me to go to the Balliol concert with her, and she had only 2 tickets and no chaperon was going[3] – as a last resort I tried Mrs B., who luckily is going, so we shall have a good time.

---

[1] It had been rumoured that Dr Hugh Allen was leaving Oxford.
[2] Hannah Martha, one of the hens at Bluntisham.
[3] The chaperon rule required that no undergraduate of a women's college should attend any social function, even in a group, unless chaperoned by an older woman. It is interesting that D.L.S. expressed no impatience about the strictness of the rule. It was understood that women were 'on probation' at Oxford and restrictions were good-humouredly accepted.

To Her Parents   Somerville College
5 May 1913

Dearest people . . .

    I have engaged a room for you in college, Mother, *provisionally*, for the week-end May 30th–June 2nd. That is about the only week that there is no particular function, as it is in the middle of Greats.[1] I want to try and arrange a tennis-party for Saturday afternoon, if we can get Gerald and one or two other men, and if you don't mind chaperoning. I have written to G. but haven't heard from him yet. Let me know if this date will do . . .

I do believe it's coming out fine. I think if it continues in this good way, I shall put on my best hat this afternoon. I have only worn it once so far. The little round one is simply *enormously* useful. It does on Sundays when it's dull, and on week-days for the Taylor[2] lectures (I find one *must* be respectable when one's the only woman or almost the only woman there, because one's so conspicuous) and keeps on in a wind, and takes up no room at concerts, and looks rather chic and coy, and is altogether a darling. . . .

People are getting fearfully agitated about Eights,[3] because the river is so flooded the boats can't get out, and they don't know what to do about it. The King[4] is coming, so of course it *would* be awful weather. . . .

[1] The Finals examination in Classics.
[2] The Taylor Institution, also known as the Taylorian, on the corner of Beaumont Street, opposite the Randolph Hotel, is named after Sir Robert Taylor (d. 1788), an architect who left a legacy for the teaching of modern languages at Oxford.
[3] Eights Week, when the college boats compete.
[4] George V. The Prince of Wales (later Edward VIII) was then an undergraduate at Oxford.

To Her Parents   Somerville College
26 May 1913   1st. Sunday after Trinity
                                        and a very hot one at that!

My dear people . . .

Eights week is over! it really was simply ripping. On Monday I had tea with Frank Brabant and graced the Balliol barge. Frank was really quite nice – much pleasanter than I expected him to be, and we had quite fun. On Wednesday we went with Mrs Dixey (another girl and I) to the Keble concert. It was glorious. . . .

Do you know, it is dreadful, but the longer I stay in Oxford, the more certain I am that I was never cut out for an academic career – I was really meant to be sociable. . . .

Yesterday we gave a garden-party to the workmen and their wives. It was most amusing. I spent the greater part of the afternoon – well, some of it anyhow – flirting on the loggia steps with a photographer who turned out to be the editor of the *Oxford Journal*. He was very easy to talk to – a trifle too easy for good breeding – and went and took a photograph of me when I wasn't looking, and had the brazen effrontery to tell me so under the nose of Miss Penrose,[1] and ask if he might send it to me. Of course I had to say he could if he liked – though I stipulated there should be no witticisms on the address-side – which involved giving him my name. Don't be alarmed – he was quite a decent sort – merely not quite quite – and we got on beautifully together and I couldn't sit on the poor dear for making himself agreeable. But won't it be a joke if the photograph comes? He said he'd only send it if it was a success. I hope he won't publish it in the *Oxford Journal*! Do you know I really *am* a vulgar child – I quite enjoyed myself. . . .

[1] Miss Emily Penrose, Principal of Somerville College.

To Catherine Godfrey   Bluntisham Rectory
22 July 1913

My dear Tony
    Do forgive me for not having answered your letter before. I have been enjoying a perfect orgie of laziness – simply lounging through the day – doing no work, taking no exercise, writing no letters, and spending my whole time puffing cigarette smoke into library novels. I am just beginning to revive.
    Yes, it was really quite fun staying with Mrs Dixey. It is a most amusing household, though. Nothing is ever dusted, nothing is punctual and nobody gets up till about 10 o'clock. As you may imagine, it quite suited me. . . .
    Do you know – you're the only person to whom I dare confess it – for a bit after I got home, I was simply home-sick for Oxford – not for college – but for that curve in the High and Radcliffe Square by moonlight, and for the people in the street and the stories about Varsity life. Talking about moonlight, on several occasions we amused ourselves by going to Wadham after dinner, and sitting in the Warden's garden under the pale rays of the tranquil moon! It was ripping. Wadham is such a perfectly shaped little college, and the garden is full of dark old trees. Dr Dixey told me lots of amusing college stories, but it wants his killing manner of telling them to make them sound anything. I'm getting gradually reconciled to being in the depths of the country with no one to speak to – and of course, it is jolly to be home – but I wish Oxford were within bicycling distance . . .
    The exam. was so funny – I was the only woman taking it, and sat, severely isolated like a leper, in one corner of the T-room at the Schools,[1] while the men occupied a quite different branch of it. The first day while looking for my desk, I wandered into the men's part

of the room, whereupon the old chap who sees you settled (not the
invigilator but the door-keeper sort of person) rushed at me with
wildly-waving arms and a terrified expression, and shooed me away
to my seclusion like an intrusive hen. . . .

Herr Jost was quite nice to me. I first of all got dreadfully muddled
with some kings and dates. When he had disentangled them for
me he said: 'I was very much surprised' (my heart sank into my
boots) 'to see that you considered Schiller's *Robbers*² a pleasing
play'. I thought to myself 'Now is the moment for an individual
touch', and relying on the fact that I had put on my best coat and
skirt and a becoming hat, I assumed my most womanly smile
and said: 'Oh don't you think it is?' – He smiled – I was encouraged to
give my reasons – he smiled and agreed. At any rate he passed
me. . . .

    With much love
    Yours ever
      Dorothy

¹ Examination Schools, a building on the south side of the High Street, on the corner of
Merton Street.
² Friedrich Schiller (1759–1805), German dramatist and poet. *Die Räuber* (The Robbers)
was his first play, begun in 1777 and finished in 1780; first performed in 1782. It is a
denunciation of tyranny.

To Catherine Godfrey   Bluntisham Rectory
29 July 1913

My dear Tony
    Very many thanks for your entertaining and sympathetic letter. It
is nice that someone understands one's feelings about Oxford and *viva
voce* examinations. Also that somebody else is not bursting herself with
work. Elsie makes me quite ill. She is steadily working through all
those books we had to take home, and I simply daren't tell her I've
done practically nothing! It's not exactly that I am idle, but I'm
interested in something else the whole time. At present I am deep in
the writing of an allegorical epic, of which I have completed the first
canto. I began it last vac., and as it is distinctly Christian in tone I
started out to mention it to Elsie, when she asked what I had been
doing. I said: 'I have started work on an epic' – she said: 'What
on earth do you want to do that for? Nobody wants to read epics.'
So I felt crushed, and took my epic elsewhere. Then I have got
to write something for M.A.S., and it has got to be in prose; I
write prose uncommonly badly, and can't get ideas. . . . About the
Encaenia¹ . . .

We got to the theatre[2] about 11 o'clock (only a quarter of an hour
late – quite good considering!) – there was straw laid down in Broad
Street as if someone was ill,[3] and the streets were simply full of people.
We went round to our entrance, the one near the Camera,[4] and joined
a long queue of women which tailed out into the street, and was kept
in order by a policeman. . . . We got splendid places – couldn't have
had better – we dodged the pillars, so that they blocked nothing. . . .
Till 12 o'clock we watched people coming in – it was really very
amusing – all in their best (*nobody* in every-day hats and cotton gloves)
– and we listened to the organ, which varied a severely classical
programme with 'Hitchy Koo'[5] (vociferously applauded) and 'Auld
Lang Syne'. Then the procession arrived – very Oxfordy and scarlet
and imposing – Spooner[6] looking as mad as usual – Dr Dixey looking
like a walrus – the (not yet) Poet Laureate[7] frightfully distinguished
and ornamental – among the doctors. The V-Chancellor[8] looked ripping – most awfully refined and mediaeval, and he has a high, melancholy, well-bred voice that just exactly suits a scarlet gown and flat
Tudor-looking black velvet cap. Then there were the new M.A.s in
their robes – the Archbishop[9] rather nice and humorous, Dillon[10] and
the other service man, looking pokerish and martial, the sweet old
Regius Professor[11] of Greek at Cambridge, very frail and doddery,
with a queer, scrunched up face like an apple, and the German chap
from Bonn, *very* German – his hair erected like a crest. – I have
just been to fetch a programme – his name was Wilcken.[12] Then Dr
Heberden,[13] with his proctors one on each side of him, started off in
Latin, to open Convocation and propose the conferring of degrees.
When he had finished, the Public Orator – namely Godley,[14] the man
who writes such screaming poetry you know, – started off to 'present'
the Honorary doctors, which meant a terrific long Latin eulogy on
each. I could follow a good deal of it, but not all. Godley is a rather
dried-up looking individual with grey hair – not suggestive of verses,
but people never do look suitable to their talents. When he'd finished,
the Vigger-Chagger[15] addressed all the assembled doctors in a sing-
song little speech, beginning something about 'Does it please you
doctors of the University that so-and-so should be admitted to such
and such a degree – *Placet ne*?' and then he took off his cap; then said
'*Placet*'[16] without leaving time for anyone to make an objection if he
wanted to, and put it on again. And when he took his cap off the
proctors took theirs off too, and when he put on his, they put on
theirs, only generally they weren't paying attention and were a little
late both times. It was awfully amusing when Prof. Wilcken was being
presented, because he being a foreigner wouldn't have understood the
English pronunciation of Latin, so everybody changed his pronunciation and tried to do it the new way,[17] and Godley did it shockingly

badly and got all his quantities wrong; Dr Heberden was much better, and looked charmingly amused at himself. After he says '*placet*' he addresses the new doctor and formally admits and invests him and all the rest of it in Latin and shakes hands with him; then the new doctor sits down with the old ones and everybody claps.

When that was all finished, Professor Warren,[18] as Professor of Poetry, delivered the Crewerian oration – in Latin of course. It goes over all the 'Varsity news of the year you know. The Latin phrases about the Prince of Wales playing football (propelling the ball with his foot) and bicycling (riding on *duplicis radiis* or *rotis*) were simply shrieking – but you will have seen all about that in the papers. (N.B. Warren is an ugly old thing. He also changed his Latin when speaking of Prof. Wilcken with comic effect.)

Then came the prizemen. They were all rather dull except the last, and the men were astonishingly well-behaved all the time. They didn't once ask the Greek people to translate, or pull the Latin verseman up for his quantities. But the Newdigate[19] was a *darling*. His poem was on 'Oxford', and he recited it so nicely. He had a very clear pleasant voice, and spoke as if he meant it. He read from the rostrum close to us, so we saw and heard splendidly. His poem was not frightfully full of genius, and was very academic in tone and form (though it was in blank verse) but there was an appealing sort of youthfulness and pathos and Oxford feeling about it that made it quite charming. As I said, he put a good deal of expression into the reciting of it – pathos a trifle oppressive, perhaps, but that is also a youthful fault. Dr Dixey said: 'I think the little beggar really felt it'. He was very nervous, and he quivered all over all the time he was reciting. Charis[20] and I fell head over ears in love with him on the spot. His name is Maurice Roy Ridley[21] – isn't it a killing name, like the hero of a six-penny novelette? He has just gone down from Balliol, so I shall see him no more – My loves are always unsatisfactory, as you know. . . .

---

[1] The name of the degree ceremony at Oxford, from the Latin, meaning consecration, dedication.

[2] The Sheldonian Theatre, where the degree ceremony is held.

[3] It was the custom to spread straw on a street near a house where someone was ill, to lessen the noise of iron-clad wheels rattling over cobblestones.

[4] The Radcliffe Camera, the central reading-room of the Bodleian Library.

[5] A popular song (words by L. Wolfe Gilbert, music by Louis F. Muir and Maurice Abrahams).

[6] The Rev. Dr W. A. Spooner (1844–1930), the celebrated Warden of New College who had a habit of accidentally transposing the first letters or parts of words and so creating what came to be known as Spoonerisms: e.g. when telling the story of a cat which fell from a window, meaning to say 'and it dropped on its paws and ran off', he said 'and it popped on its drawers . . .' The most famous example is perhaps his announcement of the first line of a hymn, 'Let conquering kings', which became 'Let kinkering congs'.

[7] Robert Bridges (1844–1930). His appointment as Poet Laureate had been announced.

[8] Charles Buller Heberden (1849–1921), Vice-Chancellor of Oxford 1910–13.

[9] The Rt Rev. Cosmo G. Lang, then Archbishop of York.

[10] The Right Hon. Arthur Henry Dillon, 17th Viscount, antiquarian and specialist in armour. The 'other service man' was Admiral Sir Reginald N. Custance, G.C.B.

[11] Henry Jackson (1839–1921), Litt.D., O.M., Fellow of Trinity College, Cambridge.

[12] Ulrich Wilcken (1862–1944), Egyptologist, pupil of Theodor Mommsen. He specialised in deciphering papyri.

[13] See Note 8.

[14] Alfred Denis Godley (1856–1925). Among his humorous poems is one which D.L.S. quotes in *The Mind of the Maker*: 'What is it that roareth thus? / Can it be a motor bus? / Yes, the reek and hideous hum / Indicant motorem bum.'

[15] The Vice-Chancellor, the distorted form being Oxford slang of the time; cf. Pragger Wagger, Prince of Wales.

[16] The Latin phrases, meaning 'does it please?' and 'it pleases' were used by D.L.S. at the end of *Gaudy Night*, where Lord Peter proposes for the last time to Harriet Vane and is accepted.

[17] Latin was pronounced in England with a 'local' accent until modern times. In the 1870s reformers began to 'restore' what they took to be the authentic ancient Roman pronunciation. The 'old' English pronunciation continued in general use longest at Oxford. At Cambridge it was kept up individually by a don at Jesus College (Freddy Brittain) well into the 1960s. It is still in use amongst doctors, lawyers and botanists and in some ceremonies, as for instance at the coronation of the queen, when the words '*vivat regina*' are not pronounced 'weewat regeena' (with a hard g), but the vs of *vivat* are sounded like vs, the i as in alive and the g of *regina* is soft.

[18] Thomas Herbert Warren, Pro-Vice-Chancellor, President of Magdalen College.

[19] The Newdigate Prize, awarded annually for a poem composed by an undergraduate, was founded by Sir Roger Newdigate in 1806.

[20] Charis Barnett, 1892–1995, (later Mrs Sidney Frankenburg), who read English Honours at Somerville.

[21] He later became a don at Balliol College and was for a time chaplain. When D.L.S. saw him again in 1935 (not having set eyes on him in the interval) she recognised him as 'the *perfect* Peter Wimsey. Height, voice, charm, smile, manner, outline of features, everything.' (See letter to Muriel St Clare Byrne, dated 6 March 1935.) Maurice Roy Ridley is thus clearly the physical origin of Lord Peter Wimsey, although his creator forgot that she had seen the original in 1913.

Fourth term October–December 1913 (Age: 20)

To Her Parents   Somerville College,
October 1913   Oxford

Dearest people

Do you mind my sitting by the fire with my feet on the mantel-piece and writing this in pencil? Because I am rather weary, after a strenuous evening – you don't? – Thank you so much –

The fancy-dress dance was yesterday evening, and I undertook to

play the violin for the Fellowship Fund. It was tiring work, but everyone was very pleased and I think it was well worth it. However, as
we didn't stop dancing till 11.30 and I didn't get to bed till nearly
one, I feel rather like dropping off the shelf now. I got myself up as
Tristram with some things out of the property cupboard. It was really
most successful. The Pen[1] was completely puzzled. She stared at me
for about five minutes and then had to be told who I was. It surprises
everyone that I make up so well as a man. It surprises me rather. . . .

  Best love to all of you
    D.

[1] Miss Emily Penrose.

To Her Parents   Somerville College
November 1913

Darlings
  Such a week of dissipation! Five times to the theatre![1] Isn't it shocking? To say nothing of rehearsals of our own play[2] and various excitements. As for work, I fear it was rather nowhere!
  Mrs Dixey went and made an engagement for Saturday, so we saw
the *Gondoliers* on Tuesday instead. They both had shocking colds (Mrs
Dixey and G[iles], I mean, not the Gondoliers) and I had a little one
(which has almost entirely disappeared by now) – but on the whole
we were a cheerful party! On Wednesday, I went on the bust and
saw *Mikado* (glorious!) in the afternoon, and *Pinafore* (the best of the
lot, I think) followed by *Trial by Jury* in the evening. On Thursday I
was dead, and refused an invitation to have tea with Mrs Price and
meet 'a very interesting man who entertains a great deal – would I
play or sing something' – and on Friday a very humorous incident
occurred. Giles, again, of course!
  Mrs Dixey had said they would probably be going to *Iolanthe*, so
on Friday afternoon I wrote to her as follows: 'Miss Godfrey and I
are going to *Iolanthe* this evening; shall you be there? shall we look
out for you? We are starting at 6.20.' So Tony, Jim and I went down
there at 6.20, and out from the middle of the queue walked Giles,
alone and rather self-conscious. 'Hullo' says I, as if I hadn't expected
to see him. 'I say', says he, 'may I come and stand with you?' 'Where's
your chaperone?' says I. 'Well, she isn't here', says he, 'but you know
this meeting is entirely accidental. Mother told me to come and stand
here till I saw someone, but she didn't say who; so I saw you!' 'Well',
says I, 'This is highly irregular, but I suppose if you insist on taking
the next place in the queue, I can't prevent you.' So he joined on,
and added that Mrs Dixey intended to come herself later, but didn't

want to stand because of her cold. So we stood all together till the
doors opened, and then bolted in. The front row of the gallery was
full, except for two very bad places at the left-hand corner. The second
row was empty, so of course Giles and I bolted from the middle and
sat there – imagine my horror when I saw Tony and Jim prancing
along and establishing themselves at the extreme end of the front row.
Before we could come to any agreement, the places were filled up all
around us! – Appalling situation for a Somerville student! – Alone
with A Man in the gallery!! We tried to keep a place for Mrs Dixey
for some time, but it shortly became evident that she was not coming.
Further, the gallery was full of Somervillians, including the Senior
Student. Giles was obsessed by the idea that I should get into a row,
and he got gloomier and gloomier and gloomier. Well, thought I, this
is going to be a cheerful evening and no mistake! So after I had vainly
endeavoured to cheer him by the assurance that it wasn't his fault or
mine, and that I shouldn't be fried in boiling oil on his account, I
reached a state of desperation, got up, and clambered along to the
Senior Student. Of course she was securely entrenched beyond a line
of youths, and you know how narrow those seats in the gallery are.
Well, I tumbled over all their large feet in turn, saying 'Excuse me',
and 'I'm sorry', and they all roared with laughter and said 'Don't
mention it, miss', and 'it's quite all right, miss'. When I got to Miss
Thompson (the S.S.);[3] of course she was sitting next to the most
bumptious fresher in college. So I laid the case before Miss T., and
asked 'could I tell my friend that it would be all right and there would
be no row, as he seemed so worried?' – Of course she roared with
laughter and said it didn't matter in the least, and what else could I
have done and the Fresher made facetious remarks which I hastily
ignored. So I clambered back over all the feet of all the youths again,
and had to say all the same things over again, and they all replied
in the same manner as before. Thus I returned and comforted Giles,
and he was quite cheerful for the rest of the evening, and I enjoyed
the play awfully, though not quite as well as *Pinafore* and *Mikado*. But
wasn't it humorous? Miss Thompson seemed exceedingly surprised
that Giles should have troubled to be worried at all – her opinion
seemed to be more or less: 'If he troubles himself for a small contre-
temps that most men would take as a spree, "why, what an unusually
nice young man this nice young man must be" '[4] – From which remark
you will probably deduce that the fifth play I saw was *Patience* – well,
your deductions would be correct. . . .

Always your very loving
Dorothy

[1] To see performances of Gilbert and Sullivan, which D.L.S. had never seen before.

[2] *The Admiral Guinea* by Robert Louis Stevenson and W. E. Henley. D.L.S. played the leading role of John Gaunt.
[3] The Senior Student.
[4] *Patience*, Act I, Bunthorne's song, beginning 'If you're anxious for to shine in the high aesthetic line', each stanza ending with a variation of 'Why, what a most particularly pure (. . .) young man this pure young man must be!' (W. S. Gilbert).

To Her Parents　　　　　　　　　　　Somerville College
December 1913

Darlings . . .

There is absolutely no news, except that an undergraduate created a sensation on Thursday night by climbing up the Martyrs' Memorial[1] and placing a certain bedroom article not usually mentioned in polite society on to the top of the cross. On Friday traffic was blocked – and the joke was that no ladders, fire-escapes or otherwise could be found of sufficient length to get it down. On Saturday I happened to be in the town at 12 o'clock, and there was really a large crowd collected, and two steeple-jack sort of people with ladders, engaged in hitching it down. It is really rather killing – but what odd ideas of humour men have. As Jim says, it would have been quite as funny if he had used a tea-kettle.

They didn't put Lloyd George in Mercury[2] – I'm so disappointed! . . .

I have succeeded in getting out of the 'Urmila' – the in-rigger tub that all freshers have to go in, and am now to be promoted to the out-riggers. Sculling is a deal more difficult than it looks – so's everything. . . .

I must go to Bach Ch. practice with Miss Bruce[3] now. So long –

Always your very loving
　　　Dorothy

[1] The Martyrs' Memorial, designed by Sir Gilbert Scott, was erected in 1841 to commemorate Latimer, Ridley and Cranmer who were burned at the stake (1555–6) for their adherence to the reformed Church of England. The prank of placing a chamber pot on the top of the memorial was a favourite among undergraduates. D.L.S. refers to it in *Busman's Honeymoon* (chapter 19), in which the Rev. Simon Goodacre confesses that he was guilty of it while at Oxford.
[2] The pond in the quad of Christ Church, in which a statue of Mercury stands. Lloyd George was then Chancellor of the Exchequer.
[3] The Hon. Alice Bruce, Vice-Principal of Somerville, 1898–1929.

Fifth term January–March 1914 (Age: 20)

To Her Parents   Somerville College
15 February 1914   Sexuagesima

Darling people . . .

On Friday I had quite an exciting day. Mr & Mrs Berthon[1] came to tea, and were very pleasant, and then he stayed on to hear the lecture Dr Allen was giving here on the music of the *Acharnians*.[2] It was a lovely lecture, the music is too glorious for words. It is by Sir H. Parry,[3] and consists of all sorts of popular tunes run together in the most marvellous way. The war-scare[4] is typified by 'A Horrible Tale I have to Tell'[5] and 'We don't want to fight, but by jingo if we do'[6] – The allies are represented by the *Marseillaise* and the Spartans by the '*Wacht am Rhein*'[7] (you perceive the adaptation of Aristophanes' topical allusions) – the Acharnians are always introduced by the 'British Grenadiers', while the farming interests are subtly conveyed by the 'Merry Peasant'.[8] It is simply wonderful the way one tune is made to turn into another. Dr Allen explained it all splendidly and played the *whole* thing through, and he had got the Coryphaeus[9] to come and sing some of the choruses. He had a beautiful voice and altogether we had a lovely hour and a half. Dr Dixey was there and came and sat next me, so my cup of content was full for the time being. . . .

It is beastly weather. I made it an excuse to neglect paying calls. Next Sunday I will really pull myself together. I am too slack to-day.

I have been told of a disease, recognised by theologians, which, if indulged, becomes a sin. It is called aboulia.[10] That is what I suffer from.

With best love
Dorothy

[1] H. E. Berthon, University Reader in French Literature and Fellow of Wadham College, whose lectures D.L.S. attended. He was the editor of *Nine French Poets: 1820–1880* (Macmillan, 1930).
[2] The Music to *The Acharnians of Aristophanes* (Leipzig, Breitkopf and Härtel, 1914).
[3] Sir Hubert Parry (1848–1918).
[4] In February 1914 fears of the coming war with Germany were prevalent.
[5] A student song of the 19th century, anonymous. (See Maria Winn, *The Fireside Book of Fun and Game Songs*, Simon and Schuster, New York, 1974.)
[6] From a Music Hall song (1878), words by G. W. Hunt: 'We don't want to fight, but by jingo if we do, / We've got the ships, we've got the men, we've got the money too; / We've fought the Bear before, and while Britons shall be true / The Russians shall not have Constantinople.'

[7] 'Die Wacht am Rhein' (The Watch on the Rhine), title of song, words by Max Schnecken-burger (1819–49).

[8] Popular piece by Schumann, from Album for the Young.

[9] The Leader of the Chorus. The Chorus in Aristophanes' play consisted of embittered and bellicose charcoal burners of Acharnae.

[10] Sloth.

To Her Parents   Somerville College
March 1914

Dearest people

Gloom has come upon me. I went to tea with the aunts at Leckford Road (Eleanor was not there) and Aunt Annie walked back with me, and thought it her duty to enquire after my soul's welfare. She will probably send you an account of my spiritual state, so I may as well prepare you. I do not at all mind discussing my soul – I do it every day – but I do not like doing it with very earnest people of narrow experience. They are so apt to be hurt, or shocked or surprised or worried. I let her down as gently as possible, but it's difficult to make people see that what you have been taught counts for nothing, and that the only things worth having are the things you find out for yourself. Also, that when so many brands of what Chesterton calls 'fancy souls' and theories of life are offered you, there is no sense in not looking pretty carefully to see what you are going in for. There are more different brands offered to us than probably there ever were to Aunt Annie. If she bothers about it, I wish you, Tootles,[1] or some-body, would just point out that we have to begin, as it were, further back than she realises. It isn't a case of 'Here is the Christian religion, the one authoritative and respectable rule of life. Take it or leave it'. It's 'Here's a muddling kind of affair called Life, and here are nineteen or twenty different explanations of it, all supported by people whose opinions are not to be sneezed at. Among them is the Christian religion in which you happen to have been brought up. Your friend so-and-so has been brought up in quite a different way of thinking; is a perfectly splendid person and thoroughly happy. What are you going to do about it?' – I'm worrying it out quietly, and whatever I get hold of will be valuable, because I've got it for myself; but really, you know, the whole question is not as simple as it looks. All this in case Aunt Annie should think fit to make any alarming statements about 'contentedly living without the means of Grace', which sounds so horrid and mediaeval somehow. . . .

With best love
   D.

Don't worry about my soul – but above all, don't let anyone else worry you about it.

I forget if I told you about the Balliol debate in my note. It was very deadly. My speech went off all right, though, and my dress was a great success.

[1] This was her nickname for her father. It is not known how it originated.

Sixth term and Vacation April–August 1914 (Age: 20–21)

To Her Parents   Somerville College
10 May 1914

Dearest people . . .

On Friday Aunt Maud took me to Elliston's to choose the evening cloak.[1] She was awfully nice about it, and most sensibly said quite openly at the beginning how much she intended to give, so that I was not made uncomfortable. I do hope you will like it. It is really rather a majestic affair. It is red brocaded velvet, lined with silk of the same shade, with sleeves of the shapeless sort that come out somewhere opposite one's waist. It has a mysterious sort of silk sling at the back, like an abortive hood, and in general appearance suggests a Whitsunday cope, tied in round the legs. I hesitated between that and a most lovely dark powder-blue one, which would have tied me less as regards the colour of frocks, but we at length rejected the blue one, on the grounds that: –

a. It was less warm than the red

b. It was rather too short for madam, seeing that madam was so tall and slim

c. It was not so pretty at the back

d. (my private reason) it was half a guinea[2] dearer. . . .

I have made myself the most *ravishing* little cap to wear in New College chapel – on the model of the one Gladys sent me. It is executed in black ribbon and net, and is *so* becoming, the Bursar thinks it is quite unsuitable for a place of worship! . . .

[1] A twenty-first birthday present.
[2] Ten shillings and sixpence (in old currency).

Dearest people

– It is over, and we are alive – that is, the choir is alive, and I have not heard of the sudden decease of Dr Allen. Probably you have seen notices. We had two evenings of acute misery, followed by one night of rapture. The Cantatas and Magnificat in New College chapel were dreadfully uncomfortable and we sang them remarkably badly. The chapel is so lofty, one can't hear what one is singing, and I know nothing more depressing than that. The solo people were quite good, especially the women, and of them, especially Hilda Foster,[1] who has a most lovely voice. We sang the Cantatas quite respectably, but the Magnificat was bad. That evening somebody told me that the last view anybody had of the Doctor, he was lying in an attitude of abandonment with his head on the piano.

On Thursday afternoon there was an excellent orchestral concert, which really went well, the choir having nothing to do with it! We had seats on the platform and of course got a good deal of double bass and trumpets and bassoons – on the other hand, it was most amusing to watch Dr Allen conducting – almost as good as having a score. He really does look terrible in a frock-coat with his hair plastered down – like a gentlemanly murderer with his portrait in the *Daily Mirror*. Also he had on a loathsome pale-green waistcoat. Why do men make themselves so hideous in public? On Thursday evening we had the three motets. The first two went simply rippingly and we were just beginning to feel so happy – when the awful catastrophe happened! In one of those tiresome places where you come in ff[2] just off the beat, the whole of the first choir, including myself, got stage-fright together and never came in at all. I have never lived through such a ghastly moment. If the earth had opened her mouth I should have been swallowed up thankfully. Through the pause we heard the Doctor. He spat at us like a cat. I didn't dare to look at him, but I believe it was a sight. For a moment which seemed hour-long I thought the whole thing wd. come to an end – then everybody in desperation sang wildly whatever notes they could hit on, and the organ came in, and by a miracle the thing rightened itself. But never have I suffered so much in a short moment. We all came home almost in tears. On Friday afternoon we turned up to a rehearsal feeling like whipped puppies. He was simply ripping about it though, said that on Thursday there had been some of the best singing that had been heard in that choir for a long time. The first choir had made fools of themselves, they appeared to have suddenly gone mad; but he supposed that human beings were subject to these aberrations at times. And the Mass was to be simply tip-top.

The Mass *was* simply tip-top . . . it was more exciting than you can possibly imagine. I have never seen anything so hot, so tired, so breathless, so excited, or, at the end, so beaming, as Dr Allen. Poor dear! He was almost dead at the end of *Cum sancto spiritu* and had to sit and pant, and pant, and pant, and in the middle of the *Sanctus* he got cramp so badly he had to drop the stick and conduct with his fists, but when all was over, he ruffled his hair up and smiled. I don't know what the audience was doing at the end, but I know that the choir went simply mad. We clapped and the men stamped and shouted till you would have thought the platform was going to collapse. He vanished through the little hole which leads down to the ante-room, and we then clapped the soloists as they came through, (politely, but without embarrassing rapture!) – and then the tenors and basses and some of the soloists hung over the stair-case making the most appalling noises to get the Doctor back again, and at last someone went down and dragged him up, hotter than ever and quite dishevelled, and we went mad again. It was glorious. I love being enthusiastic with a whole mass of people, don't you? . . .

I had to leave [a tennis party] early to hear G.K.C.[3] at the Schools. I was very agreeably surprised in him. I had been afraid he would be untidy in his person and aggressive in his manner. He was very huge and ugly, of course, but it is a nice ugliness, and he was well dressed, with plenty of nice white linen, and he looked well-brushed and put together. He had a terrible cold, poor dear, but all the same one liked his voice – it was the voice of a gentleman, and suggested not only culture but breeding. . . . His delivery, perhaps on account of the cold, was not very good – rather hesitating and slow, but he spoke very clearly. We were some distance away, and heard every syllable. His lecture was very Chestertonian, but much sounder than I had expected and not so fire-worky. He said some really excellent things. I have noted for future use, that his books ought to be read as he speaks – rather slowly, and delivering the paradoxical statements tentatively. His speaking has none of that aggressive and dogmatic quality which his writings are apt to assume when read aloud. Altogether, a most pleasant lecture. . . .

[1] A notable Bach singer, sister of Muriel Foster, also known in the same repertoire.
[2] Fortissimo.
[3] G. K. Chesterton.

TO HER PARENTS   Somerville College
7 June 1914
Darling people
    This seems to have been a terribly busy week – but a very nice one

– all this Term is being nice. I am learning to Boston,[1] and getting on quite fairly well, I think – ditto as regards punting. . . .

Tony and I have got an invitation to dine with Mr Forrest[2] on June 13th – quite a pleasant way of having a twenty-firster![3] I am looking forward to it very much, as Mrs Molyneux is chaperoning us, and we are going to have some music. . . .

We went to hear G.K.C. at the Newman Society's meeting the other night. His subject was 'Capitalism and Culture'. I thought he was quite good, but not nearly so good as he was on Romance. Where he was really splendid was when people asked him questions at the end. He was remarkably quick at answering – I don't think I ever heard anyone better, and he was very witty. Some people hated him and thought him vulgar. Others suggested he was drunk. I've heard that kind of thing about him before. It may be true that he drinks, but he certainly had his wits about him on Friday. He is said to have just 'gone over to Rome'. I hope not, because if so we shall have fewer books and different, I'm afraid. . . .

[1] A new form of waltz. It has been described as follows: 'Perhaps the essence of the new development lay in the abandonment of the purely rotatory movement of the old waltz and of the three steps of virtually even length, on which it was based, in favour of more tangential glides and even swoops.' (Quoted by John S. Peart-Binns, *Maurice B. Reckitt: A Life*, Bowerdean and Pickering, 1988, p. 94.)

[2] Arthur Forrest, a musician and member of the Bach Choir, contemporary with D.L.S. at Oxford. When war was declared he was sent out to the Dardanelles, where he died in December 1915. D.L.S. wrote a poem in his memory, 'Epitaph for a Young Musician', which was first published in the *Oxford Magazine*, 25 February 1916. It was reprinted in *Op. I*, p. 68.

[3] D.L.S. was born on 13 June 1893.

To Her Parents   Somerville College
14 June 1914

Darling people –

First of all – Tootles, dear, thank you ever, ever so much for the lovely brooch. It is just ripping – and exactly the colour I was pining for. I wore it last night, to pin on the fat rose which I bought with Aunt Mabel's money, and it just exactly matched and looked splendid. Whatever kind of stones are they? They are most fascinating. Also, it is so jolly to have a real strong, wide brooch that one can use for flowers and things of that kind. They mix the *dulce* with the *utile*[1] so well. Heaps and heaps of thanks. . . .

Tony[2] and I had a very good time at Mr Forrest's last night.[3] There were ten of us. Mrs Molyneux, and a Mrs Wright, or Right, and a French girl who is staying with Mrs Dixey, besides us; and a person

called Flex, or Flecks, or Flix, and a man called Davison, who acted
magnificently in the French play, and one called Williams, taking
history this year, who took me in to dinner, and a Mr Graham of
Oriel who played the 'cello and was rather amusing and Mr Forrest.
Mrs Molyneux seemed rather tired and depressed – perhaps she had
a headache, poor soul. She met us at the lodge and took us on. Tony
looked awfully sweet in pink, and I was really rather ornamental in
my black and red, with the rose and the shoes, and my hair consented
to go just right. We found Mrs Wright and Mlle Chapelain in a
down-stairs room where we took our things off, and when tidy, proceeded up to Mr Forrest's room, where we were introduced to everybody at once (being a little late, owing to Mrs M. having missed the
7.20 'bus) which was rather confusing. The usual awkward before-
dinner interval was bridged somehow, and I found myself trailing
down a narrow and wry-necked staircase on the arm of Mr Williams.
(This was not in Corpus, but in Wellington Square.) When we had
arrayed ourselves in a tight fit round a small table in a ditto room, I
found that I was on Mr Forrest's right. (He seems to have taken
rather a fancy to yours truly; shall I make a bid for him? He has
plenty of money and plenty of brains, and I rather think plenty of
sense, and is not more excitable than most musicians!) – Anyway,
there we were, and the party was astonishingly noisy after the soup.
Quite a pleasant little dinner – lamb and chicken, 3 vegetables, cherry
tart and something else, and something pale yellow in the wine line,
which I drank – very nice, only I've no idea what it was, and port,
which I did not drink, having, as you know, a rooted objection to it.
Mr Davison, who was sitting two away from Mr Forrest on the other
side, would insist on shouting to me about Molière across the table,
while Mr Williams and Mrs Molyneux kept up a noisy conversation
on my right and Mr Forrest, who was more pink and excited even
than usual, bawled French at Mlle Chapelain. Someone else was
talking German at the other end of the table, and as I can never hear
or make myself heard in a noise, I spent my time yelling 'what?' at
Mr Davison. At length I felt I could bear it no longer, and switched
the conversation back to Mr Williams, who was quite nice, but a
little stolid. At first he was a little difficult, and Mr Forrest was so
voluble to me that I was afraid I wasn't going to work him (Mr W.)
in at all, but at length I got hold of him all right. After dinner we
adjourned upstairs, and I talked to Mlle Chapelain, who seems an
awfully nice girl, till the men came in, and then we had music. There
was one awful moment, because Mr Davison, who is, according to
Mrs Molyneux, one of the finest amateur flute-players in England,
played a solo, and Mlle Chapelain was instantly seized with a most
awful fit of the giggles, which lasted throughout the performance. It

was all I could do to refrain from yelling myself because she was so funny, and then Mrs Dixey told me this morning that the faces I made in trying to keep from laughing added the last straw to her unseemly mirth. However, it didn't matter much, as both the performers were far too intensely pre-occupied to know what was happening. They made me sing two folk-songs and there was a trio and Mr Forrest played the piano, and by that time it was 10.50 and we had to return home.

On Wednesday we go to Mrs Molyneux's – really all the dissipations of this term! – Dance on Monday – I'll be glad to get home. . . .

[1] *dulce* and *utile*: Latin words meaning sweet and useful. The allusion is to *Ars Poetica* by Horace, her father's favourite poet:

> *Omne tulit punctum qui miscuit utile dulci,*
> *Lectorem delectando pariterque monendo.*

(He has gained every vote who has mingled profit with pleasure by equally delighting the reader and instructing him.)

[2] Catherine Godfrey.

[3] D.L.S.'s twenty-first birthday.

At the beginning of August 1914, strangely unaware of the gravity of the international situation, D.L.S. and Elsie Henderson, chaperoned by Miss Lawrance, a friend of Elsie's parents, went off to Tours, where they intended to spend six weeks. The following letters provide an eye-witness account of the situation in France during the first days of World War I.

To Her Parents
2 August 1914

39 rue Laponneraye
Tours
Sunday

Dearest people

We are here and that is about all I can say definitely; for we may find ourselves back in England in a week. I do not mean that there is any danger – there is none, but we are in a state of siege, and if Mme Larnaudie is unable to obtain sufficient provisions, we shall have to go. Just at present, though, we couldn't go if we wanted to, because the trains were all stopped yesterday, as far as the ordinary traffic is concerned; no-one and nothing is travelling in France except military transports. If our luggage had got hung up in Paris yesterday, as we were afraid for a moment it had, we might have whistled for it. . . .

Yesterday we went into the town here. It was most extraordinary. Everybody one met seemed to be in a fearful hurry, and on the other hand, all the street corners were occupied by groups of people talking about the war. Every other man had a newspaper in his hands. Soldiers and sailors were all over the place. They are not anything like as smart as our Tommies and Jack Tars,[1] and most of them look very small to English eyes, but they seem full of go. Here and there one would be greeted by a friend: '*Eh bien! vous partez alors?*' '*Oui, oui, nous partons ce soir*,'[2] shaking hands with a smile (journalistic touch!). Of course it is very different here from what it is in England – *all* the men have to go and of all ages and occupations. Our baker goes to-day, and probably the butcher to-morrow and the candlestick-maker[3] on Tuesday. Mme Larnaudie knows one person who has eight sons and sons-in-law going. There is somebody in every family. The brother of the girl here (Mme L.'s adopted daughter) is going, and she has been writing to beg him to take some permanganate of potash[4] so as not to die of drinking filthy water at any rate, but she says '*Il ne le fera pas*',[5] and if I know anything of human nature, he probably won't.

We tried to get food yesterday – in one shop we asked for two *livres* of *petit-beurres*,[6] and they would only allow one, in case there should not be enough to go round. In another place they had shut the doors and were letting the customers out one by one – they didn't want to sell any more. At the Bazar,[7] they could not give change for a 5-franc piece; however, doubtless we shall soon have some paper money to go on with. It is immensely exciting. The streets yesterday were enveloped in a thick cloud of dust from the continual rushing to and fro of motor-cars. In a restaurant it seemed odd to see the umbrella-stand stuck full of swords. Nobody may sell their horses or motors, or send them away in case they should be wanted, and we are looking forward to the possibility of having officers quartered on us.

In the circumstances, you see it is quite possible we may have to come back, if we can get back. I do hope we shall be able to stay, because it is so fearfully thrilling, but of course it wouldn't be fair to stay and eat up all Mme Larnaudie's provisions. In any case you can be certain that she and Miss Lawrance are absolutely to be trusted to do whatever is best and most prudent, and you are not to be alarmed at any reports. It is possible that communications may be cut off, in which case, of course you will not be surprised or agitated at not hearing from me.

To descend to personal matters. Owing to the delay with the luggage and other bothers, we had a beast of a journey from Havre to Paris, and poor old Elsie was quite overcome by the heat and fatigue in Paris, and is still very much knocked up with a return of the old trouble. I am very much better, and beginning to enjoy myself

immensely, if only we can stay. Mme L. is quite charming, and the
house very nice and comfortable. It is desperately hot, but there is a
very jolly little garden, with a lovely tree that one can sit under –

The milk-woman has just informed us that she may not be able to
come to-morrow, because her little horse and cart will be taken to
the front! So we shall live on condensed-milk – I suppose –

Please remember 1) that there is no danger and you are not to
worry 2) that Miss Lawrance and Mme Larnaudie are absolutely to
be trusted 3) that it is absolutely impossible to leave Tours for a week
at least in any case 4) that I am rapidly blossoming into rude health
5) that this is a delightful house to be in.

And now I'd better stop, or this letter will be awfully heavy. I hope
they won't open it, or stop it, or suppress it or anything. It will
doubtless be delayed –

Much love (bugles in the distance – the regiments are marching
this morning) –

Hope you got back all right from London on Thursday.[8]

    Dorothy

[1] British soldiers and sailors.
[2] 'Well, so you're off, then?' 'Yes, we leave this evening.'
[3] Echoing the rhyme, 'The butcher, the baker, the candlestick-maker'.
[4] A disinfectant.
[5] 'He won't do it.'
[6] A kind of French biscuit, of which they asked for two pounds.
[7] French spelling of bazaar.
[8] Her parents had gone to London to see the party off.

To Her Parents   39 rue Laponneraye
3 August 1914   Tours
                                        Monday

Dearest people

This thing is like a novel by H. G. Wells. The whole world is going
to war, and it has happened in two days! On Wednesday, nobody
here had any idea that it was coming – at any rate, as soon, or Mme
Larnaudie would have sent to put us off. Nothing was really known
till Thursday, when we had already started. Personally, I am
delighted that she was not able to warn us. You have no idea how
frightfully exciting it is being here, right in the middle of things, and
though indeed it looks as though England would soon be in the middle
of things too. But of course it is not like being in a country where a
defeat on the frontier might land the enemy in the capital in a few
hours or so.

More of our troops were moved away yesterday, and some will go to-day. At the rendez-vous, one sees the men taking leave of their families – M. Tardieu, a friend of Mme Larnaudie's, who comes very frequently to the house, arrived yesterday with a pathetic tale of an old man whose beloved horse was taken away from him for the service; of course he will never see it again, poor beast. It was licking his hands and he was weeping over its nose – The *laitière*'s[1] animal seems to have been spared so far, for we got our milk this morning. The great excitement of the day is to procure papers – they have great difficulty in getting them into the town at all – people crowd down to the station and snatch them away as soon as they arrive.

Last night's paper said definitely that the mobilisation would not be finished till August 16th, so that till then it is not of the smallest use to think about trying to move from here. When the trains are free again, we shall see what is best to be done. Miss Lawrance has written to a brother-in-law of hers, who will send someone to escort us back, if any escort should be needed. It is quite possible, of course, that travelling may be almost as usual again then, but one never knows. One must wait and see how things turn out. It certainly looks as though Germany has bitten off more than she can chew this time, but I suppose she knows her own business best. If you write, by the way, don't express much in the way of political opinions, because such are not relished by the postal authorities, and I have no idea whether letters will be respected or not.

Mlle Berthe and I took a walk yesterday along the bank of the Cher – not the Oxford variety, but the French Cher. It is a pretty river, with nice stone bridges, and bordered in a characteristic manner with willows and poplar trees. I believe that one can take boats on it quite comfortably. The Loire, though a much broader river, is very shallow here, and not apparently navigable at this season. You may imagine that we are not undertaking any expeditions. One has other things to think about; besides, there are no means of transport. The number of trams and things in the town is being reduced to-day by 50% because all the drivers etc. have gone to the front. . . .

Before I forget it, Mme Larnaudie and M. Tardieu said I was to tell my parents that I spoke French with no English accent at all. M. Tardieu was quite surprised. He says that I speak '*comme une Française qui accentue beaucoup*.'[2] It seems very odd to hear all the people in the street talking, or rather screaming to each other in French. The women hold a sort of Parliament in the morning on the doorsteps, and discuss the state of Europe with the milk-woman, and the dustman. I watched them washing their steps and the pavement this morning. Water runs along the gutter, and they hurl it over the road and over the pavement with a sort of wooden scoop on a long handle, and then brush it with a kind of flat besom. The street is pretty noisy at night just now. Last night at 12 o'clock Miss Lawrance bought a newspaper, flinging a sou[3] out of the window to the *marchand*,[4] and telling him to drop the paper in at the letter-box. I was asleep, and did not hear the transaction.

I hope to go out with Miss Lawrance some time this morning and see what I can see –

> Your always loving
> Dorothy

[1] Milk-woman's.
[2] 'Like a French woman who accentuates a great deal.'
[3] A French five centime piece, then worth about a halfpenny.
[4] Newspaper vendor.

To Her Parents
4 August 1914

> 39 rue Laponneraye
> Tours
> Tuesday
> 3rd. day of mobilisation

Dearest people –

I got the post-card you sent off on Saturday, this morning. I hope by this time some of my letters are arriving. I'm sorry about Gerald's 3rd, but I suppose it won't make very much difference to him.[1] Do you think there is any truth in the report about Linda?[2] If you were in France, she would be taken as sure as fate. The French are wonderfully patriotic. They accept all the consequences of conscription without a murmur, and seem perfectly resigned to the sacrifice of everything they possess for the good of their country. I do not think English people would ever put up with such a system, but there is such a fervour of enthusiasm here, that it seems to answer remarkably well. The organisation is quite wonderful. Each man when he has finished his military service receives a *carte* with all the details as to what he is to do in case of war – he is to go to such a place, to join such a regiment on the first, second, third day of mobilisation, as the case may be, so that when war is declared, they have only to stick up notices: 'first day of mobilisation Sunday', and everything goes like clockwork. To-morrow we are going to do our best to see one of the regiments start. We heard one of them last night at dinner, the bugles and horses and the crowd cheering them. Great things seem to be expected from England, in the newspapers and by the man in the street, or rather, the man in the ranks, for there are very few men left in the street. The husband of our *femme de ménage*[3] said yesterday before starting: If only we can count on England we'll give the

Germans a good old dressing down (*frottement*) – One feels rather
glad to be English. Of course, if we had been German, we should
have had to return immediately as best we could. They shot two men,
supposed to be spies, Germans, this morning, and they are going to
shoot the *curé* of a little village near here, who was found to have in
the *pneu*[4] of his bicycle, plans of the surrounding country, marked to
show the best spots for dropping bombs from aeroplanes. Anyway,
I'm sure traitors *ought* to be shot. We have been having a hectic time
trying to get ourselves declared as foreigners staying in Tours. We
have already been twice to the police-station, and found there a seething crowd, with one or two miserable harassed officials trying to deal
with them. While we were there yesterday, they arrested a man and
brought him in through the midst of us. He was the most awful
savage-looking brute of a man I ever saw – all shaggy hair and beard,
and a dirty brown shirt open to the waist. He had had a knock on
the head, and was not a pretty sight. Of course, everybody said he
was either a spy or a deserter, but they brought a woman in afterwards
as a witness, and I think it likely that he was merely a common thief.
It made an exciting little interlude in a long wait. We are going again
this afternoon.

We went into the Cathedral yesterday afternoon. It is very beautiful, but we could not walk round it, because Vespers was going on.
The outside, like that of every building I go to visit, is swathed in
planks and scaffolding. I forgot to tell you that while we were in Paris,
we went for a little time into Notre Dame. That is magnificent beyond
words, of course. The three great rose-windows are particularly effective, though some vandal has had the disgraceful idea of inserting a
hideous clock into the middle of the one at the west end. When Elsie
is better, I hope we shall go to service here. There is not only the
Cathedral, of course, but also other churches, particularly that of S.
Martin of Tours with his bones in it – I haven't been there yet.

A French doctor came to see Elsie yesterday, and scandalised her
very much by ordering hypodermic injections of some drug beginning
with 'coca—' – I forget the rest of the word. She said that her London
doctor was very much against the use of injections, but since he has
been treating her – or rather, leaving her alone and telling her to eat
vegetables and wait – for a year, and she, like the woman in the Bible
is no better but rather worse, it seems only reasonable that some other
method should be given a chance – especially as French doctors are
rather good at treating that kind of illness.

Yes, we had a wonderful crossing. Those turbine steamers are
simply marvellous, there is literally *no* roll whatever – it is like being
in a wonderfully smooth and quiet train. The only thing you feel is
the vibration of the screw, which makes a noise exactly like an aero-

plane. In the cabin which we had – miles up, above the water and right in the middle of the ship, you might be on dry land. It was very difficult to sleep, however, because of all the people who came on board by the boat-train at midnight, and rolled luggage up and down the passages, and stood and quarrelled in French and English just outside our door – why they all chose our door, I can't tell you, but they did, and we observed that the French and the English had quite different methods of quarrelling. The English barked shortly and ferociously at one another, and the French stood and harangued each other with fierce concentration and all speaking at once without ever taking breath. However, things quieted down at last. In the morning there was bright sunshine, and a wind fit to blow the horns off an ox – it was lovely standing on deck while we came into the harbour.

I like Miss Lawrance very much indeed. She is extremely pleasant, and an excellent person to travel with. It is odd that she always manages to come in for wars and tumults. She was in Natal during the S. African war, so she is quite accustomed to all these excitements.

1.45 – I am standing in a stuffy queue at the Mairie,[5] trying to make my declaration. We are surrounded by American women – all shouting and giving themselves terrific airs. From time to time a few officials make frantic attempts to sort us out. We have just been stirred up like whisked eggs to let some people through – the witnesses in the business of yesterday, I think.

4 o'clock – At last! I've never been so squeezed and jostled in my life, but at last it is over! The Americans screamed and talked stupidly, and the workmen smoked filthy cigarettes, and people bumped us – and then, if they didn't turn us right round in the passage and make us go in at another door, the result being that all the people who got there last went in first. I don't blame the officials, though, because they are fearfully short-handed, and all foreigners are being sent away from the coast and from the frontier and packed into the centre.

The last news we have seen is that the English fleet has been seen from the coast of France, and that General French[6] is with it. We're hoping it may be true. If only one could get English papers – or any papers for the matter of that. When you write, please give any news you can about what England is doing, and if our lads are really coming over, and above all, whether there is any reasonable chance of their coming in time.

The tea-bell has rung, so I'll stop, and someone will perhaps take this to the post –

Best love
    D.

The old chap who gave us our permits stopped to tell us how well I spoke French. He was an amiable old boy, but a bit of a dawdler.

[1] Gerald Sayers had been awarded a third-class degree, but this would not affect his appointment to a post in E. Africa in the Colonial Service.
[2] The pony at Bluntisham.
[3] Charwoman.
[4] Tyre.
[5] Town Hall.
[6] General Sir John French, leader of the British Expeditionary Force. Great Britain declared war on Germany on 4 August, the date of this letter.

To Her Parents   39 rue Laponneraye
5 August 1914   Tours

Dear people

Your wire arrived this morning at breakfast time – greatly delayed, you see. There is a notice in the post-office to say that they cannot at all guarantee the time of arrival of private telegrams. However, by this time you ought to be getting my letters. If not, they will have gone astray, but so far the post office appears to be working all right, though very slowly. There really is not the remotest need to be anxious about me. Tours is quiet enough, and the Germans are not yet at the gates of Paris, and we're determined they shall not come there. We are going in a day or two to the Préfecture[1] to get passports,[2] and I think we shall come home as soon as possible, that is to say, a few days after the railways are clear again. It will be no good to start directly the mobilisation is finished, because the crowds will be so enormous. . . .

Berthe and I have been running about the town, getting news and information about passports and so on. The old *concierge* at the Chambre des Commerçants, whither we went to see if there was anyone there to do duty for an English Consul, was excessively amiable, and learning that I was English, and wanted to know how to get home, said '*Mais nous ne vous ferons pas de mal en France, mademoiselle, c'est que nous sommes amis*'.[3] She told us of a family of ten, – seven sons and the three sons-in-law have all gone to the front. The French are really an extraordinarily plucky nation. – Troops keep on passing through Tours. At this moment there is a terrific noise of shouting in the distance. Doubtless one of the regiments is on its way to the station. The papers this morning say that the British army is being mobilised at midnight. There is a great enthusiasm for the English. The President's[4] latest address, which is excellent, full of dignity and moderation, ends with an allusion to the loyal friendship of England. It seems that M. Poincaré is the right man in the right place – immensely beloved and very capable, which is an excellent thing.

Yesterday at the police-station we witnessed a little incident not without its grim side. An elderly man and a young woman were declaring themselves:–

'*Votre nom, monsieur?*'

'*W—*'

'*Vous êtes Allemand?*'

'*Oui, monsieur.*'

'*C'est-là votre femme?*'

'*Non, monsieur – nous voyageons ensemble.*'

'*Mettons amie, alors. Vous voulez rester à Tours?*'

'*Nous voudrions passer en Espagne.*'

'*Ah! Monsieur, je vous conseille de rester jusqu' à un nouvel ordre.*'[5]

Mercifully, for English people, there is nothing but extreme politeness, though the officials are having a pretty busy time, poor souls. . . .

[1] Police station.

[2] Passports were not required for normal conditions of travel until after World War I.

[3] 'But we won't do you any harm in France, Mademoiselle, we're friends.'

[4] Raymond Poincaré (1860–1934), President of the French Republic from 1913 to 1920.

[5] 'Your name, sir?' 'W—' 'You are German?' 'Yes, sir.' 'Is that your wife with you?' 'No, sir – we are travelling together.' 'We'll say lady-friend, then. You wish to remain in Tours?' 'We'd like to go on to Spain.' 'Ah! I advise you to wait for further instruction, sir.'

To Her Parents   39 rue Laponneraye
13 August 1914   Tours

Dearest people

Letter from Mother this morning for which many thanks. There is no doubt about the successes in Belgium.[1] The temper of the Belgians has come as a terrific surprise to everybody, I think, and possibly not least to Wilhelm II. Let us hope so. Their resistance is immensely valuable to us, because it gives us time. The Belgian flag has appeared with the French, Russian and English in the streets of Tours. The really terrific enthusiasm here is of course the occupation of Mulhouse by French troops. Alsace-Lorraine are never forgotten, and the idea that we may be able to get them back arouses the man in the street to a pitch of wild excitement. Mme Larnaudie is so thrilled at the idea of seeing the end of the German nightmare, as she saw the beginning of it in 1870, that sometimes being by nature very excitable – she doesn't know what to do with herself. We have very French moments, when Mme L. and Berthe have a noisy little passage-of-arms – Mme L. wonderfully voluble and generally finding fault, and poor Berthe protesting – both talking at once, while Miss Lawrance fans herself and tries to turn the conversation, and Elsie and I sit silent. Miss L. thanks you very much for asking her to come to

Bluntisham. She herself is going to Scotland, I think, but she will have to see Elsie safely bestowed in Darlington first, wherever she goes. When I suggested that they should both come to us – we should have to have Elsie if we had Miss L. – she said something about passing a night in London. Really, I think your idea, if extended to include Elsie, is a good one, as then Elsie could have several days' rest instead of only one night, and I think I shall mention the subject again. We are not really far from London, and I suppose there are a fair number of trains running – there will be, at any rate, by the time we get home. Elsie is better at present, but of course, the things she is taking are only a sort of pick-me-up to tide her over the present crisis. One cannot effect a permanent cure of that kind of thing in a day or two. Her people at home do not seem to me really to understand how serious a matter it is, but perhaps I ought not to say that. The heat's enough to knock you down. One has to have the shutters closed practically all day. Old England for me, as far as weather goes. Mercifully, it does not seem to prevent me, as yet, from sleeping, and I turn up fresh and cheerful in the morning, to find the others jaded and hot to start with. I don't know how long I shall preserve this advantage. The streets at night and in the morning are very noisy. At night, people walking and talking and taking leave and having domestic discussions – in the morning itinerant vendors of various things, each with his own particular cry – the tomato-vendor, the milk (2 different women), the potato-vendor, the dust-man, the coal-merchant (2 of them, with two different cries), the man selling chickweed and plantains for the birds, who sings a sort of dismal little tune, and night and day the purveyors of news, each with a cry or a wind-instrument, or both. Thus, at 10.30 at night, '*Whaugh! whaugh! wau-gh! La Touraine! La Toura-a-ine! édition nouvelle! Waugh! – les nouvelles – waugh! waugh! La Touraine! – La Dépêche! Too-roo! too-ro-o-o-h! La Dépêche! édition du soir! Too-roo! – Waugh! La Toura-a-ine! – To-roo! – La Dépêche! – Waugh!*' and it dies away down the street. These are still only local rags – the Paris papers do not get here at all as yet.

I have just been talking to Miss Lawrance. We are now inclined to think that it would be best for her and Elsie to come to Bluntisham, certainly if we cross at night (which is unlikely) and can come straight on, and probably, even if we have to spend the night in London, because Bluntisham is so truly restful. I don't suppose we should sleep much in London after a long journey and voyage, and think of going straight on to the north! Miss L. has written to Havre and to S. Malo, to get information about boats etc. as soon as possible. I will let you know later. Mercifully, the irruption of one or two people more or less suddenly at Bluntisham does not mean my sleeping in

your room, or putting the visitors in the box-room. I think myself
that the quiet we wot of (!)[2] would be the best thing possible for Elsie.
She would probably rest better with us for a little time than she would
at home, especially as her mother is not very well, and could not
possibly wait on her all day. However, we shall see. They are very
grateful to you indeed for your invitation, and I think it highly probable that it will be accepted.

I'm so glad poor little Linda hasn't been taken yet – poor little
soul! – she'd never come back again. Of course, we would be thankful
to be able to give something to help, but it does seem so peculiarly
dreadful for animals. At least, they haven't commandeered the
poultry! There is a cock next door shut up in a little enclosure
with half-a-dozen hens. He makes a most awful row, and when he
stops, there is a terrible donkey in the street opposite, who makes
more noise than Jacques, and more often. Then the neighbours on
the other side have a miserable jackdaw with a clipped wing, which
flaps about all day trying to escape, and gives vent to noises at
intervals, rather like Mrs Dunham's raven, but not quite so much
so.

Oh! the heat – we are all grilling away in our bedrooms, mostly
undressed, with everything shut up, and we pant and gasp. What it
must be like on the frontier it doesn't do to think. Thank goodness,
our men are more sensibly clothed than the French or (not being
used to it) they would all give up the ghost, I should think. I haven't
heard any soldiers to-day. Perhaps most of them have gone. I do
hope that people in England are dealing severely with those German
raiders. We have a mania for not shooting people – all very well, but
sometimes one has to come down heavily. I'm sorry the Crown Prince[3]
is still intact.

   Best love to everybody
   Dorothy

[1] The defence of the Belgians of the fortress of Liège, which held out until 16 August.
[2] Wot: archaic verb (Middle English), meaning 'to know'. It is used humorously.
[3] The son of the Kaiser, known as 'little Willy'.

To Her Mother   39 rue Laponneraye
13 August 1914   Tours
                                     Evening

Dearest Mother
   I have written to you asking if we may bring Elsie to Bluntisham
for a few days before taking her on to Darlington. I felt sure at the
time that you would be glad that we should do this, but I think

perhaps, before you decide definitely, I ought to tell you the exact state of the case. She is feeling better now, and getting brighter and stronger every day as a result of the doctor's treatment, but the first few days she was really in such a bad state of collapse that we were frightened for her. The doctor has been to-night, and says that it will be safe for her to travel in 8 or 10 days if she takes it very easily but there is always the bare possibility that she *may* have another relapse after the journey. It is not at all likely that it will be anything like as bad as this one, because she will be better prepared for it by the doctor's remedies, and also we shall travel by very easy stages; but if you are afraid to have her in the house in such a condition, say so, because it will no doubt be an anxiety. I do not think there is any doubt that a rest at Bluntisham would be the very best thing possible *for her*, as she needs *rest* and *the country*, and not fatigue and the town. Because of this, I should be very glad if you could manage to have her for a little, and I know that she herself, poor child, is very much taken with the idea of going. I think the idea of quiet and coolness appeals to her, after this hot town. However, it is only fair that you should know the state of the case and be free to refuse the responsibility. Your suggestion came as a great relief to all of us – indeed, it had already occurred to me – and I do not really think there is any likelihood of her being really ill at Blunt.[1] The doctor has delivered his report to-night. It is just as we expected – not consumption[2] yet, but such a state of worn-outness that *complete rest* is absolutely necessary in order to prevent her being attacked. No games, no violent exercise of any kind – lying down continually, and a little walk perhaps every 2 hours, of a quarter of an hour or thereabouts. Lord only knows if Mrs Henderson will realise the necessity of attending to all this. Perhaps the word consumption will frighten her – I think she is one of those persons who must be frightened before they see things. Mind, there are *no symptoms* at all at present, and no danger for other people – only, without great care, something may develop – it is a damnable thing to overwork people till they get into such a state. Thank God you never let it happen to me. It is pitiful for her, poor little soul, because she is peculiarly without resources in a quiet way – i.e. she does not read with real enjoyment, cannot sew, does not care for anything that one does with one's hands. Still, there it is –

I thought it better on the whole to let you know all this – indeed, if she comes to Bluntisham, you will probably see it without being told. Needless to say, she herself knows nothing, and I shall not tell Miss Lawrance that I have told you the whole thing. She knows that I am warning you that Elsie may be ill at Bluntisham. I am marking this letter private, not because I do not wish Daddy and Auntie to know, but simply so that you may have time to think things over before people begin advising you, and also, that you may not think it is a letter full of news – I will send a different kind of letter to the others by the same post.[3]

Think it over – If you don't mind the slight risk of a botheration, I shall be more than thankful, for Elsie's sake and for that of Miss Lawrance, if she can come to Bluntisham –

Yours with very best love
Dorothy

[1] Bluntisham.
[2] The contemporary term for tuberculosis, a prevalent disease at the time and usually fatal.
[3] See preceding letter.

D.L.S., Miss Lawrance and Elsie Henderson left Tours on about 21 or 22 August and arrived at Bluntisham Rectory on the twenty-fifth. There are no letters extant for the intervening period. Her guests remained at Bluntisham until the twenty-eighth. D.L.S. returned to Oxford in October, to find it filled with Belgian refugees.

Seventh term October–November 1914 (Age: 21)

To Her Parents   Somerville College
25 October 1914   Oxford

Dearest people

Well, as for Uncle Cecil, Mother, you have the satisfaction of saying that you told us so. I'm not in the least surprised. I think it's bad luck on Gwen. Has the bride-elect[1] any money? I suppose Gerald will be up some time this month. I must try and see him. . . .

Yesterday afternoon at Miss Penrose's At Home a very charming Belgian lady came, the wife of a Louvain professor, who managed to save the one MS which was saved from the library there. He happened to have the book out, working at it, when he was told that the Germans were coming, and he and his wife and two tiny children had just time to get away, with as much luggage as he could carry in his hand. So, instead of any clothing for himself, he insisted on his wife's putting in this book, which he has brought with him to England. It is a unique copy of something or other, and of course unreplaceable.

This morning, as Barney[2] and I were starting off for church we ran into a whole party of Belgians in Walton Street, who wanted to be

directed to S. Aloysius. It was rather complicated from there, so as
we had started in extra good time, I offered to take them by a short
cut through Somerville. Till that moment I had seen only a woman
and a man with a map of Oxford – As soon as I spoke, however, the
woman waved her umbrella wildly, crying '*C'est par ici!*'[3] and two *huge*
fat women arrived, gesticulating and protesting from the other side
of the street. I gathered them in, and in the distance we beheld other
scattered units turning round, and pointing, and crying '*Par là!*'[4] The
street seemed to be stacked with Belgians going to S. Aloysius. I
piloted my lot along – One of the women was '*ma tante*', and very
rheumatic, and could only go *very* slowly, so we must have been
exceedingly humorous to behold. I left them at the gate, and went
off to S. Barnabas on my bicycle, after carefully indicating the exact
position of the church – but how many there were of them, or how
long the procession through Somerville became, I didn't stop to
see! . . .

Yes – I think we ought to take Belgians, if we can get them to come
to such a God-forsaken spot. People here are being simply ripping
about them.

[1] Cecil Sayers had recently become engaged to be married for the third time.
[2] Probably Charis Barnett, a contemporary at Somerville.
[3] 'It's this way!'
[4] 'That way!'

To Her Parents   Somerville College
1 November 1914   All Saints Day

Dearest people . . .

I've seen a fair amount of Belgians and people – there is going to
be an At Home for them here on the 14th. which I am to attend,
among other French-speaking persons – How are your people going
on? Remember that you must always say 'monsieur' and 'madame'
in every sentence, even when speaking to the gas-fitter and his wife
or at least, they do in Republican France, I daresay they don't in
Belgium. The class distinction there is so terrific that even the refugees
won't speak to anybody whom they wouldn't 'know' in their own
country.

This makes things very difficult for the Committee. One aristocratic
lady actually objected to Miss Pamela Bruce, who is head of the
committee, because she said she had seen her riding a bicycle (a thing
only done in Belgium by shopgirls, apparently!) and she said that,
though Miss Bruce had been very kind, she really felt she could not

associate with her so we had to trot out Miss Bruce's pedigree, and point out that she was an 'Honourable' and the daughter of a lord,[1] and the lady was pacified . . .

[1] She was the daughter of the 1st Baron Aberdare and the older sister of the Vice-Principal of Somerville.

To Her Parents   Somerville College
8 November 1914

Dearest people

This has been a flurried week – yesterday I helped to see a family of nine Belgians with their two maids into a house which the Bursar and Miss Phillpotts, assisted by the Senior Student, Elsie and myself had furnished in a week with borrowed furniture. It was a humorous job. You should have seen Lady Mary Murray's cook explaining the kitchen range to us in English, Miss Jones and myself explaining to Madame Rüdder in French, and Madame Rüdder passing the explanation on in Flemish to the cook and housemaid! It was like a page out of *Punch*. They are a very nice family. I am going this week with Miss Jones to call on them – I spent all yesterday morning buying pails and scrubbing-brushes at the sixpence-halfpenny shop, and being thoroughly domestic.

Thank you very much indeed for the lovely cakes. Please tell Auntie how greatly they are appreciated; I am quite famous for them here, all my friends rejoice in them, and they are a most enormous saving. Things go on as usual. Bach Choir last Monday was rather hectic and the Doctor's eyes were very green, which is always a bad sign. . . . Did I tell you the perfect thing the Doctor said about the basses and their tone being like liquorice? 'very thick and very slowly elastic'? I believe I did. . . .

To Her Parents
November 1914   Somerville College
                                                        First Sunday in Advent

Dearest family

This week's just about jolly well put the lid on. It's been one wild scrum. Chiefly H.P.A.'s[1] fault. He picked me out on Monday to be one of the students to illustrate Sir W. Parratt's[2] lecture on War Music on Tuesday – indeed, I'm swollen with pride because as far as I can make out, he picked *me* himself, and left the secretary to choose the others. Anyway we practised at his home on Wednesday and Friday and are going again this afternoon – and on Wednesday there was only 1 copy between us, and we had to get it copied out by Friday and then practise it, and they're appalling 15th. and 16th. c. things – one about Agincourt in some wild old mode, and the other about Marignan[3] – all vomm, vom, fari-rari-la-la, trique traque, pati-pata and other fearful sounds, intended to represent the noise of battle. So you see, life is a strain just at present. I'm going to screw up my courage to ask him to lecture next term for Lit. Phil.[4] I've no idea whether he'll take kindly to the idea or not . . .

We had a sermon this morning about the Society for the Propagation of the Gospel, which has depressed me. However, I was pleased, because the preacher said we were to pray that God would do away the shortcomings of missionaries. He added that our own attempts at converting other people were generally blundering, and that when our friends tried to convert us, we usually dismissed their attempts as well-meaning but painful. He added that it was very important that missionaries should inculcate the doctrine of Purgatory, and encouraged us by a story to the effect that some cultured Indians, on hearing the Athanasian creed fully explained (I suppose by a High Churchman) exclaimed 'Well! if that is the philosophy of your creed, we cannot stand against it'!

I must stop now, and practise the Battle of Marignan for 10 minutes . . .

[1] Dr Hugh Percy Allen.
[2] Sir Walter Parratt (1841–1924), organist, teacher and composer. He was appointed Master of the Queen's Musick in 1893 and Professor of Music at Oxford in 1908.
[3] The battle of Marignan was fought on 13–14 September 1515 between the French, led by Francis I, and the Swiss. The French were victorious.
[4] The Literary and Philosophical Society of Somerville College.

Eighth term January–March 1915 (Age: 21)

To Her Parents   Somerville College
7 February 1915   Sunday

Dearest people . . .

Daddy, dear – you are most awfully good and generous to me – I don't quite know what to do about it. The difficulty is, getting something which will enable one to put away a little money for one's declining years, so to speak – and there *are* no jobs in Oxford that I can hear of – and it's such a question whether it's worth while wasting (so to speak) a year. If I worked for a B. Litt.[1] or anything, it would mean fees, and expense and even then wouldn't lead to anything very paying. Just at the moment, too, I am fed up with careers and learning, and don't seem able to cope with the subject, so I'm going to leave it alone for a little and see how I feel about it in a few weeks' time. But ever so many thanks – and if of course I could stay in Oxford a bit longer, I should be very glad. . . .

I am now coping with the Doctor[2] on another tack – he seems inclined to add me to a long procession of little tame cats who have adorned his organ-loft in succession. This is a nuisance, because I do not want to be anybody's tame cat. – Don't be perturbed, and for Heaven's sake don't think anything horrid about him – but I understand from Mrs Molyneux that he gets fancies for patronising people. But by that glad star which danced at my birth, I'll not dance to his piping! He's an old ass, though – he nearly lost the chrysophase ring Aunt Maud gave me, the other day, by fooling about with it and almost dropping it down between the organ-pedals. Imagine Aunt Maud's face, if she heard what had become of it! I've an idea I've conveyed some horrid impression with these remarks without intending it – and I may be flattering myself over-much! – and in all circumstances he's a perfect dear and one would trust him round the world and back again – Still, out of his own subject, I can meet him on an equality, and I will – only he must be ridden on the snaffle till I've got him here to lecture! – Bless him! – Everyone thinks it's an awful achievement to have got him to come at all –

Balliol Concert[3] this evening – rather a good one, I think.

Best love
    Dorothy

[1] Bachelor of Letters, Oxford post-graduate degree, between the B.A. and the D.Phil. (Doctor of Philosophy).
[2] H. P. Allen.
[3] Balliol concerts were founded in 1885 and still exist. (Cf. *Gaudy Night*, chapter 23.)

When D.L.S. returned to Oxford for her ninth and last term, Somerville College had been commandeered as a hospital for wounded officers. The students were accommodated at Oriel, either in the college itself or in lodgings.

In June of this year D.L.S. sat for her final examinations and achieved a first class. This qualified her, as was the case at that period with all women candidates at Oxford, only to a 'title to a degree'. (The matter was rectified in 1920, when D.L.S. was among the first batch of women on whom an Oxford degree was officially conferred.) She had taken French Honours, specialising in the mediaeval period. This involved a study of Old French, in which she was tutored by Miss Mildred Pope. Of the mediaeval texts she studied, two made a special impression on her. They were the eleventh-century epic, the Chanson de Roland, *and the twelfth-century romance* Tristan *by the Anglo-Norman poet, Thomas. She was later to translate both these works.*

Ninth term and Vacation May–December 1915 (Age: 21–22)

TO HER PARENTS   St Mary Hall
2 May 1915   Oriel College
                                              Oxford

Dearest people

I'm so sorry I haven't been able to write before, but I have been very busy with various things. It is great fun being at Oriel, though it has its draw-backs of course – such as having to be very careful to stick on a hat when one goes two paces from the door, and not shouting in the bathrooms because it can be heard all over the quad. and half-way down the streets. Legends and tales are already growing up. A really charming one is this. When we came here we were much taken aback to find that there were no keys at all to the bathroom doors. (Note: the baths *et hoc genus omne*[1] are of course outside, and buried at an incredible depth beneath the earth, and the windows give partly on to the High and partly on to Oriel Street.) One student, entering the bathroom cried out to a friend in the passage: 'Oh! I can't lock the door!' Voice from the street: 'It doesn't matter this time, dearie.' A dusty-looking old person, standing in Oriel Street, and seeing one of our students walking in, in rather a dusty state, carrying a bunch of marigolds, was heard to ejaculate: 'What a horrid sight!' We dine in the old hall of S. Mary's, which was Oriel's J.C.R.,[2] and our common-room is, I believe, that of the professors and people – or someone's library, I forget which. They are lovely rooms. My own room looks out on the High, exactly opposite St Mary's. It is really far more comfortable than my Somerville room, because there are more shelves and drawers to put one's things in. The moving has been managed most marvellously – they brought everything along, and lost practically nothing on the way. I have been having a great time trying to get the bicycles into order,[3] but it is done now, and I think Miss Penrose and Miss Walton are pleased with the way I coped with the situation. . . .

We had a gorgeous May Day yesterday.[4] We brought a punt down to Magdalen the afternoon before, and at a quarter to 5 we fetched it, and heard the hymn from the river, and then punted down the New Cut into the Isis and got armfuls of glorious marigolds. We had

Dorothy aged about five, with her hoop *(Marion E. Wade Center)*

Dorothy, possibly acting in *Coriolanus* at the Godolphin *(Marion E. Wade Center)*

Amateur theatricals at Bluntisham: from left to right Miss Hamilton, the French au pair girl, Dorothy and Betty Osborne *(Marion E. Wade Center)*

Lewis Waller as Henry V *(John Culme)*

Teachers at the Godolphin School, 1909. From left to right, top row: Miss White, Miss Brett, Miss Isaacson; second row, Miss Westlake, Miss Fehmer *(The Godolphin School)*

Hugh Allen as Dorothy knew him *(reproduced from a photograph published by Oxford University Press)*

Dorothy imitating Hugh Allen *(Jack Reading)*

Punting with Muriel St Clare Byrne at Oxford *(Jack Reading)*

On holiday in Yorkshire with Muriel Jaeger, soon after the birth of John Anthony *(Jack Reading)*

Dorothy in 1917, a photograph kept by Leonard Hodgson *(Mrs Brigid Somerset)*

a huge breakfast on the way of course. Then we punted right up to Somerville boat house, – and got back about 10.30. The swan is sitting just by Parsons' Pleasure,[5] but the old gentleman[6] was quite polite. . . .

[1] Latin euphemism: 'and all that sort of thing'.
[2] Junior Common Room.
[3] D.L.S. was Somerville 'bicycle secretary'.
[4] At 6 a.m. on May Morning a Latin hymn is sung by the choristers on the top of the bell-tower of Magdalen College, after which the bells are rung. People gathering for the occasion then go off to breakfast with one another on the river. (See *Gaudy Night*, chapter 11.)
[5] A bathing-place for men where no swimming clothes are worn.
[6] The male swan.

To Her Parents
16 May 1915   St Mary Hall
                                        Sunday after the Ascension

Dearest people . . .

Yesterday I went with a friend to a play given with no scenery or anything by some Belgian actors in the Sheldonian. It was Verhæren's[1] *Le Cloître*, and really awfully fine, though owing to the theatre being only half full it was very difficult to hear anything. The man who took the chief part was a really ripping actor.

I have been talking to Miss Pope about jobs in France, and have come to the conclusion that I had rather have a nursing post than do relief work. I do not think the work is much harder, and it would be more definite. Also, they do not like taking people under 24 for Relief (re-patriation etc.). Miss Jones, who is making a great success of her job, seems to think that they are simply crying out over there for nurses who can speak French. So I propose, if possible, if you will allow me, and if I find that I am physically fit, to take a month's training in August at any hospital that will take me. This would cost, I suppose, from £10–15 – then I could go abroad in September. I am going to write to Miss Jones in a day or two, and ask her to try and find me a post in France (conditionally, of course, on the hospital here thinking me fit, and my being able to stand the training) – as it is much easier to get an English hospital to train one if one can point to a definite post which is waiting for one in France. Dr Kempe[2] didn't say I'd got any permanent weakness left in my lungs, did he? It would be the most confounded nuisance to be chucked out as unfit. Of course, in one way I should hate nursing – hard labour and horrors – but I should be frightfully glad to have done it, and to have done something *real* for the first time in my life. And it's better than peasants

and babies and local administration and inspecting drains, which is
what one does on the other job. . . .

¹ Emile Verhaeren (1885–1916), Belgian poet, playwright and critic. His play *Le Cloître*
(The Cloister) was first published in 1900. D.L.S. refers to his poem 'Le Carillon' in *The
Nine Tailors*, II, 'The Sixth Part'.
² The doctor who attended her at the Godolphin when she had double pneumonia
resulting from measles.

To Muriel Jaeger¹   Bluntisham Rectory
27 July 1915

Dearest Jimmy –
    I've been meaning to write for ages, but something's generally
cropped up to prevent me – sometimes real obstacles and sometimes
just blue devils, so I'm sending you a 'souvenir' as the soldiers say
of the last meeting of M.A.S. as a propitiatory offering. . . .
    Just at present I'm simply struggling with Oxford fever, with the
help of Franz Schubert and J. S. Bach. I feel a strong repulsion from
all books, but am attracted by music, so I'm practising violently. One
can't sit glooming while trying to play a Bach prelude correctly – at
least, not when one plays the piano as rottenly as I do. I have also
found Betty Osborne very willing to play classical stuff with me, so
I've taken the fiddle up again. But oh! my dear! I *do* want Oxford.
If I've not got a job which keeps me stuck elsewhere this autumn I
shan't be able to keep away from the place.
    But peace! enough of this. Nothing much has been happening,
except that my cousin from the front and my uncle from the front
have each paid us a visit, with their respective wives. Both (the men,
not the wives) have got nervous breakdown, one has neuritis and the
other has damaged his eye gazing at aeroplanes. Jolly business, war.
Both seem uncommonly gloomy over the prospect, but I don't know
how far they can really judge. I'm rather glad they're gone, because
I do so hate everlasting war-talk, and I'm always in terror of Mother
getting another of her nervous attacks. She was on the verge of one
the night my uncle arrived. And they are so terrifying, because she
loses control over her speech and limbs. Nothing very dreadful
happened this time though, but it is always a most worrying
possibility. . . .
    I must stop, because I've got a lot of letters to write. A word about
the 'Last Castle'.² I've sent it just as it is, because you know what
it's all about, and for outside consumption it would want lots and
lots of expanding and altering. I've only cast in some more lyrics,
and added the scoffing labels of the various 'schools' which we used

to patronise. Good old M.A.S. We got some fun out of it, didn't we?

Lots of love, Jim dear, and write sometimes, won't you?

Ever yours
Dorothy

[1] Muriel Jaeger (1892–1969), a member of the Mutual Admiration Society, read English at Somerville. For many years she was one of D.L.S.'s closest friends and gave her moral support while she was at work on her first novel, *Whose Body?* This may be seen from the dedication: 'To M.J. / Dear Jim: / This book is your fault. If it had not been for your brutal insistence, Lord Peter would never have staggered through to the end of this enquiry. Pray consider that he thanks you with his accustomed suavity. Yours ever, D.L.S.'
[2] A series of poems later included in *Op. I* (Blackwell, 1916).

To Muriel Jaeger   Bluntisham Rectory
26 September 1915

Dearest Jim

Ever so many thanks for your letter and the sonnet, which I like immensely, not only because of the charming and undeserved compliment to myself but for the whole sentiment and expression . . . Miss Kempson for one would agree with you or me or whichever of us it was. I mean that while we keep on writing to each other about the good old days and thinking about them, it doesn't do to spend one's whole time planning to get back to Oxford or to see each other again. Not that any of us is likely to do that, unless it is I. So much for that . . .

On Tuesday I'm going up to stay the night with Charis, and buy clothing. It will be nice seeing her again, though I'm afraid she'll be in a depressed state. It is terrible for them to have lost the brother – Donald, his name was, wasn't it? – She wrote me a perfectly ripping letter, in answer to my feeble *de mortuis*.[1] I think it's wonderful how kindly people receive one's condolences. I'm sure if I was in trouble I should hate all the letters saying all the same things – but perhaps I shouldn't when it came to the point.

Talking of condolence, I have just received a despairing missive from Giles Dixey. Nothing is right and everything is all wrong. He hates his work, his colonel, his fellow-officers and his men. He can't write poetry. He's bored with everything. His young woman (I gather, he does not say so) is unpropitious, and 'everything seems so little worth while'!!!! There's a state of mind singularly likely to appeal to my sympathies! The amount of womanliness and sympathy generally I've been required to pour out lately is quite wonderful . . . Bother these suicidal egotists! Not that Giles would think or talk of suicide;

he wouldn't think it respectable. He assured me in moving terms at the end of his letter that he was not really conceited. (He is.) Somebody has been rubbing it into him apparently. God forgive me though for calling anybody conceited – I've suffered too much from the accusation myself. Is a prig the same thing? Because that's what he is. Please tell me next time you write how you define priggishness, and is it conceit, or isn't it rather a kind of inelasticity?

This morning I got a letter from Arthur Forrest – you remember about him, don't you? I had written to bid him God-speed, learning he was ordered out to the Dardanelles. He wrote on the eve of sailing – an awfully nice letter – only the nice letters are so horribly pathetic. He hates the whole thing, I think, but takes it very high-spiritedly. His one idea seems to be to get back to his musical work at Oxford. I hope to Heaven he may, but the very mention of the Dardanelles turns me cold . . .

I have no news of the 'Lay'[2] and I don't know whether the book is out yet, or whether it isn't coming out at all, whether they will send me a copy or whether they won't. Like a fool I forgot to ask for my proofs, or I should have known . . . I've only been doing technical work since – rondeaux and a ballade chiefly – excellent practice – I still hammer at J. S. Bach, but I can read a little now. I've just finished the life of R. L. Stevenson.[3] What a perfectly topping man he was. I also read *The Master of Ballantrae* for the first time; grim, but very satisfactory. It amused me to find that I could practise Prof. Rudler's 'dynamic method' with some success, for having finished the book I said to myself 'That resurrection scene was the first bit of the book to be thought of, and all the former disappearances were constructed to lead up to it' – and I could see the whole making of the story as clear as glass.[4] Then, reading the *Life* I found my views exactly, or almost exactly, confirmed by R.L.S. – If only I had his patience, to work and re-work my productions. He was a little wonder – I'm glad you like the bit about 'Something shifting nightly'[5] – it's rather a favourite of mine, and if I say it slowly to myself, I get the creeps. I wrote it one day in New College, after refusing an invitation to the organ-loft. Do you like the poem 'Symbol'?[6] Charis read it in D. Rowe's copy, and said she liked it immensely, and that it rang perfectly true; so I was pleased, because she is unhappily in a position to judge.

I say, this beastly new postal rate of only 1 oz. for a penny will weigh heavily on some of us, I'm thinking. We shall find ourselves going back to the ghastly old days when one crossed and re-crossed one's letters. – I have an aunt[7] who at present conducts her whole correspondence, practically, on halfpenny post-cards. She is a stricken woman. I chuckle myself, because I very seldom send postcards, and

I *do* dislike this sort of thing, to which she is prone: 'Went to B. to-day, saw D.'s new c. and s. Very pretty. E. *a vendu sa maison. Pas très bien* but more when I see you about this. H. says she does not think it is *true* about D. and the F.'s, but of course we all know that S.F. is sometimes *un peu difficile.* I saw J.K. and he *entirely* confirms what G. told us, *Nous verrons.* Met L. on Sat: *enthusiastic* about a *certain plan*! Love to D. and H. and hope to see them at B. before long.' and so on. All very tightly squeezed in and like a jig-saw puzzle to read, though perfectly plain to the postman and servants.

Mind you write soon, so that we can get in as many lengthy epistles as possible before the rates change! I shall certainly try for Oxford next term.

> Ever your most loving
> Dorothy

[1] From the Latin, *de mortuis nihil nisi bonum* (nothing save good concerning the dead).
[2] D.L.S. had offered her series of poems, collectively entitled 'Lay', to *Oxford Poetry*, 1915, a volume edited by G. D. H. Cole and T. W. Earp, published by Blackwell. It was accepted and later reprinted in *Op. I.*
[3] Robert Louis Stevenson (1850–94). The biography is probably that by Graham Balfour (1901).
[4] Cf. *Whose Body?*, chapter 10, in which the ingenuous medical student, Mr Piggott says: 'Lord Peter had a funny way of talking about books . . . as if the author had confided in him beforehand, and told him how the story was put together, and which bit was written first.'
[5] A phrase from the penultimate section of the multiple poem 'The Last Castle', published in *Op. I*: 'Thus was our singing':
> . . . for this was like the noise
> Of something shifting nightly at the root
> Of a tall pleasure-house . . .
[6] The ninth item in 'The Last Castle', representing the 'Pre-Raphaelite School', beginning:
> I found him in the church-yard
> My brother who had died,
> With white lilies above him,
> And a hemlock by his side.
[7] Aunt Gertrude Sayers, whose epistolary style D.L.S. imitated in the letters of Miss Climpson.

To Dorothy Rowe[1]   Bluntisham Rectory
8 October 1915

My dear Tiddler –
   I have been meaning for days to write and tell you how I got on in London, but like a procrastinating ass I kept putting it off, and writing you out poems instead, which I am now sending. It is a bulky package, but you are not to feel bound either to read or to admire them. The rondeaux especially are the merest technical exercises in

most cases – trying different shapes and models with different lengths of line and arrangements of rime and refrain – none original, as you will see. They are the sort of things one either tears up when done, or keeps filed for reference in an alphabetical list. The last poem 'Matter of Brittany' was written merely for enjoyment. I thought I was tired of 'Oxfords' and 'Alma Maters' and 'Going-downs' and 'To a Leader of Mens'[2] and things that meant a powerful lot, and terseness and pregnancy and dignity and so on, so I thought I'd just revel a bit in the dear old obvious glories of scarlet cloaks and dragons and Otherworld Journeys, and in the clank and gurgle of alliteration, and the gorgeousness of proper names. So you are to read it in this spirit, please, if possible at night and by the fire.

Well, I contrived to get to London in the end, though later than I hoped, because of a violent cold. Charis and Hilda[3] were most awfully good to me, and it was simply topping seeing them again. Tony[4] came for a night, as I dare say you have heard, and we all lay on the floor, round a gas-stove with no gas in it for fear of zepps., and the eider-downs and pillows all over us, and talked late, and pretended we were at college. Then Tony and I went to bed side by side, and talked yet later. She seems terrifically overwhelmed with work at Blackheath, I don't know how she will be able to stand it. I thought she was looking very well at the moment, but of course she had only had a little over a week of it. – Charis is quite wonderful, the way she 'carries on' with things; can't think how she does it; of course, one can't help feeling Dobbin[5] in every corner of the house. C. is perfectly charming with the two little girls, isn't she? They keep her strenuously occupied, that's something – I got my coat and skirt, with the kind and expert help of Charis and Hilda. It is all black, with a short front and long straight back to the coat and high collar; the skirt is simply fascinating – band, and deep hip-yoke, and wide skirt with two most attractive little pleats in front and full pleats at the back. 5 and a half guineas, reduced for me from 6 and a half.[6] Then we bought a black velvet hat at Whiteley's for seven shillings and a pink rose for eighteen pence, and Hilda did the trimming in a most fetching manner. . . .

Did Charis tell you my story of the old lady on the moving staircase? If she did, don't read this. I'd never been on one before, so Charis told me how to step on to it, which I did, and she stood beside me, holding my arm, lest I should get giddy or anything. So, standing still abreast, we took up rather a lot of room and blocked up the stairs. Suddenly an old lady pushed violently past me from behind, and muttering 'I must get down this thing quickly, I'm always sick if I don't' hurled herself to the bottom in a series of goat-like leaps.[7] Anything more reassuring to a neophyte! . . .

I hope you aren't working yourself too hard – I bet you are – Love to everybody and please write some time.

H. P. Rallentando[8]

[1] Dorothy Hanbury Rowe (1892–1988), a contemporary of D.L.S. at Somerville and a member of the Mutual Admiration Society. She taught English at Bournemouth High School and directed an amateur theatre.

[2] All these poems, including 'The Matter of Brittany', were published in *Op. I*.

[3] Charis's sister.

[4] Catherine Godfrey.

[5] The nickname for Charis's brother, Donald, who had been killed in the war.

[6] A guinea was twenty-one shillings (old currency).

[7] When moving staircases were first introduced into department stores, assistants stood by with brandy in case any customer felt faint.

[8] The pseudonym which D.L.S. used when she impersonated Hugh Percy Allen in the Going-Down Play in 1915. She also used it as a pen-name for her poem in the style of Browning, 'Thomas Angulo's Death', which won the prize awarded by *The Saturday Westminster Gazette*, 20 May 1916, p. 9.

To Catherine Godfrey   Bluntisham Rectory
23 November 1915

Dearest Tony

I'm going to try teaching after all. Tell me what you think. I got sick of hanging about, and I thought it wouldn't do any harm to try, say, a year of teaching, so I sent to the Joint Agency for notices of Boys' and Girls' schools. On Saturday I pattered up to town to see (1) a mistress of a private school at Harrow, (2) a mistress of a public school[1] at Hull. I didn't like the first one as much as I had liked her letter because she was chatterboxy and smiled too much, and I was afraid the job might be rather a soft one. But I rather wanted to be near London. So she said she was seeing other people, and would write on Monday, and would I accept if she offered it? I said I was seeing other people, and couldn't promise, but it certainly was a great point being near town, though I should have preferred a non-resident post. However, I said I thought I should accept it if nothing happened in the meantime. I then trotted away to Berners Hotel, Berners Street and asked for Miss Elliott,[2] and a tall person in a musquash coat and becoming hat flew out, and caught me, and carried me into the drawing-room, and began to talk. She said that the High School at Hull had been run by the same H.M. with no ideas for 26 years, and had suffered in consequence, and that the London Council which runs it (it is some kind of church school) had now appointed her (Miss Elliott) and she had had to begin by making a clean sweep of the fossilised staff (all unqualified!), and was beginning in January to reorganise the whole thing and work it up again. (At the word 'reorganise' the Bicycle

Secretary lifted her head and snuffed the air like an old war-horse.) She said she had only been there about 6 weeks, and had already put the girls into a uniform, abolishing short sleeves and blue silk dresses, and tied their hair back! She then said that I was the sort of person she wanted, experience or none – that she was starting off with practically a whole new staff of young, qualified women, that she would want me to arrange and take the whole of the French – and in short, offered me the post straight off – £120 p.a. non-resident.

The first moment I saw her I didn't like her, but afterwards I did. She is tall and not very old, with lovely red hair, and uncommonly nicely dressed, under the musquash coat, in a black velvet gown with fur at the neck. She is a friend of Miss E. C. Jones! I didn't accept straight off, but I came back and told the family, and then wrote to Harrow to say I couldn't come, and to Miss Elliott to say I would. I considered that:

1. it was a public school and non-resident.
2. it was definitely offered to me.
3. if I couldn't get London I didn't mind where I went.
4. if I refused both posts I should have all the bother again, and I liked Miss Elliott better than Miss Robinson.
5. the idea of starting with a new staff was attractive.
6. also, I should be helping to make a tradition and not living up to one (or trying to).
7. if Miss Elliott made a success with the school, and I with her, it wouldn't be a bad thing to have done and the job seemed rather in my line.

So I accepted, and now I'm trembling rather. She says she intends the staff to be introduced to nice people in Hull. There is an advisory Committee there with charming people on it, and she means to encourage social relations between them and the staff. So it may not be so bad.

Tony dear, do write and say what you think, and forgive me for being so long-winded about it. Mercifully, whatever happens, I have a home to return to, so if it's very awful, I can go. But don't you think in a way it's rather nice not to be sucked into an already highly efficient machine, which has been working at high pressure for years? I haven't heard any details from Miss E. yet. I shall get them to-morrow, probably . . .

 Your loving
 Dorothy

The Harrow post was offered me after all – Have I done well? Terrible thought.

---

[1] Actually a local education authority school.

[2] Ethel Mary Linda Elliott held an Honours degree in Classics of Manchester University. She had previously taught at Manchester High School for Girls and at Bridlington High School for Girls. At the time of her appointment as headmistress of Hull High School she was forty-three years of age.

1916–1920

In Search of a Career

On 18 January 1916 D.L.S. went to Hull to take up her post as Modern Language mistress at the High School. Her chief responsibility was to teach French but for a time she also taught German. She encouraged her pupils to write plays in French and to act scenes from Molière's Les Précieuses Ridicules. *She also volunteered to organise a choir, which she conducted herself. She joined the Hull Vocal Society and took part in performances, though sadly missing the standard of the Oxford Bach Choir and the conducting of Hugh Allen.*

She continued to write poetry and began to translate the Chanson de Roland. *At the end of 1916 Op. I, her first book of poems, was published. During the Christmas vacation she discussed with her father the possibility of entering the firm of Blackwell's in Oxford as an apprentice, to learn the publishing business. An agreement was reached and by the end of April 1917, having taught for four terms at Hull, D.L.S. was back in Oxford.*

Hull: January 1916–April 1917 (Age: 22–23)

To Her Parents   80 Westbourne Avenue
?30 January 1916   Hull

Dearest people . . .
My first week has passed with no important mishap! Miss Elliott really is a dear, and very jolly and friendly with the staff. There is a nice little person, called Miss Biggs, who teaches Science, and seems to have taken a fancy to me, so we trot about together. She is musical, and we have joined the Hull Vocal Society together. The conductor, Dr Smith, is what is usually called a 'sound musician' – after H.P. his conducting, as such, is of course not conducting at all – however, he seems a pleasant little gentleman, and I daresay it will be quite amusing. Poor little chap, he heard yesterday that one of his sons had

been killed at the front. He was giving an Organ Recital at All Saints', and we went to it, only to hear that it had to be put off, owing to the son's death. So I don't know whether there will be a practice to-morrow or not. We are doing Coleridge-Taylor's 'Tale of Old Japan'.[1]

The girls in this school seem really very nice, but they have been rottenly taught, and have no idea how to think for themselves. But we shall change all that, I hope. The Maths mistress has turned up, I am glad to say, and has taken the German off my hands, so I have now got all the French, from the first form to the sixth; which suits me much better. Do you think you could find my *Chanson de Roland* in *modern French*? It is a thinnish buff book, picked out in blue, and should be on one of the middle shelves of my book-case. Don't confuse it with Clédat's edition of the *Chanson* in *Old* French, with no blue on the cover, but about the same size, and with lots of pencil notes in the margin. It is the Modern French translation which I want for my VI form people to look at, if you would please be so good as to send it. . . .

I have discovered why my landlady does things so nicely – she was cook in a good house before she married. It does make such a difference. I felt sure she must have been in service, and asked her – The other sort never know how to set a table. . . .

I don't think Hull is a bad city, though ugly and *dreadfully* dirty – I mean in the way of smuts and things. It is full of cinemas, and has at least one decent café and quite good shops. Miss Biggs and I are trying to find the 'Highest' church – no one can direct us to it, because it is at present housed in a Mission Chapel while a new church is being built, but I obtained more definite news of it just before dinner to-day, and hope to run it to earth next Sunday. The Church of S. Trinity is enormous, – the Hull people say it is the largest parish church in England, but I believe Yarmouth beats it by an inch or two. . . .

So long –

Best love from
    D.

[1] 'A Tale of Old Japan', a cantata by S. Coleridge-Taylor (1875–1912), on a poem by Alfred Noyes (1880–1958), was published by Novello and Company in 1911, price two shillings and sixpence. A copy of the original octavo edition, inscribed 'M. Bourne, 687 Holds Road, Hull' and dated 17 January 1916, indicates that rehearsals had begun by then. (This copy was discovered in 1994 in a second-hand bookshop in Cambridge.)

To Muriel Jaeger   80 Westbourne Avenue
6 February 1916   Hull

Darling Jimmy,

This is the seventh letter I've written to-day, so please excuse its being feeble.

I always funk writing to people about a new place, because one has to say the same thing over and over again, and can't give a proper idea of anything. Also, one feels shaken out of touch with things and people, till one has settled down a bit.

First of all, I have delightful rooms and a delightful landlady. So that's all right. Also, the Headmistress is a dear, for all her red hair – and it is lovely hair too, – and treats the staff as friends and play-mates. One goes to the theatre with her, and takes her to the cinema, and she laughs at everything that happens, in school and out of it, and so do all of us. We are a most hilarious staff.

So far so good. But the work –! Jim – I have always been so decently taught most things that I simply had no idea how ignorant people could be. These unhappy children have never been encouraged – encouraged? – never been *allowed* to use their brains. They can say a few things by rote, but as for giving the reasons for a rule, or translating a word in more ways than one according to circumstances – nay, even as for conceiving that there could be a reason for a rule, or more ways than one of translating a word – their poor dear minds are a blank. Sometimes I simply dare not ask a question, for I feel that the whole structure of their knowledge is reared upon a foundation of Leave-ill-alone, and propped up by the support called Ask-no-questions, and that if once I pull that support away, all the rotten beams and rafters will come rattling down about my ears. The VIth form has never heard of Corneille, Racine or Pascal – one girl vaguely 'thinks' that she once read something of Molière's – title unknown, and anyway she didn't read it in school. They have been reading *La Mare au Diable*[1] in class for two terms, so I suggested they should write an easy free composition about it. An awful groan followed this suggestion, and I discovered that they had been reading and reading away without ever understanding a word of what they read. The other forms wallow in a darkness full of hurtling compound tenses and grim, dim pronominal forms, and are continuously bewildered. It will take me ages and ages to learn how to make myself clear to them. At present I am always sailing over their heads, because they don't know the meaning of quite simple English words, like 'emphatic', or of ordinary grammatical terms, like 'relative' and 'antecedent'. Heavens, I suppose it will all come right in time.

But by that time I expect I shall have gone,[2] because my brain will be growing rusty, and I can't afford that.

The rest of the staff are quite nice, but not, I think, particularly striking. There is a S. Hilda's woman and a Newnham girl – the rest are from the younger Universities. . . .

The Zepps.[3] got pretty close to you on Monday, didn't they, damn them! We had a scare here, of course. The buzzers went, and all the lights were put out. I was down singing with the Hull Vocal Society (a very different thing from the Bach Choir) – when it happened, and we all had to bundle out and crawl home in the pitchy dark. I had about a mile to go, but was escorted by another member of the Chorus. I sat up till 1, and then got bored and went to bed, to be woken up at 2.30 by a blooming buzzer which meant that they had gone. . . .

How is Oxford?[4] Please greet Skimmery quad., S. Mary's chime, Magdalen Spire, Tom Tower and New College Chapel from me. . . .

Ever your very loving
John Gaunt
of the good ship *Arethusa*

[1] 'The Devil's Pond', by George Sand, pseudonym of Amandine-Aurore Lucie Dupin, French novelist (1804–76). *La Mare au Diable*, first published in 1846, consists of short stories and sketches about the countryside.
[2] Already in the second month of her first term at Hull D.L.S. was thinking of leaving.
[3] Zeppelins.
[4] Muriel Jaeger was completing her final year at Oxford.

To Her Parents   80 Westbourne Avenue
5 April 1916   Hull

Dearest people –
I have bought a pair of boots.

This is the real news of the week. A Zeppelin has been brought down in the Thames, and my poems have been accepted by Blackwell, but the importance of both these events is eclipsed by my boots.

They have a black patent golosh, and elegant fawn cloth tops. They have a black stripe at the back (rather wide) and two little stripes in the front (rather narrow) and they lace up with black laces, and they cost – well, quite a little.

They are superlative boots. . . .

The poems I sent Blackwell were 'Alma Mater', 'The Last Castle' and some odd lyrics, but I daresay I shall choose different ones for the book. It can't appear for months and months as it comes at least 5th on the list if not later.[1]

The Choir is learning Mendelssohn, and doing rather well considering. I rather think I'm going to take on all the school singing in the near future. . . .

[1] The volume, *Op. I*, was published by Basil Blackwell on 28 December 1916, in a limited edition of 350 copies, as No. 9 in a series entitled *Adventurers All*. The poems she mentions were included in it.

To Muriel Jaeger   1 Balmoral Terrace
11 April 1916   Woodlands Road
                                          Darlington[1]

Dearest Jim –

This is just a line to tell you how much I love you, and that Blackwell has accepted 'The Last Castle', 'Alma Mater' and some odd lyrics to publish in his 'Adventurers All' series – devoted to the works of young poets. So that if we agree about copyright, concerning which I have just written to him, I shall be a real published author at the cost of £5 to myself, which is paid back to me as soon as the sales cover the cost of production. These terms seem very fair – If there are any profits, Blackwell and I share them in proportion to the risk taken by each. This also seems fair. Of course, there may be difficulty about the copyright, but I've consulted various people, who all agree that I must secure it, so I've written firmly to that effect. . . .

I haven't time for more than just this line – Oh yes! and to ask you whether, if the Zepps. blow me up, you would accept, in conjunction with D. Rowe and Tony, the charge of my MSS with full powers as to publishing or destroying, but not letting anything be published at the expense of pious relations? I'd be frightfully grateful if I knew that things would be attended to, and nobody cd. do it as well as M.A.S.[2] . . .

[1] D.L.S. was staying with Elsie Henderson.
[2] Mutual Admiration Society.

To Her Parents   80 Westbourne Avenue
25 May 1916   Hull

Dearest people –

The news is, that my journey to Oxford will be made without a single twinge of conscience, and without costing me a penny, as I have just won a 3-guinea prize in the *Westminster Gazette* for 50 lines of verse – an imitation of Browning on a subject from *Don Quixote*.[1] Most convenient. Tony drew my attention to the competition, and sent me the result to-day. I have not finished with the copy, but you will find it in the *Saturday Westminster* for May 20th – or I will send it to you later. I think 3 guineas should do Oxford well, with quite a nice little margin. . . .

[1] Entitled 'The Prize Fragment. Fragments of an Unpublished Poem by Robert Browning', *The Saturday Westminster Gazette*, 20 May 1916, p. 9. D.L.S. used the pseudonym H. P. Rallentando once again.

To MURIEL JAEGER   80 Westbourne Avenue
26 June 1916   Hull

Dearest Jim . . .
    I left you severely alone during Schools and the Going-down Play
– *Do* say the latter wasn't as nice as ours – But I hope both were
truly enjoyable . . .
    I've been slogging away at the *Chanson*,[1] but I haven't made much
of it. I've sent it to Miss Barry[2] – to Watford, as I wasn't sure if she'd
be in Oxford or not. I've tried doing the rhymes, and have got through
20 *laisses*,[3] but it's the devil. Make her show, or send it you, if she
hasn't done so – but I don't think you'll find much to say to it. Of
course, it needs a lot of working over. Chanted aloud *in the bath-room*
it doesn't sound so bad. . . .

[1] The *Chanson de Roland*.
[2] Florence Barry (1880–1955), a research graduate at Somerville. She became head of the English department at Clapham High School. D.L.S. deputised for her there in the winter term of 1921.
[3] i.e. stanzas. D.L.S. was attempting a rhymed translation. She later said this version was 'very bad' (in 'The Translation of Verse', *The Poetry of Search and the Poetry of Statement*, Gollancz, 1963, p. 127) and at a second attempt translated the *laisses* with end-words in assonance instead of rhyme, in keeping with the original. This version, dedicated to the memory of Mildred Pope, was published as a Penguin Classic in 1957.

To F. J. H. JENKINSON[1]   Bluntisham Rectory
3 August 1916   St Ives
                                    Hunts

Dear Sir,
    I am writing to you to know whether, and on what terms, I can
be admitted as a reader in the Cambridge University Library. I have
taken a final Honour School in the University of Oxford, where I was
a reader in the Bodleian. During the next seven weeks, I should be
glad to have access to works on the French Language and Literature,
particularly texts from the *Chanson de Roland* to the Renaissance, and
the works of modern authors, such as [J.] Bédier and G. Paris[2] on
the same period. I should be greatly obliged if you would tell me
what are the proper steps to take to this end, and whether a

recommendation from a Cambridge MA would be required. May I
beg the favour of an early reply?

> I am, dear Sir,
> yours faithfully,
>   (Miss) D. L. Sayers

[1] Librarian of the Cambridge University Library.
[2] Joseph Bédier (1864–1938) and Gaston Paris (1839–1903), authorities on mediaeval
French literature.

To MURIEL JAEGER   Bluntisham Rectory
5 August 1916   St Ives
                                                   Hunts

Dearest James –
   I *am* so glad you can come – Wednesday will do beautifully – We're
all looking forward –
   It's doubly fortunate, as we've just had alarms and excursions –
Large bald patch on my head – and of course I thought of ring-worm,
as the school has been full of it. Doctor however convinced that it is
an obscure nervous disease, resulting from mental strain or shock.
Roland in danger for some time – me in wrathful tears. Eventually
put down to shock of Zeppelin raids – and really I shouldn't wonder.
Treatment prescribed: Exercise and freedom from worry. So you see,
you come as a sort of heaven-sent messenger to take me for walks!
   Roland is in his 68th *laisse* – a little rough-edged but going strong,
and the obstacle in -art, finding there was no business doing, has
settled peacefully down and worked itself off in -ise[1] – with practically
no difficulty. A little kindness and putting their hair in papers[2] does
wonders for them . . .

>   Ever your devoted
>   H. P. Rallentando

[1] Words ending in -ise were easier to rhyme than words ending in -art.
[2] Echo of Lewis Carroll, *Through the Looking-Glass*, chapter 9: 'A little kindness – and
putting her hair in papers – would do wonders with her –' (The Red Queen to Alice,
about the White Queen).

To HER PARENTS   80 Westbourne Avenue
10 October ?1916   Hull

Dearest people . . .
   Life is tiring, but William[1] has ceased his attentions for the moment.
And it appears that we have now got new [deleted by censor] which
will blow any enemy aliens which come within [deleted by censor] of

us into [deleted by censor] pieces. That sort of thing. Cheer-oh!

I'm glad the new organist is a success. Service at S. Mary's has been very adventurous lately, as the American organ gave up the other evening after 10 years' brutal slavery, and began to cipher on a loud low note in a most disconcerting manner, during a Solemn Evensong of S. Francis. On Sunday last it started off all right, and then busted again just as we were beginning the psalms. The performer agitatedly pulled out the upper set of stops, and the psalms proceeded, playing entirely on the upper octave, with an unsupported effect impossible to realise unless you'd heard it, particularly as the choir clean lost their heads, and the congregation was quite bewildered – the result being that no one ever began a psalm, but tumbled in, faint but pursuing at intervals during the first two verses. The organist and the verger then fled with a candle into the organ-loft, where various pipes, in process of erection, were lying ghostily around. The choir, abandoned to its devices, meanwhile suffered from a difference of opinion as to which set of responses was suitable to the circumstances, but the stronger part eventually imposed Tallis.[2] These were punctuated by spookish whistles on somewhere about C3 from the rudimentary organ. Suddenly, the hymn being announced, we blared away into 'Blessed City, heavenly Salem', on some very loud brass pipes and shrill high reeds, thus completing the nervous shock to those members of the congregation who had not known that there were any bits of organ handy, and who had not been able to watch the consultation in the organ-loft. After which Mr Scott preached a loud and impassioned sermon, becoming quite breathless with rage at heartless employers and people who made money out of the war, and arousing (actually) stern groans of approval from somebody in the front benches, just like an election or a Welsh revival. The Vicar was absent, being indisposed. . . .

We are going to do Bach's 'Sing ye to the Lord' at the Vocal.[3] Oh! Hugh Percy!

Best love –
Dorothy

No news from Blackwell!

[1] i.e. the Kaiser.
[2] Thomas Tallis (? 1520–85), organist and composer.
[3] Hull Vocal Society.

To Muriel Jaeger   80 Westbourne Avenue
14 November 1916   Hull

Dearest James –

I'm so sorry I haven't written before – It wasn't pride and 'ortiness,[1]
but just having a lot to do. Instead of writing now I ought to be

1) correcting Va's[2] books
2) writing a lecture for the VI[3]
3) preparing a paper on 'The Way to the Other World'[4] to be read
to the Association of Assistant Mistresses –
but I damn well shan't! . . .

Don't talk so about Zepp. raids. They are hell. My landlady, who
is not very strong, got a sort of attack of the shudders last time – I
thought she would be ill. I had never seen fear before – believe me
it is brutal, bestial and utterly degrading. I should say it was the one
experience which is neither good for man nor beast. Pah! As usual,
I was the only person in the place who had any spirits handy. . . .

I must stop now, and scribble a line home –

Your loving
      H. P. Rallentando

[1] Haughtiness.
[2] Form 5A.
[3] The sixth form.
[4] A lecture on the Celtic tradition of Other-World journeys. (See Barbara Reynolds,
Dorothy L. Sayers: Her Life and Soul, chapter 13, pp. 187–9, Hodder and Stoughton, 1993.)

To Her Parents   80 Westbourne Avenue
25 January 1917   Hull
                                       S. Paul

Dearest people –

Just a line to say that I have received a most kind and sympathetic
letter from 'Mr Basil', telling me everything about the publishing
business, including a dissertation on business morality. I feel that the
work would suit me exactly, and that I should like him to work under.
As you are so very kind and generous, Tootles dear, as to give me
this further opportunity, I think it very likely that I shall accept it.[1]
There is *no future* in teaching, and I think that I might really make
something of publishing. I have given a provisional notice to Miss
Elliott, and shall go at Easter, if other things are satisfactory – The
one point which troubles me is this: What will happen to me if 'Mr
Basil' is called up? I have written to him about this – it would not
do to risk being stranded. . . .

[1] Her father was able to meet the financial commitment, having recently been offered the living in Christchurch, Cambridgeshire, at a higher stipend.

To MURIEL JAEGER   80 Westbourne Avenue
8 March 1917   Hull

Darling James . . .

Well, now, everything is settled. . . . On April 29th, I enter on a year's pupilage with Basil Henry Blackwell, who undertakes, in the words of our agreement, 'to instruct the pupil fully in the mystery of publishing', 'on consideration of receiving the sum of £100, to be repaid at the weekly rate of £2.'

Mr B. is a darling – he *looks* about 17 – but he has a young wife, and a yet younger baby, so I suppose he is more than that. I went to Oxford one week-end to see him. He is not very tall, and very slight, and he has hair of a warm mouse-colour, only rather more reddish than mouse – which forms a lock, or wave on one side of the parting. His forehead is pleasing, being rather low and broad – his eyes grey and bright, with rimless pince-nez. (His sight is not good.) His complexion is palish, and I should say that he would probably freckle if exposed to the sun. His mouth is fine, merry and pleasant in expression – his chin pointed, giving an air of great alertness to his countenance. In his drawing-room is a large sofa full of cushions, on which he has a habit of sitting sideways, his feet drawn up upon the seat, and his hands clasped about his knees. He smokes a pipe with a curly stem – his teeth and ears I neglected to notice, but I suppose that they are good, as they did not obtrude themselves in any distasteful manner upon my attention. The action of his hands in taking down one of the volumes with which his shelves are so liberally stocked, is caressing and sightly. His voice is quick, nervous and somewhat high, and his conversation lively and full of humour. I find I have omitted to mention that he wears his hair slightly long, but not sufficiently so to lay him open to aspersion of being *silly* or *Byronic*. His dress when I saw him was a grey suit, with a soft shirt and purple tie. For walking he had a loose coat approaching the khaki in colour, a soft green hat, and a muffler of the Merton College boating colours (Purple and White). He obtained a Second Class in the School of Literae Humaniores, and rowed in his College Eight; his enfeebled sight, however, and an unfortunate liability to attacks of *sunstroke* and *malarial fever*, have relegated him to the class C3 under the present military arrangement. He has a white dog called *John* and a white cat called *Michael*. . . .

James – I am to have a dear little room, perched high up in Blackwell's shop, and looking down upon the Cæsars[1] – Bless them!

My duties will be the writing of letters, the reading of MSS and the learning of the whole business, from discount to the 3-colour process. It's going to be fun – but strenuous. I shan't get any holidays, I suppose, except Bank Holiday and early closing day – but let's hope I shan't want them. It's immoral to take up a job solely for the amount of time one can spend away from it, which is what most of us do with teaching.

These holidays will be awfully strenuous, for the family is moving to Upwell.[2] We *shall* have a lovely chase round! And Lord knows when we shall all meet again, Jim – but anyway, Oxford is within reasonable distance of town.[3] . . .

Ever your loving
H. P. Rallentando

[1] The heads of Roman Emperors adorning the Sheldonian Theatre, opposite Blackwell's shop.
[2] A town near Christchurch.
[3] Muriel Jaeger had left Oxford and taken a job in London.

Return to Oxford: April 1917–June 1919 (Age: 23–26)

To Her Parents   17 Long Wall Street
28 April 1917   Oxford

Dearest People

Here I am, safe and sound, after quite a pleasant journey on the whole, though my train did not catch the Oxford one at Cambridge. The reason is, that the latter, which used to depart at 11.25, now departs at 11 precisely. However, I went into the town and mouched about, and had lunch, and a long conversation with Mr Heffer,[1] who was as amiable and witty as usual.

My rooms are very nice, and I hope I shall be able to stop in them. Mrs Nicholson entered quite sensibly into the money problem, and I hope we shall be able to work it out. There is a beautiful view of the deer-park from my bedroom, and the same, though not so good because on the ground floor, from the sitting-room. The staircase window looks upon New College Chapel, and the garden is tucked in under the Old Walls, so I am rather jollily placed as far as Oxford goes.

Muriel Byrne[2] also came up yesterday, and we are going shares in a punt, which will be jolly, and much less expensive than if I hired on my own account. . . .

Basil's shop is now full of women,[3] and he opens at 10 and shuts at 4.30. He has a lovely tale about one of the girls, a Miss King. He selected her, as being a rather stupid, painstaking person, to go through a new catalogue, and send a copy thereof to all the authors concerned. At the end of the morning she returned in great distress and said, 'I've found them all, sir, except Mr Aristotle, I can't find his address anywhere.' Basil, being a beast, said: 'Oh! how odd – you had better ask Mr X— he knows all about the addresses.' So Miss King trailed away to Mr X—, and returned, puzzled, and said: 'Mr X— doesn't know, sir, and he laughed.' So Basil replied with great gravity, 'You had better try Fenimore' (the office-boy). Away went Miss King to try Fenimore, and returning, still more puzzled, said, 'Fenimore laughed, sir, and said he thought Mr Aristotle was in receipt of an old-age pension.' So Basil said: 'Oh, well, I shouldn't bother any more about him, Miss King, perhaps he has moved.' – Next day, when Miss King arrived at the office, she said: 'I *was* a silly yesterday, about Mr Aristotle. I said to Mother when I got home, "Mother, Why does everybody laugh when I ask for the address of Mr Aristotle?" And she said, "Why, you silly, he's one of those old stone men outside the shop".'

With best love
Yours cheerfully
Dorothy

[1] Mr Ernest Heffer, the founder of the well-known Cambridge bookshop.
[2] Muriel St Clare Byrne (1895–1983), O.B.E., became a close friend and collaborated with D.L.S. on the play *Busman's Honeymoon*. She graduated in English at Somerville.
[3] Members of staff, the men having been called up.

To Her Mother   17 Long Wall Street
? June 1917   Oxford

Dearest Mother . . .

I have had a very full time this week – something on every day. On Thursday I made the acquaintance of two perfectly charming Australian Tommies,[1] whom I picked up in the Botanical Gardens and took on the river. They are perfect dears – such absolute natural gentlemen, making themselves perfectly at home, without the least familiarity and with no stupid shyness. I took them again on Friday, and pretty weary I was at the end of it, as I couldn't get hold of anyone else and so of course had to do all the punting. This afternoon I've got them (unless anything goes wrong) for the river and tea, but I have also roped in a perfectly delightful padre, – viz. the Vice Principal[2] of Teddy Hall,[3] who is a friend of B.H.B.'s[4] – to come and help with the boat. He is most charming, and won my heart yesterday

by coming into the office and telling me how much he liked *Op. I* –
which (good man!) he had bought. . . .

The toil is a daily joy. Yes, the tonic seems to me quite a good one
– I really think my hair's getting a bit stronger. Probably, too, it's
partly having a healthier life and less worry. . . .

Your ever loving Dorothy

[1] Non-commissioned soldiers.
[2] The Rev. Leonard Hodgson (1889–1968, later Regius Professor of Divinity at Oxford.
(See Barbara Reynolds op. cit., pp. 78–9.)
[3] St Edmund Hall.
[4] Basil Henry Blackwell.

To Her Mother   17 Long Wall Street
11 June 1917   Oxford

Dear Mother

Yesterday ended rather unexpectedly! I went to the Basils' for supper, as I told you, and in the middle, in dropped the Rev. the Vice-
Principal of Teddy Hall, unexpectedly and à propos of nothing,
apparently. After surprising his hosts by 1) his arrival 2) his absent-
mindedness 3) his refusal to have supper or state what brought him
4) dropping innumerable knives and forks while helping to clear, he
succeeded in cornering me in the drawing-room after supper, while
Basil and Christine were making coffee, and Mme Jarintzov[1] was I
don't know where, and informed me that he loved me with his whole
heart and would I marry him? –!!! – My elegant and maidenly reply,
to the best of my recollection was 'Oh Lord!' – and I nearly fainted
into the nearest chair – seeing I've met him four or five times at most,
and only twice to talk to at any length.

I had just time to tell him that I had never for a second thought
of considering him in that connection, and that I certainly did not
care for him, – but that I could not forbid him to see me – as I barely
knew what he was like – and that wouldn't be fair to him – and
remembered to say that he had done me a great honour, when enter
Basil, innocently, with a box of cigarettes. I swooped on him and tore
one out of his hands and lighted it – and Mr Hodgson said with
exaggerated fervour, that it was just what he was longing for, and
the situation was saved. It *was* funny! Mr Hodgson then fled, leaving
B. and C. entirely mystified – whereon B. ran after him to pour some
lengthy and exciting and hideous scandal into his ear. For the rest of
the evening I listened to Mme Jarintzov reading translations from
the Russian, and offered suggestions with idiotic excitement (rather
good suggestions) and yelled with laughter.

At the hall-door I departed, parrying Basil's expressions of bewilderment at 'old Leonard's' inexplicable appearance, and rode off, only to be overtaken by the said Leonard on a bicycle, to apologise (well he might!) for his extraordinary precipitation. He then said all the same things over again, and I said the same things over again, and so ends the history of my first proposal. It has humorous features!

After all, it's nice to think anybody should care for one as much as that – I can't tell you anything about him – I don't know him!

What a day!

Your loving
    Dorothy

Don't get agitated! I'll never marry a man I don't care for!

¹ A Russian author who was offering a book on Russian poetry to Blackwell's.

To Her Parents   17 Long Walk
19 June 1917

Dearest People

I have just written to the Rev. Leonard to tell him that I can't marry him. Beastly job, but had to be done. I can't tell you why I can't, because he's very nice and extremely good, but I don't love him, and there's an end. It was borne in on me that there *was* an end – you know the way you worry about a thing and suddenly one morning you wake up and find that it has gone and settled itself irrevocably, apparently without your own interference.

Basil Blackwell has been wonderfully kind. I didn't know a man could be so good. . . .

To Her Mother   17 Long Wall St.
11 July 1917   Oxford

Dearest Mother

Thank you ever so much for your letter. I, too, feel dreadfully wicked, not having written. It isn't that life is uninteresting, but the interest is made up of so many odd little details, that there isn't really a lot to write and tell people about. Quaint remarks of B.H.B.'s, dreadful theological arguments with him, pleasant books to be looked up in the Bod.¹ with a view to reprinting, discussion of format and price for a new series – all tremendously interesting, but they don't make very good material for letter writing. . . .

Leonard Hodgson is going down in a day or two, God be thanked! Why a man can't shut up and stay away when he isn't wanted I cannot conceive. It bores me dreadfully to have him perpetually coming to tea in the office, and looking like a Good Friday cod. You never would believe me when I dissected my character for your benefit, but I was right about myself. To have somebody devoted to me arouses all my worst feelings. I *loathe* being deferred to. I *abominate* being waited on. It *infuriates* me to feel that my words are numbered and my actions watched. I want somebody to fight with! . . .

I'm tremendously busy just now in all my odd moments translating the *Tristan*.[2] I think I told you Basil was going to publish it[3] – probably in the Spring. At least, he liked what he saw of it, but I am going to show him some more and ask him again, because I rather doubt if it will be a commercial success. . . .

Rather an exciting gentleman is coming (all being well) on Friday to stay on my landlady's drawing-room floor for a week. He is a distinguished mathematician and architect, called Bligh Bond,[4] but the most entertaining thing about him is that he and a friend of his, while digging for antiquarian remains at Glastonbury, got some astonishing information, by automatic writing, from spirits purporting to be those of certain Glastonbury monks, who lived at the time of the Dissolution of the Monasteries. The surprising part of it is that many of the indications given as foundations, plans etc. have subsequently been proved correct. We are going to publish some of his results, and he is coming on Friday to tell us all about it, and to show us the script. He is not really the medium, but his friend, so I don't suppose we shall get any actual communications, but we intend to have a shot. So if you don't hear from me for a *very, very* long time, you may conclude that I have been absorbed into the Infinite, or carried off like Dr Faustus. Bond is an odd little chap – certainly not a charlatan, though he may be mistaken. Anyhow, he makes no claims whatever.

I have hired the piano for 6 months for £3. I think the entertainment one gets from having something handy to strum on is cheap at the price. . . .

Please take care of yourself.

Your ever-loving and very happy Dorothy

[1] The Bodleian Library.
[2] By the Anglo-Norman poet, Thomas.
[3] Basil Blackwell changed his mind. Two sections of the translation were published in *Modern Languages* in June and August 1920. The entire translation, entitled *Tristan in Brittany*, was eventually published in 1929 by Ernest Benn.
[4] F. Bligh Bond, F.R.I.B.A. (1864–1945), author of *The Mystery of Glaston*. He excavated at Glastonbury under the Committee of Inspection appointed by the Council of the Somerset Archaeological Society.

To Her Parents   17 Long Wall
2 August 1917   Oxford

Dearest People . . .
Did you begin to think Mr Bligh Bond had absorbed me into the
absolute? He is the oddest little gentleman, very mild and inoffensive
in manner – just like a bird to look at, and he sits and talks about
the 4th dimension, and the mathematical relation of form to colour,
till you don't know if you're on your head or your heels. In practical
matters he is rather helpless – and very amusing about his spooks,
who really are rather wonderful. I must tell you all about it when I
get home – He entirely won the hearts of the Blackwells, and told
them hair-raising tales of how he and the Head of the Psychical
Research Society are sent for to haunted houses, to Sherlock-Holmes
about for the haunters![1] I didn't know such people really existed –
but apparently they do – and it seems to take up quite a large part
of Bond's time. Otherwise he is an architect and greatly did I love
him while he was here, for he took me over the Cathedral one afternoon, and showed me how it grew – a very different thing from seeing
it with a guide.
Tristan is getting along pretty well. Did I tell you I am hoping to
get it out in the Spring? It is hard work, though, and of course, as I
am at the office all day I am not generally able to give quite my
freshest brain-work to it; so I fear my presentation of Thomas to the
world will be less adequate than I should have liked. However, one
can but do what one can. . . .

[1] D.L.S. used what she learnt about fraudulent mediums from Bligh Bond in her novel
Strong Poison (chapter 16).

To Her Mother   B. H. Blackwell, Publisher
5 February 1918   50 & 51 Broad Street
                                                  Oxford

Dearest Mother . . .
I've just been talking to Basil. He says exactly what I've expected
he would say: that he wants me to stay, but that the business can't
afford to pay me more than I am getting now, i.e. £2 a week, at
present, that is. Now, of course, that isn't enough to live on, and
though he will undertake to shove my screw up the minute he can
afford to do so, naturally, no one can say when that will be, under
these miserable war conditions. (If he should be called up, as I suppose he must be some time if the war goes on, I shall stay on to run
the business part of it, and of course on a larger screw, so *that* needn't

worry us!) – Of course, it's a young business, and he's a young man, and he may make good or he may not; he is full of ideas, but hampered, of course, by lack of capital and this everlasting God-damned war! If all went well, however, I should of course get a steadily rising screw and eventually a share in the profits – and it is to be remembered that in this case, I should be in the thing as part of the management – more or less – instead of being just an employee, as I should be anywhere else. That has its appeal to me, because I don't really care about money provided I can rub along comfortably, but I do like to be on a friendly footing with people, and to have my finger in their pies! You know my reasons for wishing to stay in Oxford, and not go to London just at present. If B.H.B. makes his way as he hopes, he will go to London eventually, (as well as Oxford) – in which case I should go with him, (or else have a larger part of the job here) – so I might get there in the end after all – My chief reason for wanting to stay is that I am happy here, and that's the great thing – and I'm tired of knocking about and starting in with new people, and all that. So that, unless you say you think I'd better not, I shall tell Basil that I will hold on for better or for worse – for a bit anyway. You see, if things become impossible, I shall only be *better* off at the end of, say, another year's experience, than I am now, as far as getting a job with another house is concerned. – So you see, Tootles, there I am! But it means living beyond my income for a bit – or rather, Tootles dear, accepting your offer of a larger allowance, which I didn't want to do – I mean, I didn't want to, on the principle that one ought to get one's living wage – not because I want to be purse-proud and independent! . . .

To Her Parents   B. H. Blackwell, Publisher
? April 1918   50 & 51 Broad Street
                                   Oxford

Dearest People
    A quite offensively busy and important young woman snatches a few minutes of her valuable time to write a letter! I always love being left in charge for the first day or two, and afterwards I loathe it, and long for Basil to come back. Such is life!
    Ever so many thanks for the lovely daffodils. They arrived in splendid condition, and look gloriously fresh this morning. There were such a lot – Mrs Nicholson was struck dumb. 'Are they out of your garden, do you think?' says she. ''Deed, yes,' says I – 'it's a very big garden.' – 'We had a very big garden,' says she, full of past grandeur, 'but not to that extent.' – 'Well,' says I, careless-like, 'that depends – ours is about three acres.' 'Oh,' says she, with her ideas suddenly

enlarged, 'that *is* big!' – Indeed, there was such a lovely lot that after I had filled the room I had still a nice bunch left, so, 'a gracious action is a good investment,' thinks I to myself, and off and took them to Mrs Brabant, who was tremendously pleased with them and with the attention. . . .

I had a very delightful week-end with Jim,[1] who was full of ghastly information about starvation horrors in Germany and Austria. She is in the Statistics Dept. at the Ministry of Food, and those two countries are part of her special province, so I think her information is reliable. She says that Germany and Austria (especially) are unthinkably worse off than we are – and that the Ukraine wheat, even when they get it – for the transport is broken down and much of the stores damaged – will all have to be used for Austria (which is eating wood-pulp!) and that none will be available for Germany. Also it appears that the German 'discipline' has quite broken down in the interior, and that they are only held together by the inertia of exhaustion which prevents a split. If we can successfully hold up this offensive, she thinks they will have to come to terms for economic reasons. On the other hand, our food shortage is very real, and will get worse; also that every 3 months of war now adds a year to the tale of lean years which will follow the declaration of peace.

In all probability tea will not be rationed.

Oh, about the Orchestra – Tootles, dear, how could you think I could give up the Choir? Nay indeed, but I shall sing on Mondays and play[2] on Wednesdays, and sing in combined concerts (unless I have a cold) and play in Orchestral concerts, and all will be gas and gaiters.[3] . . .

Glad you like Jane Austen, Tootles; she's one of the people about whom there is no question at all. I read *Northanger Abbey* for the first time the other day, and Lord! it was good.

I must stop now, and have lunch, and then do a few thousand things –

Heaps of love, D.

[1] Muriel Jaeger.
[2] D.L.S. was keeping up her violin-playing.
[3] A quotation from Dickens which D.L.S. was fond of using. (*Nicholas Nickleby*, chapter 49: the Gentleman in the Small-clothes, professing his love for Mrs Nickleby says: 'She is come at last – at last – and all is gas and gaiters.') E. C. Bentley's Philip Trent uses it also, in *Trent's Last Case* (1913), chapter 14.

To Her Parents   B. H. Blackwell, Publisher
19 April 1918   50 & 51 Broad Street
                                  Oxford

Dearest People

So you have heard bombs fall at last! All experience! But it is an entertainment that palls upon repetition, so I hope you may have no more of it. I heard about the flyer's collision with S. Ives steeple – bad luck on everybody concerned; it seems odd that with all the sky to fly in, he should pitch upon – or against – that one thin spike, poor dear!

I had a jolly time last week at Kingham with two friends. It was very cold and windy, but we occupied ourselves in the construction of nonsense verses before a large wood fire, and were exceedingly merry, and I returned to work much refreshed. Basil is back, and all goes well. . . .

I do not think that anybody need be in the least ashamed of conscientious objections to killing people – provided that the objections are really conscientious ones – and one has no right whatever to say that any person's convictions are not honest until they are proved dishonest. I think that to argue from that position that one must not assist the country, even in the way of food-production, is illogical, while one continues to eat the country's food, and I think (personally) that it is wrong, and, in fact, chiefly due to spiritual pride – but it is not in any way base, where the opinions are genuine. I don't discuss the matter with Margaret,[1] because it would lead to no good – but nothing but harm can come of construing people's motives uncharitably. I speak and feel strongly about the matter, since I had Ivy[2] to tea the other day, who, without the least knowledge of the people or the matter, assumed, quite gratuitously, that Mr Stevens'[3] opinions were a pretence to cover up cowardice, and who would hear not a word to the contrary. People who prefer to believe the worst of others will breed war and religious persecutions while the world lasts. The only thing one can do is to leave these people to work out the belief that is in them; if it is evil, it will defeat itself; if of God, it ought not to be, and cannot be defeated; only I would insist that these persons should logically follow up their principles, and if they will not help to produce a potato under conscription which might nourish a fighting man, neither should they eat wheat which has been brought over-seas under the protection of fighting men enlisted under conscription; and I would let them read the books of Plato. – That is my opinion for what it is worth . . .

I've written some more *Catholic Tales*[4] – I wish I could get a publisher for them. I think I'll try the Society of SS. Peter and Paul –

But I don't think they'd take them. I've been reading Bunyan – *Holy War* and *Grace Abounding*. Wonderful man – such style!

> Best love
> **D.**

[1] Her cousin Margaret Leigh, who was a pacifist and had been doing house-to-house propaganda.
[2] Ivy Shrimpton.
[3] Margaret Leigh's fiancé, who was a Quaker.
[4] See n. 2 to following letter.

To Her Parents   B. H. Blackwell, Publisher
14 June 1918   50 & 51 Broad Street
                                  Oxford

Dearest People
    May I just write one letter to you all, to say one large, loud and collective 'Thank you' for the very generous cheques![1] Most useful, I need not say – They shall buy all sorts of useful and decorative things. . . .
    I hope [my new book] won't horrify you, but I'd better warn you about it! Basil is doing it and is very keen on it. It is called *Catholic Tales*,[2] and all the poems are about Christ. Some people think it 'wonderful' and some think it 'blasphemous'. Of course, it may fall quite flat – but on the other hand, it is quite possible that some mugwumps may object to it like anything. You won't mind being the parents and aunt of a notoriety, if that should happen, will you? I can assure you that it is intended at any rate to be the expression of reverent belief – but some people find it hard to allow that faith, if lively, can be reverent – But I dare say, nobody will take any notice of it. Anyhow, it's jolly well *got* to be published . . .
    Best love, dear people, and again *many* thanks to everybody.

> Your loving
> Dorothy

Oh! Heaps of gratitude for the BUTTER.

[1] D.L.S. had just had her twenty-fifth birthday, on 13 June.
[2] *Catholic Tales and Christian Songs*, her second volume of poetry, was published by Basil Blackwell in October 1918 in an edition of 1,000 copies, price three shillings.

To Her Mother   Acland Home[1]
Saturday, ?July 1918

Dearest Mother

I'm afraid you must have had a perfectly awful time getting home yesterday – Here it rained and rained and rained and rained! I thought of you sitting bleakly in Bletchley station without even the comfort of a waiting-room fire. Anyhow, I hope you got to your journey's end safely, and found all well at home.

It was so jolly having you here to come and see me, and I missed you awfully yesterday. I was altogether deserted, for it seems that my nurse and another, who is her particular friend (one should never have particular friends) had a really epic bust-up with Sister (poor soul!) yesterday, and flounced out of the home (or were requested to leave) altogether – or at least 'till Matron' (and the Saturnian reign)[2] 'comes back'. So all is excitement and confusion. I am at present being run by two nurses, one of whom is always looking in, and being surprised to find that I have already been washed, dressed, put to bed, got up or what not, by the other. However, perhaps they will settle some time which of them I belong to. They are both very nice, and I am so much better now that I am only rather amused. But, my word! what little haunts of peace these Nursing Homes are! – Of course, I'm not supposed to know anything about it, but I get all my information from the night nurse. And I may say that altogether I am in no way surprised. My abandonment was enlivened yesterday by (a) some lovely pink ramblers from Biddy Mee (b) jasmine and roses from Maud Dixey (I adore jasmine) (c) half-an-hour's barefaced flirtation from Mr Whitelock,[3] with an account of how many cities he has been wicked in, in the course of his life. I cannot understand why men always think to make an impression by boasting of what devils they are – everybody sees through it – but they will cling to their belief in it – and if they are too young and innocent to have committed any devilries, they invent them (and everybody sees through that!).

I am reading *Sir Charles Grandison* – I must say Richardson[4] is a wonderfully good observer, when he doesn't waste time in flatulent moralities –

Good-bye – Your ever loving and amused
    Dorothy

[1] D.L.S. was in the Acland Nursing Home in Oxford, where she had had her appendix removed. Her mother had been to visit her.
[2] Reference to Virgil's IVth Eclogue: '*Iam redit et virgo, redeunt Saturnia regna*' (Now the virgin returns and Saturnian rule is restored).
[3] The surgeon, who had performed the operation. His name is also spelled Whitelocke.

He was then a major, later promoted colonel, a married man with a grown-up daughter.
⁴ Samuel Richardson (1689–1761). *Sir Charles Grandison* (1753–4) is the last of his three epistolary novels, the other two being *Pamela* and *Clarissa*.

To Her Parents   Acland Home
No date, but ? July 1918   Oxford

Dearest People . . .

I think, Mummy, I will tell [Mr Whitelock] your opinion of him, and see what he says. The other day he told me he liked me because I was human, and called me a wicked little girl; yesterday he said he had finally decided that I was *not* human, and this morning informed me I had the face of a mediaeval saint. Why he should have followed this up by hugging me, I don't know – it seems inconsistent! – to-morrow he will probably kiss me, and I shall box his ears, and we shall part on excellent terms. I love having some one to fool with, meeting on entirely equal terms, and seeing which can joke the other down. The moment one person begins to be even a trifle in earnest, the whole thing is spoilt. You remember Alice (in *Through the Looking-Glass*)'s favourite game was: 'Nurse, let's pretend!' – It's the only game worth playing. I said all this to Basil once . . . and he said: 'But Melly,[1] love-making isn't a *game*, you know' – and all I could say was: 'It is, to me.' . . .

There is a dear little boy here – about 7 or 8, I should think, called Christopher Jay, who has had an op. He is a great favourite with everybody, and yesterday, having nothing to do, and his bed being in the glass corridor, I went down and made his acquaintance, and played 'Snap' with him and his nurse. After I'd been there a little time, he turned and said, with the manner of a young man out on his own, with a most engaging smile, –

'Will you meet me again?'

So I am going to meet him again this afternoon.

End of the chronicle of the love-affairs of

> Your affectionate
> Dorothy

[1] It is not known why Basil Blackwell called her by this nickname. It does not appear anywhere else.

To Muriel Jaeger   50 & 51 Broad Street
2 October 1918   Oxford

My dear James . . .

Ever so many thanks for your kind services[1] in the matter of *Catholic*

Tales. This should be out very soon indeed now, being all worked off, and ready for binding as soon as we can get a nice cover-paper. I enclose a rough pull of the very beautiful cover block, drawn and cut by Gabriel Pippet. He is a well-known artist, and a well-known Papist, so that his work should add greatly to the value of the book. – I am glad to find that very few Catholics seem to find offence in the book. I was very glad to have your friend's opinion. It will (the book, I mean) go to the papers she mentions – also all the other Roman and Anglican productions – the edition will be 1000, so we can shove it about a bit, and Fr Bernard Vaughan shall certainly have it – also the Bp of London.[2]

About the *Church Times* – do you mean that you are certain of being able to review it in that organ? If so, don't slate it, because the C.T. is the organ of the High Church Party, and I'd as soon have 'em with me as against me – but having got it nicely reviewed there, you couldn't do better than write a furious letter from 'Pew-holder' or 'Via Media', wondering how they could possibly allow so much as the name of the vile production to sully their pages. However, you must of course follow your own inclination and conscience in the matter. Anything said is better than nothing said.

Oxford is to be socially regenerated as soon as term begins. I have bought a door-curtain and two pounds of wax candles for a start. Also, I have promoted myself from a tin whistle to a flageolet with six keys!

My good Colonel[3] was a little taken aback by our list of conversation topics. But I was in a brisk, unkissable mood that night. This afternoon I call on his wife. How complicated our latter-day civilisation is! . . .

Good news from abroad, what!
Very busy and in great haste

Much love
H.P.R.

[1] Muriel Jaeger had agreed to conspire with D.L.S. to start a dispute in the press concerning the orthodoxy or otherwise of *Catholic Tales and Christian Songs*, in order to promote interest and sales.
[2] The Rt Rev. A. F. Winnington-Ingram, D.D.
[3] Colonel Whitelocke, the surgeon.

To Her Parents   B. H. Blackwell, Publisher
28 October 1918   50 & 51 Broad Street
                                        Oxford

Dearest People
So sorry I haven't written before – I was steeped in the melancholy

which follows 'flu', but I've now recovered, thank-you. – Yes, I'm taking a tonic – don't believe in 'em much, though! – I've had to put off my All-Hallows party – that's been my chief grief, but one can't give hilarious parties with people dropping dead all round one![1] Lots and lots of people are dropping dead – they get pneumonia and are never seen alive again. It's like being in London when the Plague was on – People are all right one minute, and the next they fall down in the street and are carried away! I'm rather glad to have had it, as I got it so mildly, because I'm safe now and can go where I like.

Have your *Catholic Tales* arrived yet? I'm greatly pleased with the book's appearance. I am having some prospectuses done. I hope it may sell –

Margaret has got 'flu' now – rather worse than I did, I think, but nothing dangerous so far. Aunt Maud has been most awfully good –

Everybody is down at Blackwell's, and everything's in a ghastly mess!

In great haste
D.

Mind you don't get the germ down there!

[1] The Spanish influenza epidemic of 1918 is said to have killed more people than World War I. D.L.S. appears to have had a slight attack of it.

To Her Father   17 Long Wall
20 November 1918

Dearest Tootles

Ever so many thanks for your letter and P.O.[1] Now that I have a moment I can explain about Sir H. Warren.[2] When your card arrived about him, I had already despatched him a copy, as to the Professor of Poetry, and he acknowledged it to me; but he doesn't like it – I'm afraid he's shocked. He 'doesn't like the Black Magic style – especially applied to Such Themes'! Poor dear! The only poem he could bear was 'Christus Triumphus'.[3]

I had a most charming letter from Canon A. C. England (formerly of S. Mary's, Hull) about it, which particularly cheers me because he is so good and simple a man, and not in the least an 'intellectual'. '. . . Your very charming book. I like it very much indeed and congratulate you on your *Magnum Opus*. It is very like you – and I can see you in it all. What I like about it, is the freshness and naturalness of it all' – (!) Against which, *The Weekly Dispatch* – the only review which has as yet come through, complains of 'artificiality', but says nevertheless: 'Dorothy L. Sayers must be taken into consideration when one speaks of young poets.'

The French Class – no, I get nothing for it; you may pigeon-hole it under 'Peace-work' or 'Reconstruction'. It consists in teaching the elements of the language to elementary teachers who want to know something about France.[4] . . .

[1] Postal order.
[2] The Professor of Poetry at Oxford. (Cf. p. 79.)
[3] Entitled 'The Triumph of Christ', p. 9 of *Catholic Tales and Christian Songs*.
[4] Another instance of D.L.S.'s teaching experience.

To Muriel Jaeger   17 Long Wall
22 November 1918

Dearest James

I hasten to tell you that I have some expectations of a really scrumptious row in the *New Witness*.[1] . . . If you could reply to this review[2] when it appears, or if you could get a friend (a Papist for preference) to do so, it would be most exciting and make the book go like wildfire. . . .

The point about the 'Symbol' is the difficult one. It would have to be made clear that the real kind of symbol is that which is itself the supreme instance of what it symbolises – something which *is* – and by simply *being* symbolises the truth by which it is – e.g. an arch is a *real* symbol of the truth that complete rest can be obtained by continual and unremitting exertion. Incense, e.g., on the other hand, is only an arbitrary symbol of prayer. So that, while I commit myself unreservedly to the reality of Christ (literal flesh and blood of Man; complete Eternity, power, etc. etc. and pre-existence as God) – I do not see that anybody must be committed to a dogmatic opinion of any sort about Osiris or Pan. They may be real powers; they may have been men; or fancies; – but they attest a conviction among all sorts of people that God, *the* God, must suffer (to take only one point). Christ came and suffered – always suffered from the foundation of the world of course, but the world saw it when He came in the flesh. – And why Osiris should not typify this as well as the Jewish scapegoat, I can't understand.

Tell me if you feel ready to tackle all this, and we'll concoct a scheme – against the review's appearance – if it does appear. . . .

[1] A journal founded by Cecil Chesterton and later taken over by his brother G. K.
[2] D.L.S. had heard that Theodore Maynard, a Catholic poet, intended to review *Catholic Tales and Christian Songs* unfavourably in *The New Witness*.

To Muriel Jaeger   17 Long Wall
26 November 1918   Oxford

Dearest James . . .

I say! There's one delightful stunt we might do if Maynard really denies any pre-Christian revelation to the heathen. You (or a hired myrmidon) shall write in somewhat these terms:

'We know, of course, that "Salvation is of the Jews", but is it really necessary to take this so literally exclusively as Mr Maynard seems to think? Surely it is time the Church at large was freed from that Old Testament bondage which we connect with the Reformation. The Church of Rome has always held that Virgil at any rate was a Prophet of Christ, and must we deny the working of the Holy Spirit in such men as Plato, Socrates and Marcus Aurelius (or anybody else who sounds well) in order to restrict operations to Moses and Isaiah? I note with regret these Semitic leanings so prevalent in the modern world, and it is not, Sir, in *The New Witness* that I should have expected to find them upheld.' *The New W.* is *violently* anti-Semitic – and I think if we could manage in one breath to call *The New Witness* a Jew, and Maynard a Protestant, we should make several people very angry indeed. Of course the above letter is only a suggestion, and would have to be better put.

Meanwhile, I intend to write a dignified letter saying: 'In view of the doubts cast by Mr Maynard upon my orthodoxy I beg you will give publicity to the following statement:' Then quote such portions of the Creed as may seem fitting, saying 'I believe this, that and the other' – and adding, 'understanding these words in the sense in which the Catholic Church has always understood them and in no other'. I shall then stand aside, while you people fight out the meaning of the Creeds among you. What think you?

Oh, James, I hope it comes off! . . .

This term has been very busy ever since the 'flu went away. I find myself getting addled in the head, and intend to do a little quiet work at the Radder[1] during evenings in Vacation, working up the poems of Thomas Lovell Beddoes[2] – just to keep my brain from degenerating.

Yours in love and mirth
    Dorothy L. Sayers

[1] The Radcliffe Library, or Camera.
[2] Thomas Lovell Beddoes (1803–49), poet. His best-known work is *Death's Jest Book*, published posthumously in 1850. D.L.S. had discovered his poetry while still at Bluntisham. Writing to Ivy Shrimpton on 15 April 1908, at the age of fourteen, she said that his favourite subject was 'death treated in a gruesome manner'. She found his poems 'curious and ghastly' and was impressed by their 'grimness'. She used quotations from his work as epigraphs for the chapters of *Have His Carcase* and devoted several pages of *The Mind of the Maker* to an appreciation of his fragmented work.

To Her Mother   17 Long Wall
28 November 1918

Dearest Mother . . .

Many thanks for sending Mrs Osborne's comments on *Catholic Tales* – they are more appreciative than I should have expected, I think. It is extraordinary the way no two people agree about which of the poems are revolting and which are not. I quote from the letter of a man I scarcely know, but met once or twice at Basil's, – himself an author.

'The whole thing is a great achievement – and it's so masculine, so full of vim. It's so soaked in piety too. I don't mean the sloppy goodiness which so often annexes the term, but *pietas* . . . I love the nursery rhymes. I read Bo-Peep[1] the other evening to a friend, and his comment was: "Rather doubtful taste" – And I thought him rather an intelligent person before! However, I have now a criterion of stuffiness. I shall test my appreciation of my friends on the whet-stone (is the metaphor all right?) of Bo-Peep: and if they pass the test they shall be admitted to the innermost circle. One can't pick out individual poems, besides it's rather impertinent, but *Christ the Companion, Desdichado, Justus Judex*[2] appeal to me most. But they're all wonderful, and strike such a new, fresh note' –

There, you see! Just the 2 poems that one person hates, another person loves – so there you are. I reckoned last night that if I had removed all the poems anyone objected to, there would be perhaps half a dozen left in the book.

I heard two pleasant things last night. a) That Henry Ley[3] . . . has set to music my carol 'When All the Saints',[4] and wishes, I suppose, either to perform it here, or to publish it, or both. Either would be an excellent advertisement. I am to meet him shortly *chez* Mrs Moly-neux, and talk it over. b) That Hugh Percy intends to have '*Quittez Pasteurs*' (a beautiful old French Carol) publicly performed with an English adaptation of the words, which I wrote[5] (primarily for Mrs M[olyneux], but offered to him, in hopes he might use them). I'm rather pleased about both these things. They don't mean money, but they do mean a step towards getting known. I suppose the Carol will be done at the Carol Concert on the Sunday before Christmas. On Christmas Eve, I am singing for Mrs M. in the Hospitals, and I am also playing 2nd fiddle for her in a small orchestra, which will give concerts to wounded men every day for a week beginning on Boxing Day – so it looks as if Christmas were going to be a strenuous season! I shall have to take a tonic, what? to keep going on. I only hope it won't be such fearsome weather as last year, when everybody was ill! . . .

Best love to all
Your rattled but on the whole quite pleased with life
Dorothy

[1] 'Fair Shepherd', p. 39 of *Catholic Tales and Christian Songs*.
[2] pp. 10, 17 and 20 of *Catholic Tales and Christian Songs*.
[3] Henry George Ley (1887–1962), pupil of Walter Parratt, organist at Christ Church, Oxford. He was also a pianist and a composer. In 1926 he became precentor at Eton College.
[4] Entitled 'Carol for Oxford' in *Catholic Tales and Christian Songs*, p. 42. Nothing is known of Henry Ley's setting.
[5] Nothing is known of this adaptation.

To Her Parents   17 Long Wall
14 January 1919

Dearest People

I've just been having German measles, and from all the beastly fuss you'd have thought it was the Plague. I wasn't ill at all, and it's all quite ridiculous, but it happens to be a notifiable disease, and the Farrers[1] had to rush off with the boy because of their absurd school rules, and you never knew of such a disturbance. Dr Steedman was furious with Mrs N.[2] (who seemed to think it would prejudice her letting for the whole next term) – he said: 'I could barely restrain myself from calling her an ignorant old fool.'! (I'm glad he *did* restrain himself – it wouldn't have improved matters.) Anyway, I'm to bathe to-morrow in Condy's fluid, and then he says I shall be quite free of infection, but I'm not to go back to the office, because if anybody there gets German measles within the next 6 months they'll say it was me. So being thus cut off from my work, and not wanting to be a leper, I'm going to seize this God-sent opportunity for doing what I wanted very much to do, and going into Retreat for a few days. I'm getting so dusty and scuffling in the spiritual region I really thought I never *should* get straight again – so it's just as well – I never thought I'd get time for such a thing, but doubtless 'all is for the best', as Laura Godfrey[3] would say. So I shall be at the Convent of the Holy Name, Newlands, Malvern from Thursday to Tuesday, in case I'm urgently wanted. I'm going to cut clear away and have no letters sent on or anything, and as for my controversy with Theodore Maynard in the *New Witness*, it can stew in its own juice for a week. Controversy is bad for the spirit, however enlivening to the wits. . . .

[1] Fellow lodgers at 17 Long Wall.
[2] Mrs Nicholson, the landlady.
[3] A member of the Godfrey family who lived in Bluntisham.

To Her Father   B. H. Blackwell, Publisher
22 January 1919   50 & 51 Broad Street
                                                 Oxford

Dearest Tootles

I'm afraid the time has come when I must really move from 17
Long Wall, and ask you to help me with rooms! Mrs Nicholson has
been horrid lately, especially over the German measles – but the chief
thing is that now the 'Varsity is back, I shall be continually having
it cast in my teeth that I am not an undergraduate, and how much
better it would be for her if I were. I can't bear to live in an atmosphere
of petty insults and disagreeable hints.

The crowning point was reached, I think, when she said, as I told
you, that she had lost £3 by my illness. I drew her a cheque for
the amount and handed it to her on the morning I left for Malvern
– and would you believe it? she took it, and never even said
'Thank-you'!

The trouble is that very few people want a permanent woman. All
the licensed houses want to get their old University connection again,
so I am determined that I will go to an unlicensed house, or it will
only be the same thing over again. Even these are as a rule not keen
to have permanent people – and *everything* is bound to be far more
expensive than what I have been paying. Well, the upshot is that I
have found a most charming little set of 3 rooms in 5 Bath Place[1] –
(not the same woman Mother went to see, but next door). They are
unlicensed, and the landlady is anxious to have a permanent person,
and would be very willing to take me. The sitting-room is a little
smaller than my present one, but very delightful, and on the first
floor, and there would be quite room for my furniture and pictures.
Mrs Walklett seems a good, kind person, and I have had golden
opinions of her from various people. I feel sure I should be far happier
with her, esp. under present circumstances. She has a daughter who
helps to run the house, and apparently does not mind work, or noise,
or late hours. She prefers to cater for one, and a man[2] I know who
lives there says that she is generous with food and cooks quite well,
and is very clean.

Well now, the price for this convenient situation and accommodat-
ing disposition is £2.10[3] a week, inclusive of everything except coal,
which is 2 / 6[4] a week. Of course I pay for my own coal now, so that
would probably come to much the same thing in the end.

Tootles dear, shall I take these rooms? – I don't think I should get
anything better, and I *don't* want to leave Oxford. I wish everything
wasn't so difficult. – I'm having some wounded soldiers to tea this
afternoon, and Mrs N. is being a pig as usual. How anybody can

grudge anything to wounded men I cannot understand! – Anyhow, I'm buying every scrap of the food, and she need not grumble –

Tootles dear – say I may go away and be happy! – I really do think that Mrs Walklett will be nice – because I think she would be glad to have me –

I'm ever so glad you've got a car again. I look forward to seeing you in Oxford ere long.

> Your loving
> Dorothy

¹ Hilaire Belloc had previously lived there.
² Eric Whelpton, who was to become an important person in her life. (See introduction to letters from France p. 154.)
³ Two pounds and ten shillings (old currency).
⁴ Two shillings and sixpence (old currency).

To Her Mother   [As from] 5 Bath Place
12 February 1919   Oxford

Darling Mother

Oh! so strenuous! I move house to-morrow – in great pomp and publicity, on a hand cart at 9 in the morning. I've got my own proper set of rooms after all. God knows how I'm going to squeeze everything into the sitting-room, for it is much smaller than No. 17, but I dare say I shall be able to manage. The real drawback is gas instead of electric light, but I hope to be able to work an oil lamp in time. Nobody could be more obliging than Mrs Walklett about shifting her own furniture and pictures. The walls are a pleasant golden-buff. My door-curtain will, I think, make two, as the doors are very narrow, so as to cover also the door leading to my bedroom – But oh! my bill at Elliston's! – Oxford is crammed with people, and there is going to be plenty of social life this term and next – I'm going to establish a *salon* every Thursday evening during term – Frank Brabant is keen and is going to bring nice people, and I'm going to get hold of Shaw and other musical swells, and it ought to be really jolly nice. The upshot is, however, that I can no longer be quite destitute of an evening gown – I haven't had one for 6 years at least! – So I'm getting one made by Mrs Brabant's dressmaker. She is quite good, I think, and her charges very reasonable. It is of blue charmeuse, with a ninon top, and a little silver trimming – i.e. a wide belt, and a fringed end to the sash. It will cost rather under 5 guineas all told, which is not bad, and it is a beautiful material that will remake or dye well. Then my red cloak is being re-lined with primrose! and done up with a monster fur collar and sleeves. And who is the fur collar and sleeves, think you? Why, poor dear Percival, whom I never wear now, as stoles are out of fashion! So he's going to be chopped up and take on a new lease of life as an evening cloak. Isn't it a good thought? . . .

To Her Parents   5 Bath Place
14 February 1919   Oxford

Dearest People

You'll be wondering whether I'm here all right, and what it's like. Well, I am – after a tremendous business moving yesterday – and so far I am very happy, though of course it's early days yet. My room is simply delightful! When the curtains are up it will be quite perfect, and although it is so small, there seems to be really more room in it than there was in the other, because its shape is such that I can have the sofa right against the wall, and yet not too far from the fire. We had a terrible job getting Mrs Dawson's piano upstairs – there was a ghastly quarter of an hour when I thought it would never be able to be got in, and then I *should* have been done! but it was managed at last, with awful difficulty. I tipped the men heavily, and indeed they deserved it. My pictures look absolutely perfect – much better than they did at No. 17. There is not at present room for my books, but Mr Walklett is presently going to put up a new shelf. Meanwhile I store things most comfortably in the spare room, though I miss not having any sort of spare shelves in the sitting-room. My bed is very comfy, and the hot-water bottle last night was as hot as hot. I cannot say Mrs W. cooks as well as Mrs N. – she rather inclines to the greasy! – but as you know, provided food is wholesome and plentiful I don't mind very much, and it certainly is that. It remains to be seen whether she will try to make a lot of money out of me. – I parted company with Mrs N. in the most friendly manner, and gave her a little extra in the cheque, to save the buying of a memorial tea-pot or jam-jar. She was most amiable the last few days, all things considered.

I say, dearies, *do* come and see me in my new abode. You've got a car now! Only wait till the curtains are fixed!

The social regeneration of Oxford is well in hand. I have such a lot of engagements of one kind and another I begin to feel quite twirly in the head, but it's all very jolly. I hope to give a rather good musical party, either next Thursday or another, with Mr Shaw, who is a brilliant pianist. I have written to ask him to come next Thursday, but I don't know if he will. The only social difficulty which besets me is that I know various people with whom *I* get on very well, but who don't always fit each other! However, everybody has to cope with that. Mrs Brabant is such a darling, and so kind and reliable to fall back on in any difficulty – I like her more and more. Another most charming person, whom I am getting to know very well is Dr Chance.[1] I forget if I have mentioned her before. She lives at 2 Bath Place, and is *so* nice. To-morrow evening I am entertaining two advanced young poets, Osbert and Sacheverell Sitwell![2] They came into Blackwells this morning looking such fearful bloods that I had to invite them quickly, before I got frightened. I believe they are very good company, and anyway, B.H.B. wants to get hold of Sachie, and I think I can do that for him . . .

I think the love-affair is petering out satisfactorily, thank-you.[3]

> Yours full of life and love
> Dorothy . . .

[1] Dr Alice Chance, a medical practitioner, who became a friend, and whose advice D.L.S. later sought.
[2] The writers, Sir Osbert Sitwell Bt (1892–1969) and his brother Sacheverell (1897–1988), who succeeded to the baronetcy in 1969. They attended a meeting of D.L.S.'s Rhyme Club, but they were unresponsive.
[3] Doreen Wallace (1897–1959), the future novelist and friend of D.L.S., had fallen in love with Eric Whelpton, who did not reciprocate. D.L.S. acted as adviser and confidante and fell in love with Whelpton herself.

To Her Parents   5 Bath Place
21 February 1919   Holywell

Dearest People

I simply haven't had a moment till now in which to answer your letter, and thank Tootles for his most kind and welcome cheque. I am thoroughly established here now, and feel as if I'd lived here all my Oxford life, except that I am still too much in love with my room to be quite an old stager. I bid fair to become quite silly about it! It is really delightful, and so absolutely all my own – no pictures of anyone else's, and no furniture, except a table, sofa and 3 chairs – rather nice too, (the chairs) and not part of an 'elegant suite'. There are all kinds of funny little comforts and advantages about the place, which one can't explain till one sees them – one of them is having plenty of room to hang and store clothes – and there is a 'glory-hole' which holds a) oddments b) hats most usefully. I'm very well looked after, without being bothered – one doesn't have to make conversation with the landlady at all hours of the day, and one can come in and out unquestioned at any hour of the day or night. There's glory for you![1] The gas isn't really half bad on the whole, and I can have a lamp if I like to write and read by – and fetch it myself without fuss!

Last night I had a really delightful 'salon' – at least, I hope people enjoyed themselves – they seemed to! I got Mrs Molyneux to play the fiddle, and Mr Shaw of Keble, who is one of the most brilliant pianists I know, to come and play, and I had Miss Potts and a friend of hers, D. Newcomen and Mona Price, and Giles, and a very nice fellow (in the technical sense of the word) from Wadham, called Wade-Gery, and Dr Chance came in later. Do you know, I think I must make rather a good hostess, because people all seem to get talking and jolly at once when they're here.

My evening dress came this evening and my cloak last night. They *do* look nice! The cloak especially looks so opulent I have ado to know myself! There's nothing like fur to look rich! The little dress is quite simple of course, but a most beautiful colour, and looks very rich and good – which it is. The colour-scheme – passed with applause by Captain Whelpton – is most exciting – blue frock – red cloak lined with primrose, and black fur. By the way, I don't believe I ever told you about Whelpton. He lives in the house.[2] . . .

Did I tell you that I was singing next Sunday in a small private performance of the six Parry motets, 'Songs of Farewell'?[3] It is the combined Christ Church and New College choirs, reinforced by a few female altos, Allen conducting. It is really very jolly – they are beautiful little works – one or two of them quite great little works.

Oh I must stop – what a lot of jaw and all about myself!

Your loving D.

[1] Quotation from Humpty Dumpty.
[2] For Eric Whelpton's account of his years at Oxford and in Verneuil, see *The Making of a European* (London, Johnson, 1974, pp. 120–42).
[3] Then very recent. The last had been composed the previous year.

To Her Mother   5 Bath Place
28 May 1919

Dearest Mother

Thank you ever so much for your letter and all your welcome parcels. The narcissus are simply lovely. I am very glad to have my old cotton frock to knock about in this hot weather. By the way, I've meant every time to say and always forgotten, how splendidly Mrs C.[1] washed my check shirt; please congratulate her.

Eights week – and I am small-mindedly depressed because on this occasion the gods come down from town and up from the country, and the half-gods (that's me) are left at home – But there! This has been a week of minor infuriations. (No, I've missed no more property.) The world is full of tiresome people and damnable bills, and I haven't got enough work to do.[2] I'm dreadfully sorry to be so full of grumps, but I feel as if I'd come to a blank wall, and I've lost grip. It will pass off, of course, and I knew it would happen – but I'm rather bored with this place just at present. If I come home at the end of term, can we go off somewhere and see some mountains or something? Do! – By the way, I had one of the Sisters from the St Name,[3] Malvern, here the other day, and she said we could go there any time except in August.

Glad Gerald is all right – I am writing to him; he's an odd lad. I don't suppose there is anything very much behind that barrier; I'm beginning to think that in the majority of cases these immense fortifications are merely camouflage and mean nothing. He always did have a poor opinion of women – but how shouldn't he?

By the way, I hear that Roger Dixey has come home with frightfully bad shell-shock. It seems a bit late in the day for it to have overtaken him, but I suppose the accumulated strain has been too much for him. It often seems to happen that way to the finest soldiers. Poor lad! – I only had this very vaguely from the Brabants, and I haven't seen Giles or Roger – I gather Roger is terrified to see anybody.[4]

We had an awful muddle about going to town last week, and eventually I got stung in the face by a horse-fly, and didn't go. So I shall have to rush up on Friday morning and down again in the afternoon. I am going to Dorothy Wilding[5] in Regent St. She charges about 3 guineas for 6, I believe and 4 guineas for a dozen, so it seems cheaper to have a dozen. She is a really good person – Oxford is perfectly useless for photographs – they don't know how to take or mount them – this woman is an artist.

The Bach Choir affair is going to be an immense one – sorry you can't get up for it. Mind you do some time –

I say, do forgive all this grousing and depression – Don't worry – it'll all come out in the wash, and I've really nothing to grouse at!

Heaps of love
Dorothy

[1] Mrs Chapman.
[2] In April D.L.S. had entered into a new arrangement with Blackwells, whereby she would undertake only piece work. She hoped to eke out her income by coaching and free-lance journalism.
[3] The Convent of the Holy Name, where D.L.S. had gone on a retreat after having German measles.
[4] D.L.S. had thus close knowledge of shell-shock when she inflicted it on Lord Peter Wimsey.
[5] A well-known photographer of the time.

To Her Mother   5 Bath Place
6 June 1919   Holywell

Darling Mother

Thank you ever so much for your jolly letter – it's so awfully understanding – bucked me up no end as Egerton Clarke[1] would say. Your
diagnosis is pretty true – it is the lack of regular work that's done me,
and – not that I've got tired of my friends but – that some of them have
got very tired of me. Not the men – I'll say that for them – nor all the
women, but some of them – and just at the moment when, having nothing much to do I particularly wanted people to talk to. That's the sort
of thing that happens, but can't be helped. It's a great deal because
some of them are too busy to think about anything or anybody, or go
anywhere. Then I simply loathe spending such an awful lot of money
and making none – it gets to be a kind of nightmare especially in the
morning – damnable feeling of being no earthly use to anyone. And
yesterday the awful arrival at breakfast of a hideous great bill from
Elliston's for the last two quarters – 16 guineas! – Sixteen! – and I don't
believe I got a solitary unnecessary thing except my Renaissance robe!
– just put the lid on, – so I've written violently to various people to see
if I can get a holiday job of any kind – coaching in a family or something.
If I get my board and lodging and something over for a month or two
it'll save a bit. If only I don't have to pay for these rooms all the Vac.
People always tell you they have no difficulty about letting rooms until
you want to sub-let them, and then they say they can't – and the old
girl, though kind, is uncommon sharp in the dollars. Mr Rayner and
Mr McInnes told me last night that she bled them for friends in Eights
week, and I simply laughed. There's just one solitary advantage about
being a woman – people simply dare not overcharge one as much as
they would if one were a man – that's why they don't like women.

But altogether, I shouldn't be surprised if I cut Oxford before long.
I want a thorough change. Look here, should you mind awfully if I
went to France for a bit, supposing I can get a job? I've never been,
except for those 3 weeks, and it's quite ridiculous that I shouldn't –
and an absolute change of everything – language, way of life, times
of meals – everything – would be rather a relief. And it's not awfully
far off – at least, it won't be after they've finished with all this silly
business of passports and things. Not that I've got any definite post
in view, but just that I'm looking out for possibilities in that way. . . .

Mrs Brown has made my white river suit very well, the blue and
white check is going to be charming. More expense! Oh damn!

    Your distracted
    Dorothy

[1] One of her contemporaries at Oxford and a friend of Eric Whelpton's.

Between April 1917 and June 1919 the state of mind of D.L.S. had moved from elation to depression. She had reason to feel depressed. She had given up a steady, well-paid teaching post for an apprenticeship with Basil Blackwell, which led nowhere. Her delight at being back in Oxford faded as she found herself with less and less reason for being there. Her health had not been good: appendicitis, Spanish influenza (though a light attack) and German measles in two years had undermined her natural resilience. Although she had published a second volume of verse and had set herself to make social and cultural contacts, she began to feel more and more out of things. To add to her troubles, she had fallen in love and this time it was no game of 'let's pretend'. Her feelings were deeply involved.

Eric Whelpton (1894–1981), who had been invalided out of the army, returned to Oxford as an undergraduate at Hertford College in May 1918. His good looks and frail state of health made him a romantic figure and he had a number of women admirers. In May 1919, having been awarded a war degree, he took a post teaching English at L'Ecole des Roches, a boarding-school in Normandy. While there he set up an agency for organising exchange visits of French and English boys and needed a bi-lingual assistant. D.L.S. wrote to him to say she would like to find work in France. He offered her the post.

Although she was then twenty-six years old it was thought desirable that her parents should meet the man for whom she would be working abroad. Accordingly, as the following letter shows, Eric Whelpton paid a visit to the rectory in Christchurch. (For further details, including Eric Whelpton's own account of the visit, see Barbara Reynolds, Dorothy L. Sayers: Her Life and Soul, *ed. cit., chapter 5, pp. 86–96.)*

France: September 1919–September 1920
(Age: 26–27)

To ERIC WHELPTON   80 Westbourne Avenue[1]
29 July 1919   Hull

Dear Mr Whelpton
    Many thanks for your kind letter, in which you seem to have thought of everything. I was just going to ask you about the bicycle. I will track the Cycle Touring Club to its lair without delay, and cope with the passports and things.
    This is just to say that I feel sure the family will be charmed to inspect you at Christchurch on the 16th. – Are you aware that the 17th is a Sunday, and that you will have to hear Dad preach (being the 3rd Sunday in the month)? – No! I recollect, you never go to church, so it's all right. If you really don't mind coping with a Sunday in our midst, of course we shall simply love to have you, and then I

will return with you on Monday, if that pleases you. I will tell them
about it at home, and will you please let me know in good time where
you will be coming from on the 16th, so that Dad can arrange to
fetch you from the nearest available point. Christchurch is the last
place God made, and when He'd finished he found He'd forgotten
the staircase! . . .

Very sincerely yours,
    Dorothy L. Sayers

[1] D.L.S. had gone to Hull to visit her friends at the High School.

To Her Mother   Le Vallon
5 September 1919   Ecole des Roches

Dearest Mater . . .
    Please don't miss me too much because it makes me feel so criminal,
and really I'm only a day's journey away – a little farther than Oxford,
but not much and in an incomparably better climate. To-day has
been a simply wonderful day – like July – I bicycled to a wood a few
kilos. away, and basked gloriously with a book.
    We are gradually establishing matters in the office. Whelpton is a
funny, vague soul in some ways, but as quick as lightning in others
– he grasped and improved my card-index stunt in about 2 minutes.
It is killing to think of him and me sitting decorously opposite one
another at meals, chatting politely with the housemaster and his wife,
and calling each other 'Monsieur' and 'Mademoiselle'. He is rather
charming to all these people, and obviously popular with many of
the boys – those that are here, that is – but they are only about twenty
– poor devils who failed in their exam. and are now doing it again.
    Oh! by the way, you will be glad to know that the food is excellent,
and almost too plentiful. During the holidays G.E.W.[1] and I are
allowed *petit déjeuner* in bed for a treat! – permission of which we avail
ourselves with gratitude and alacrity. (This sounds as if we had it in
bed together, but I didn't mean that, though I believe he is sleeping
in this house *pro tem.*!) In term I shall have to arise, I'm afraid, but
as one goes early to bed, it works out much the same thing in the
end.
    When school begins, I am to be given a class of boys to the end
that I may teach them to act an English play. I've been writing to
D. Rowe for suggestions – she will probably know as well as anyone
what material is available. It ought to be rather good fun, I think, as
I am told they all speak English quite well.
    To-morrow I lunch with M. and Mme Marty – the house-master
here, you know. M. Marty is very nice I should think, though he

alarms me a little in the office. I think he probably worships efficiency. Madame is charming so far as I have seen anything of her; I shall know more about them to-morrow. I shall also have to call on the headmaster's wife, whom so far I have only just been presented to – as you know, out here a newcomer calls on the residents.[2] . . .

[1] George Eric Whelpton.
[2] The reverse was true of English etiquette.

To Her Parents   Le Vallon
? October 1919   Les Roches
                                       Verneuil sur Avre

Dearest People

Here I am again, safe and more or less sound, after what was really a very fatiguing journey.[1] I caught the universal cold *en voyage*, but am now very much recovered, after a day in bed, except that I have completely lost my voice. This is irritating, but as I feel perfectly well in myself I don't mind much. Poor old G.E.W. does have the most rotten luck. He pitched off his bicycle yesterday – whether he fainted and fell off or fell off and fainted he can't remember – which is a pity as it's an important point as far as his disease is concerned. Anyhow, he pitched on the point of his right shoulder and put it out, and he's pretty bad, poor laddie. The doctors and people have been pulling him about all day, and it must hurt like the devil. He's very plucky about pain, but if it gets too bad he faints, and of course he can't sleep at all, so we're in for a pretty cheerful week. It's like Bath Place over again, except that I'd fifty times rather have to deal with a sprained shoulder than with nameless nervous attacks.[2] But this is such a damned uncomfortable country for anybody sprained or hurt – no sofas, or *large* arm chairs. How I long for good old G.K.C.[3] or for the Chesterfield at 5 Bath Place. . . .

[1] One of D.L.S.' duties as Whelpton's assistant was to escort boys to England and France, as part of the exchange organised by the Bureau.
[2] Whelpton was subject to fainting attacks and had once fainted in D.L.S.' sitting-room in Bath Place.
[3] Her capacious armchair at Somerville, which she named 'G.K.C.' after Chesterton's girth.

To Her Mother   Bureau International d'Education
22 October 1919   Les Roches, Verneuil (Eure)

Dearest Mother

Just a line to thank you for your letter and assure you that I'm all right again and thoroughly cheerful, my voice found (not my despatch-case, alas!) and all well – that I am exceedingly warm in bed, and that though the house is cold at present we are to have the central heating in the course of a week or so, and then we shall be very cosy. It's only the coal-transport difficulty which has prevented us from having it before. G.E.W. is also very much better – shoulder almost well again – he did have a rotten time for a few days, poor laddie!

I'm busily working away at the viola in my spare time, and find that I can manage quite well with it, so as to be of assistance in the orchestra, and I even managed to read through a César Franck quintette[1] last night with some of the musical lights of this place. It's very jolly doing that kind of work – really for the first time, as I never had the opportunity of doing any chamber music before. The Hills (the music-master[2] and his wife, you know) want me to do some quartets with them too, to which I'm looking forward, as I like them both very much. . . .

[1] There is only one César Franck quintet, in F minor (1879), for piano, two violins, viola and cello.

[2] Francis J. Hill, who later taught at Marlborough College.

To Her Parents   Le Vallon
2 November 1919   Les Roches, Verneuil sur Avre

Dearest People

Just a note to tell you that I am alive and very well – that the house is warmed and all is gas and gaiters. It's just as well it *is* warmed for to-day it started snowing at Mass and is still snowing at 5 p.m. G.E.W. is well and sends you his love – He has been a little trying the last few days, because on Weds. I read him a lecture on his general behaviour which first of all made him thoroughly ill, and has since produced a spasm of sentimentality, but he suddenly perceived this morning, of his own accord, that he was growing fatuous! So I hope for amendment. Generally speaking, he behaves very well, and is easy enough to get on with. I hope to be home in England about Dec. 18, and I've promised to spend a day in Town fooling around with Himself. . . . After that I'll either come home, or make some arrangement; it depends on what people I've got to see. I'd rather like to go to Oxford, if you could join me there for a few days. There are various people I'd like to see there, and it's convenient for confessions and things – awful arrears to be made up after all these excommunicate months![1] Do you know when term ends at Oxford? Because I hear they're doing the Mass in B minor in the Bach Choir, and if I could possibly come in for that, I'd almost let everything slide for the chance of singing it again – but I expect I'll be too late, as I can't get over before the 16th at the earliest, and shall have to return on the 27th at the latest, to let my masters get away. I don't believe I'm really entitled to a holiday beyond a day or two, but G.E.W. seems determined to wangle me one, so I expect he will.

I'm continuing to like everybody very much and have lots to do, especially a good deal of chamber music, one way and another, which rejoices me. Fortunately I'm good enough to play either viola or 2nd fiddle in anybody's quartet, and not good enough to want to play 1st fiddle or take anybody's place, so that I am on excellent terms with both factions of a very jealous and deeply divided body of musicians. How delightful and how smooth is the golden road of mediocrity! and how amusing it is to hear both sides of a quarrel! . . .

For the moment Himself has taken a violent fancy to the black jumper with the Tudor rose, and the hair turned under, so I run about the school looking like an Italian page; I'm sure the authorities must think me frivolous. However, there is a girl here with really bobbed hair, so that's a shade more frivolous still. You will be interested to hear also that I have:

pretty hands
a nice neck
beautiful shoulders
good legs!
good ankles!! (at this point I began to think him really besotted; the rest is true)
a good temper
and
a bit of the devil in me!
So you see that the life of a private secretary is not without its amusements! . . .

I'm going to get up *Vice Versa*[2] with some of my little boys; they seem very keen, and I think they will thoroughly enjoy it. . . .

I'm sure you look jolly nice in your new hat and sports coat – I'm coming to look at 'em at Christmas, Mother darling. – By the way, G.E.W. likes you so much, and says yours is the best appointed house he's ever stayed in! There, now purr!

Lots of love
Your
Dorothy

[1] This indicates that D.L.S., by then a High Anglican, went regularly to confession when she was in England.

[2] By F. Anstey, pseudonym of Thomas Anstey Guthrie (1856–1934), author of novels and dialogues. *Vice Versa* (1882), is the story of Mr Bultitude, who is transformed by magic into the physical semblance of his son, and vice versa. C. S. Lewis evidently read this book as a boy; he calls the bear in *That Hideous Strength* Mr Bultitude.

On 23 November 1919 D.L.S. wrote to tell her parents that a young unmarried woman on the staff of the school had become pregnant. Her mother refused to help her and in her desperation she was considering an abortion. D.L.S. was horrified and knowing that Whelpton had relatives in Paris who were involved in welfare work she told him about the case. He managed to find accommodation and assistance for her in Paris, where D.L.S. visited her several times.

To Her Parents   Les Roches
23 November 1919   Verneuil sur Avre

Dearest People,

I'm so sorry I've not written before, but the last few days have been very full one way and another. I hope you've got my card telling you that I shouldn't be home till January some time. It sounds a long way off, but it is really rather complicated, and I'll be able to get home for certain. I shall spend a couple of days in Paris at Christmas – hear midnight Mass at Notre Dame – get my own affairs settled at St George's – hear High Mass at St Sulpice or the Ste Chapelle, and go and see some of G.E.W.'s friends. Then in Jan. I shall be free to devote myself to my family and friends – So probably everything is for the best in the best of all possible worlds.

We've got our tragedy out of the house and away to Paris, and it's to be hoped the baby will turn out well, for I'm jolly well responsible for its existence, if anybody is! Nice sort of responsibility to take on, eh? I had to get G.E.W.'s assistance in the end, and between us, with the help of a charming woman here, we got the girl into the right hands, and I'm hoping she'll stick it out and not let us down, but it's a long time ahead, poor soul, and she's bound to get depressed. However, I mean to keep an eye on her – also an excellent relative of G.E.W.'s in Paris is interesting herself. It's all a long and very silly story – that's the disheartening thing – these stories always are so trivial – nothing at all inspiring about them. I tell the girl that she's now got the one and only chance to make a good job of the whole silly business. The man is an odd creature – a Russian Jew, God save us! – one of these war muddles – a 'lonely soldier' introduced by somebody, and the girl with a vulgar mother and a bad home – a grubby muddle, and everybody in the soup together. The mother simply refused to have her home, and the man turned up the same day and offered to do away with the evidences – I did have a time! However, I swore by all my gods that someone anyhow would see her through, and G.E.W. and I worked like blazes, and I think all is going to turn out well. Thank God Himself's a man one can trust at a pinch – because the thing was getting jolly difficult. But he knew the right person to help here, and he produced the good lady in Paris – So you see we two irresponsible young people are resolutely founding a family in a morganatic kind of a way! However, we're not going to have any crimes committed, that's the chief thing.

Curious country, this, ain't it? But as G.E.W. says, what's to be expected when you get such mixtures – a Russian Jew and an Italian-English French-speaking girl, flung by the force of circumstances into each other's arms in the streets of Mentone? – The girl who has come to replace the delinquent (smuggled away on the score of some disease invented by a discreet doctor!) – is very charming and pretty – I hope she won't turn out to have any tragedies – I'm getting fed up with the part of sympathiser. It was funny, all the time the above business was going on, I had G.E.W. in one of his worst 'states of mind' – blethering, poor dear, about his bad health and his blighted ambitions, and the girl who had failed him, and how he didn't think he'd ever be able to marry, and how he was envious of the slackers all round who could knock round and do things and he tied by the leg here – and, finally, how he had no business to be telling me all this, but I was the only person who ever understood – with his head buried on my knees and making me smell of brilliantine in the most compromising manner! . . .

To Her Parents   Les Roches
7 December 1919

Darling people . . .
    I've had a rather tiring week – two Thursdays running I careered about Paris – but I'm distinctly cheerier now. I saw Adèle Camons both times, and did my darndest with all the moral force at my command to prevent her from re-entangling herself with the father of the child. Why doesn't he marry her? My dear, because he hasn't, and never had, the faintest intention of marrying her – He's a nasty Russian Jew, the son of people well-known for having got their money in very dirty ways – one of those men who kiss and preserve a masterly silence on all important points. He's ready, it seems, to acknowledge the child, but as, in French law, recognition of paternity carries with it very important rights, I am of the opinion that it would be well to

wait and see what the man's intentions and character are, before delivering the child over to him. Better grow up in poverty than with rotten moral standards. As things stand she has the chance of wiping out the sin and turning it into good, but if she lets the man into it again, she may only do more harm. She has now a number of very good friends in Paris, and a good prospect of work and assistance, and I hope she will do well. I couldn't with any conscience advise anybody to force a man into a marriage he doesn't want; nothing but misery could come of it – especially if he's a rotten sort. No, I didn't let the head people here get wind of it – at least I hope they didn't, though that sort of thing is hard to hide. Of course, G.E.W., who could see a needle in a bunch of hay through a brick wall, had suspected the truth long before I told him. In any case, nobody could possibly compel her people to take her home again, as she is over age and has been earning her living for some years – Besides, what a life! If they came round – and I have hopes that they may – well and good, but till then, she is probably better off, even in Paris. The only thing I dread for her there is loneliness and idleness – I make a point of seeing her whenever I go, and I shall stay a couple of nights with her at Christmas. A friend of hers has gone away and left her her flat for a few months, which is very convenient, and the same friend has promised to look after her when her time comes.

G.E.W. goes to England on Wednesday for a week, and after that will put in a fortnight's holiday on the Riviera. I'm very thankful, as he's about at the end of his tether, poor lad. – Worn out and difficult to help. . . . I do my best with him – it's not always easy, as I well knew it wouldn't be – and I don't know that my head is particularly well screwed on where Captain Eric Whelpton is concerned, but I promise you that if I find I'm hurting him, I'll leave him like a shot. I didn't come over here to add to his burdens. But I think if it wasn't me it would be somebody else, and I'd rather it was me, because I do mean well by him, and don't want to land him in difficulties or exploit his temperament to titillate my vanity, as some people might do who were thoughtless. – All this sounds very solemn, doesn't it? . . .

The boys of the Vallon gave a play yesterday which was very good – they are very good actors. M. Marty, G.E.W. and myself are plotting to do *The Taming of the Shrew* next term, with me in the title-rôle and Himself as Petruchio (Note the characteristic modesty with which we cast ourselves for the leading parts!) It probably won't come off – if it does, I shall probably get my costumes made in England, where they will cost rather less. I can do with two – one for the wedding scene, and the other for the rest of the play. . . .

(Please use discretion in reading this letter aloud!)
Dearest Mother
   Please forgive me for not having written for such a long time. The
fact is I didn't quite know what to write, because I was going through
rather a difficult moment, and when one is worried and puzzled it's
hard to say anything. However, we had a crisis last night and an
explanation this morning, and all is well. At least, we are right with
one another, and that's the chief thing. I daresay you gathered pretty
well when I was last at home that the situation had its difficulties.
Everything became so odd last fortnight that I thought I was becoming a nuisance, and offered to go, because I thought I was fighting a
losing battle; however, this morning it was made [clear] that whoever
the fight was up against Eric and I are pulling on the same side, so
that there's nothing to be ashamed of, if a lot to be coped with. We
are both rather estimable people and the whole thing would be most
heroic and pathetic if one didn't see the comic side of it. Anyway, we
both nobly shouldered our own share of the blame – in fact, Eric
claimed it all, but to tell the truth I have been partly responsible –
and at present mutual admiration stands at par. The intention is to
try back for the old position; I have my doubts about the possibility
of this kind of 'feats and exercises', but shall of course loyally co-
operate as far as I can. Don't you worry; it's all experience, and
nobody is permanently damaged! It would make rather a jolly movie
one of these days. I've received a tribute to my behaviour too which
was worth having. So that's something. All over now, and perfectly
better, thanks.
   It's a pity it all had to happen now, because Eric got thoroughly
knocked up and out playing in a silly football match on Shrove Tuesday and has been rather a wreck ever since. However, there's no
doubt he's far better than last term and happier, I think, on the
whole. He is going to Paris to-morrow for four days which will do
him good and clear the air.
   The week after I hope to go myself for the Sunday to hear Beethoven's Mass in D minor[1] which is being given somewhere or other.
Mr Hill is going to try and get hold of the score beforehand so that
we can read it and know a little about it. I shall go and see Adèle
Camons, who is finally detached, I believe and hope, from her brute
of a man, and doing as well as can be expected in the way of working
out existence on her own lines. Tell Dad that I have actually been
persuaded . . . to learn Bridge, and am told I show signs of making
a good player one of these days! Last night (owing to the crisis!) I

blithely flung away two trumps, wasted two other useful cards and lost us 4 tricks in spades (of all things), but that was owing to mental pre-occupation. . . .

[1] *Sic*. Mass in D, otherwise called the *Missa Solemnis*.

To Her Parents   Le Vallon
3 July 1920

Dearest People

I simply haven't been able to write! There's been a lot of work – this old Bureau is going to boom one day! G.E.W. came back from Florence[1] last week and has now gone again to England with boys, leaving me with all the work plus his classes, so I'm pretty occupied as this is the busy season. I'm pleased about the Bureau. M. Marty and I, profiting by the fretful G.E.W.'s absence, are devoting a little time to quiet inspection of the accounts, which might be much worse, as far as I can see. Yesterday was a field-day, in which I perpetrated 23 letters and 7 post-cards. To-day is calmer, but there really is a lot of stuff going through. G.E.W. is seeing people in town about the Bureau and incidentally about me – but I shouldn't be surprised if I stayed on here till Christmas – if they make it worth my while, that is. So please don't expect anything of any kind till you hear that it's settled. I shall be in town for a couple of days about the 20th of this month – with boys of course.

What do you think I've done with my birthday money? Made a daring speculation, and bought a very decent viola for the equivalent at the present rate of change of about £7. I ought either to be able to sell it at a profit in England, or sell my fiddle for a good deal more than I gave for it. When I'm in town I mean to look for the opportunity of doing some quartette playing. The Hills advise me to stick to the violin, and say I could make money by playing in bands and things, but I don't quite know. I'm rather inclined to sell it on the whole. One can always borrow a violin, but a good viola cheap is a useful thing to have.

The other really important piece of news is that Adèle Camons' war-baby has arrived all right, and is a boy, I'm glad to say. Adèle had a bad time, but seems all right now and very glad to have the infant. I'm so thankful it's all right, because now she can really make good, and will have something to fill her life. She will be looked after by the State for a month or two, and then will have to find some work. I expect to be able to help her to this, if nothing turns up in other ways. The father is doing his part by assisting with money etc.

but I'm very thankful she didn't marry him – as a matter of fact he never suggested it – as I don't think he is any great shakes.

I must stop now and write to her. . . .

[1] Eric Whelpton had decided to become a partner in a house agency in Florence. He suggested to D.L.S. that she should take over the Bureau and offered to sell her his interest in it for £40. For a time she was tempted: 'It's not every day one can buy a show of one's own for £40!' she wrote to her parents. She wondered if she could interest the Anglo-French Society in the venture. If so, she could run it from London.

To Her Parents   The Craven Hotel
23 July 1920   Craven Street
                                             Strand

Dearest Mother

Ever so many thanks for your letter – And first of all I'll explain why I can't come to Cambridge. I've been occupied in town till to-day and I've got a certain sum of money to live on at the Bureau's expense till Tuesday. Town being expensive, it's cheaper for me to go down to-day to stay till Tues. morning with D. Rowe. And why D. Rowe and not you? Why, because, by a very humorous chance, on my way over (a delightful journey by the way) I met a Cinema producer,[1] to whom I talked about writing scenarios for Cinema. He said it was a frightfully paying business if one had the knack, and gave me a lot of tips, and finally mentioned a book by Blasco Ibañez,[2] and said he particularly wanted to produce that story and that if I liked to make a scenario and send it to him, he would (if it was any use) be almost certain to get a manager to take it. Now I couldn't do it alone, but D. Rowe and I could make something of it together, so I got the book – hunted all over London for it! – and am carrying it off in triumph, in the hope of *perhaps* making £80! – or anyway, getting some idea of whether one could make money that way or not. Of course, the man may be a boaster, or a fraud or anything, but he *seemed* a nice honest creature, and anyhow it seems to be well worth trying. Consequently, I thought D. and I could most profitably put in 4 days studying the book and knocking a scheme together. I shall almost certainly be back in a month or so and may spend a short time at home, as the affairs of the B.I.E.[3] and Anglo-French Soc. are still thoroughly undecided. . . . So there you are. – In the circs., I thought it better to go to B'mouth[4] and save my money, make a shot at the Cinema thing, and see you in September. . . .

[1] His name was Cyril Mannering.
[2] *Blood and Sand*. Vicente Blasco Ibañez (1867–1928), Spanish novelist, is best known for *The Four Horsemen of the Apocalypse*. Mannering was pleased with the scenario which D.L.S.

produced but he had omitted to discover whether the film rights of the book were free. Nevertheless, she continued to write film scenarios for him. It is not known whether any were accepted.
[3] Bureau International d'Education.
[4] Bournemouth.

To Her Mother   Le Vallon
18 August 1920

Dearest Mother –
   I've been feeling a dreadful pig not having written for such a long time, but my mind seems to have gone blank! I suppose it's because I don't know what I'm going to do. I seem to have a lot of irons in the fire and not to be at all certain which I'm going to pull out. They're all interesting irons in their way, but I shall probably end by falling among all my stools (mixed metaphor). Anyhow, I've agreed to hold up the chin of this old business till the end of September, so that I shall really be able to talk things over properly with M. Marty. He may want me to stay on till December, but all these things depend on other people. As a matter of fact, I believe the only way in which I could get a real hold on the B.I.E. would be by becoming a partner, when they couldn't turn me out and I should have a right to dictate – but I haven't quite enough confidence in myself to ask Tootles to risk money. Yet the thing grows, and I do believe that with money and energy and a headquarters in London it would be a jolly good thing. M. Davray seems disinclined to commit himself in any way – but I'm not sure that the best thing for *me* wouldn't be to hang on a bit longer till we see how that connection is going to pan out. Then if another of my irons comes to anything it might solve the whole problem – but that's a very vague iron indeed. So I feel unsettled and sleepy – very sleepy – unfortunately just as I ought to be most energetic! Such is life! It comes of its being so hot here. One goes about in a single garment, and spends as much time as possible in the swimming-bath – though I'm a rotten swimmer and loathe diving.
   I think Jim really enjoyed her time here. She's passed her journalistic exam. and thinks she has got a fair job in town, but she doesn't seem frightfully enthusiastic about it. It is the sub-editorship of a new paper,[1] and sounds all right, but she doesn't seem to care much about the people who are running it, which is a great drawback. I thought she seemed a great deal happier and better in health when she was here. I think she ought to do rather well in journalism if she gets a good start. . . .
   How are your domestic affairs going? . . . I think I should send Adèle Camons over to you as cook-help, as soon as she was strong

enough. She cooks splendidly – but unfortunately it's the housemaid that's lacking. Seriously, I don't suppose such a work of charity would appeal to you? I'm rather worried as to what the girl is to do with herself when she has to leave the home. She has a friend in Paris who has promised to look after her, but she's a curious, vague sort of woman, and though she's been very good to her, I don't know that she's very reliable. If there was any real difficulty, could I count on you to shelter her for a bit in exchange for services? I don't suppose there'll be any necessity, but one never knows. I'm determined to make a good job of Adèle, and it's *after* the crisis that people need help most – which is what so many people won't understand. One's got to keep on standing by. I've just got the notice of the Degree fees,[2] which I enclose. I've told them I want Oct. 14th if possible, because my movements are so uncertain after the beginning of October – but really, of course, because I want so much to be in the first batch. It will be so much more amusing. That will mean a day or two in England, but I don't think, even if I'm still here next term, that M. Marty will make any difficulty about letting me go. I shall probably have to be over again before that with boys. I believe I could do that silly old crossing in my sleep now. (Last time I crossed we all had to sleep on deck, the boat was so full!) – I'm not sure I shan't end by getting a taste for a wandering life. At the moment I'm divided between that and London. Next time I'm in town I'm going to look up my Cinema man, and see if there's anything doing there.

By the way – don't worry about me. I'm all right, only puzzled for the moment. If I don't write, it's a kind of impatience at having nothing definite to say. I feel you must think me a fool – but it's a little complicated.

Your loving
Dorothy

[1] *Time and Tide.*
[2] Oxford University had just consented to confer degrees on women. On 14 October 1920 D.L.S. was among the first batch of women to be formally invested first with a B.A. and immediately afterwards with an M.A.

1920–1925

The Difficult Years

On her return from France, D.L.S. decided to look for work in London. She had set her mind against teaching as a profession and knew that she wanted, above all, to write. Her parents were willing to help her financially until she could support herself. It was a period of economic stagnation and unemployment. She put a good face on things when writing to her parents, but in reality the outlook was bleak.

London: October 1920–November 1925 (Age: 27–32)

To Her Parents   96 Belgrave Rd S.W.
3 October 1920

Dearest People –
 This is just to say that I really haven't anything very definite to tell you – I have several irons that seem to be heating up finely, but there are 'ifs' still attached to them, and I won't tell you lots of details in case nothing comes off and everybody is disappointed. However, there seem to be plenty of opportunities going about, anyhow, and so far I have had great good luck. More than ever, though, I realise the paramount necessity of always being on the spot – I feel as if I hardly dared leave London for a second. Of course I am going to Oxford on the 13th for my degree – Christine Blackwell is putting me up – and then I hope to come on home for about a week. If one of my 'irons' comes out as I hope I shall be able to do this without much risk. In the meantime I am really enjoying running about and looking for things.... I saw Mr Mannering on Friday. He was immensely pleased with my scenario of *The Matador*[1] – but of course, now all the work has to begin – the first necessity is to get the author's permission, and it is quite possible that somebody else has bagged

the rights already, so it won't do to count at all on that. However, what Mr Mannering says encourages me to go on trying. . . .

These are really desperately hard times for literary people. Jim seems to be quite enjoying her work, but is already thinking of crying aloud for more salary. If I turn out to be wealthy enough, Jim and I want to take a flat together – but of course flats and rooms are frightfully difficult to find at the moment. . . .

[1] Based on the novel *Blood and Sand*.

To Her Parents   Craven Hotel
26 October 1920   Craven Street
                                        Strand, W.C.1

Dearest People

This is first of all to thank you, Tootles, very much for your letter and the £5 note. I hope Poland[1] will soon pay up, in which case I can pay my debts, but in the meantime the extra quid or so will come in very useful.

Now for my affairs. I've fixed up to take a very nice unfurnished room at the top of a sort of Ladies' Club in S. George's Square, S.W.,[2] quite close to where Jim is, but a much nicer house, all freshly done up. It's run by a very nice woman – a lady, which is something. Now the immediate question is furniture. I've bought an excellent camp bed, slightly damaged, for 35 shillings, which no one can call out-of-the-way, and Jim can lend me an arm-chair and table which are at present being housed by somebody else (all this is very complicated!) – By the way, you will see I've had to give up the flat idea for the present. Nothing seemed doing, and also Jim has quarrelled with her employer and flung up her job. I think myself she has behaved very foolishly, but it's no good telling her that. If one wants to chuck a job, one should always do it in such a manner as to get a testimonial out of the people, but in this case Jim and the good lady seem to have been mutually rude to one another, so that's no good. In the circumstances I'm quite glad to be out of the flat idea, as it would have been a bit precarious. At present I shall be paying thirty shillings a week for the room and £1 a week for 'partial board' (7 breakfasts and 2 dinners a week and lunch on Sunday) – so that when I'm getting £10 a week or so from the Poles I shall be well off. . . .

[1] D.L.S. and her father had undertaken to translate certain documents from French relating to Poland. No details are known of this work.
[2] D.L.S. was to place Miss Climpson in a top flat at 97a St George's Square in *Unnatural Death* (chapter 3).

To Her Parents   S. Anne's[1]
31 October 1920   Surrey Rd,
                                                  Bournemouth

Dearest Mother and Tootles

I've been trying to write to you for days, but for one thing I've been simply slaving at the demography of Poland whenever I had a moment and for another, things kept coming from you by every post, and I waited to thank you for the whole lot collectively. . . .

I say, Tootles, Poland seems to be a little gold-mine. I'll do the new MS., because corrections, though beastly are very quick work. I don't see why this kind of job shouldn't go on for ever! – Just at present I want all the money I can lay my hands on to furnish etc. – later on we will divide the spoils.

Dorothy is very busy as usual getting up private theatricals. . . .

The house is full of lovely early Victorian frocks – for the play *Trelawney of the Wells*.[2] There is an evening dress of flowered puce silk which suits me down to the ground. When I have made my pile out of Poland I shall have an evening dress like that – slipping right off one's shoulders, and with a crinoline – It would make such a sensation when everybody else was in hobbled skirts! . . .

[1] D.L.S. had gone to stay with Dorothy Rowe.
[2] By Sir Arthur Pinero (1855–1934). *Trelawney of the Wells* was first published in 1897.

To Her Parents   36 St George's Sq.
3 December 1920   S.W.1

Dearest People,

Just a line only – I am in a very cross state, having just been behaved very rude to by my landlady. I've given notice, but having paid till the end of the month, don't know if I can move just yet. Don't worry – she can't do me no harm, but she's a stupid old woman who drives everybody out of the house by her temper. So if my letters are few and far between for a bit, you'll know I'm busy house-hunting again. I've heard of a rather beautiful room that I might be able to get, but I don't know. I've made the acquaintance, through Jim, of a Mrs McKillop – a very nice woman, whom Aunt Maud knows very well. She is hunting for rooms for herself, and told me about the one I'm going to try for, and I think she might be useful to me in lots of ways. Jim knew her at the Ministry; she is, I believe, a distinguished statistician – but none the less is very humorous and delightful. She is musical, too, and has asked me to go round and play with her sometimes. As she is going to be in London till Easter at least, she ought to be rather a nice person to know. . . .

Miss Barry[1] – a college acquaintance – wants me to undertake some [teaching] at Clapham High School as her deputy for a month or so in January. I shall probably accept, as is prudent, if they intend to pay decently, but if there should be another Polish book after this one it will make things a bit of a rush. Still, one must seize what comes and do what one can with it. Better too much to do than too little. . . .

[1] Florence Barry, nicknamed 'Jack', head of the English department at Clapham High School.

To Her Parents   36 St George's Square
7 December 1920   S.W.1

Dearest People –

The die is cast and I am departing on Thursday to 44 Mecklenburg Square W.C.1, where I think I shall be much happier. I made a bad mistake over this old lady, but I shall have paid for it, and it's done with, and we won't talk about it any more. It is a great pity, because in some ways the house suited me very well, being so clean and nicely kept and so well placed, close to Jim and to Lucy[1] (comparatively) but the truth is that Miss Latch's temper is so diabolical that it really almost amounts to possession. Nobody could be pleasanter when she is pleasant or more obliging, but when she is annoyed, she loses all control of herself, and shouts and is most insolent. And she will inter-fere – all her servants leave after a very short time, and most of the lodgers I have seen have gone off in a fury. Poor old beggar – I'm sorry for her, with this great house on her hands and nobody in it – but her rents are too high and she won't try to be amiable.

The place I am going to will be very different, and a success, I hope. It is the room Mrs McKillop saw and liked so much – a lovely Georgian room, with three great windows – alas! would that I could afford curtains to them! – perhaps I shall in time – and a balcony looking onto the square.[2] There is an open fireplace, and the last tenant has thoughtfully left some coal behind, which I can take over at a valuation – and there is a gas-ring. The only drawback is, no electric light, but I shall get a little oil-lamp, which will look very nice. It is a beautiful big room, far larger than the one I am in now, and costs less money. The landlady is a curious, eccentric-looking person with short hair – the opposite of Miss Latch in every way – and thoroughly understands that one wants to be quite independent. That is really all I want – to be left alone, and I can't think why people won't leave me! – Well, there it is, and mercifully, thanks to the blessed old Poles I have enough money to do the move (per a greengrocer in Bloomsbury).

Now to cheerfuller subjects. Mrs McKillop (see above and my last) has just asked me to tea. I think she likes me and means to be kind to me, and ask me to meet people. I am looking forward to going, and having some music with her.

I've taken on the Clapham work, so that if there should be no more Poles I shall have something to keep going on. I've also got some new ideas.[3] . . .

[1] The wife of her cousin Raymond Sayers.
[2] Cf. *Gaudy Night*, beginning of chapter 1: 'Harriet Vane sat at her writing-table and stared out into Mecklenburg Square.'
[3] She was beginning to create Lord Peter Wimsey.

To HER MOTHER   44 Mecklenburg[1] Square
9 December 1920   W.C.1

Dearest Mother

Just a hurried line to thank you most awfully for your letter and welcome present. I am installed in my new quarters, and think I shall like them very much, though I and my little belongings look rather lost in this vast space at present. I am asking Basil to send up my *Venus*,[2] and I do very much hope I shall be able to stay here. I'm going to try hard, and have written to Dr Cros to ask if there are to be any more Poles to do.

I parted with Miss Latch rather triumphantly on the whole. She did her best to make me pay a lot of money she wasn't entitled to on a ridiculous pretext, but on my referring her to my solicitor – an imposing though fabulous figure – she climbed down, and contented herself with charging one shilling and sixpence for the loan of a bed-spread – which small and malevolent satisfaction I did not grudge her.

Don't ever think I'm not feeding myself well – Food is my most sinful extravagance. I am just going out to get a huge dinner in Soho for two shillings and threepence (beer extra)! . . .

[1] *Sic*: D.L.S.'s spelling of Mecklenburgh.
[2] A print of Botticelli's *Birth of Venus*, which she had bought in Oxford.

To HER MOTHER   44 Mecklenburg Square
14 December 1920   W.C.1

Dearest Mother –

Thank you so much for your letter. I will try and write – though you know one's hand and shoulder simply ache with writing after a few hours with the Poles (sounds like the title of a missionary lecture!) and one feels one would rather do anything than write. But you've axed a lot of questions one way and another, which I'll try and answer.

My landlady – very nice – one never sees her. Only occasionally, just as one is hurrying away to an appointment, she wanders out and engages one in a discussion of art, literature or domestic economy. She keeps herself *to* herself as the saying goes and lets her lodgers alone – I'm afraid there wouldn't be any room in this house to put you up if you came to town – it's full from attic to basement, but I expect I could find you something in the neighbourhood if you gave me a little notice. There is a very nice woman who does the cleaning and washing-up for a moderate stipend. I have discovered that the one really vital necessity for living in unfurnished digs is a frying-pan. I bought one the other day, and have just been illustrating my favourite theory – the superiority of the trained mind, no matter what its training has been. Although I can't remember ever having had a frying-pan in my hand before, there was nothing wrong with the eggs I had this evening – or at least, if there was, it was only a sort of urban flavour which wasn't my fault. Of course, if it was ever possible to send new-laid rustic eggs by post – but there!

I admit the coldness of the weather, and of the room. I can only say that I am none the worse for it, though I shall be glad to get some curtains up when I can afford it. Just at the moment there is a slight hitch in my finances, owing to a letter from the Poles being apparently delayed in transit. . . . Anyway, my present landlady, Miss James, to whom I mentioned that the Poles hadn't turned up, merely replied sweetly – 'Oh, it'll be all right – you needn't pay anything here, and I will lend you money with pleasure if you need it. Be sure to ask me if you're short.' She really seems a model sort of landlady. . . .

I'm rather swanking about, because the other day I sent a long poem to the *London Mercury*, which is a particularly swell sort of monthly, run by tip-top people, and they actually accepted [it] by return of post, in an autograph post-card from J. C. Squire,[1] calling it 'that delightful thing'! I believe they pay very well, but I shall have to wait for the money, as Squire says there will be some delay about printing it. I suppose they are made up months ahead.

I saw Ray and Lucy the other day – stodging out to Battersea[2] all in my smartest clothes in the vilest of weather. Fortunately there is a 'bus which goes all the way.[3]

I simply must stop now, my right shoulder has a positive pain in it from so much scribing.

The *Venus* has started from Oxford to adorn my chimney-piece.

Ever your loving
       Dorothy

[1] J. C. Squire (1884–1959) was the editor of the *London Mercury* from 1919–31. The poem, elaborate in structure, entitled 'Obsequies for Music', was published in *London Mercury* III, January 1921, pp. 249–53.
[2] Battersea is used as a setting for events in *Whose Body?*
[3] As Sir Reuben Levy discovers. (See *Whose Body?*, chapter 13.)

Some time in 1921 D.L.S. met the American writer John Cournos. Of Russian Jewish origin, he was born in Kiev in 1881. When he was ten his family emigrated to Philadelphia. He had a deprived childhood, leaving school at the age of twelve to work in a spinning factory. At fourteen he obtained a job as an office-boy with the Philadelphia Record *and rose to be assistant editor. In 1912 he decided to try his fortune as a free-lance in England, where he interviewed a number of leading personalities. In 1917 he was appointed a member of the Anglo-Russian Commission to Petrograd and later worked for the Foreign Office and the Ministry of Information. His first novel,* The Mask, *was published in 1919. He was a regular contributor to literary journals and was recognised as a poet of the Imagist movement. Among his published works are nine novels, two plays, an autobiography, fifteen volumes of translation, eight anthologies and a volume of poetry.*

D.L.S. had never met anyone like him. Twelve years younger, she became infatuated with him and longed to marry him and have children by him. Cournos professed to be opposed to marriage on principle and to be unwilling to bring children into the world. He wished to consummate the affair and to use contraceptives. D.L.S. would not agree and put an end to their relationship. Cournos returned to the USA and married Helen Kestner Satterthwaite, the author of detective novels under the pseudonym of Sybil Norton. She was a widow and the mother of two children. The situation has a parallel in the relationship between Philip Boyes and Harriet Vane in Strong Poison. *Cournos made detailed use of it (even quoting from D.L.S.'s letters) in his seventh novel,* The Devil is an English Gentleman *(Farrar and Rinehart, New York, 1932). He died in 1966.*

To Her Mother   44 Mecklenburg Square
22 January 1921   W.C.1

Dearest Mother –
   Ever so many thanks for the parcel and the lovely eggs, which are
a great joy – I'm in a great hurry, because I'm doing the Clapham
work and the Poles, and of course have chosen this moment to be
visited with ideas for a detective story and a Grand Guignol play,
neither of which will certainly ever get written.[1] – Delighted with your
last remarks about the *Obsequies*[2] – they go to support – what I have
always maintained – that you can never judge of a poet's life by his
works! The most cynical passages of that gloomy work were written
at the beginning of my second year at College. Now then! what have
you to say to that? – My detective story begins brightly with a fat
lady found dead in her bath with nothing on but her pince-nez. Now,
why did she wear pince-nez in her bath? If you can guess, you will
be in a position to lay hands upon the murderer, but he's a very cool
and cunning fellow. The Grand Guignol ends with a poisoned kiss!
– Lucy and Jim and I are going to the Little Theatre on Saturday
week – I hear that this new series of plays surpasses everything else
in grisliness. . . .

[1] The detective story turned into *Whose Body?* Nothing is known of the Grand Guignol
play. (Guignol is the chief character of a French puppet show. 'Grand Guignol' is a term
applied to a theatre which puts on plays of a gruesome nature.)
[2] Her poem 'Obsequies for Music', which J. C. Squire had accepted for the *London Mercury*.

To Her Mother   44 Mecklenburg Square
15 March 1921   W.C.1

Darling Mother –
   O dear me! What a cross letter! I laughed over it dreadfully. However, in the main I agree with you. You needn't be surprised at finding
Raymond a bit of a bore – I know nobody who doesn't, except Lucy
of course. All one can say is, that he is such a kind old bore, it doesn't
matter. But I must say I wish he wouldn't give long résumés of plays
and books and forget the point till after he's finished – I had tea with
Aunt G.[1] to-day, and she said the same as you about Lucy's dressing
– I expect she thinks it doesn't matter in the country, or when she
goes to see Aunt G., because she really can look very nice indeed if
she likes – not good-looking at all, of course, but quite smart. I think
it's rather a shame to go to poor old Aunt G. in all one's oldest clothes
– I always make a point – unless it's very wet, of course – of sticking
on my best bib and tucker to go to East Putney as much as if it was
to the Ritz.[2] I'm sure it pleases her, and she always notices . . .

I had a most delightful week-end with Gwen and Colin.[3] I don't think you need be too sorry for Gwen. She seems to me to be *most* happy in her married life and singularly sensible and wise in her handling of Colin. I don't think I could do with him as a husband myself, because of his perpetual thirst for improving his own mind and hers and everybody's about him, but she takes it humorously – and has even embodied his little foibles in a short story, which she read us, and which shows much more observation and analysis than I should have expected. I must admit, too, that he is singularly fair-minded, and ready to accept her criticism – in fact, it is quite a little mutual admiration society, very pretty to watch. John is really a beautiful baby, and quite singularly good and intelligent. Gwen was rather foolish in doing too much when she was in London a little time ago and knocked herself up a bit, but she seems all right now, and all I can say is, that if I can spin about and build rockeries when (or if ever) I'm seven months with child, I shall consider myself fortunate. Perhaps she doesn't rest quite enough, but she says that if she felt bound to consider herself a sort of invalid, she'd get frightfully moped, especially with Colin away all the week, so I dare say she is right. Anyway, I notice that the people like Christine Blackwell and Madame Marty, who skip around till the last moment, always seem to have the jolliest babies.

Jim has gone off to stay with her mother in Bournemouth for a little. It is just as well, because she had been getting very 'down' about things lately, and had developed a sort of blood-poisoning, due to rundownness, I expect. She is a problem. She's rather like Eric in a way – never liking what she's doing at the moment because she thinks she ought to be doing something grander. One can't do anything for those people – they have to learn by experience. I should think Bournemouth would do her good. Oddly enough, she really isn't as good at roughing it in rooms as I am. She really likes comfort and needs it, of course, being much more delicate than I am – but she doesn't know in the least how to make herself comfortable.

My Poles are good for another £45 or so anyhow, so I'm just going on and not worrying. I'm a great believer in things 'turning up'. I should have been called Micawber.

I suddenly had the idea the other day of seeing whether I had quite forgotten all my German, so I got hold of a modern novel and started in to read it. I found that my vocabulary wasn't as extensive as it might be, but I was really surprised to find how easily I could read – though of course, after all these years, I can't get along nearly as *fast* as I do with French or English. The book happened to be extraordinarily good, and very interesting. It is about Berlin in the last year of the War, – very terrible, but gives one some idea of what

Germany went through. We, of course, never even began to feel the
pinch of war. I am sorry we are making such asses of ourselves at
the moment – Simons[4] is a man of sense. I don't blame Lloyd George
– he is doing his best to restrain France, who is dingo-mad about
indemnities. Anyway, we may be quite sure that whoever pays the
50% export duty it won't be Germany – her manufacturers will simply
raise the export prices of produce to cover the difference, and the net
result will be the further depression of the already depressed trade of
Europe. However, I don't believe France cares what happens as long
as she can squeeze the Germans.

So sorry your neuralgia has been bad – I hope it's better now. I
shall have to come home for a few days presently and collect some
books, but I mustn't leave my Poles for the moment – they were very
good and patient while I was doing the Clapham job, and I don't
want to annoy them.

> Best love –
> Dorothy

[1] Aunt Gertrude Sayers.
[2] In a previous letter to her parents D.L.S. had written: 'Oh, yes! one small excitement!
I had tea at the Ritz on Thursday! Guess with whom? . . . No, you are quite wrong – it's
somebody you never saw or heard of. – No, I won't tell you. It's so nice to have a little
mystery.' The mystery was never divulged.
[3] Raymond's sister and her husband, Colin Hutchinson.
[4] *Sic*: John Allsebrook Simon, 1st Viscount Simon (1873–1954).

To Her Parents   44 Mecklenburg Square
No date, but March 1921   W.C.1
                                  Sunday – Lent 5
                                  (forgotten the date)

Dearest People . . .

Having nothing to do this afternoon I strayed into the National Portrait Gallery[1] - I'd never been there before, and had no idea it was so
interesting. One sees practically all the famous people one's ever heard
of – but, my God! what a plain set of women Mrs Browning, Charlotte
Brontë and George Eliot were! They are all hung together, and they're
a depressing sight. C.B. is the nicest – but *such* a bumpy, shiny forehead
– obviously she used no powder! George Eliot has an arresting face, but
rather unpleasant, I think – an ugly, sensual mouth and hard, pale eyes.
As for E.B.B.,[2] she has a sort of goblin face. The most attractive portrait
in the gallery is, I think, Collier's famous one of Darwin. He is hung
quite close to Newman, whose face quite haunts one, it is so pitifully
harried and worried and bullied-looking. They've got a sketch of him
downstairs next-door to Pusey, who looks to have settled down with

aggressive firmness into an argumentative position – Newman's appearance certainly offers no argument for secession. The funniest thing there is a portrait of Bulwer Lytton, portrayed in a striking attitude and a sort of rococo fancy get-up, all over luxuriant black side-whiskers, in a garden! There is also a bust of Queen Elizabeth off her tomb. My hat! She was an ugly old girl!

It is pouring with rain – Hang! I shall not go out to supper. I shall fry an egg.

> With best love
>   Dorothy

[1] Where her own portrait, by Sir William Hutchison, now hangs.
[2] Elizabeth Barrett Browning.

To Her Parents   44 Mecklenburg Square
1 July 1921   W.C.1

Dearest People

Please, I'm sorry I haven't written for such a long time. Things have been very up-and-down and tiresome and pleasant, and I've never known from one minute to another whether I was in high spirits or the depth of gloom.[1] I think if I could get a job I should be more or less permanently in the high spirits, as socially all is going well – lots of parties – theatre and a night-club (!!) last week, teas and things this week, lunch at the Ritz next week, distinguished persons like X ... and Y ... and J. C. Squire coming to tea with me, and so on. Even a victim or so and a gift or so – in a very mild way. Nothing is wrong but the financial side, and I somehow feel, if only I can hang on long enough, I can get on top of that. But oh! 'Tis difficult.

Eleanor Chase is living in town, and we have renewed acquaintance. She is nice and is fond of me, I believe, but she is still what I call tasteless, and that annoys me. I do hate being patronised and advised. It's a pity, because she and I used to be great friends,[2] and I feel she'd like to be still. I think Cambridge rather permanently spoilt her by making her too efficient. That's their way at Girton. . . .

[1] This was the period of her affair with John Cournos.
[2] At the Godolphin School.

To Her Mother   44 Mecklenburg Square
16 July 1921   W.C.1

Dearest Mother –

I'm sorry I haven't written for so long – but I've been waiting for something cheerful to write about. Except for my lunch at the Ritz, which was very pleasant, and a few social things like that, everything has been accursed! Not only do the Poles appear to have more or less dried up, but I can't get my last cheque out of them, though I've written to ask what has happened to it. I suppose it will turn up some time, for they've been very good about payments so far. I've got one friend who *may*, in time and so on, be able to get me into touch with cinema people, and another woman will show some of my work to an editor, but all these things take time, and in the ghastly heat we've been having, I simply haven't had the strength to put pen to paper. I've been wanting to get out of London, and wrote to Dorothy Rowe a week ago, to know if she could have me, thinking the sea would be pleasant, and I could come on to Christchurch later, when the house was freer, but Dorothy hasn't answered – and what is the next move in that case? I can't get the work I want, nor the money I want, nor (consequently) the clothes I want, nor the holiday I want, nor the man I want!![1] – In spite of all these drawbacks, I remain obstinately in the rudest health, when everybody else is played out in the drought. And then people tell me about girls who are oppressed and embarrassed by the possession of an income of £300 a-year, and feel they ought not to have it, and ought to be doing slum-work and being useful to society. I call that pure egotism and spiritual pride. How thankfully would you or I support life under a load of similar embarrassments!

J. C. Squire came to tea the other day, and was, like a Jane Austen hero, 'perfectly amiable', though very drowsy with the heat. I fed him on ices, and he said he hoped I would invite him again, which was flattering, but not pecuniarily helpful – rather the reverse. I wish he'd print that poem he's got of mine, and pay for it! . . .

As for Jim Jaeger, she is a mystery. She is still here, with no job, living, I imagine, entirely on her people, or somebody, and writing something mysterious, which she won't say anything about to anybody. I suspect her of a novel, like everybody else. A novel seems the thing to write now-a-days. I wish I had the application for it. Unfortunately, novels seldom interest me, even to read, and the thought of grinding one out is fearful![2]

I'm so sorry to be depressing and depressed! I dare say it's partly the weather. Don't worry. I'll come home before I starve.

Your loving
Dorothy

[1] i.e. John Cournos, whom she wanted to marry.
[2] D.L.S. was evidently distinguishing between novels and detective stories, of which she read a great many. At this very period she was writing what eventually became *Whose Body?*

To Her Mother   44 Mecklenburg Square
27 July 1921   W.C.1

Dearest Mother

Many thanks for your letter. I'm going down to a friend at Loughton[1] for a few days next Tuesday, and then shall come on home – probably to stay for some time, as I have let my room to Egerton Clarke.[2] I vaguely suggested to Jim Jaeger that she should come[3] some time, but she seems undecided as to plans, and I'll tell her we can't have her at present. I'm inviting a friend[4] for the end of September, but ten to one he won't be able to come. I'll let you know as soon as I hear.

I've been having 'remnant mania' rather badly, and spending such cash as I have on making jumpers at about half-a-crown apiece. It's really wonderful how cheaply one can clothe one's self nowadays if one puts one's mind to it. And I'm going to make delightful under-clothing, all over little purple parrots! I am really awfully domesticated when I like – but I do continue to hate cooking things![5]

On second thoughts, and re-reading your letter, I will give the friend the choice of the end of August or the end of September. He'll be no trouble if he does come, being used to living under pretty uncomfortable conditions and asking nothing but kind treatment – and in any case, he's extremely problematical. He is *not* the young man who entertains me at the Ritz, and will not expect Ritz standards.

I'll be glad to get out of Town for a bit, especially as practically everybody has now left. Also, I'm feeling a bit strenuous, and ready for a rest-cure. . . .

[1] Loughton is in Essex. The friend's name was Mrs Pendred.
[2] A contemporary at Oxford, who also worked for Eric Whelpton at l'Ecole des Roches while D.L.S. was there.
[3] To the rectory at Christchurch.
[4] i.e. John Cournos. This is her first direct mention of him.
[5] But she enjoyed cooking dinners for guests; cf. letter dated 24 July 1922.

To Her Mother   44 Mecklenburg Square
7 October 1921   W.C.1

Dearest Mother

I seize the moment while the iron is heating to write this over-due letter. Life is being very pleasant in spasms . . . Lord Peter is nearly ready to be typed,[1] but I'm feeling rather disgusted with him now he's done. However, that's nothing unusual. I'm going to try him on one or two publishers I have slight influence with, but I don't suppose anything will come of it. No job as yet. Jim is working away on some story or other. I'm trying to write this in the interval of laundering, and it doesn't make for lucidity or consecutiveness. John writes, 'Your mother and dad appear to be quite charming people from your accounts and I shall certainly have to contrive to meet them some day. But perhaps they won't like *The Wall*[2] as well, or the handwriting on it may prove to be a little terrifying.' You must tell me what you think. Personally I think *The Wall* is not nearly so alarming as John thinks it is. Why do all men love to make themselves out such wonderful devils when they aren't anything of the sort? John imagines he's a terrible person! . . .

[1] Her first detective novel was finished but still lacked a title. She had completed it at Christchurch in August and September. This was the period when she had invited John Cournos to stay, but he did not accept. Her parents never in fact met him.
[2] His second novel. D.L.S. had persuaded her parents to read his first novel, *The Mask*, and they appear to have been complimentary about it.

To Her Mother   44 Mecklenburg Square
8 November 1921   W.C.1

Dearest Mother –
    Thanks so much for your jolly letter. What with the dentist and the new Lord Peter[1] and other things I've been a bit tied up this week . . .
    Lord Peter[2] is being typed, and will be ready early next week. I expect he'll cost about £7, curse him! . . . I've been promised introductions to various publishers, but I don't suppose anything will ever come of it. I really haven't the least confidence in the stuff, which is a pity, because I really enjoy turning it out. John was 'nice' enough Friday week in a general way, but I fear he has no sympathy with Lord Peter, being the kind of man who takes his writing seriously and spells Art with a capital A. Norman,[3] on the other hand, is very helpful. I was delighted with a dictum of Philip Guedalla's[4] in the *Daily News*: 'The detective story is the normal recreation of noble minds.' It makes me feel ever so noble! Norman and Jim and I are going to see the grimlies at the Little Theatre on Friday, in the hope of getting the fan-tods[5] if possible! My latest social acquaintance is an ex-convict,[6] so you see I'm getting on! . . .
    I spend all my time reading or writing crimes in the Museum![7] Nice life, isn't it? – I've done the coroner's direction to the jury[8] to-day, and I feel quite exhausted. . . .

[1] She had begun work on *Clouds of Witness*.
[2] Her first novel, soon to be entitled *Whose Body?*
[3] Norman Davey, novelist, author of *The Pilgrim of a Smile* (1921), a novel which D.L.S. much admired and recommended to her father. It was republished by Penguin Books in 1936. It contains a character named Major Bunter.

[4] An essayist and historian (1889–1944).
[5] Slang for cold shivers.
[6] Cf. Lord Peter's ex-convict friend, Rumm, in *Strong Poison* (chapter 13).
[7] The Reading Room of the British Museum, later known as the British Library.
[8] *Clouds of Witness*, conclusion of chapter 1.

To Her Mother   British Museum
No date, but November 1921   Tuesday

Dearest Mother –

Forgive me for not having written more quickly to thank you for
your very, very kind cheque. It is jolly to have paid off that silly little
account and to be straight again.

Fairly straight, at least – but, oh dear! I'm rather distressed at
present, because Miss James[1] seems to want me to turn out a good
deal sooner than I expected. In her last conversation she said
December 5th, which is very near, and I shall either have to find
somewhere else to live – without either money or job! or else give up
beloved London and return ignominiously home. I hoped I should
be able to stay on till Xmas, by which time I might have known a
little more about prospects. As it is, even if, on the 5th, I warehoused
the furniture and came away for a time, it would be rather futile, as
I shall really want to be in town just now to try if there really is the
smallest chance of getting Lord Peter published. Mind you, I haven't
much hopes of him, but after spending so much time on him, and
getting him typed (I'm afraid the bill for that will have to go home
too) it would be absurd not to make *some* energetic effort to place
him. The typist is dawdling over him, it seems to me, but as I haven't
the cash handy I bear up! But when he *does* arrive I ought to trot
him round to various publishers before giving up altogether. – If only
he'd sell! – Though in that case, I'm afraid he could never be 'only
a jolly extra', because as a matter of fact, it takes all one's time and
energy to invent even bad, sensational stories. But there is a market
for detective literature if one can get in, and he might go some way
towards providing bread and cheese. But it's not a bit of use counting
on him, I'm afraid. So few things get accepted – and every time I
look at him, he seems more feeble. – I do wish, my dear, I wasn't
such a hopelessly shaky investment. Do forgive me, and say what you
think I'd better do. . . .

Nothing has happened to me except one very jolly evening with
Norman and Charles Scott Stokes at the play. I dined with Norman
at Isola Bella and we went on to see the Grands Guignols at the Little
Theatre (my treat to him – because he had really given me such a
lot of hospitality and small presents) and Charles joined us at the

theatre. I'd been gloomy and grinding away at a new story and pov-
erty-stricken and bothered for ever so long, and it was good to let out
for one night, and look nice and be taken everywhere in taxis. I do
hope to goodness Norman isn't going to get devoted or anything,
though. That would be the culmination of all tiresomeness! I don't
think there's anything in it, though – I think it's just that he is the
sort that naturally expresses itself in gifts and compliments. What a
bother everything is, isn't it? . . .

    I'm thankful I got a few good garments while I could afford them.
I really shan't need to spend anything much on clothes this winter.

    This is a dreadful letter – full of money – your money! I ought to
be thinking out a murder. But what's the good, unless I can publish
it?

    Yours gratefully and affectionately, but full of wrath against a harsh
world

    With much love
        Dorothy

¹ Her landlady, who was moving.

TO HER PARENTS   44 Mecklenburg Square
24 November 1921   W.C.1

Dearest People . . .

    I have now received proof that 'Lord Peter' is very saleable, but I
anticipate difficulty from the publisher with whom I am at present
negotiating as to terms. If they make an offer at all, they will probably
try to bully me into selling the copyright, which I should on all
accounts be exceedingly unwilling to do. Especially, it would greatly
damage the success of the series, if I produced subsequent Lord
Peters. I shall have to go cautiously, and not accept any offer because
I am flurried into it. I know I shall have both your moral and material
support in this. I am sending the book to a second publisher to see
if I can get an offer of better terms, and I have yet a third and fourth
up my sleeve if the second isn't satisfactory. Of course all this will
take time, but I feel sure it is the best course. I shall take the advice
either of an agent or a solicitor or a person used to the malpractice
of publishers before signing any agreement. If the worst should come
to the worst and I should have to sell the copyright I shall probably
get about £100; on a royalty basis I should get less to begin with –
probably less in the end on that one edition, but the sale of copyright
includes American, foreign, serial and dramatic and film rights – also
cheap editions, and unless things look very black indeed, I shall not
let those go for £100. Of course, the whole thing may fall through: I

have not yet had an offer from the publishers in question, only the reader's opinion; but that was enthusiastic. There seems no reason why I should not get proper terms.

In the second place, I believe I have been very fortunate about getting new rooms. Jim, who kindly offered to look for rooms for me while I was at school,[1] saw for me, and I went and saw afterwards, a delightful little set of three rooms in Gt James St, just the other side of Mecklenburg Sq. They consist of sitting-room, bedroom and kitchen, with use of a new bathroom and lav., which are just being put in. The rent is £70 – only £5 more than I am paying for the one room. It is a long lease – 3 years – but no difficulty will be made about subletting to a proper person, so that in case I had to leave I should make, rather than lose, upon the rooms. It is very easy to let small sets just now – indeed, the difficulty is still to get hold of them. I feel that, if no hitch occurs about this set, I shall have been amazingly lucky. The rooms are quite small, but very pretty, being entirely panelled in white, which has just been repainted and done up. The man told me yesterday that they had written to my references, and that if they were satisfactory I should have the first offer of the rooms.

So you see that, *if* all goes well, I am very favourably placed. Lord Peter is still my chief anxiety, but I am quite sure now that there *is* money in him. I was worried for fear I might have produced a complete white elephant. . . .

I am writing this in prep.! I like this school as schools go; they feed you well and treat you well. The headmistress and staff are particularly nice, and I like the girls, though one or two forms have obviously been giving my unhappy predecessor a hell of a time. At 10 minutes past 12 precisely, I shall proceed to mete out frightfulness in Up. IVa where it is badly needed. The Upper V German division, supposed to be tartars, have come to heel in the most charming way; I wonder if they have anything in pickle for me! . . .

[1] She had taken a temporary job at the Haberdashers' School for Girls in Acton, West London. (The school moved to Elstree, Hertfordshire in 1974.) She entered on her appointment on 17 November and left on 14 December 1921. The salary was six guineas a week. In the same year she had taken temporary work at Clapham High School (for one month) and at South Hampstead High School for two weeks.

To Her Mother   c / o Miss Jaeger
19 December 1921   35 Cambridge Place
                                                     Praed St. W.

Dearest Mother –

Please forgive my not having written sooner. I have been in such a terrible rush, finishing off the Acton job, and then hurrying about to get and make curtains etc. for the flat and pack up and so on. I have been rather tired and depressed mostly at the end of the day, and there is no news of Lord Peter. . . .

Nobody can feel more acutely than I do the unsatisfactoriness of my financial position. I wish I could get a reasonable job, or that I could know one way or another whether I shall be able to make money by writing. I applied, as you wished, for the Bromley[1] job, but the Headmistress thought, and I agreed with her, that it really was too far out for me. I should have had to get up at 7 every morning and start on a long train journey, and get back, with luck, perhaps, at 6 p.m. The post itself was a hard one, with an average of 6 lessons a day, and all large classes. I daresay another temporary will turn up – this is a sickly term! – If not, I shall sell those fiddles, and, with the money I still have, I can live this term, if Tootles can let me have the rent. They demand rents in advance, the blighters! I made a fuss on principle, but I imagine a large percentage of Bloomsbury residents habitually abscond without paying, and it makes them careful. This lot is due Xmas Day – i.e. a fortnight after. During the next three months I shall hope to get some definite offer for Lord Peter. If any shark offers to buy the copyright, I will ask you again whether I shall accept it or not. It would be a perfectly scandalous arrangement, but perhaps it would be worth it to me, to save this perpetual worry.

If you like, I'll make a sporting offer – that if you can manage to help me to keep going till next summer, then, if Lord Peter is still unsold, I will chuck the whole thing, confess myself beaten, and take a permanent teaching job. There will be a Mod. Lang.[2] post vacant then at Acton, and I feel certain that if I were to apply for it, Miss Sproules[3] would give me the preference over any other candidate, and I have liked teaching at Acton better than in any other school I have ever struck. Will you think over this suggestion? – I hope it mayn't come to that. – One reason why I am so keen about Lord Peter is that writing him keeps my mind thoroughly occupied, and prevents me from wanting too badly the kind of life I *do* want, and see no chance of getting.[4] . . .

Yours ever with love, and apologies for being such a failure

Ever your grateful
Dorothy

[1] In Kent.
[2] Modern Languages, involving the teaching of French and German.
[3] On the appointment form, in the space headed 'Post, if any, taken up after leaving the School', Miss Sproules (or her secretary) had entered: 'Became v. well known as writer and speaker.'
[4] In an article entitled 'How I Came to Invent the Character of Lord Peter Wimsey' (*Harcourt Brace News*, New York, vol. 1, 15 July 1936, pp. 1–2), D.L.S. wrote: 'Lord Peter's

large income . . . I deliberately gave him. After all it cost me nothing and at that time I was particularly hard up and it gave me pleasure to spend his fortune for him. When I was dissatisfied with my single unfurnished room I took a luxurious flat for him in Picca-dilly. When my cheap rug got a hole in it, I ordered him an Aubusson carpet. When I had no money to pay my bus fare I presented him with a Daimler double-six, upholstered in a style of sober magnificence, and when I felt dull I let him drive it.'

To Her Mother
31 December 1921

24 Great James St[1]
W.C.1

Darling Mother –

Just a line to thank you a thousand times for the splendid consign-ment of cutlery. I feel a regular housewife – and really, all these things are rather interesting. I'm glad you remembered my preference for the knives which fulfil their destiny as cutting instruments; I hope I shall be able to keep them clean, and not rub them into daggers, or those curious shapes with a thin waist and a blob on the end that one boot-boy – was it the toothsome Eric Wallace? – used to give us at Bluntisham.[2]

Also much thanks for the table cloths, which will be a great help. I'm glad Tootles is coming up on Monday, because I'm really in love with the flat, and I hope he will be, too, though it's so tiny, he will hardly be able to stand upright in it.[3] I'm greatly pleased with my new curtains, which are of a very loud colour and pattern, and which I bought in fear and trembling at Barkers. My pictures are going to look lovely on my white-panelled walls. I haven't finished staining the floor yet. – You'd laugh to see me tackling all these domestic jobs; I really think I don't do them so badly, all things considered. The worst job was cleaning the gas-stove, which had been left filthy – but I look rather well scrubbing the kitchen floor, too. I'm going to get a woman in presently, but I'm not hurrying to fix up with her, till I've got everything perfectly straight, and know precisely how much I want her to do.

I've got terrible arrears of letters to make up, so forgive this hurried screed. Life is made a burden to me at the moment by an Irish stew two rooms off, which must not on any account be allowed to boil – I keep on thinking it's boiling itself on the sly, and rush away to supervise it!

Heaps of love. All news to Tootles on Monday.

Your ever grateful
Dorothy

The wooden spoon most active in the matter of the stew.

[1] This is the earliest extant letter written from this address, where D.L.S. was to live until 1929, when she moved to Witham, Essex, though keeping on the London flat for visits to town.
[2] Before the days of stainless steel, knives had to be rubbed clean with emery powder on a knife-board. This tended to change their shape.
[3] Her father was over six feet tall.

To Her Mother   24 Great James St
18 January 1922   W.C.1

Dearest Mother –

At last I've time to thank you for your generous cheque. I've got a nice little black coat-frock at Derry and Tom's, and a splendid black corduroy skirt, which ought to be no end useful. I'll see what can be done about the coat. The frock is very plain and simple, but a beautiful gaberdine. I like black things to be plain, don't you?

Aunt G. has just been to lunch. . . . By a sort of miracle, the lunch (roast ribs of beef with roast potatoes followed by a rice pudding) turned out very well; I was a bit doubtful, rice puddings being dubious affairs. However, she was quite impressed. She also liked the flat very much, and was most discreet about not barging into the kitchen just when I was clawing things out of the oven. I've got one or two little labour-saving gadgets which she greatly admired, including the multiple steamer aforementioned, and a sort of patent claw for lifting hot tins out of the oven – a useful device which I must bring some time for Annie, as it saves many burnt fingers and greasy cloths; it is particularly handy for basting. I'm beginning to think that my bent is domesticity after all. Do come up and stay with me some time and I'll jolly well show you!

'Lord Peter' still hangs fire; I've asked Ward Lock's man to tea, in hopes I may be able to poke the directors through him. I gather they like the book, but wail that times are bad and they can't take risks on unknown authors – the old story! I've put in an advertisement about the fiddle, and hope something may come of it.

John turned up the other day and was all right, though deeply buried in *Babel*.[1] He and I have had a difference, though, on a point of practical Christianity (to which he strongly objects!)[2] and I may hear no more of him. . . .

[1] John Cournos's third novel.
[2] The 'difference' concerned the use of contraceptives. (See her letters to John Cournos.)

To Her Parents   24 Great James St
14 February 1922   W.C.1

Dearest People –

I've nothing cheery to say, except that the Rowes have asked me
to go down to Bournemouth for a week or so; so I'm departing on
the 25th, leaving Cournos (who has finished the great work at last –
130,000 words, good gad!) to keep the flat warm in my absence.[1] I
couldn't let it for so short a time, and it will save his money, so it
seems a convenient arrangement. . . .

No good news of Lord Peter. I got exasperated, and sent him to
an agent – who immediately died! I think of advertising him as 'the
book that killed an agent'. . . .

So sorry Aunt Maud isn't over her trouble yet – the cold is trying.
You must be frozen down there. My little flat is warm, except when
the wind is in the east! – Thank you enormously for the splendid
stores of butter etc. I can't quite keep up with the consumption of
tea – I've got enough now to last me a bit, so please don't send any
next week. – I've got a pair of sheets for John, and pillow-cases, which
I bought cheap in the sales, by way of having a pair for any stray
guest. If he stays here very long he might have the others as they
return from the wash, but I dare say he won't be here more than a
week. I hope he won't leave the cupboards full of mouldy sandwiches,
as Egerton did! . . .

[1] The 'difference' mentioned in the preceding letter did not prevent John Cournos from
taking advantage of this offer.

To Muriel Jaeger   24 Great James St
undated fragment ?1922   W.C.1

. . . Norman Davey rolled up (literally, in a taxi) on Thursday, *dreadfully* cross. He'd been lunching with a man who, instead of listening
to what N.D. had to say about himself, had thoughtlessly endeavoured
to tell him his own views about something, and I was told, with an
engaging frankness, that I was expected to act as an antidote! Thus
encouraged, I did my best, with, I may say, very satisfactory results
as far as the gentleman's temper was concerned. The following dialogue took place at parting:–

He (*at the front door*) – Will you come and have lunch with me some
day?
She (*opening the door*) I should be delighted.

He. Will you really? That will be splendid.

She (*offering an elegant hand*) I will remember not to talk to you.

He. You never do. (*On the door-step*) You let *me* talk to *you*.

She. Alas! All my little wiles are seen through.

He. That's what's so nice. You are one of those delightful women who know how to manage a man –

She (*curtseys*)

He. – the kind of woman I love.

(*Exeunt severally*)

Even allowing for the fact that the gentleman had lunched heavily, I think I must have succeeded in concealing my natural disposition in a manner which does more credit to my dramatic powers than to my religious principles.

(Talking of religious principles, I have been greatly fortified and encouraged by reading Benjamin Kidd's *Science of Power*.[1] How delightful to find one man who really understands what women think of his sex!) . . .

[1] Benjamin Kidd (1858–1916), Irish sociologist, special correspondent of *The Times*, was the author of *Social Evolution* (1894, translated into ten languages), *Principles of Western Civilization* (1902) and *The Principal Laws of Sociology* (1909). *The Science of Power*, published two years after his death, contains two chapters on the future influence of women on society: 'Woman the Psychic Centre' (8) and 'The Mind of Woman' (9).

To Her Mother   24 Great James St
20 February 1922   W.C.1

Dearest Mother

Ever so many thanks for your two letters and the butter etc. etc., and to Tootles for his generous offer to pay my fare. As to what is going to happen to me, I know nothing – but I have promised that if nothing turns up before the summer I will look for a school job. I'll stick to that.

Dear – I've got a charwoman, who is perfectly reliable, to do for John while he's here – she has been doing a little work each week for me – but who in the world, except John, is going to be 'about the flat' while I'm away? A flat isn't rooms – it's a house – you go out and lock it up and take the key with you. The sheets will be as safe as the pictures or the furniture. Many thanks for sending them. J. will be here 10 days or a fortnight, and I will explain to him about them. . . .

John was here to dinner last night – a very dainty dinner, though I say it; though he was too tired to do it full justice. He is exhausted with his work on *Babel*, and was hoping to be able to take a complete

rest. Unhappily, his American sales of *The Wall* have turned out badly
– owing, as *he* says, to the slackness, deliberate or otherwise, of the
publisher – and he is short of the money he had counted on, and has
to go on working. He has no kind parents to fall back on, you see –
in fact, all *his* people do is to clamour for money. And he has worked
so hard, and suffered so much – he deserves something better of
life. . . .

TO HER PARENTS   S. Anne's[1]
3 March 1922   Surrey Road
                                                Bournemouth

Dearest People . . .
   I'm enjoying myself greatly as usual. I came away from town in
deep gloom, because Hill,[2] who offered me £8 or £9 last year for my
fiddle, simply refused to look at it this year at all – so that source of
cash is done away, unless I can get rid of it privately. However, for
a few days I am dismissing all thoughts of £.s.d.![3] I've got hold of Sir
Arthur Marshall,[4] whom I've mentioned to you as a barrister and
Liberal political light, and pumped him for all sorts of information
for the new story[5] I'm writing, which has been hung up for some time
for lack of legal details. He is being simply sweet about it, and taking
a tremendous interest in working out the details. It's a very unusual
case – a peer tried for murder – of course before the House of Lords
– and he didn't know the procedure himself when I asked; but he
made a point of finding out all about it yesterday from Lord Russell[6]
(who was tried for bigamy some time ago), and took me out to coffee
this morning and simply filled me up with priceless information. Also
he has promised to take me some time when there is an interesting
case on in the Lords to show me what it looks like. He says it's very
jolly to see – all the Lords in their robes, and counsel in full dress
with full-bottomed wigs! He's such an old dear – sometimes people
just giggle and make fun of one instead of giving one useful information.
   John is established in No. 24, and enjoying himself, I hope. I'm
glad to have him there, as he is a decent, responsible body, and will
keep things nice. . . .

[1] The address of Dorothy Rowe.
[2] The music teacher at Ecole des Roches.
[3] Pounds, shillings and pence.
[4] Sir Arthur Marshall (1870–1956).
[5] *Clouds of Witness* (T. Fisher Unwin, 1926).
[6] The second husband of Elizabeth Mary, by her first marriage Countess von Arnim,
author of *Elizabeth and her German Garden, Enchanted April* and other novels.

To Her Parents   24 Great James St
26 April 1922   W.C.1

Dearest People

I've been hoping to have something pleasing to write about, but
nothing has happened, except that I've seen my agent[1] again and he
still seems very confident that he will be able to get Lord Peter off
with somebody. I'm rather worried because the Poles haven't paid
me – they now owe me £14 and I ought to have had it 3 weeks ago.
I hope they've not gone bankrupt again! I remember there was a long
pause about this time last year, but it's very irritating to be hard up
when one really has plenty of money! However, doubtless they will
fork out before long.

My new pupil seems quite an intelligent girl, and I think I shall
be able to cope with the work all right. If so, there may be other
pupils from the same source. It is a 'crammers' in Baker St (nice and
handy) and I very much like the people who run it. On the whole,
the financial situation seems a trifle more hopeful than it did a month
or two ago, though just at the minute, owing to the Poles, it's a bit
straitened.

My new Lord Peter book is going to be a corker, only I'm held up
by some legal details. I have written to Sir Arthur Marshall for assistance, but he hasn't answered yet. Perhaps he is away from home,
because I'm sure he'd help willingly. He has been awfully decent
about it so far and given a lot of useful assistance, but I have involved
myself in a murder trial in the House of Lords, which is no joke. The
immediate trouble is a question about the relevancy of some evidence,
which is of vital importance to the plot, so I'm a bit stuck till I get
counsel's advice upon it. . . .

Oh, dear! I *do* hope something will come of Lord Peter! I really
feel that if an agent is really keen upon him it must mean that he *has*
monetary possibilities, because it is not to an agent's interest to stuff
himself with dud authors. And I have plenty of ideas for other books
if this first one gets taken. After all, I'm sure writing is much more
my job than office work or teaching. I don't mind these separate
coachings, such as the one I'm doing now, but big classes of youthful
people are not in my line[2] . . .

[1] Andrew Dakers.
[2] So far as is known, this was the last of D.L.S.' teaching jobs.

*Among the many jobs for which D.L.S. had been applying was one as a copy-
writer with the advertising firm of S. H. Benson. For two months she heard*

nothing. Then in May she was offered a job for a trial period at a salary of £4 a week. In June the appointment was confirmed. This was a turning point. She remained with Benson's for nine years.

To Her Parents   24 Great James St
24 May 1922   W.C.1

Dearest People –

It is hot – it was hot yesterday and it will be hot to-morrow. I am exhausted with trying to find arguments for using tea and margarine. I am infuriated with Hutchinsons, who are *still* humming and hawing over 'Lord Peter', and have calmly demanded a synopsis of the second book before they decide on the first. Brutes!

The office is all right, and fairly cool. The people are quite decent. I've no idea whether I shall make anything of this business. The man who cuts my copy about is perfectly amiable, but that's sometimes a bad sign. I'll know better later on – I have a room to myself, thank goodness!

I had a lovely time with Norman last week, and looked uncommon nice, thanks to Tootles' very generous cheques. It really is a dream of a frock! – Norman is much thinner, which is a good thing in some ways, but he doesn't look well and complains of still getting bad attacks of pain.

I've waited to write to know a) about this work b) about Lord Peter (curse him!) or I'd have written before to thank you, Tootles, for the money and your awfully kind letter, and whoever sent the asparagus for that excellent thought. Norman is coming to dinner at the flat on Friday. If this weather goes on, he will be allowed nothing but hors d'oeuvres and mayonnaise sauce!

    With much love
      Your own
        Dorothy

To Her Parents   24 Great James St
1 June 1922   W.C.1

Darling People –

I don't know whether you have observed that it is extremely hot. In London, the warmth is distinctly noticeable. The roofs and pavements store up each day's heat and add it to that of the next. My office is under the roof. When I go out, the pavement is under my feet. I am hot. I have taken off all my clothing but the bare necessary for decency.

I am going to Oxford for Whitsun. I hoped it would be cooler there, but John says he is positively withered with heat. But then I don't think he goes on the river. I shall go on the river, and the mosquitoes will raise large lumps on my hands and legs and neck and face. – I shall be staying with Mrs Brabant. . . .

I enclose an advt. for *Sailor Savouries*, which was the first bit of copy I drew up, and has now made its appearance. It is all lies from beginning to end – at least, a tissue of exaggeration. I did some things on 'Lytup' Handbags which are more amusing. You shall have them when they appear. But this is just to show you that I really am doing a little work at least.

I don't know whether they are finding my work satisfactory. Mr Jayne blue-pencils a good deal of it. He is rather a dear, and very kind and human – but sometimes those nice polite people are just being nice and polite, and politely bow you away at the end of the month's trial. So I don't know. But Mr Jayne has just 'taken to' a scheme of mine for advertising tobacco, and perhaps that is a good sign. – Mr Green, the head of the department, I don't see. He interviewed me on the first day, and has since avoided me. . . .

To Her Mother   24 Great James St
13 June 1922   W.C.1

Darling Mother –

Thank you ever so very much for your birthday present and good wishes. Bless you lots of times!

I had an awful good time in Oxford, running about everywhere and seeing everybody. Mrs Brabant sent you her love, and was frightfully sorry to have missed you when you called. I saw Aunt Maud and Margaret, who both looked and seemed rather jaded with the heat. They seemed to think that Dorothy Scott Stokes and I, who had come down from baking London to find coolness, looked fresher and fitter than anybody they'd seen for a long time! I believe town must be rather a healthy place after all. – I saw Miss Penrose, who was uncommonly gracious – also Dr Chance, whom I think you've heard of, and who seemed pleased to see and talk scandal with somebody who hadn't the North Oxford point of view. I think she finds Oxford rather a tiresome and gossipy place, as undoubtedly it is for a singularly attractive woman on her own. As usual she is besieged with admirers and doesn't really seem to want any of them!

I have got a lodger! – The mice were getting so bad in my kitchen that I asked my char to find me a kitten, and she has just produced one. It arrived to-day – a vulgar little tabby Tom, but very quick and lively. I should think he would be a very good mouser. He will be a bit of a nuisance just at first till he settles down, as I have to be out so much, but he will soon get used to things. I shall either call him Peter, after Lord Peter, or Agag, because he walks delicately.[1]

I have received the enclosed from Dakers.[2] I suppose I shall have to get another copy typed, as I only had the two originally, one of which is already in America and the other with Hutchinson's. If Benson's keep me on, I shall have no great difficulty in paying for it. I'll get it done cheaply this time – if also nastily, *tant pis!*[3] Of course, if I could place the book in America and do well with it there, England wouldn't matter. The sales this side simply don't count in comparison – so I think it's worth while to try everything.

I don't know about Benson's yet. Sometimes I think they mean to fire me! – to-day Mr Jayne muttered something about what was likely to happen in July, which sounded hopeful – but that may have been an oversight. He also passed two bits of copy without alteration, which is all to the good. But I'll know on Saturday.

Meanwhile I enclose the Poles' cheque for £8 which I promised to send Dad when he was so generous about my new frock. I'm sorry there's been so much delay, but they didn't send it till Whit Monday.

I saw John in Oxford and he paid a flying visit to town yesterday. I don't think it could have been he you saw in the Café – if you mean the Cadena – for that isn't one of his haunts. His publishers are likewise being tiresome fellows, but he is undaunted, and is planning a vast poem (!!) and another novel (!!!).

Norman is in France. Meyerstein[4] came in the other night and read me 2000 odd lines of a mediaeval poem, which took him till 1 a.m. – me sitting sewing and listening, and feeling that tight feeling coming on all over my face! Still, it was quite a jolly poem.

I must stop now and write a line to Aunt Mabel.

Ever your loving and grateful
    Dorothy

[1] 'Then said Samuel, Bring ye hither to me Agag the king of Amalekites. And Agag came unto him delicately' (1 Samuel XV, 32). The Dowager Duchess of Denver has a cat called Agag. (See *Busman's Honeymoon*, Epithalamion II.)
[2] Andrew Dakers, her agent.
[3] So much the worse, who cares?
[4] E. H. W. Meyerstein (1889–1952), a contemporary of hers at Oxford.

To Her Parents   24 Great James St
15 June 1922   W.C.1

Dearest People –

Just a line to say that all is gas and gaiters. Benson's want me to stay on, and Mr Jayne tells me I am doing extraordinarily well and that I have 'every quality which makes for success in advertising', and that very few people have those qualities. He added that though at present I hadn't enough experience to command more than £4 a week, the question of salary would come along in due course, and I should get a rise before very long. – So I'm actually settled in a job, and quite a nice job with prospects, too. I feel so surprised I hardly know myself, but it's a tremendous relief. And I want to thank you again and again ever so much for the wonderful patience with which you've stood by while everything was so unsatisfactory, – never cursed me or told me I was a failure, and have forked out such a lot of money and been altogether ripping to me. . . .

As regards money now. I'm going to suggest, Tootles, that while I'm getting £4, perhaps you would like to pay me an allowance to cover the rent and nothing else, till I see exactly how expenses work out. Then when I am getting more, I hope to be able to release you from all financial responsibility concerning me. Tell me how this strikes you.

Hutchinson's are still nibbling, but won't say anything definite.

With lots of love
    Yours cheerily
        Dorothy

To Her Parents   24 Great James St
19 July 1922   W.C.1

Dearest People –

It's sweet of you to jubilate, but don't jubilate too loud or too soon! There are lots of slips between literary cups and the public lips. The result of Liveright's[1] American offer, which includes the Canadian rights, has been to make Hutchinson's withdraw theirs, since they refuse to publish without the Canadian rights. However, we should have turned him (Hutchinson) down in any case, as his contract was not satisfactory when it eventually turned up. Meanwhile, of course, Liveright's offer is only by cable, and may turn out to have snags in it when his amplifying letter arrives next week. And in any case, we've got to begin all over again in England, though with the added prestige of the American offer behind us. And in any case, publication in

America secures my copyright here. So you see how slow and complicated it all is. I have asked my agent to come to dinner next week,
and hope to get more details out of him then. I think he is working
very hard for [me] and looking after my interests well. . . .

[1] Boni and Liveright, the American publishers, brought out the first edition of *Whose
Body?* in 1923.

To Her Mother   24 Great James St
24 July 1922   W.C.1

Dearest Mother . . .
   I had John to dinner on Saturday – and the dinner was *perfect*. I
had 5 courses, and they were all thoroughly successful, and none of
them came out of tins – except the jelly mixture, of course – Here is
the menu:–

Wines and Liqueurs	*Dinner*
Vermouth	*Hors d' Oeuvre*
French: *Noilly-Prat*	Grape-fruit *rafraîchi*
Italian: *Martinazzi*	(on ice with whipped cream)
Wine	*Potage*
Red Spanish Burgundy	*Consommé aux vermicelles*

Rôti
Beefsteak *à l'anglaise*
Potatoes
Salad
Dessert
Fruit jelly with cream
(natural fruit in calves-foot orange jelly)
Savoury
Baked mushrooms
en casserole
Coffee *Grand Marnier Cordon Rouge*

Ain't I a little wonder? On Wednesday I propose to give Mrs Pendred
and Mr Dakers the following:–

Hors d' Oeuvre	*Rôti*
Variés	*Côtelettes de mouton garnies*
Potage	Potatoes
Tomato Cream	*Petits pois*
Entrée	*Dessert*
Mayonnaise Egg	Fruit salad *au vin blanc*

Wines, coffee and liqueur as before. I do *love* cooking nice dinners! . . .

Best love
    Dorothy

To Her Mother   24 Great James St
27 July 1922   W.C.1

Dearest Mother . . .

Mr Dakers came to dinner last night with great *éclat* and success.
My dear, though I says it, it was a damned good dinner! Mrs Pendred
(the friend I mentioned) came early and helped me to get all the
courses ready, and really there were very few waits considering. Mr
D. charmed me very much by troubling to turn up in evening dress,[1]
in which he looks thoroughly ornamental. After dinner we had a lively
discussion of many things – werewolves, religion, marriage, fashions
in dress and the mechanicalness of the present civilisation, and separated, well pleased, about midnight.

He tells me that the American publisher has written about *Lord
Peter* and it is all quite satisfactory, so the matter is clinched and
settled. So that's all perfect and splendid, and I shall get $250 anyhow,
whether it's a success or not. That will only be on publication, of
course, which won't be quite yet, as they will try to get it taken as a
serial first. If they succeed in that, there will be quite a lot of dollars
forthcoming – but of course, I don't know whether the magazine
people will think the story will serialise well. – $250 is between £50
and £60 at the present rate of exchange.

There's a good deal of work on hand at the office now, and most
people are away, so I'm kept busy. Mr Green tells me I'm doing very
well. There is a new girl coming soon, so I shall no longer be the
little stranger. . . .

[1] i.e. tails and white tie, a compliment indeed.

To Her Parents   24 Great James St
28 November 1922   W.C.1

Dearest People –

I'm sorry I've been so long a-writing, but now I've begun I don't
seem to have much to say, except that my fur coat[1] is a great joy
in this frosty weather, and makes me quite oblivious of changes of
temperature. It looks very jolly, too, and everybody admires it
greatly. . . .

I'm feeling a bit dull just at present – so many people seem to be away – especially all my new friends. John hasn't so much as sent me a post-card since he went,[2] though I hear from Dakers that he is alive and well, only very busy . . . Mrs Pendred is a very good friend to me, and I go round there a lot. . . .

The office is always an amusement – I was really wonderfully lucky to get a job that suited me so well. Of course, some days are dull with nothing doing (to-day, for instance) but others are full of energy and rush – and all the people continue to be nice to me. So let's thank Heaven for the good things and put up with the rest as best we may.

I *knew* Aunt Maud and Margaret wouldn't be comfortable in a French family – however, they're there for a year, and they'll have to shake down. Of course the W.C. opens out of the kitchen – where should it open out of? They ought to be thankful it doesn't open out of the larder. The red-and-white checked American cloth[3] on the table is the regular thing in the bourgeois household – it was used everywhere at Les Roches and is perfectly recognised as a part of French social life. . . .

[1] A Christmas present from her mother.
[2] D.L.S. had put an end to the affair and John Cournos had returned to the USA.
[3] Oilcloth.

Left lonely by the departure of John Cournos, who had not 'sent her so much as a post-card', D.L.S. made friends with a man who was staying with the tenants in the flat above hers. This was Bill White, a car salesman and motor engineer. Frustrated by her inconclusive relationship with Cournos, she entered into a casual affair, which neither she nor Bill intended to be permanent. It resulted in the birth of a son, John Anthony, on 3 January 1924, in Southbourne, Hampshire. It is not known why she chose this area. Southbourne is near Bournemouth, where Dorothy Rowe lived, but the latter said she knew nothing of the son until after D.L.S.' death.

To Her Mother   24 Great James St
18 December 1922   W.C.1

Dearest Mother –

Don't faint – I am coming home for Xmas on Saturday with a man and a motor-cycle, with request that you will kindly give same a kind welcome and a few words of friendly cheer.

It's not anyone you know – it's a poor devil who has been staying with the people above me, and whom I chummed up with one week-end, finding him left lonely, so to speak, and he's been very prettily grateful and has taken me out a lot on the bike. But he simply has not a red cent or a roof, and his job has gone bankrupt for the moment – the job being motors – so that, though he can always get petrol for nothing (hence the joy-rides) – he can get nothing else – and one can't eat petrol or sleep in it. That being so, and his friends departing for Xmas, and the poor blighter's own home being in some ungodly and far-off place, and him obliged to be in town again after Xmas – and so on – I said, Would he save me my train fares home in exchange for his board and lodging, so to speak. He was really extraordinarily grateful! – My God! I've been lonely and poor enough alone in London to know what it feels like – and I know you'll have a fellow-feeling for the jobless. – So expect us some time Saturday – Don't be alarmed – he's an absolutely rock-bottom, first-class driver with safety attachment, and all that. Brooklands is his native heath, so to speak – engine-trouble an agreeable excuse for a wayside cigarette – no more. His name is Bill White and I can vouch for his behaviour. Intellect isn't exactly his strong point – I mean, literary intellect – he knows all about cars, and how to sail a boat and so on – and in fact he's the last person you'd ever expect me to bring home, but he's really quite amiable, and will be desperately grateful for a roof over his head . . .

To Her Mother   24 Great James St
8 January 1923   W.C.1

Dearest Mother –

Many thanks for letter and washing. There really isn't any news, except that I've got my arm-chair and it's a beauty. The only drawback is that it's nearly as big as the flat! It was a 12-guinea one, and the Midland let me have it for £9.9.0,[1] in consideration of my being at Benson's.

Otherwise nothing very much, except that I've fed Bill[2] and gone out with him and seen Dorothy Scott Stokes and other people, and bought a few necessary garments. (And à propos of feeding Bill, I'm getting more and more ingenious in the cookery line!) I haven't had time yet to go and see about your tea-pot without a spout, but I haven't forgotten it, or Annie's pan-lifter.

Things are much as usual at the office. Mr Greene has cut short his holiday for some reason, and returned to-day. I don't anticipate any rise in salary at present, as I hear that times are rather bad, and we have lost two important accounts lately. However, we shall see. At present my ambition is to present Mr Jayne with 20 pieces of margarine copy at once! I've done 15 – but I'm afraid he'll ask for them before I complete my score.

There's to be an office dance on the 25th – so I'll have to get a few more lessons out of Bill. Yes, he is getting an occasional week's wages now – enough to pay for an attic in a revolting slum off Theobald's Rd. *My* neighbourhood is aristocratic by comparison! . . .

[1] Nine guineas (*i.e.* nine pounds and nine shillings).
[2] The relationship with Bill White was now established and he had become dependent on D.L.S. for meals.

To Her Parents   S. H. Benson
26 January 1923   Kingsway Hall
                                                        Kingsway

Dearest People –

All is well – the dance[1] went off excellently last night. Too many women, but Bill came and did his duty nobly! I'm full of yawns, and can't seem to find anything to say about Colman's Starch,[2] which is the commodity I am supposed to be advertising. When I have said 'Polish those collars off in no time', and 'Beware of Stickfast Starch', I seem to be at the end of my available headlines.

Bill is working as a fitter now on a small weekly wage – though, honestly, if I didn't feed him pretty regularly I don't quite know what would happen to him, poor wretch! However, he's a good little soul, and very easily kept amused, and has promised to stain my sitting-room floor for me, which is a great joy. I've now got two beautiful Persian rugs, which look ever so jolly, and match the curtains very well. The armchair is covered in black and gold, very good for not showing the dirt. . . .

I'm having too busy a time to get on with the new Lord Peter stories. Otherwise all is well.

Best love to all
  Dorothy

[1] At S. H. Benson's, to which Bill White went as D.L.S.' partner.
[2] She was writing from the office.

To Her Mother   24 Great James St
15 February 1923   W.C.1

Dearest Mother . . .

Nothing much has happened to me, except that Bill has stained
my sitting-room floor for me and it looks very nice. We had arranged
with Laura[1] and her boy and Norman Davey to go and dance last
night at Cricklewood.[2] Laura has been taking lessons and the boy
too, and she was very keen on 'humanising' Norman and 'making
him' come out and be ordinary and less superior and so on, so we
arranged to go, and N.D. took a preliminary private dancing-lesson.
So Bill, after a hard day's manual labour at his shop, and I, after the
usual office grind, came home, washed and changed, had our dinner
quickly and went round to pick up the others. Lo! and behold! there
they were, lounging round the fire in an atmosphere you could cut
with a knife, saying 'Oh, it was such a foggy evening and Cricklewood
was so far and they didn't want to go and weren't dressed and they'd
quite decided in their own minds that we shouldn't want to go either
and "do be matey, Dorothy, and sit down and be comfortable with
us."' And Norman, roasting his posterior before the fire and looking
all sleek and oily saying in a haw-haw voice that it really was horrid
out-of-doors – this to Bill, who'd been testing motor-cycles all day in
fog and rain and inches deep of liquid mud. I was so angry, I could
hardly speak, and I found afterwards that Bill was just as bad – and
I told Norman not to try and come the heavy over me, and the whole
lot of them that they were damned unsporting and Bill and I stormed
out of the house and went to Hammersmith Palais de Danse[3] alone
– and my blood's boiling still. I hate these soft-gutted people. And
Laura, with all her talk about humanising Norman, simply taking
the line of least resistance and treating Bill and me like a couple of
fools – after we'd taken all that trouble – I'm going to speak my mind
next time I see any of that crowd!

Did I tell you I'd heavily snubbed J. C. Squire about Christmas-
time? I forget. Anyway, months ago I asked him to tea, and he neither
came nor wrote, so I thought he was damn rude and let him slide.
Towards Christmas he wrote as follows: 'Dear Miss Sayers. Are you
still about? If so, may I come and have tea with you?' I thought this
was adding insult to injury, so replied 'Alas, you are too late. Months
ago when I asked you, you neither wrote nor came, and now I am
at work every week-day. But if you would really like to see me and
hear the story of How I Sold My Book in America, could we not meet
one day at lunch?' – No answer for a long time, and I thought he
was thoroughly offended at the snubbing tone of my letter, but a day
or two ago I got an invitation to lunch for next Tuesday! I graciously

accepted, begging him to appoint a spot that I could get to, not too far from Kingsway Hall, and received the reply that the great man would call for me at Benson's in person on Tuesday at one o'clock! – Treat 'em rough, that's the way, what? I *won't* have people rude to me, I don't care what they're editors of.

'Lord Peter' – the name of the book is called *Haddock's Eyes*, but that's only what it's called, you know[4] – the book really *is Whose Body?* – will be published in the States this Spring, I believe. . . .

[1] It is not known who Laura was.
[2] In north-west London. A palais de danse in Cricklewood is mentioned in the short story, 'The Unsolved Puzzle of the Man with No Face', *Lord Peter Views the Body* (Gollancz, 1928).
[3] In west London.
[4] Cf. Lewis Carroll, *Through the Looking-Glass*, chapter 8. Quoting Lewis Carroll was evidently a family habit.

TO HER PARENTS   24 Great James St
5 June 1923[1]   W.C.1

Dearest People –

So glad you approve of *Whose Body?* – Many thanks for helpful list of misprints. There wouldn't have been so many if I had been able to see a review proof. However, it doesn't matter, and I'll be able to see that the English edition is all right. By the way, I'm not sending any copies of the American edition to aunts etc., because it would be a great mistake to set anyone talking about it or trying to get hold of it before it is obtainable in England. So till then, we'll keep quiet about it.

I've found a place to go and write in – a friend of mine was there, and says they do you proud for thirty-five shillings a week (2 rooms), which is cheap enough. It is

c / o Mrs Bowler
    Hyde Cottage
    Bovingdon
    Herts –

I decided in the end that I must have a place fairly near town, so that I can run up and consult the B. Museum in case of necessity. It is a very awkward thing to be cut off from one's references; I found this with *Whose Body?* and the new book[2] is much more complicated. I shall be glad to get away, as this weather, combined with the coldness of the office, has given me a beast of a cold. . . .

[1] By this date D.L.S. must have known she was pregnant. Her holiday gave her an opportunity to think about her predicament. She decided to have the baby but to keep

its existence a secret from her family and friends. This decision had a crucial effect on
the rest of her life.
² She was still working on *Clouds of Witness*.

To Her Mother   24 Great James St
8 June 1923   W.C.1

Dearest Mother –
    Thank you very, very much for your birthday present.¹ As soon as
I get back to town I shall buy something suitable to whatever weather
is then current! – I'm so glad you enjoyed *Whose Body?* – the scene
with Sir Julian Freke² is one of my own favourites, so I'm glad it
thrilled you!
    You'll be rejoiced to hear that Mr Greene has come up to the
scratch and raised my screw another 30 bob³ – quite right, of course,
but still, pleasing! – Also I shall now be entitled to the bonus when
it falls due, so I'm not doing so badly!
    My cold is almost quite gone, thank you – only a bit of cough
remains, which will speedily clear off now the weather shows signs of
warming up. I go off to-morrow to Bovingdon, with a bag of books
in one hand and my cat in the other – the perfect travelling spinster!
I'll write again from there –
    With best love to everyone and again many, many thanks

    Your loving
    Dorothy

¹ D.L.S. was now thirty years old.
² Chapter 11.
³ Shillings.

To Her Parents   Kingsway Hall
No date, but 17? August 1923

Dearest People –
    Mustard again!¹ It is astonishing that they should want so many
advertisements for mustard. However, let's hope that's the end of it
for a bit. We seem to have a lot of work just at present – all the better
– more spoils for the staff to divide.
    Yes, I know I looked charming² when Aunt G. saw me. I always
make a point of looking charming for my relations, since 1) they like
it 2) they are more critical than one's friends 3) they always write a
'Report of Interview'. Besides, if one is not pinched for money one
can easily look nice! – By the way, Lord Peter proves disappointing.
He looked like really booming at one time in America, but he hasn't

– so I must stick to the mustard for a few years more at any rate.[3] However, L.P. has done better than most first novels. So I can't complain. . . .

I wish I could write a good detective play – that's where the money is![4] . . .

[1] D.L.S. had evidently included an advertisement for Colman's mustard, for which she was responsible. This was the period of the famous Mustard Club campaign.
[2] By now she was about five months pregnant.
[3] She was planning to give up her job at Benson's as soon as she could rely on her earnings from writing. This she eventually did, in 1929.
[4] She did so in 1936 (*Busman's Honeymoon*).

To Her Mother   Kingsway Hall
2 November 1923

Dearest Mother –

Thanks most frightfully for the vests – They're beautiful, but, my dear, I wish you wouldn't. Honestly, I find it very difficult to wear woolly things now-a-days. Wool always seems to give me such awful colds. I think I get too hot,[1] except on absolutely piercing days. It seems to take all the go out of me! That's why I've gone back for the moment to my old combs.[2] The short ones are all right – nobody wants legs these days – but London is so much hotter than the country. For bitter weather – but then we never really get it! Dear, *don't* keep on giving me wool, though it's sweet of you.

Look here – I'm awfully rushed and rather bothered. Don't come up till the Spring – I want to get things straightened out, and I can't do that till I get my accounts from America and England and have got my new book into the Press both sides of the Atlantic. Just now I simply couldn't give my mind to anybody or anything.

Don't expect me at Xmas – At Easter I hope to see you with a settled scheme of things, but just at present I'm too 'hot and bothered' to cope. I've got all sorts of irons in the fire – When I'm clear, come up by all means – At present you'd hardly see me!

I've seen nobody much lately. N.D.[3] burst in on me the other evening, and I had to pretend his book wasn't as bad as it really is! . . .

[1] D.L.S.'s pregnant body was providing its own central heating.
[2] Combinations.
[3] Norman Davey. He must surely have been aware of her condition. She was by then seven months pregnant. Her quarrel with him was evidently forgotten.

To Her Mother   24 Great James St[1]
11 December 1923   W.C.1

Dearest Mother –

Many thanks for letter – No news. . . .

Yes, Aunt M.[2] read *Whose Body?* all right and wrote a very nice letter about it. I've tried already to joggle Fisher Unwin into greater activity, but one can't do much with these people. . . .

Lord Peter[3] is still in trouble over a bit of evidence that I don't know how to work in, but all these problems solve themselves in time if one doesn't worry about them too much.

I'm afraid I can't absolutely say off-hand what clothes I want – I haven't settled my spring colours yet! May I think about it and let you know. I expect he'd[4] like it to be something large and definite – not things like gloves and stockings, which are what one really is always wanting. If I had a little idea how much he suggests going to, it would help a lot – could you tactfully discover? I find brown suits me better than I thought it did – but I don't know if it will be fashionable again next year.

Agag[5] sends love – Your loving Dorothy

[1] D.L.S. was now in Hampshire. She had let her flat and arranged with her tenant to send on her post and to post for her in London letters which she sent ready stamped. In this way she concealed from her family and friends that she had left London.
[2] Aunt Maud Leigh.
[3] In *Clouds of Witness*, on which she continued to work in Hampshire.
[4] Presumably her father.
[5] It is unlikely he was in Hampshire with her. Her tenant must have been looking after him in her absence. This is a nice touch of deception.

In thinking over her problem, D.L.S. must have considered, among other solutions, the possibility of asking her cousin, Ivy Shrimpton, to foster the child. She and her mother, Aunt Amy, had earned their livelihood in this way for some years and were experienced and reliable. On the other hand, there was the disadvantage of the close relationship and the likelihood that the truth would reach her parents. It is possible that D.L.S. had made other arrangements and that these fell through or that she changed her mind at the last moment. It is difficult otherwise to explain why she waited so long before writing to her cousin.

Dearest Ivy

Thank you very much indeed for your letter and the delightful
pussy. I have been wanting for some time to write to you on a matter
of business. There's an infant I'm very anxious you should have the
charge of, and I hope very much indeed you'll be able to take it. It
isn't actually there yet, but will be before many days are over. It
won't have any legal father, poor little soul, but I know you would
be all the more willing to help give it the best possible start in life on
that account. The parents want to do the very best for it, and will be
ready and willing to pay whatever your usual terms are, and probably
something over. They especially want it to have affection rather than
pomp! I know that nobody could do better for it that way than you.
I am very personally interested in the matter, and will tell you more
about it later on, or when I see you as I hope to do before too long.
The point is – what would be the earliest possible moment at which
you could take it? At present everything depends on the girl's not
losing her job. Everything has been most discreetly managed – her
retirement from public life is accounted for by 'illness' – but naturally
she can't turn up back at work plus a baby – at least, not without
letting stacks and stacks of people into the secret, which might then
leak out. So you see, the sooner she could dump the infant on you
and clear back to work, the more chance there [is] of there being
money to support it, and both parents are working – one of them
alone couldn't do much to support it. From the mother's history it
should be an extremely healthy child, having given not the slightest
trouble or bad time so far, and I understand the doctor thinks everything should go easily. It will be a little gent (or lady as the case may
be) on both sides,² and would probably be in your charge for some
years – till circumstances enable the mother to take it herself. I think
you would find it a paying proposition, and I do very much hope
that you will be able to help in the matter, as I feel that nobody could
do better for it than you. Indeed, I'd ask you to make a very special
effort in the matter – it is so great a relief to feel that somebody really
trustworthy will have the child, – its mother is counting much on my
cousin!

Please let me know by return of post whether you can manage it
by hook or by crook – and if so, the earliest moment at which you
could take it, and what your terms would be. I can guarantee the
payments – and you would be given an entirely free hand in such
matters as doctors, clothing, and necessaries of every kind.

I am rather in a hurry as usual, so can only say how glad I am you like Lord Peter. There will be a new adventure of his very soon. Why do you want that wretched pretty girl? She is the ruin of any detective story! However, there is a love-affair (of a sort) in the new book.[3]

My very best love to Aunt Amy – and don't fail us over the baby!

Your loving
> Dorothy

[1] D.L.S. was writing from Hampshire. See note to letter dated 11 December 1923.
[2] This indicates that she considered the baby's father, Bill White, socially acceptable. If she had not done so she would not have invited him home or introduced him to her friends.
[3] *Clouds of Witness.*

To Ivy Shrimpton   24 Great James St
6 January 1924   W.C.1

Dearest Ivy –
Excuse hasty note – Have been waiting to give you definite news. Your baby arrived on Jan 3rd[1] – a sturdy little boy, and will be brought to you with all paraphernalia and particulars on or about Jan 30th. Terms quite satisfactory. Ever so glad you can take him. Will let you know further –

Best love
> Dorothy

[1] John Anthony was born at Tuckton Lodge Maternity Home, Iford Lane, Southbourne. His birth was registered on 28 January in Christchurch, a suburb of Bournemouth.

To Her Mother   24 Great James St[1]
22 January 1924   W.C.1

Dearest Mother
Thanks so much for your very amusing letter[2] . . . I heard from Aunt G. at Xmas, when she characteristically – and so kindly – sent me quite a pretty little scent-spray for my handbag, filled with a kind of lavender-water so rank and vile that after repeated washings of the bottle it still stank like a skunk and made my bedroom almost unfit for habitation! It is so strange that people can't tell good scent from bad! But this is by the way – She told me then that she was giving up her Brighton room – but as one of the chief reasons she mentioned to me was the expense, I rather wonder at her going in for what is obviously a still more costly arrangement at Highgate. But there! – Of course all Aunt G.'s geese are swans at first sight – *My* opinion is

that the moment she ever has to do with anybody else's servants, it will all be U.P.[3] before you can say knife. . . .

Lord Peter nears completion, but I had to re-write a couple of chapters[4] owing to a change of plan, which has thrown him back a good bit. – Weather awful, as you say – but so far I have contracted neither 'flu nor measles nor any other prevalent disease. . . .

[1] D.L.S. was still at Tuckton Lodge. The baby was three weeks old. This is the first (extant) letter to her mother since the birth.
[2] It had been sent on by the tenant from the London flat.
[3] Up, finished.
[4] She did so in the nursing home.

TO IVY SHRIMPTON   Tuckton Lodge
27 January 1924   Southbourne
                                                     Hampshire

Dearest Ivy –

I am bringing the boy to you myself on Wednesday. Owing to the strike we shall probably have to come by road, so expect us at your door[1] some time in the afternoon. As I shall try to get up to town by train the same night I may only be able to stay a minute or two so am enclosing confidential particulars which I had intended to give you by word of mouth. I know you are the most discreet woman in the world – will you read them first yourself, and only tell Aunt Amy about it if, on consideration, you think fit. I trust your discretion absolutely.

    Yours affectionately
        Dorothy

[Letter enclosed. On envelope]: *Strictly confidential*
                            Particulars about Baby

27 January 1924

My dear – Everything I told you about the boy is absolutely true – only I didn't tell you he was my own! – I won't go into the whole story – think the best you can of me – I know it won't make you love the boy any the less. He is really a fine little chap, – I can't feel too bad about it myself now, because it will be so jolly to have him later on. I'm 30 now, and it didn't seem at all likely I should marry – and I shall have something for my latter age anyway. But never mind me – don't think about it, but just be fond of the little chap. I wouldn't like to send him to anybody but you, because I know I can trust you absolutely to give him everything which I can't give him these first years.

I didn't tell you straight away for two reasons: 1. I thought you would be able to tell me more frankly about terms, and whether it would be convenient for you to have him, if you thought he was someone else's. 2. I have no idea what Aunt Amy will feel about it. If you think it would distress her very much there is no need to tell her – you have a quite plausible story to account for my interest in him. Please use your own judgement. Whatever you do will be right.

They know nothing about it at home, and they must know nothing. It would grieve them quite unnecessarily. You know, it's not the kind of ill-doing that Mother has any sympathy for, – she isn't either a man-lover or a baby-worshipper, – so I see no reason whatever for distressing them. So please, not a word of any kind to Christchurch. By the time I want the boy, they will be too old, if they are still alive, to worry much about anything, and they must have these last years in peace. I know you can be as silent as the grave, and I trust you to be so in this case.

The boy will have to be registered in my name, of course, but I think he may as well be known by his father's, which is as non-committal and common as blackberries – so to you and the world he'll be John Anthony White.[2] For certain reasons, that isn't the name I'm using here,[3] so I haven't been able to mark his things.

I'm afraid you'll have a job with him at first – food etc., because he has been breast-fed. They said it would be better to give him a good start in the natural way and then let him struggle with the change of food than to bottle-feed him from the beginning. He is very greedy and seems to have a pretty sturdy little inside, so I hope you'll be able to get him started without too much trouble. You will know what to try. If you need anything more expensive, or doctors or advice, or anything in the world for him, let me know. I can manage it. – He is rather noisy and excitable – you'll find it doesn't do to nurse him or pet him too much, or he'll keep you at it all day and night. He's accustomed to be stuck down in bed when he yowls and taken no notice of – so be stern with him.

He has been circumcised, by the doctor's advice, and I think you will find his little insides in good working order.

I'll tell you anything else there's time for when I see you –

Good-bye till then, my dear – and be good to my son!
    Dorothy

---

[1] Ivy and her mother (Aunt Amy) then lived in Cowley, outside Oxford. There were other foster children in the house, including a girl named Isobel Tovey, aged about six, a ready-made sister who became very fond of the baby.

[2] D.L.S. must surely have remembered that White had once been an important name to her.

[3] It is not known what name she used at the maternity home.

To Ivy Shrimpton   24 Great James St
1 February 1924   W.C.1

Dearest Ivy

Thank you ever so much for your letter, which it was a great relief to get, as I couldn't help thinking of poor little Algy perhaps yelling himself into fits and being sick, and all kinds of horrors! But I really think he's a determined sort of kid and *means* to live! – I say, you will be awfully careful to see that his little works work regular, won't you? (Of course, what does the woman think? Parents always fuss!) – I firmly believe that why some of the Leigh family take such a pessimistic view of things – notably Mother – is because they are everlastingly tied up inside, or dosing themselves! And Algy has started by being so good that way that I hope he's taking after me in that respect. . . .

I was a bit weary yesterday, because I came home to find that the fool I'd let my flat to had locked up the keys inside the flat, and my charlady, who had intended to leave her set with a friend before going to the Cinema, forgot them, and went off with them in her pocket, so I had to find a Cinema too, and sit there till she came home!!! How sweet of Isobel to be so fond of the infant. I'm glad he didn't simply howl the house down in the night. Let me know if there's anything you want, and send me a report from time to time.

Thank you, dears, ever and ever so much. It's splendid to know he's being so much loved and cared for –

    Your grateful
    Dorothy

To Ivy Shrimpton   24 Great James St
6 February 1924   W.C.1

Dearest Ivy –

I'm so sorry you should have been worried by that little trouble – quite right to get the doctor – and it's useful to have his opinion of J. anyhow. There is always a little discharge from the navel for some time after birth, and he had been wearing his binder till quite shortly before he came to you, but it (the discharge) appeared to have ceased, so Nurse left it off. No doubt it will be better for him to keep it on a little longer. He is so active and yells so loudly that no doubt he puts extra strain on his little self. Never hesitate to call in advice whenever you're in the least worried or puzzled about anything – I expect the change of food will throw him back for about a couple of months, so you mustn't get alarmed about that. I know only too well that I've put a lot of responsibility on you with the weaning, and I was, as I told you, considerably bothered about it, but I couldn't very well insist upon my own ideas in the face of expert opinion! It seems to me that you are doing wonderfully well with him – I expected you would have far more trouble, and that the poor little beggar would be half-starved before you could find anything to suit him. So don't think I shall be unduly worried by any loss of weight or anything of that kind. I know it's bound to happen – I'll give you a month or two before I come along and look at him! – I'm glad he appears to have the full use of his senses.

I am quite all right – well back into my stride at the office, where they were all charmed to see me, and very sympathetic about my 'illness' – Well, well! As you say, there seems to be a fate in things.

Thank you so much for all you are doing – don't worry too much when little things happen – they're bound to. Get the doctor whenever you like (it won't break me!) and carry on.

With regard to my premature decease. If it should occur before that of my people I think they will have to be told, because in that case they would probably wish to do what they could – and they might even be glad of John in my absence. Otherwise I am arranging for guardians, but I must wait a little till I find out whether his father wants to have anything to do with it. He can't do anything very material, but when he gets over his present feeling of helpless rage and misery about the matter, he may wish for a certain measure of recognition. I hope to get this settled up before long – but if I rush things I may ruin every thing!

    Yours ever affectionately
      Dorothy

To Ivy Shrimpton   24 Great James St
No date, but February 1924   W.C.1

Dearest Ivy –

Afraid Sunday is off – Traffic strikes and things make people want to keep their cars and not lend them to people to go and see their offspring – lawful or otherwise! I'm so glad I came down and saw the young man last Sunday, and saw him getting so big and looking so jolly. Don't think I'm worrying over his looking pale or anything

– the fact is, I was so taken aback at having left a scarlet infant and finding a white one that it quite startled me for a moment!

As to the other point – Whoever suffers over this business I'm quite clear it mustn't be John Anthony. If the poor little soul has to be fatherless, at least he mustn't be motherless. I think Isobel had better suppose I've adopted him or something of that kind, and if she does let anything out to Aunt Maud or anyone it can't be helped. They can suppose I 'take an interest' in him – it wouldn't be the first time.[1] As regards J.A. himself, I daresay he won't give things away himself just at present. If he does, it can't be helped – I've done what I could to spare people's feelings, but it can't be carried to the point of letting the kid lose anything he might be having. The father side of the question can wait; it's not likely to become acute for some time. Let me know what you think, but I do very strongly feel that as the boy has got a mother, he should have one properly, so to speak –

Just heard by the wireless that there is to be no tube strike – I was looking forward to being the only person in the office to-morrow!

Goodbye,
Best love
  Dorothy

[1] She was probably referring to the interest she took in Adèle's baby. Adoption was not made legal in England until 1926.

To Ivy Shrimpton   24 Great James St
21 February 1924   W.C.1

Dearest Ivy

Very many thanks for your letter, which I was very glad to get, though knowing quite well, of course, that no news was good news. I'm ever so glad to hear that Algy – beg his pardon, John – is getting on so well; I think you are doing wonders with him. I really *can't* believe he's gained a whole pound! – perhaps his clothes weigh a bit more than the health lady's[1] average! – but obviously he is gaining steadily, which, with the change of food, is really fine. Never mind about the doctor – they will turn up and you can't prevent 'em, as you say. At least, perhaps the panel system[2] does – but the only difference is that then you can't get hold of them, whereas the other way you can't get rid of them! Anyhow, it's just as well to have an eye kept on J.A. – Nurse told me you would probably get a little soreness in those regions – she says it is because bottle-food somehow always has more acid in it – perhaps it's the fruit-juice or something – than natural food. Anyhow, it can't be helped. She always kept him heavily vaselined to prevent chafing or sticking – I expect you do this. I heard from her the other day, and she was greatly pleased to hear he was doing so well, and said, like Dr Russell, that that little discharge was nothing to worry about. – Oh! about the doctor – perhaps the simplest way would be if you sent me an account[3] at the end of each month for any little extras all together, so that it could be paid at the same time as the general fee. – I thought you would find those nappies all right for the present – in fact, I felt that any more 'gumblesomeness' would probably make him bow-legged!! I say, I hope you've observed what nice, flat ears I've made him. I gave special thought and trouble to their construction – so if I catch you putting him into round caps that give him elephant-flaps there'll be *such* trouble!!! . . .

Of *course* he'll pull off, untie or poke his fingers through anything which gives him the least opportunity. I told you he would!

It's really sweet of Isobel to be so fond of him – and I expect, as you say, he will be spoilt. On your own heads be it! for my impression is that he means to turn out a handful! –

I suggest coming down to have a look at him one Sunday towards the end of next month. By that time you'll feel that you've had time to get him in shape, so to speak, and will have got over the immediate trials of weaning and so on.

> With best love and gratitude
>   Your affectionate
>   Dorothy

[1] The health visitor.
[2] A system of health care, funded by the rates, in existence before 1945. Doctors in private practice accepted a number of patients 'on the panel'.
[3] D.L.S. had arranged for Ivy to register the baby as a private patient.

To Ivy Shrimpton   24 Great James St
1 March 1924   W.C.1

Dearest Ivy –

Herewith cheque for £3.5.0 to cover March fee and Dr Stick-in-the-Mud. This is all, isn't it?[1]

No news, as I wrote so recently, except that John's father is, exactly as I hoped, beginning to feel less sore and take a little pride and interest, so I think my 'don't rush' attitude is justifying itself. I showed him your last letter, and he said 'what an awfully nice woman she must be'[2] – (meaning you). He is really 'coming round' quicker than

I thought he ever would – after all, small babies aren't in themselves very attractive to the male mind.

    With best love to you all
      Your ever affectionate
        Dorothy

[1] At this stage D.L.S. paid Ivy Shrimpton £3 a month for fostering the baby. The extra five shillings was the doctor's fee.
[2] These are the only known words of John Anthony's father. There are no letters extant between him and D.L.S.

To Ivy Shrimpton   27 Great James St[1]
29 April 1924   W.C.1

Dear Ivy
    Here's the money. Is everything all right? I saw the Christchurch people at Easter – nearly told Mother, but Aunt M[abel] makes everything very difficult. Better to wait – besides, things are being very rotten here for the time being. Thank you for your unfailing sympathy and discretion – 'Bide the time' is a good motto – I've always found that if one waits questions solve themselves! Dad very delighted with his wireless set. Poor little J.A. – I hardly know whether I love him or hate him – but he's happy enough so far, anyhow –

    D.

[1] The handwriting of this letter is large and uncontrolled, as was the case when D.L.S. was under emotional stress. She has given her address mistakenly as 27 Great James St. The visit to her parents, the first since the baby's birth, has upset her.

To Ivy Shrimpton   [As from] 24 Great James St
2 May 1924   W.C.1

Dear Ivy
    Many thanks for letter. Glad everything is all right. Don't take any notice of my moods. I had just told J.'s father to go to hell – he's always behaved fairly badly and finally became intolerable, so I thought he'd better push off.[1] I was feeling rather annoyed at the time. – Of course I knew going home would be rather a trial, but it had to be done, so there it was. I can't see that I should do any good by telling them at the present moment. It would be a great worry and embarrassment to them, and I should have to answer a lot of questions which are better left alone. Everybody has not your valuable gift of silence. And if I was being sympathised with and bothered I should want to throw

J.A. out of the window. As it is I can't see that anyone suffers but myself so far, and therefore, so far so good.

Glad J. is progressing – I don't know why he should kick you in the face, or pull Isobel's hair but if he bites the hand that feeds him it's probably an hereditary failing (she said bitterly!). His interest in the kitchen clock is intriguing. Is it the tick? I wish he'd be a mechanically-minded child – I hope he doesn't intend to be musical or artistic – I'm so bored with writers and people like that. He's got a big head – he ought to have something in it, oughtn't he? Anyhow, there doesn't seem to be any fear now that he's deaf, blind or imbecile, though I'm sure, considering the little pampering he got before he was born and the worry I was in, I wonder he has any faculties at all! Let me know when he wants clothes or anything –

In haste – (there's an awful lot of work coming into this office!) –

Hope all your colds are better again. If I wrote 27 it was just bad writing! I'm still at 24.

> Best love
> Dorothy

[1] From this date on D.L.S. gave up all hope that her son's father would take any interest in the child. He never in fact set eyes on him. (Source: John Anthony Fleming in conversation with editor.)

To Ivy Shrimpton   24 Great James St
7 July 1924   W.C.1

Dearest Ivy –

How perfectly brilliant of John Anthony![1] The much inferior child of one of my friends has only just managed the top ones with much difficulty at 10 months, having produced the bottom two at eight. I do hope I haven't perpetrated an infant phenomenon or anything! It's a great testimonial to you, too. Cheers! . . .

[1] Ivy had reported that John Anthony, aged six months, had cut several teeth, both top and bottom.

To Her Mother   24 Great James St
13 June 1922   W.C.1

Dearest Mother –

Ever so many thanks for your good wishes and the cheque, which will come in most useful to excuse a late extravagance in the way of stockings! Please thank Aunt Mabel also very much indeed for her present which arrived this morning. It is very sweet of you both.

So glad you enjoyed your stay in town. – I must tell you something (damn this pen!) about Aunt G. which strikes me as frightfully funny, somehow! It was when we went to the Cinema. I came over to [her] with the tickets and she said 'Got them all right?' I replied with a grimace, 'Yes – had to get rather expensive ones though.' To which she replied: 'Ah! Splendid! You're the right sort about money' – with the greatest satisfaction. – Of course, I know Aunt G. would like to be able to spend money if she could, most generously, and it wasn't actually a lot that the tickets cost, but the casual cheerfulness with which Aunt G. disposed of *my* cash made me hoot with suppressed laughter all afternoon! Compared, I mean with the amazing satisfaction it gives her to cause Aunt Jessie to save a halfpenny on a tram-fare.

I am going, I hope, to the North of Yorkshire in July to get Lord Peter finished amid his proper surrounding[1] – though this does not mean that I am aspiring to be the new Emily Brontë – so don't think it. . . .

[1] Much of the action of *Clouds of Witness* is set in Yorkshire.

On her return from holiday in North Yorkshire with Muriel Jaeger, D.L.S. heard that John Cournos was back in England and that he was married. She had heard nothing from him since he departed for the USA in October 1922. The news must have distressed her for he had always maintained that he was opposed to marriage on principle. Moreover, he had married an author of detective fiction, a form of writing for which he had hurtfully expressed contempt. Nevertheless she yielded to an impulse to renew contact with him.

To John Cournos   24 Great James St
22 August 1924   W.C.1

I say – wasn't I clever. Nobody knew – and don't tell anybody, please. Didn't even have to chuck my job!

Dear John,
  I've heard you're married – I hope you are very very happy, with someone you can really love.
  I went over the rocks. As you know, I was going there rapidly, but I preferred it shouldn't be with you, but with somebody I didn't really care twopence for. I couldn't have stood a catastrophe with you. It was a worse catastrophe than I intended, because I went and had a young son (thank God, it wasn't a daughter!) and the man's affection couldn't stand that strain and he chucked me and went off with

someone else! So I don't quite know what I'm going to do with the infant, but he's a very nice one!

Both of us did what we swore we'd never do, you see – I do hope your experiment turned out better than mine. You needn't bother about answering this unless you like, but somehow I've always felt I should like you to know. I hope you're ever so happy –

Dorothy

To Her Mother   24 Great James St
25 August 1924   W.C.1

Dearest Mother –

Now how would you advertise the Midland Furnishing Co? Or Waverly Oats? or anything? I really begin to believe that all the ideas in the world have been used up. I have taken to photography again as a hobby – *it needs no words*!! I'm sick of words and writing and everything that has to do therewith.

I've lunched with Gerald, given him dinner and dined and danced with him. So you see we are doing our duty by one another – amiably, though without undue enthusiasm. In fact, we get on very well on a basis of mutual courtesy too frequently lacking in families. He had relaxed so far as to be able to exchange improper stories with me – a great stride, as I recollect that in the old days his tales were merely tedious. But I *cannot* hear what he says. I never could and never shall.

Our holiday was a good one, in spite of the weather, but I came back after walking about 5 hours a day and getting a huge appetite, and promptly dropped all exercise. Result: Biliousness! I think holidays are really a great mistake. . . .

To Ivy Shrimpton   Kingsway Hall
9 October 1924

Dearest Ivy –

I will try and come down on Saturday afternoon – I see there is a good train getting in about 3.

Many thanks for letter – I don't know how you can call J.A. a sweet little thing – he sounds a perfect little horror. Don't you let him howl to be the centre of attraction – he's going to grow up exactly like his beast of a father! – Anyhow, I'm glad he's such a good advertisement. I always knew he was going to be frightfully tough and obstreperous –

There have been a lot of babies produced (respectably, of course) by office people lately – all girls! What's the matter with the people??? See you Saturday –

Love to all –
    D.L.S.

I don't believe that about his talking – I'll believe the teeth, but I do not believe he is an infant prodigy!

To John Cournos   24 Great James St
27 October 1924[1]   W.C.1

My dear John –
    Have I really succeeded in astonishing you! And you who used to boast that you knew me better than I knew myself! – But if you really didn't *know* to what a desperate limit of endurance I had been pushed, you should never put a woman into your books again, for very lack of understanding! 'But why not me?' (He said with true masculine vanity.) Because (she replied) the one thing worse than bearing the child of a man you hate would be being condemned to be childless by the man you loved. So now you can sit down and apportion the praise and the blame and the motives and consequences for your next plot. – God bless you, man, I didn't want *his* son – that I've got one only goes to show that Nature refuses to be driven out, even with pitchforks – or other implements. However, since I suppose it is something to come out of such a hell with one's reason, one's health and one's job intact, I will accept your congratulations.
    I tried to answer your letter before, but the result would not have made pleasant reading. To be frank, I'm badly disappointed. I wrote because I understood from somebody (who said they'd seen it in the papers), that you had really been generous to somebody after all, and I was sorry I'd misjudged you. But now you say that is an error – and when I ask if you are happy, you reply with a shallow brutality about babies. Look here, John – when I see men callously and cheerfully denying women the full use of their bodies, while insisting with sobs and howls on the satisfaction of their own, I simply can't find it heroic, or kind, or anything but pretty rotten and feeble. Of course I know no woman wants to have bastard children – but that's why it's so jolly mean to take advantage of it. You see, I *know* now, what I only was sure of before, that the difference between the fruitful and the barren body is just that between conscious health and unconscious – what shall I call it? – uneasiness, discomfort, something that isn't

quite health. Please take this from me – I have bought the right to
say it to you. The fact is, I'm afraid, that I'm the person you are
always talking about and don't like when you meet her – a really
rather primitive woman. I mean, I really do feel (not think, certainly,
but feel) it disgraceful to be barren, or to give birth to girls (all girls,
I mean – obviously there must be some) – and I'm disgustingly robust
and happy-go-lucky about the actual process. And coarse and greedy
like the women in the comic mediaeval stories. And really quite
shameless. If I could have found a man to my measure, I could have
put a torch to the world. Would you like to find me one, even
now?

Now why in the world should you want to meet me? Last time we
met, you told me with brutal frankness that you had no use for my
conversation. Do you think my misfortunes will have added new lustre
to my wit? Or am I to provide you with material for a new chapter
of John Gombarov's philosophy? If I saw you, I should probably
only cry – and I've been crying for about 3 years now and am heartily
weary of the exercise. Or do you just want to know 'How *did* I do it?'
– I can tell you that, without wallowing in sentimental misery in an
atmosphere of toasted tea-cake. To carry it through one needs two
things: a) guts, b) iron health. I was away from my job exactly 8
weeks.[2] The day I met you in Southampton Row was the day I left
London 'on account of illness'. When I came back, I was congratu-
lated on looking so much fatter than when I left.[3] You can put that
in a book if you like; no one will believe it.

These trifling vicissitudes have, as you may guess, somewhat
delayed my new book.[4] There are limits to even my creative energy.
However, the original *Lord Peter* behaved like a trump in the way of
paying doctors' bills, which was as well, since the individual who has
the honour of being my son's father is penniless – and, indeed, somewhat indebted to me. Meanwhile, the younger generation displays a
physical strength and general precocity which are quite alarming. I
don't know what I shall do if he turns out an infant prodigy of any
kind. It is very irritating to have no one to whom I can boast about
him, but I'm afraid you don't sound as though you would be a very
sympathetic listener. It's a 'ard world – peopled by savage women
and tame men, isn't it, my civilised friend? – Don't grudge me that
gibe – you can laugh at me if you like – the world's great lover – out
of a job!

Dorothy

[1] Date added in handwriting of John Cournos.
[2] John Anthony was born on 3 January 1924. D.L.S. returned to Benson's on 1 February.
This means that she met John Cournos in Southampton Row at the end of the preceding

November. She was then eight months pregnant. Her success in concealing her condition, both at the office and from Cournos, is difficult to explain. Out of doors, the fur coat given her by her parents the previous Christmas must have been part of the solution. They had also given her a waterproof cloak. In the office she probably wore loose, flowing garments during the later stages. Even so, it seems unlikely that no-one at Benson's was aware of her condition, unless, as sometimes happens, she carried the baby exceptionally high under the rib cage.

[3] This is not surprising. D.L.S. had breast-fed the baby for three weeks and the fluids of her body had not yet stabilised. From then on her metabolism appears to have changed. From being slim, almost thin, she gradually became stout.

[4] *Clouds of Witness.*

To JOHN COURNOS   24 Great James St
4 December 1924   W.C.1

Dear John –

I kept your letter for a week before I read it, because I do so hate getting worked up – it's such headachey work going to the office after howling all night – but I feel better this evening. The Beast's[1] present female plumped down at the table next me in a restaurant, and while I was most tactfully not seeing her she accidentally flung an entire cup of tea into my lap and had to apologise, which must have been horrid for her, poor thing.

I meant to get a rise out of you when I said you oughtn't to write about women, but I didn't expect to nerve you to such an outburst of wrath and oracularity! And all about nothing, too! I said *if* you didn't foresee what was going to happen, you didn't understand and oughtn't, etc. Well, *did* you or *didn't* you? You are magnificently vague about the 'short story'[2] – I understand with awe that it's a 'revelation' and that 'the author' (I like this 3rd person touch) 'understood only too well' and so on, but what did it say? Attaboy! Come across with the goods if you've got 'em, there's no need to be so grand about it. Lord love you, I don't mind how many stories you write about me, so long as I'm not compelled to read them.[3] Or even J. Gombarov's sermons. But be human. Spare me your maxims!

You are the most unscrupulous commentator and perverter of texts I ever met. How can you say I laid stress on the old complaint that women are misunderstood? Now, can you see me saying anything so harmless and silly? – I said that certain men – you're one, the Beast's another – behave pretty callously as regards the crying need of a woman for children, which is physical completion for a woman as t'other side of the business is for a man. So you do, and I don't think any the better of you for it. And that for all your talk about being free to live and love naturally, the first thing you insist on is, the use of every dirty trick invented by civilisation to avoid the natural result. Well, didn't you? don't you?

Now for the grand maxims! – Gosh! my dear, they don't mean anything, do they? They're quite incomprehensible to me, anyhow, except as vague generalisations too shadowy for argument. 1) Savage woman and civilised do.[4] with primitive instincts. A difference between them – certainly – in what? Physiology, tradition, custom, opportunity, desires, taboos, colour, size, shape, – what do you mean? A general proposition like that means nothing. The resemblance I trace between myself and the more primitive type of woman was this: I wanted to have children, quite normally and ordinarily. I wanted yours, and as you repeatedly refused, I chucked the whole business.[5] I didn't want the Beast's, but having got it, I felt perfectly affectionate to the Beast, and would have stuck to him faithfully if he hadn't so to speak turned round and stamped on me. I told you then, and tell you now, that romantic love is not important, but bodily comfort and decency is. I think indifference to romance and dislike of sterility are on the whole, primitive traits, but whether they are 'savage' or 'primitive' only, or what the difference is or if you would approve of them more if they were whichever you think they aren't, I really don't know, because I don't know what you are pronouncing about.

2. Deeds not words. Yes, indeed. I don't think you've ever been quite fair to me about that. Remembering that I wanted your children – ought I to have come to you, nominally on your own terms, while secretly planning to cheat you into giving me children, which I could easily have done if I'd liked? It may interest you to know that I actually gave the plan my serious consideration, but decided it wouldn't be fair to burden you, especially as at that time I was practically penniless. Besides, I really did want to live decently, and spare my parents (they still know nothing) and I *was* untouched – and you very encouragingly prefaced your invitation with the assurance that you did not love me and wouldn't stick to me. Deeds, certainly. If you'd wanted me, you'd have taken me. The Beast did – to do him justice. And indeed, if you'd wanted me you'd have got me – the Beast did. Do *try* to be just about this.

3. 'The great lover is never out of a job.' Do you mean I ought just to be a common harlot? Because I'm afraid that would be a bit rough on my people and my son. Or do you only mean I didn't love you? Well, I did, in the only way I know. I paid you the biggest compliment I knew how; and you stood to me for something jolly fine – only there is always that taint of the 'rubber-shop' now. And you condescend to find my wit improved? It was always there – only you drilled and sermonised the poor thing out of existence. I was really fond of you and afraid of you. You were a rotten companion for a poor girl. You

wouldn't go to the theatre and you wouldn't talk nonsense – can you imagine me sitting on *your* knee turning out impromptu limericks, each obscener than the last? – I'm reckless now, having nothing to lose, and you seem to like rudeness. I'm sorry you found our last conversation dull. It was rather too desperately exciting for me – the last whack that chucked me over the cliff. Well, if we meet, I'll be witty – and don't you offer me any more maxims. Women hate 'em. Be a brute if you like, but *be personal* and you'll be irresistible. Come off Sinai – I'm damned if I'll be patronised any longer.

Final problem: Tea or no tea? It's going to hurt me like hell to see you, because Judah with all thy faults I love thee still, and as you've no use for me I must be in a very stupid and false and painful position. And I *won't* be made to cry in teashops. But if you like to come here, I will see you. And ask any questions you like – I can't imagine the question I would not readily and frankly answer. But for Christ's sake, no generalities. Good God! – do you think I am unsexed?

What *is* your letter all about? – It worries me, because it makes me feel you've got some obscure grudge somewhere, and I don't know what it is. I really am quite bewildered. – It quite honestly amazes me that you should even have been interested to the point of writing a short story. *Is* there a personal feeling behind all this – of any sort?

D.

[1] Her way of referring to Bill White when writing to Cournos.
[2] It is not known whether this short story is extant.
[3] It is not known whether she ever read *The Devil is an English Gentleman*.
[4] Ditto.
[5] From this it is clear that it was D.L.S. who brought the affair to an end.

To JOHN COURNOS   24 Great James St
25 January 1925   W.C.1

Dear John –
You asked me to write – so I will, as it's rather a relief to write to someone who knows about things – even though you always snub me with a crushing reference to my 'long letter', as though you found it a tedium beyond words. However, I shan't really know whether you read it or not, provided your answer is sufficiently diplomatic. Like Disraeli's message to Mallock,[1] you know. 'Tell him I am taking a holiday at Hughenden. How I wish that my solitude might be peopled by the bright creations of Mr Mallock's fancy!' – when he hadn't read a word of it.

Well, my 'bright creations' really are done with for the moment. The cursed book[2] – associated with every sort of humiliation and

misery – is actually finished, – and five short stories as well. On
Tuesday I shall cart them down to Dakers. They nearly fill a suitcase
(4 copies of the book and 3 of the stories) – I hope he'll be pleased
to see them. Nobody will like the book, though there are good things
in it. One story still remains to be done, but it will be time enough
before the rest of the series is placed and I don't want to hang them
up any longer.

So, Uncle Pandarus – you can send Troilus[3] along when you like.
I am at leisure to devote my attention to him. The sooner the better
in some ways. If 'twere done . . .'twere well it were done quickly.

Though in some ways I loathe the idea of starting all over again.
It makes such a slave of one. And in a sense, I am learning to cope
with loneliness. I'm used to it now, and it frets me less than in the
days when you knew me. – Still, a companion would be good.

Troilus *must* be companionable. A companion is more necessary
really, than a lover. Desires don't worry me much. If I see you or
Bill (the Beast, you know)[4] I have a sleepless night and am disgustingly sick(!) but that's about all it comes to. (That's really why I
made such a fuss about seeing you, really, – not just sulkiness. The
next day was horrid. If I stood up I was sick and if I ate anything I
was sick, so I had to stay in bed – fortunately it was Sunday!! I had
to cut Bill right out for the same reason – it interferes with one's
work. So if I'm not always over and above ready to see old loves,
you'll understand why! Nerves, I suppose – the solar plexus, or something, like being sea-sick!!) – Anyhow.

The companion part is so necessary, because, you see, it's such a
lonely, dreary job having a lover. One has to rely on him for all
companionship, because one's entirely cut off from one's friends. One
can't have them meet him, because it isn't cricket to force them to
know anybody they wouldn't approve of if they knew – and it isn't
really fair to let them go on knowing one under false pretences, either.[5]
And besides, it's so dirty to be always telling lies, one just drops
seeing them. One can't be open about it, because it would end by
getting round to one's family somehow. So you see, the lover has to
be companionable. – Only there again – if he was too nice one would
fall in love with him, and that would be vile. As you know, I don't
think I could face all that sordid secrecy over anybody I really cared
for. It simply spoils everything. One can't be ecstatic about something
which involves telling lies to one's charwoman! At least, I can't. Bill's
girl seems to be able to – but then she's dreadfully common, with a
voice like a rasp and a hard little mouth. She suits him perfectly, so
I suppose it's all right – what you once said you wanted yourself –
the superior chorus-girl type – but I don't suppose you want to be
reminded of that, under the circumstances.

No – but if Troilus was decent and kind, and companionable, and would take an interest in things, I daresay I could stick it. Only he mustn't be superior, or make one feel it's a crime to be rather a dab at doing cross-words and taking photographs. I take rather fine photographs. I meant to show them to you when you were here, but I didn't dare confess to it! It's odd that I get on so much better with you when you aren't there. I suppose what I had for you was one of those sort of abject hero-worships, and that was why all the back-stairs part of the business was so completely unthinkable. A dirty job always seems to need dirty tools, doesn't it? – I made no bones about it, you see. I always looked on it as a dirty job and I always shall. Even putting things 'right' by subsequent marriage would never quite take the taste out of one's mouth I fancy – I'm afraid this doesn't sound very encouraging for Troilus – but if I made up my mind to it, I'd do the square thing by him all the same. And I really can be enormously entertaining – more so than you know, because I have always been strained and uncomfortable when you've seen me.

I don't seem to be able to get off the subject – but I've nothing much else to think about. I can't tell you about my job, for you hate the very name of it – besides there's nothing to tell.

I met a woman the other day, who has just divorced her husband. She has one boy of 10. She was a complete stranger, so I told her about my Anthony.[6] She merely envied me having no father to lay claim to the child! I really began to feel it *was* rather enviable. I suppose the contemplation of other people's misfortunes is a really delightful occupation, for I'm sure we both felt happier after that exchange of confidence. I wish I could make some money, though – and I do think I ought to get hold of some man to help me to handle the kid later on. Another job for Troilus, poor thing!

Oh, by the way, I've had my hair cut, so I don't need to look hideous at night now with it screwed up into beastly little rats-tail plaits. Bill always objected to those. Of course, my hair is thin and ugly anyhow, and it doesn't look awfully nice short, but it isn't bad. It all came out, too, after Anthony was born – that was another misery – and is only just coming right again. Anyway, I'm sure Troilus would have hated the tight plaits and they've gone! I don't really know why I had it done, except that it was such a beastly fag having to do it every night however racked with tiredness one was.

Do you think the Americans will be interested in the thing in my book about the trial of a Peer in the House of Lords? Nobody has ever put such a trial into a novel before that I know of (except perhaps an impeachment in a costume novel – I think it's unique in a detective story). It may appeal to their itch for British antiques. It might be a good thing to write out a few notes about previous cases (they're very rare) and let Liveright[7] disseminate a few discreet paragraphs in the press about the time the book appears, if it ever does appear. What do you think?[8] – Of course, if *only* some British peer would seize the moment of the book's appearance really to commit a crime it would be magnificent, but they're a law-abiding lot on the whole, and I'm afraid it wouldn't do to count on it.[9] Dear me! If only the thrice-necessary Troilus were to hand, I might try it on him and see how he reacted. – I spent a beautiful sunny afternoon in the B.M.[10] today, reading up the trials of Lord Cardigan and Lord Pembroke. Lord P. was a splendid picture of London night life in 1678. He had a row with a man in a pub in the Haymarket and knocked him down and kicked him. The man died and Lord P. was had up for murder. It turned out that the victim was subject to 'fits' and perpetually drunk – his family physician complained that when he offered him a 'glister'[11] for his bowels he rudely replied that he would rather have small beer (!). So there was some doubt whether the death was not due to natural causes. Anyway, the Lords brought it in manslaughter, and the culprit 'pleaded his clergy'[12] and so got off scot free!!! The whole tale is characteristic!

This is another 'long' letter – all about myself. I am so interested in myself, you see. – Reply with a brief note all about yourself – Give my love to Troilus –

D.L.S.

[1] W. H. Mallock (1849–1923), satirist and anti-progressive.
[2] *Clouds of Witness.*
[3] By now John Cournos had been to visit D.L.S. They had evidently discussed the possibility of finding a husband or a lover for her. She refers to Cournos as Pandarus and to the possible husband or lover as Troilus, after the story of Troilus and Cressida. Lord Peter Wimsey was to call his mother's brother 'Uncle Pandarus' because of his pleasure in playing the go-between.
[4] This is evidently the first mention of Bill's name to Cournos.
[5] She had introduced Bill to Norman Davey and to several other friends.
[6] She usually refers to her son as Anthony in her letters to Cournos, though she calls him John in her letters to Ivy Shrimpton and that was the name by which she continued to call him.
[7] Boni and Liveright, American publishers, who brought out the first edition of *Whose Body?* in 1923.
[8] Cournos wrote 'No!' in the margin.
[9] The last occasion on which a peer was tried in the House of Lords occurred *c.* 1932. The charge was motor manslaughter.
[10] i.e. The Reading Room of the British Museum.
[11] Obsolete for clyster, a medicine injected into the rectum.
[12] In mediaeval times the clergy were exempt from the penalties of secular justice. To mitigate the rigours of the criminal law, which imposed the death penalty for most crimes, the courts permitted any literate person to 'plead his clergy', i.e. claim to be exempt from punishment under their jurisdiction. By the late seventeenth century this way of avoiding punishment was available to all.

To John Cournos   [24 Great James St
No date; beginning missing; ?January 1925   W.C.1]

Thus heartened, I can proceed to the discussion of your other perversities –

I'm sorry you don't like being put in the same sentence with Bill – I suppose it's a blow to your vanity, but still, from some points of view, all men have much in common, you know. I'm sure *he* wouldn't object to the juxtaposition. He read *Babel*[1] and admired it enormously – and I'm sure he has a higher opinion of me than you have, and ·that's a great point in his favour. But as to making me sick – oh dear! You entirely mistake me! I'm always sick if I cry very much – especially if I've been physically worked up. What the hell do you mean by saying 'it was not you that had been the cause of this very practice'? Passion *fulfilled* has no power to produce the phenomenon, passion repressed, yes! – (and you go on 'which is not at all uncommon to women who love indiscreetly; you will be blaming me for Anthony next'? What *do* you mean? If you are implying that I can't carry a child without being sick in the morning like any anaemic, nerve-wracked, constipated, suburban imbecile of a half-baked, under-sexed, rotten-bodied, strait-corseted, flat-bellied, up-to-date, semi-female degener-ate, then you are offering an insult to my truly magnificent body which, as I believe Sairey Gamp[2] says somewhere, lambs could not pardon nor worms forget. If not, I don't know to what unnatural abominations you are referring, but I assure you that Bill never caused any sickness in me except by abandoning me. I think you must mean something so nasty I don't even know what it is.

As for the 'backstairs' question – I'm afraid my hero-worship was perhaps not *quite* so abject as that of the lady to whom you refer. I mean that, though doubtless you feel that your company would be sufficient 'reward' to compensate for any amount of spiritual filth, I'm afraid that if it excluded frankness and friendship and children and so on, it would be but a maimed thing. You broke your own image in my heart, you see. You stood to me for beauty and truth – and you demanded ugliness, barrenness – and it seems now that even in doing so, you were just lying. You told me over and over again, 'I cannot marry anyone', 'I will not be responsible for anybody's life', 'I will not be responsible for bringing any lives into the world', 'I do not love you', – my dear, you stripped love down to the merest and most brutal physical contact – it is nothing – any man would do for that. I said to myself: 'There is nothing I can give him, beyond what the first harlot in the street could provide. Our life would be one dirty shift after another, with nothing in it but an agony of emptiness for both of us.' I could not associate ugliness with you – then. I daresay

I wanted too much – I could not be content with less than your love and your children and our own happy acknowledgement of each other to the world. You now say you would have given me all those – but at the time you went out of your way to insist that you would give me none of them. – Remember that I had some ideals left then – I hadn't the advantage of being married or divorced or shop-soiled. I believed everything you said to me in those days and if words mean anything, yours meant that you would not love me, you would never marry or have children. – By the way, having 'retired in contemplation' of your wife's previous matrimonial experience, I am led to ask: 'Are the girl of 8 and the boy of 10 the fruits of the first or second marriage?' and to add that the results of my contemplation are, don't put off your own efforts in that direction too long, unless you want to add wife-murder to your pastimes. I had rather a hard job with Anthony, at 30 years of age, though of course that wouldn't apply so strongly to a tripara. Still, recollect the old song that 'Lovers wish themselves unborn when all their joys are in their eyes.'[3]

My son's names are John Anthony, chosen by Bill and myself.

As to Troilus – the companionship is certainly the most important part, but for his own sake, let him be a sturdy fellow. I regret that you are 'temporarily' mortgaged (at least, I don't know that I do, but as you refer to it as a 'misfortune' I will politely concur in that regret) – but really, as I've said, *as a companion* you aren't my choice. With you I should always have had to put my days in pawn to my nights, but you would have broken either my heart or my spirit, and I'm getting too old to contemplate such a result again. I'm not hard to companion, really. Bill filled the bill quite fairly well, you know.[4] Of *course* I should like two best. Did I never loose on you my famous epigram: '*Qu'on devrait avoir des maris comme des chemises – un de jour et un de nuit*'?[5] Only it would be so complicated in its working. I once started to concoct a tale, about a law which was passed, compelling people to marry in sets of four – the night husband lived with the day wife, you see, and his day wife slept with the other husband. To have any sort of spiritual or intellectual passion for your night partner would be as big an infringement as sleeping with your day partner. You had adjacent flats, and went upstairs (or down as the case might be) after your morning bath – 12 hour shifts, so to speak. The ingenuity of the arrangement is seen when you realise that each man had to bring up the other man's children – this made a lot of difficulty in the cases where the day husband was in financial difficulties and the night husband prolific. But it had points. If the night husband of A (a greedily passionate woman) had exerted himself to the point of exhausted irritability, he didn't have to spend the day with her. No. He went up to the placid and amiable B, and a new face looked at him over the teapot. While B's night partner, who might find her too motherly and dull in the daytime, could go and be re-stimulated by converse with the electric A. The real difficulty would be that before you could get married you'd have to find three other partners – and of course the housing question would be a trouble too, especially nowadays. It would have made a delightful book, though, and some day, perhaps, I shall write it. But for me, personally, the day question is the most important – at night all cats are grey,[6] as the wise Frenchmen say. . . . [continuation missing]

[1] John Cournos' third novel.
[2] Sarah Gamp, the nurse in Dickens's *Martin Chuzzlewit*. Her colleague, Betsey Prig, casts doubt on the existence of Mrs Harris ('I don't believe there's no sich person') and Mrs Gamp says indignantly to Mr Sweedlepipes: 'But the words she spoke of Mrs Harris, lambs could not forgive . . . nor worms forget' (chapter 49).
[3] Source unknown.
[4] John Cournos wrote in the margin: 'A clerk might!'
[5] That one should have husbands as one has shirts: one for day and one for night.
[6] John Cournos wrote in the margin: 'Make your choice by day'.

To John Cournos   [24 Great James St
No date; beginning missing; ? January 1925   W.C.1]

. . . broadminded. Love sits more happily at meat with the publicans and sinners than with eligible Pharisees with water-tight minds.

You sneer at the word 'bargain', but the thing itself, to my mind, is a fine one – an open exchange between equals. It would be good to find the man to whom one could say: 'Let us try this thing out – I have done so-and-so but I can offer you such and such. If we find we get on together, let's make a permanent job of it.' You make the whole thing seem so much more sordid than it need be. Is it any wonder that women are frequently accused of being hypocrites, when men like you insist on and prescribe hypocrisy?

Then again, if it is a husband you are looking for, the 'requirements' are very different. A lover must be a companion, because he cuts one off from the world; a husband need only be a lover, because one then remains in touch with the world and can get companionship from one's friends. With a lover, all sorts of complications arise – restrictions of time and place, non-interference with business, precautionary measures from the rubber-shop, and a definite understanding that one can accept no favours or presents and so on. With a husband, his interests are my interests, his home my home, his time my time and love can be free and careless. You are right in supposing that it is a husband I really want, because I become impatient of the beastly restrictions which 'free love' imposes. I have a careless rage for life, and secrecy tends to make me bad-tempered. – All the same, I think the man should know what sort of person he has to do with, and I should simply loathe to think that you had given anyone a wrong impression of me.

Give me a man that's human and careless and loves life, and one who can enjoy the rough-and-tumble of passion. I like to die spitting and swearing, you know, and I'm no mean wrestler! But there again – precautionary measures cramp the style. Bah! if you had chosen I would have given you three sons by this time – but you are one that will do your wooing and begetting by proxy.

I trust your book goes well. For myself, I am tired of books. I say! For God's sake don't pick me out a highbrow! Marrying a highbrow (or living with one) would be like marrying one's own shop. Couldn't you make it a stockbroker or an explorer or a safebreaker or an engineer or something? Still, that's a minor consideration – I can be interested in anything. Only, if it's a husband, see that he's a lover; if a lover, that he's a companion.

Now, which of us do you *really* think is the more cynical, O divine Perfection?

D.

Post-script

I re-open this on returning from the film *Peter Pan*, to submit to you a very serious difficulty!

Supposing one is ever able to give Anthony a home and a parent or two – will it become necessary to his peace of mind to see *Peter Pan*? Will he feel a pariah if he is the only child who has never seen *Peter Pan*?

Because I absolutely refuse to take him. I am quite unable to sit through a Barrie play without grinding my teeth. There is a kind of leering unwholesomeness about the Barrie mentality which makes me "eave"[1] – I could not sit and receive it with the serious approval which children demand.

It looks like another job for Troilus. But here is the serious difficulty. I could not live for a week with anyone who could sit through a Barrie play and *not* grind his teeth!

Is there any way out of this dilemma?

Has any child ever been heard of that does not like *Peter Pan*? In that case, one might gamble on Anthony's being that child.

But –

Is a child who does not like *Peter Pan* a monster?

I should not like to be a mother to a monster.

Please give me your opinion on this agitating question.

[1] i.e. vomit.

To John Cournos   24 Great James St
5 February 1925[1]   W.C.1

I've just discovered that my clothes were on fire! Not a desperate
tragedy, though – I'm sorry – that would really have been something
for you to enjoy – only rather a nasty smell of burnt wool. If I'd been
wearing cotton there'd have been a really lovely blaze.

[Letter continues]   Wednesday the somethingth
Dear John –
   I really must give an immediate answer to your highly entertaining
letter. To begin with, of course, while sending you my deepest sympathy and all that, I am charmed to hear that your step-children –
(No, no – it's no use your trying to lay claim to them by proxy – not
the slightest credit attaches to you in the matter – I may say 'my son'
but you must not say 'my daughter') are behaving in this complicated
and distressing fashion. Of course, a really juicy murder, explosion,
fire, flood or act of God would be still more thrilling – still, appendicitis is very painful and expensive. I had it in 1918 – I admit having
rather enjoyed it after the first two days, but then I didn't have to
foot the bill. Pray proceed to break your leg or lose your money, and
I shall become quite attached to you!
   I went down to see Anthony on Sunday. He is very ugly, I think,
but brutally strong and horribly intelligent. He has cut nearly all his
teeth, which at his age is preposterous, and can stand up and say
'Bow-wow' and so on. He kindly consented to sit on my knee without
howling, which, from him, is a great concession. He destroys everything he touches and his aunt says he is a little demon. I really think
Troilus is rather needed.
   Dakers received the new book and the 5 new stories and promptly
'retired sick'. *Post hoc* – I hope, not *propter hoc*.[2] Officially it is 'flu. Ah,
no! I can't write for low-brows. It's the merry high-brows who like
my books, those who feel, like Philip Guedalla, that 'the detective
story is the normal recreation of noble minds'.

   Yours
      D.

No – appendicitis is far preferable to liking *Peter Pan* – the knife can
cure the one for ever, but Barrie-itis is a deformity of the soul which
no treatment can remove.

[1] Date added in Cournos' handwriting.
[2] Latin, 'after this', 'on account of this', meaning 'subsequently, I hope, not in consequence'.

To John Cournos   24 Great James St
22 February 1925   W.C.1

Dear John –

I suppose I ought to apologise for writing to you in so much anger[1]
– but that sneer about Anthony's name was just a bit below the belt,
wasn't it? – I know I have said some bitter things to you, but you
have rather encouraged that dreary kind of wit than otherwise. I am
sorry if any of it was unjustifiable. It must have been bad indeed if
it deserved that stab.

Another thing, Bill may be a bad lot, but he was my man and I
can't let anybody abuse him but me. He was placed in an intolerable
position, because he had no power to put matters right, and he was
gallingly in my debt. It must be dreadful to be indebted to a woman
who doesn't love you, and to have accidentally messed things up for
her as well. And he was not responsible for the original break between
us. I can't explain that part, because it involves other people, but
you must take it from me that there were very great excuses for him.
I believe the girl he is now living with is very fond of him and he of
her, and that he is kind and faithful to her. To be just, I never meant
him to be more than what he wanted to be – an episode. If it had
not been for the accident of Anthony I couldn't have blamed him for
leaving me. He is not a good man, but he never deceived me – I
understood from you that you, also, only wanted to be an episode,
and I didn't want *you* to be that. I am sorry if I mistook the things
you said – they didn't seem capable of any other interpretation – but
as I have been so bitterly punished by God already, need you really
dance on the body?

If you want to dance – then dance over the fact that Brandt[2] doesn't
like the new book[3] and that I shall either have to chuck it up or
re-write great chunks of it – and you can imagine how much I shall
enjoy going over that old ground again. – I hope Anthony and I don't
come to the workhouse! but it's so hard to work. It frightens me to
be so unhappy – I thought it would get better, but I think every day
is worse than the last, and I'm always afraid they'll chuck me out of
the office because I'm working so badly. And I haven't even the last
resort of doing away with myself, because what would poor Anthony
do then, poor thing?

I asked you to help me, and I still want help, you don't know how
badly – but I simply can't pretend to be impervious to jibes. I know
it's very unattractive to be miserable and I've tried hard to be merry
and bright and all that sort of thing, but words that sound all right
when life's all right sound pretty harsh when you're down. I'm afraid
my nerve's gone a bit. And I'm no good at 'making use of' people.

If you can help me, I shall be very grateful to you, but I can't pay *too* heavy a price for your help. Don't make a jest of my love for you, because truly it isn't fair, and leave poor Bill alone – poor Beast!

Silence of course is your strongest weapon. If you don't answer, I won't bother you with any more letters.[4]

Dorothy

[1] The 'angry' letter is not extant.
[2] The American agent.
[3] *Clouds of Witness*.
[4] But she did.

To JOHN COURNOS   24 Great James St
28 March 1925   W.C.1

Dear John – oh! dear, John!

Am I to conclude from your haughty silence that, while you 'do not mind' being thought cruel or a liar, you do object to being thought a trifle comic? It looks like an almost human side to your stern and rugged character.

Meanwhile, John Anthony and I are struggling to bear up. We have decided not to starve after all, but to buy a motor-cycle, having lifted $1500 off *Detective Stories* (less 10% commission). We excuse the extravagance by saying it will save Mother's fares to Oxford.

Cheer up, anyway – I may get smashed up on the thing – wouldn't that be nice? – and never smile again!

Merrily yours
D.L.S.

To IVY SHRIMPTON   24 Great James St
15 April 1925   W.C.1

Dearest Ivy –

Your last letter made me feel very anxious about Aunt Amy, and in fact, a letter to you asking for more news was in my hand ready to post, when I heard from Mother that she was dead. I needn't say how very, very sorry I am. You will miss her terribly. Considering she had really lived to a great age, I think it is wonderful how lively and jolly she always was – always when I saw her, at any rate.

Look here. Is J.A. going to be in the way? Because, if so, I will hunt round and try to stick him somewhere else – *pro tem*, I hope, as I shouldn't feel half so cheery about him with anybody but you? I don't know if I can find anything at short notice, but I expect it's possible. I thought that if Mother should ask you to go down to Christchurch for a time or anything, you might feel you'd like to get rid of him. Please let me know.

If, later, you think of getting a room in town, or want to come up here and look round or anything, you know I can always put you up in a makeshift kind of way.

Oh! – if things should become acutely difficult, you can always shove J.A. off onto Mother and tell her, and I'll weigh in and explain, only I feel it would be rather a nuisance, what with Aunt Mab and the parish and everything, and I'd really rather wait till later on, if possible. Tell me what Mother thinks of him! –

My dear, I haven't said enough how awfully sorry I am. But believe it.

> Your loving
> Dorothy

To John Cournos   24 Great James St
17 April 1925   W.C.1

Dear Uncle P –

So, Uncle Pandarus, less hopeful than Diogenes, has abandoned his search for an honest man! –

Anyhow, you need not be jealous! I can't sell short stories either. The $1500 was for serial rights. And may you get treble as much for your forthcoming work!

I appreciate your mediaeval attitude – about things moved by machinery. (It is shared by one of my bosses at the office, who is a perfect Oxford Don in every way.) But I do not think it would be very practical to keep a horse in Bloomsbury. One would be rather confined to the suburbs or Hyde Park for one's exercise. I really prefer the open fields. Also a horse would eat a great deal – oats are much dearer than petrol. And it is much easier to ride a motor-cycle than a horse, unless one has been brought up to horseflesh, as I have not. And the garage fee would be larger, though of course one would save on insurance and registration. Anyway, I'm afraid I shall have to be content with the less aesthetic motor-cycle, and you can buy a horse for your wife.

I shall probably be running about the Cotswolds during your bachelor fortnight in Town, except perhaps for the first few days of it. Unless I take my holiday the last fortnight in May, which is rather a risk as regards weather. Unless, indeed, I am thrown out in my arrangements by John Anthony. My aunt has died suddenly, and it is a question whether my cousin will be able to go on looking after him, which may cause a great deal of difficulty. However, it's no good worrying. I shall probably find something else if the worst comes to the worst. If I am going to be in Town I will let you know, so that if you want to come and see me, you will not come to an empty flat. If not, I will convey your greetings to the country – You're a complete fraud, you know. If you don't like modern conveniences, why the hell do you stagger from hotel to boarding-house all the time, when you could have a country cottage without even drains in it? Horse, indeed! Then why do your travelling on the Métro?

    D.L.S.

To Ivy Shrimpton   24 Great James St
17 April 1925   W.C.1

Dearest Ivy –

Thanks for your letter. I'm afraid J.A. does complicate the problem rather. If you can hang on a bit, I'll try and see if there's a possibility of dumping him somewhere. It should be possible, and there are one or two people I can ask. If we told Mother, she'd want to help, and I don't want to be helped. J.'s my look-out entirely, and it's feeble if I can't manage without help – financially that, I mean –

As regards you – I don't altogether grasp what Mother means by 'giving up the children and going out.' Going where and as what? – I can't help thinking you'd rather hate living alone in rooms, and resident jobs aren't all jam. And it would have to be something to do with children, wouldn't it, if you were to like the work? Do you yourself want, do you think, really, to keep them (quite apart from the John complication)? – Would you be lonely without Isobel?

I rather feel that if you could manage to go on with them, in rooms (not necessarily Mrs Munt's – what a name!) or possibly, as you suggest, in a Convent, you would like that better, because you would go on being your own mistress, which I find a very great consideration, personally. (N.B. Convents are not frightfully good about food and heating as a rule!) Of course, I am in complete ignorance of the financial facts which are all-important. I'll try and come along – not this week-end, but next, if I can manage it, and try and bring some ideas with me. Perhaps by that time you will have seen your lawyer, and will know how things stand.

Of course I don't think you ought to have bothered about asking me down. It would have made things very complicated with Mother there! And I can remember Aunt Amy much more happily just sitting on her sofa, playing with John Anthony.

Hang on half a jiff – We'll find a way out – straight, we will!

Your loving, and always most grateful
    Dorothy

To Ivy Shrimpton   24 Great James St
20 April 1925   W.C.1

Dearest Ivy . . .

Of course I shouldn't think of suddenly snatching John Anthony
away from you while his small fee was still needed, and I certainly
don't want to take him away at all. I would far rather you had him.
Only I should like you to feel free to do whatever you felt best for
yourself, and I have just written to an old college friend who is a sort
of trained authority on babies, and who might very probably know
of some person who would take charge of him in case you found it
impossible. It is always better, I feel, to have a line of retreat open,
though I can't say too often that I want him to be with you and
should be very sorry indeed to hand him over to anyone else. In any
case, I wouldn't think of making any change till you desired it.
So you may rest quite assured of J.A. so long as you want to keep
him.

I will certainly come down when I can. I may wait to hear if this
friend has anything interesting to suggest, but I will try to come next
Sunday if possible. Don't expect me definitely, however, unless I write
again. If it isn't next Sunday it will be the Sunday after.

With best love to you all
    Yours affectionately
      Dorothy

To Her Mother   24 Great James St
24 April 1925   W.C.1

Dearest Mother . . .

I expect you had a very trying time down at Cowley.[1] I have written
to Ivy, and hope to go and see her soon. My advice, for what it is
worth, would differ from yours, I think. I fear that, except with the
very poorest and most uncomfortable sort of people, Ivy would find
it extremely difficult to get a job as a nurse or anything to do with
children, as training is of paramount importance now-a-days. Nor do
I think she would take readily to the yoke of servitude after so many
years of independence. If she can possibly carry on, and get enough

children to take care of to enable her to employ some help in the house, I think she would probably do better, as she undoubtedly has a marked talent for that kind of work. I have written to a friend of mine who is an expert in maternity and child-welfare work, and she agrees with what I have just said about the difficulty in the way of the untrained person. However, when I see Ivy, I shall no doubt hear more.

>   With best love
>   Dorothy

[1] Mrs Sayers had been to Cowley to help Ivy with arrangements for her mother's funeral.

To Her Mother   24 Great James St
28 April 1925   W.C.1

Dearest Mother . . .

I went down to Oxford on Sunday and saw Ivy. We talked about her plans, and considered that for the time being it would be well for her to try living with the Munts, or rather the daughter, Mrs What's her name,[1] and see how she got on. Ivy spoke with great gratitude of the kindness of Mrs M. and the daughter, but as you say, she can't seem to rid herself of the idea that these people are of different clay from herself, which is really a pity. She keeps on lamenting that the children should have to mix with Mrs (the daughter's) children – but really, except for the increased chance of picking up illnesses, of course, I don't see why not. Really, in these days, very few children, even in a humble class, are actually coarse or rough. Ivy told me that the Munts had been devoted to Uncle Henry and would have done anything for him. Ivy said he was 'very fond of making friends he shouldn't have', but when I enquired into this, I found she only meant people below their own social status (save the mark!) and not, as I was beginning to think from her horrifying way of speaking, gamblers, drunkards or footpads! It is a pity that she and Aunt Amy should have let Mrs Munt see that they felt like that, because there really seems to have been no necessity, and one can't but sympathise after all with the poor woman for wanting to use her own house. However, Ivy seems willing to try and get on with the daughter now, and certainly the rooms are *extremely* reasonable, so I think she had better try and see how it works. If not, of course, she can try for a place, though I fancy it would be rather more difficult to get than you realise. People's requirements have become much more exacting of late years. I think she would be sorry to give up the children and the girl would hate leaving her – though no doubt she

will have to sometime. The baby,[2] I gather, can, if necessary, be
disposed of, if time is given to make arrangements.

I think Ivy was no end grateful to you for going down and helping
her. I don't know what she would have done without you. . . .

[1] Mrs Spiller.
[2] Her own child!

To John Cournos   29 June 1925

Hope your letter wasn't one of your coy communications to which
silence gives consent (– or otherwise!), as I haven't felt dismal enough
to grapple with it yet!

I seem to have sold 4 short stories out of 5, and I didn't care much
for the 5th myself – so it might be worse.

If anything ever *is* urgent, say it on a post-card – then I shall see
it whatever mood I'm in!

  D.L.S.

To Her Mother   24 Great James St
No date, but July 1925   W.C.1

Dearest Mother –

Many thanks for letter. So sorry to hear Dad is still feeling seedy.
I've been sleeping rottenly too just lately[1] – I think it's the heat.
Anyway, after some weeks of being depressed well-nigh to tears, the
coolth set in and I revived completely. So perhaps he will do likewise.
The thunderstorms, as thunderstorms, were very jolly, but they didn't
do their job and clear the air. . . .

I'm engaged in cutting the new book for publication, after a severe
struggle with Unwin. We tried hard to make him refuse it, but he
wouldn't. I don't blame him. It's very good. In the end we came to
a compromise. The result of all this literary activity is a large addition
to one's income-tax – no great incentive to energy. . . .

[1] She had been worrying about what to do about John Anthony if Ivy gave up fostering
children. The situation had now been resolved. Ivy had decided to continue.

To John Cournos   24 Great James St
13 August 1925   W.C.1

Dear John –

I've only just read your last letter – I hadn't the courage to make
myself miserable before, but I happen to be miserable on a totally

Roy Ridley, 'the *perfect* Peter Wimsey'. *(Balliol College)*

BUDGET SECRETS LEAK
"SEALED LIPS" GOVT. COMING UNSTUCK? ASKS PUBLIC.

Mr Sherlock Holmes, M. Hercule Poirot and Lord Peter Wimsey have the matter in hand.

The Low cartoon from the *Evening Standard* and letters of protest *(Marion E. Wade Center)*

Witham
2.5.36

Dear Muriel,
Please ask Mrs Allen whether a Devil Low cartoon is not fame indeed!

Yrs ever — D

My dear Miss Byrne,
Pray assure our theatrical friends (dear people, but so impulsive) that I would not be seen dead in such checks. Nor do I care for this kind of collar & tie.

Very sincerely yours Peter Wimsey

Dear Miss Byrne
My husband has not got
Rabbit-teeth
Ys Harriet Wimsey

Dear Madam,
Having only just recovered from a fainting fit, I beg leave to state my opinion that this is a Low cartoon.
Yours respectfully
Mervyn Bunter

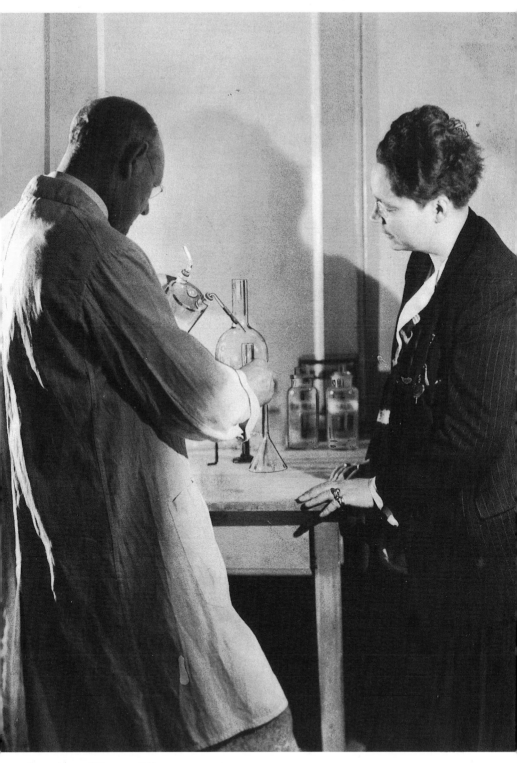

Dorothy and Eustace Barton concocting synthetic muscarine *(Marion E. Wade Center)*

With Helen Simpson at the Detection Club *(Mrs Clemence Hamilton)*

different account tonight, so one may as well be hanged for a sheep as a lamb. Sorry to have missed you when you called – as I hadn't read the letter, I didn't know you were in Town. Anyway, you might have let me have a post-card.

It is because you can indulge in 'good-natured fun' and not know that it hurts – well, there are things that decent men don't jeer at, see? – However, if it was just stupidity, I will withdraw 'cad',[1] and accept the apology. I don't know what you mean by feeling on 'the old footing' again. I know no very happy sort of footing we ever were on.

My dear, 'wanting the gesture to come without threat or persuasion' is all right – but you could hardly expect it to come without your making it a little easy. Do think – I was utterly inexperienced – passionately wanting to be loved and to be faithful, and deliberately you told me over and over again that you did not love me, did not want fidelity – that you had nothing for me but animal passion and 'kindly feeling'. – *Now*, I know, it's different – I'm so battered about that even decent kindness would be a boon beyond price. But *then* I still had some hope and some faith and the desire for better things. But I swear that if you had offered me love – or even asked for love – you should have had everything. Not easily, because I did not want to commit so bitter a sin – but you never asked me to love you – never said a word to me of anything but bodily desire.

It is perfectly true that you could never have been the companion to me that Bill was – but it's not true that I didn't take any interest in your pursuits.[2] So far as I knew what they were and you gave me a chance, I did. I tried desperately hard to be allowed to – but what were they? You never asked me to go and do anything with you, or for you – never told me anything – I don't know now what your interests are, really. – Yes, I admit that you went to cinemas (and that it was a fearful job to find a piece you would condescend to see, as I remember excellently on one occasion, having tramped half London with a bad blister on my heel before you would settle down) – but I seldom remember your being very cheery there. – And how stupid you are! it wasn't that I wanted to dance – I wanted somebody to think I was worth teaching to dance. I'd never been treated as a woman – only as a kind of literary freak – I wanted somebody to want *me* to do things – not to have to ask. – I should have been – I was – terrified to try, because I never had lived a natural girl's life[3] – but of course I wanted to be persuaded – And in the bigger matter as well – I longed to be over-borne, like any Victorian fool – so young, you'll say, I was – even at 28! If only you knew how pathetically ready I was to be moulded into any set of interests! – Bill knew, of course – even now he understands me far better than anyone else. I did meet him the other day and we are friends – he seems hopelessly wrapped up in the present girl, by the way – but she is one of those thin-lipped women, and I am wondering!

– My *dear*! What dreadful priggishness to put that sort of thing in *Who's Who*! You should be above wanting to *épater le bourgeois*![4]

One last thing – your post-script. That, I have not deserved. Absolute and utter faithfulness to the claims of lover or husband is a kind of fanaticism with me. So much so that if, for example, after the 'episode' I mentioned to you, some Troilus or other had turned up, I would no more have thought of entering into any kind of engagement till I had a formal release, than I would think of blowing my nose with my fingers. I have a very rigid code about that. Take Bill – however faithless he was to me, I considered myself bound to him till he told me in so many words that he had no use for me. But your sneers at faithful women have, I must say, bitten pretty deeply into me, and I am afraid, now, to offer faithfulness to anybody. I never suggested that I should be unfaithful. I only gave *you* licence to be so if you wished, if that was what you wanted. But I did want marriage – if for no other reason, in order that when you got tired of me (as you said you would), you should not have, like poor old Bill, the eternal reproach of having put a life-long handicap upon me. I desired that, as far as possible, I should go bound and you go free. If you remember, I offered to marry you by English law only, so that you could be free in your own country.

It is the more dangerous that you – for it *was* you – should so have undermined the ideal of fidelity in me, that I *have* a Hyde personality as well as a Jekyll. It would be very easy for me to be completely 'episodic' – hence my early and persistent desire to bind myself. I could very readily have become the complete courtesan – though I think I should always be faithful to the affair while it lasted, even so. I don't want to let Hyde kill Jekyll though – that was one reason why I wanted a Troilus so badly.

That question is again becoming acute. I don't quite know what to do about it. The original suggestion which I made to you, and which you afterwards rejected in favour of a husband-hunting scheme, still appears to me to be the best, but as you are now unwilling to further it, I shall have to try some other way. I am so terrified of emotion, now, and it makes me feel so ill and work so badly, that a quite business-like beginning would be easiest for me. Perhaps, on consideration, you will be able to think of something, if the thing still interests you at all.

Oh! by the way – I wasn't referring to standing in theatre queues. I once asked you – as a little act of courtesy that would give great pleasure, and make the situation easier for me – to do some little thing for poor little old Miss James,[5] who was very good to me in her queer way – I think it was to call or send a post-card. I remember that you promised to do it, and then got out of it. That was all – but it *donnait à penser.*[6]

The motor-bike is fine. It is strange that the beauty of machinery has no appeal to you. Though I know nothing about it, I am able to appreciate it, and it really gives me very great pleasure to feel the engine purring along in the lovely, velvety way that means that everything is exquisitely adjusted and happy together. Of course, Bill taught me that too to a great extent. I didn't think much about it before, but his enthusiasm in the old days was infectious, and since I have had the little 'bus, I've developed a great affection for her, the dear! Quite apart from that, it is good to be able to get out of London and see the country so easily and inexpensively. Why do you waste your time hating so many fascinating and marvellous things?

Well, well – the prizes all go to the women who 'play their cards well' – but if they can only be won in that way, I would rather lose the game. But do you really believe that any woman gives herself to an unmarried man *except* with the hope and intention of marrying him if possible? (I don't mean paid prostitutes, or demoralised sort of people.) Don't you believe it. *None* of them do – not in England at any rate. But the silly ones admit it, and the clever ones bide their time – make themselves indispensable first, and then *se font prier.*[7] Clever – but I can't do it.

I will send this to Dakers,[8] as I don't quite know where you are. If you are still in London and wish to call, will you send me a post-card first so that I may be in.

Dorothy L. Sayers

[1] The letter in which she calls him a cad is not extant.
[2] D.L.S. had written at the top of the page: 'I *did* jolly well read *Babel* in two nights – 120,000 words.'
[3] Her social life at Oxford had been normal and happy and she had learned to dance.
[4] To shock the middle class. Part of the entry was as follows: '*Educ.* left school at 13, self-taught. Lived in a Russian village until tenth year.'
[5] Probably her landlady in Mecklenburgh Square.
[6] Made one think.
[7] Play hard to get.
[8] Andrew Dakers was also Cournos' agent.

To John Cournos
18 October 1925

24 Great James St
W.C.1

Dear John[1]

Many thanks – My attention had, as a matter of fact, already been

drawn to it[2] and I was intending to purchase it, so that I am indebted
to you for saving me six useful pennies.

It is certainly admirable – one of the soundest and most useful
pieces of constructive criticism I have met with for a long time. G.K.C.
has put his finger at once on the central difficulty of detective fiction
– that if you make your solution too obscure and unexpected, the
reader is annoyed and says: 'Oh, well! that's not fair; nobody could
have been expected to guess that.' Whereas, if you make it too logical
and necessary, the reader is again annoyed and says: 'Rotten story;
I guessed the murderer straight away.' It is a most delicate problem
of balance, and has only very seldom been solved *perfectly*. His remarks
on the manner of introducing the criminal are especially valuable –
should be read over and over again and laid to heart. And though,
on the whole, I do not care for a love-interest in a detective story,
there is a great deal in what he says about its usefulness as camouflage.
In fact, I think the reason why it is so seldom successful is because
it is unnecessarily foisted onto a story which would be complete without it – as in those sentimental intrusions which I deprecate (and
skip) in Austin Freeman's[3] otherwise admirable work. In the stories
in which it is successful it forms an integral part of the plot, as in
that incomparable classic *The Moonstone*,[4] where the whole story
revolves about the loves of two dissimilar (but both admirably-drawn)
women for Franklin Blake. Bentley[5] has used it well, also, in *Trent's
Last Case* – the matrimonial relations of Mr and Mrs Manderson (very
restrained and good) – the splendidly-managed 'red herring' of the
supposed intrigue between Mrs Manderson and Marlowe – and
Trent's own love for Mrs M., which prevents him from accusing
Marlowe, and provides a plausible *cheville*[6] to connect the two parts
of the story.

G.K.C. is, of course, a determined upholder of the strictly classic
form of the mystery story – not only in theory but in practice, in
which point he is superior to Conan Doyle, who (as he admits in one
of the *Sherlock Holmes* tales, I forget at the moment which) sometimes
departs from the academic ideal. 'The thing that we realise must be
the thing that we recognise; that is, it must be something previously
known, and it ought to be something prominently displayed.' That
excellent sentence should be illuminated in letters of gold and hung
above the desk of every mystery-story writer. In other words, there
should *never* be any clue in the hands of the detective which is not
also in the hands of the reader. Sherlock should never 'pick up certain
small objects which he placed carefully in an envelope'. We must
know *what* the objects are. When the elucidation comes, the reader
ought to say, in a burst of self-reproach: 'Why, of *course*! I ought to
have seen that for myself – it was staring me in the face!' The *Father*

Brown story of the 'The Invisible Man' is an excellent instance in point. The trouble is, that writers tend, after a time, always to work to the same formula, so that, after reading half a dozen stories by one man, one begins to see the formula and solve the thing automatically by $(a + b)(a - b)$. Baroness Orczy,[7] who is another severe classic in method, though not in style, has unfortunately spoilt her work by too rigid an adherence to a single formula. – But there! once started on the fascinating subject of technique, one could go on for hours. – Anyway, I am glad you appreciate the brilliance of that article. Oh, dear! I should like to annotate every paragraph of it with examples, awful and otherwise.

There is 'meat', too, in his calling it not only a trick but a 'craft' of writing mystery stories. It does give just that curious satisfaction which the exercise of cunning craftsmanship always gives to the worker. It is almost as satisfying as working with one's hands. It is rather like laying a mosaic – putting each piece apparently meaningless and detached – into its place, until one suddenly sees the thing as a consistent picture. Like mosaic, too, I believe it to be on the whole most effective when done in the flat and on rather broad lines. Even in *The Moonstone*, though the characterisation is sound and good, it is not intricate and not altogether in the round. The Conan Doyle, Freeman Wills Crofts,[8] and Austin Freeman methods are all strictly two-dimensional, and, I think, the better for it. The story[9] I am preparing to start on at the moment shows signs of becoming 'round', and for that reason I am rather nervous of it; probably I shall try to keep it, at least, in no more than high relief. But I may, of course, make a dead failure of it, because it is a very difficult thing to do. It means combining the appeal to the emotions with the appeal to the intellect, and I'm afraid it means foregoing the appeal to the Tired Business Man and the Tired Journalist who, like yourself, do not want to flog their jaded intellects over the craftily-constructed detective story!

D.L.S.

[1] This letter is so different from her other letters to Cournos that it is probable that 'Troilus' had now entered her life in the person of her future husband, Atherton Fleming.
[2] An article by G. K. Chesterton, 'How to Write a Dectective Story', published in *G.K.'s Weekly*, 17 October 1925. It is evident that Cournos posted it to her immediately. (See Barbara Reynolds 'G. K. Chesterton and Dorothy L. Sayers', *The Chesterton Review*, Volume X, No. 2, May 1984, pp. 136–57.)
[3] R. Austin Freeman (1862–1943).
[4] By Wilkie Collins (1824–89). *The Moonstone* was first published in 1868.
[5] E. C. Bentley (1875–1956). His detective novel, *Trent's Last Case*, was first published in 1913.
[6] Peg, pin.

[7] Baroness Orczy (1865–1947) playwright and novelist of Hungarian origin, creator of the Scarlet Pimpernel and author of three volumes of detective stories.

[8] (1879–1957).

[9] *Unnatural Death*, published in 1927.

To Ivy Shrimpton   24 Great James St
13 November 1925   W.C.1

Dearest Ivy –

Sorry I've been such a time answering your letter. The last week or two seem to have been exceptionally busy and *mouvementé*[1] – the biggest thrill being caused by a very nice, particularly quiet and inoffensive little man in our department falling down between the platform and a moving train at Baker St.[2] For some inscrutable reason he was not killed, neither was his skull cracked nor any limb broken; nor, though his spectacles were smashed to atoms and his face cut, were his eyes in any way injured. All that happened was that his ribs were buckled up, like a bicycle wheel when you hit the kerb hard, and he is now getting along splendidly, thank-you, and is expecting to be allowed to sit up in his room on Sunday (the accident having occurred last Thursday week). So you see it is not only on the open road or to mad motor-cyclists that troubles happen! The funny thing was, I had been saying only the day before it occurred that life was very dull, and that I wished some exciting disaster would occur to somebody! It just shows that one shouldn't start wishing things! All the same, I admit to having thoroughly enjoyed the sensation, as soon as I knew no permanent damage had been done. Such is human nature!! . . .

[1] Eventful.

[2] Cf. the incident of Dr Garfield in *Murder Must Advertise*, chapter 15.

1926–1929

Marriage, Maturity and the Beginnings of Success

In 1926 D.L.S. married Atherton Fleming, known as 'Mac', a journalist and motoring correspondent, working for the News of the World. *It is not known how or when they met. Mac had been married previously and had two daughters, but his wife had obtained a divorce. Born in 1881, he had served as war correspondent during the Boer War and was a Captain in World War I, in which he was wounded and gassed. In 1919 he published a short book,* How to See the Battlefields, *describing the conditions under which the Royal Army Service Corps functioned in the field. He was a good photographer and a painter and he had raced cars at Brooklands. He was also an expert cook. He died in 1950.*

London: March 1926–November 1929 (Age: 32–36)

To Ivy Shrimpton 24 Great James St
15 March 1926 W.C.1

Dearest Ivy . . .
   Something has (in Mr Micawber's phrase) 'turned up' which seems to promise a solution for one part of our problem at least, though not of your immediate bother.[1] I am getting married to a man – (naturally, it would be to a man, not a peacock or an elephant) – who seems quite satisfied to throw the eye of affection and responsibility over John Anthony in the future. This seems to settle the difficulty we felt as to his needing a boys' school and a firm hand in a month or two! It doesn't mean that we can do with him as a permanent resident yet a-while, because we shall both be keeping on working, so we want you to carry on as at present, please. But it will mean that there is

somebody else to look to in case of accident and so forth. – I'm hoping we shall get down and see you ere long and jaw the whole matter over. In the meantime we shall have to turn our minds to the housing problem – we too, as there's no room for two in my flat. But when we meet, we'll go over the whole question. One can't really do it on paper. The whole thing has happened very suddenly, and I haven't told anybody but you, not wanting a fuss, so pray you say nothing till you hear further. I *will not* have Aunt G. all over us! Anyhow, marriages are one's own business.

I'm ever so sorry your silly old cold still hangs about. I'm afraid J.A. and Co. are rather too much for you – but oh! my dear, do stick to us! I'm certain it'll work out excellently in the end if we can only just wait and not have to bungle things by rushing them. I'll do everything I can to help. Is money all right? I may be able to spare a bit more presently, but of course, moving and things are going to be expensive just at the moment –

I'll come down just as soon as I possibly can.

By the way, the name will be Fleming. It goes quite nicely with both mine and J.A.'s, I think – though I shall probably still use my maiden name for most things – e.g. books and business.

> Yours rather hurriedly with lots of love
> Dorothy

¹ Ivy was looking for somewhere to live.

To Ivy Shrimpton   24 Great James St
18 March 1926   W.C.1

Dearest Ivy –

Thank you ever so much for your long and sympathetic letter. I'm so glad you are pleased about it all. We shall probably be able to persuade the Registrar to hook us up in about three weeks' time, and then we will come down together and see you. Good God, no, don't be on ceremony – that would be fatal! Mac is perfectly get-on-able-with and disposed to think the world of you for being so decent to me. I do think perhaps he wouldn't like tinned milk, so we will indulge him in a penn'orth¹ of cow. He is rather an authority, by the way, on good things to eat, which suits me to a T(ea) or indeed any other meal! . . .

No, I haven't told them at Christchurch yet – I don't want a fuss – and oh, lord! what about Aunt G. when it does come out! I'll tell them presently all right.

Sorry J.A. is such a little devil, but Mac says he likes them like that, so it's all to the good. He says he is looking forward immensely to seeing you all and meantime sends kindest regards.

Best love
    D.

We aren't having a honeymoon – just doing it in the Mr Wemmick[2] style: 'Hullo! here's a church.[3] Let's get married.'

[1] Pennyworth.
[2] Clerk to Mr Jaggers in Dickens's *Great Expectations*, who marries Miss Skiffins, 'seeming to do it all without preparation' (chapter 55).
[3] There could be no question of a church. The remarriage of divorced persons was not then permitted in the Church of England.

To Ivy Shrimpton   24 Great James St
1 April 1926   W.C.1

Dearest Ivy . . .
    If all goes well, I shall be married on Monday or Tuesday.[1] I'm letting them know at home in a day or two, Aunt G. and Aunt Maud having now cleared off from Christchurch. Mother tells me that Uncle Cecil and Flo are getting a judicial separation, him havin' been a-carryin' on with a female in the back garden – naughty old man! I feel rather inclined to congratulate him on retaining so much youthful energy. At his time of life, a romantic affair in the potting-shed when everyone has gone to bed seems such a damp, rheumatic kind of job! . . .

[1] Dorothy L. Sayers and Atherton Oswold Fleming were married on 13 April 1926 in the Registry Office at 53 Clerkenwell Road, London, E.C.1.

To Her Mother   24 Great James St
8 April 1926   W.C.1

Dearest Mother,
    I don't believe I ever thanked you for my 'Easter Egg', which was extremely rude of me. I do so now, with a great deal of gratitude. It came in very handy over the holiday.
    I regret to say that I laughed exceeding loud over your graphic description of the latest Uncle Cecil imbroglio! At his time of life, and with his infirmities, I feel it argues a great deal of vitality and energy of spirits to go carrying on with a female in a damp potting-shed o'nights. So unromantic a situation! So rheumatic a climate! So late an hour! So fine an indifference to the ridicule of the irreverent! Naughty boy! Bow-wow! Let him consider himself dug in the ribs. I

am sorry, certainly, for the unfortunate Flo, who will, I'm sure, be much better without him – not so much on account of the lady in the back garden, as because of his financial unreliability as to which point you and Dad also are well advised to keep clear. I can't help grinning at the thought of the double appeal to you to interfere in the matrimonial gallimaufry.[1] It's a pity you don't really enjoy these family excitements in the true Sayers fashion. Aunt G. will have something fresh to think and talk about, anyway. Honestly, why take it too seriously? *Qu'ils se débrouillent*, as the French say - let 'em pick out their own tangle. I can't see that it can be anything but a good thing for Flo to be quit of the whole show – Raymond and Gerald[2] are well out of the way where it can't affect them, and Gwen[3] has already cut loose and has other interests to think about.

In the meantime, I am getting married on Tuesday (weather permitting!) to a man named Fleming, who is at the moment Motoring Correspondent to the *News of the World*, and otherwise engaged in journalism. No money, but a good job, 42[4] and otherwise eminently suitable and all that. I think you will rather like him. He was Special War Correspondent to the *Sunday Chronicle* during the War and to *Black and White* during the Boer War (which seems so much in the dim ages now that I sometimes think he must have written dispatches in his cradle, but I suppose it's not so long ago as that really), and is therefore quite the 'old soldier'. I didn't mention this before, because it's our own business and I don't want an avalanche of interrogation from all sorts of people; so I thought I'd wait till Aunt G. and Aunt Maud had cleared off from Christchurch, as it might have been awkward for you to have them there and not tell them. Now you will be able to say with perfect truth that you didn't tell them because you didn't know yourself. For God's sake don't 'announce' it to Osbornes and Godfreys[5] and people – just let it trickle out casually at subsequent times. No flowers by request! – If all is well, we propose coming down to Christchurch at Whitsun and making an exhibition of ourselves then! I am going on with my job, and there will be no honeymoon. We are tucking into my flat for the moment, till we can find something suitable with a little more room in it. This is rather a difficult quest, as we both want to remain central. Our present position is ideal, being equally handy for Fleet St. and Kingsway. Of course, I am keeping my own name for all business purposes, such as writing books and signing cheques. A change would mean so much bother and confusion with contracts and royalties.

Which reminds me that *Clouds of Witness* has had a really extraordinarily good press. Of course there is no news yet about sales. Equally, of course, for all future books I shall have Fleet St. in my pocket. Observe with what business acumen I have picked a partner!!! I

enclose a very grubby press photo of said partner in the act of presenting a 'pot' to the winner of last year's Six Days.[6] He is the cleaner
of the two, the one in plus-fours. He is called Mac to his friends and
you, because, of course, one could not call a person Atherton, any
more than Adolphus or Marmaduke.[7] You might let me have the
photo back some time. I shall have a better one presently.

Best love
    D.

[1] Absurd muddle.
[2] The two sons of Cecil Sayers by his first wife. Flo was his third wife.
[3] Sister of Gerald and Raymond.
[4] He would actually be forty-five in November of that year. D.L.S. would be thirty-three
in June.
[5] Friends in Bluntisham.
[6] International Six Days Trial, an annual motor-cycling event.
[7] The juxtaposition of Adolphus and Marmaduke recurs in *Unnatural Death* (chapter 17).

To Her Mother   24 Great James St
10 April 1926   W.C.1

Dearest Mother –
    You are a very sensible woman, and your attitude in this matter
is all I could desire!! That is just what I wanted you to do – keep
things quiet till it's all over. It's *our* funeral! Tell Dad that I'm afraid
a notice in *The Times* would be the very last thing we should think of
having. It would bring a horde of the very people we particularly
wish to avoid – Mac's Fleet St. acquaintances and family friends and
all the imbeciles who ever were at school or college with me. Sorry
and all that! – Please thank Dad very very much for his cheque. It
will be most useful. One doesn't seem able to get married, even in
the quietest way, without expense! Strange!
    Mac says he's sure from your letter that you are just the sort of
woman he likes. . . .
    I am being married in green.[1]

Best love
    D.

[1] Her mother had evidently asked what she planned to wear for the occasion.

To Her Mother   24 Great James St
14 April 1926   W.C.1

Dearest Mother –

Meant to send you a card last night, but nobody had any stamps and we had all over-eaten and over-drunk ourselves. I understand that, the news having seeped out, the whole of Fleet St., incapably drunk, decorated the bar of the 'Falstaff' last night, and for all I know they are still there.

We were 'turned off' as the hangman says, in the salubrious purlieus of the Registrar's office in the Clerkenwell Road, which was decorated with aged posters, headed WARNING and CAUTION, and threatening fines and imprisonment. However, this seemed chiefly to concern persons under 21 years of age.

Will you please thank Mrs C.[1] very very much for her sweet letter – I don't feel I can write a proper reply at full length, but I appreciated her kindness and good wishes very much. She writes an uncommonly good letter, as a matter of fact.

    Best love from us both
       D.

[1] Mrs Chapman, the wife of the gardener at Christchurch Rectory, who was himself the son of the gardener who had worked for the Sayers family at Bluntisham. He had recently died.

To Her Mother   24 Great James St
23 April 1926   W.C.1

Dearest Mother –

Many thanks for your letter. I'm glad you had champagne on the 13th – not that it's a wine I've much use for personally, it's too thin and windy and you can't get nearly as much exhilaration out of it as you can from a good Burgundy. Still, there's no doubt it has a fine appearance as it creams out of the bottle – and why Aunt Mabel shouldn't have some I can't think, for it's a very harmless wine, when taken in moderation. I'm glad your hand has not lost the art of drawing corks.

Sorry you are having such a hard time with spring-cleaning, though no doubt, as you say, the atmosphere is less thunderous without the Daisy–Chapman feud. And the old carpets and things have always looked jolly nice whenever I've come home to them. Our flat would give you a fit by the muddle it's in with all Mac's things piled in on top of mine, but he seems to have taken a fancy to it, so there we are for the present, and if he's satisfied, I'm sure I'm only too thankful to be spared the fag of moving. . . .

Mac sends his love – he really feels he ought to write to you, but doesn't really quite know what to say. I told him to keep it till he sees you.

Best love
D.

To Ivy Shrimpton   24 Great James St
26 May 1926   W.C.1

Dearest Ivy –

We really are going to make an effort to come down to Cowley to-morrow, but last week-end's beautiful weather seems to have disappeared completely, and you mustn't expect us if it's beastly. Mac isn't very keen on an open side-car in the rain – and I don't altogether blame him! He hasn't been frightfully well lately, either – so I'm not exactly a free agent in the matter. Indeed, I've been hoping several times to be able to come but it couldn't be done.

Last week-end we had of course to go down to Christchurch. Luckily the three days were gorgeous and the 'bus ran finely, having just been overhauled from top to bottom, so our visit was quite a success. I took Mother in the side-car for a short run and she was ever so sporting – seemed thoroughly to enjoy going fast.

Here's hoping – but don't count!

Best love
Dorothy

To Her Mother   24 Great James St
31 May 1926   W.C.1

Dearest Mother –

Please forgive my not having written at once to thank you for the beautiful napkins and rings. They are very, very nice ones and ought to last a long time (the napkins, I mean). I've no doubt the man was quite right in saying the rings were solid silver – in fact, being hall-marked, they must be. 'Solid' doesn't mean that the rings are solid – that's only their way of putting it. It just means that there's no more than the statutory amount of alloy in the silver. Similarly, a solid gold bangle is usually a thin shell of gold filled with nothingness, as you promptly discover if you will only drop your bracelet on the floor and step on it – a course I do not recommend. Anyhow, the rings are charming – please tell Mrs C. and the girls that *their* presents also are in constant use.

We went to Oxford yesterday and looked in on Ivy, who was very pleased to see us and thought Mac very nice.[1] We also looked up Miss Penrose, who is retiring in December. She was exactly the same as ever, and really seemed thoroughly pleased in her quaint way with the attention. – I rode back in the side-car tenderly clasping a magnificent ham of very special home-cured quality, bought by Mac at a very special home-curing place he knows in Henley.[2] This was all very excellent, except, of course, that we have no utensil in the flat large enough to boil the said ham in. Consequently, I had to rush to Selfridge's to-day at lunch-time to buy a suitable thing – and after the man had offered me a young copper made of cast-iron and an iron enamelled pan costing 25 shillings, I began to think it would turn out rather an expensive ham. However, I pointed out that we only intended to boil hams from time to time, and not to make a daily habit of it, and we compromised on a tin fish-kettle of much smaller price and incidentally handier. So tonight we shall sit round bathed in the savour of boiling ham. . . .

[1] This was Mac's first introduction to John Anthony, then aged two years and five months.
[2] Cf. Lord Peter Wimsey's words on home-cured ham in *Unnatural Death* (1927), the discussion of the curing of hams in *The Five Red Herrings* (1931), and the episode of the purchase of a ham in *Have His Carcase* (1932).

To Her Mother   24 Great James St
11 June 1926   W.C.1

Dearest Mother –
Very many thanks for your letter and good wishes. We will try to go on being happy and good – particularly if the weather will consent to brighten up, as we find climatic conditions affect the temper! The *Daily Mail* forecast offers a faint hope of a moderately decent first half to our holiday, which starts on June 26th; after that, things are apparently to become progressively worse. We intend to go to a country inn, in a not-too-hilly country (on account of the Ner-a-Car's[1] modest climbing powers) and stray about the countryside when fine and write stories when wet, in the hope of making the holidays pay for themselves. . . .

I am sending another Lord Peter[2] along – it is rather dull, but

Pearson's doesn't like anything really grimly.[3] The old book[4] is a real one – I picked it up for 5 shillings, exactly as described.

Best love to all
    from Mac and Dorothy

[1] A make of motorcycle with a side-car.
[2] 'The Learned Adventure of the Dragon's Head', first published in *Pearson's*, vol. 61, June 1926, pp. 557–66; later included in *Lord Peter Views the Body* (Gollancz, 12 November 1928).
[3] Archaic form of adj. grim.
[4] Sebastian Münster's *Cosmographia Universalis*, published at Basel in 1540.

To Her Mother   24 Great James St
12 July 1926   W.C.1

Dearest Mother –

Here we are home again and ready to receive the leopard[1] as soon as you can send him on. Will he come by post? Oh, yes – he won't be extraordinarily bulky, I suppose. I hope he is all right.

We had a very jolly holiday in the New Forest – only disturbed by a little friction now and again because I am quite determined to reserve the right occasionally to drive my own bike. Of course, when the other person can do a thing much better than you can, it is rather boring for them to sit in the side-car and watch you bungling, but after all, there must be a little give-and-take, and I've seen enough of the results in your case of not being able to get about independently to hang on like grim death to my own liberties. Of course, I know that it is always nerve-wracking to be driven by other people – I pass my time blinking agitatedly when Mac takes corners in racing style and bores alarmingly through traffic – and it's far worse for him, because I know he is a good driver while he hasn't the same comforting knowledge about me. Still, unless one gets a little practice, one will remain a bad driver to the end of one's days! Anyway, I think that with a little necessary firmness and patience the situation will clear itself up all right.

It was very beautiful in the Forest and we had very good weather on the whole – the first week was gorgeous. We liked the hotel very well, too. I was dreadfully disappointed, though, because Mac's miserable tummy was all upset the whole time, and didn't take to the hotel food. It is very worrying that he doesn't seem to get right. He ought to take more care, though I know it is a great nuisance always having to be careful what one eats. However, he was feeling so rotten yesterday that he has determined to go very steady for a bit and really try to get himself fit and behave as a doctor would approve. After all, when one has once been badly gassed one cannot expect to go on quite as usual; I suppose one should be grateful to be alive at all.

The Ner-a-Car went down and came home splendidly, though she gave us a good deal of trouble while we were there. At last we took her completely to pieces and vetted all her innards, and now she seems to be in excellent trim. . . .

[1] A leopard skin rug, a wedding present from her cousin Gerald Sayers, who had taken a post in the East African Colonial Service.

To Ivy Shrimpton   24 Great James St
21 July 1926   W.C.1

Dearest Ivy –

I'm afraid that if any wish was expressed on our part for a country cottage it must have been a pious hope of Mac's (for I cannot imagine a situation less desirable to me personally, who hate the country and love the town – though I suppose, some time, if we grow rich, it may come to banishment for me!) – In any case, it would be absolutely impossible at the moment, since how could we live in Banbury and earn our living in Town? Even week-ends are the devil, so long as I am obliged to be in Kingsway at 9.30 of a Monday morning. I'm very sorry if anything we may have said misled you.

As regards the cottage itself, it would of course be infinitely better for you and the children if you could manage something of the sort, and from what the letter says, the rent does not appear to be excessive for the size of the place. You would have to look into it carefully, of course – the 'attics', for example, may be livable, or they may be box-rooms under the roof. But if all is well, I do not see why, if I were to give you, say £4 a month instead of £3 (as I had already determined to do before many months were over), you should not be able to manage it – especially as you might very well let two of the rooms, and, possibly contrive to cover the rent with them, if it were possible to let them furnished. (As you say, it is a pity you had to let so much of the furniture go – still, you might very likely let them unfurnished and get about half the rent that way at least.) And then, of course, there would be room to take another infant – only in that case, you would have to have help with the work. I think the thing is well worth looking into at any rate, don't you? – I should not try to disguise from the landlady that you would be bringing the children, as any concealment might make difficulties afterwards about the lease. She asked particularly, you see, of whom the household consists. Perhaps it might even be a good move to take Isobel with you to see her – she (Isobel, I mean) is very nice and quiet when 'on view' and doesn't look like anybody liable to scratch the paint! (I shouldn't take John – he does!)

I'm sorry not to be more helpful, but so much depends on the place itself. I should certainly go and have a look at it if I were you. Of course moving etc. is a nuisance and expense. No doubt we could help a little there, though we are still in rather a muddle financially, owing to Mac's income-tax debts and the expense of alterations to the flat, new furniture, telephones, etc.

We would come down and look at it with you, but we have just sold the Ner-a-Car and are 'busless in the interval between that and a more powerful outfit.

In haste, with much love
    Dorothy

To Her Mother   24 Great James St
19 August 1926   W.C.1

Dearest Mother . . .

We have now got a conveyance – paid for it last night but it isn't delivered yet. Mac hated the side-car so much that I had to consent to a small car. I am rather distressed about it, because, though it was very cheap to buy, I'm afraid, what with garage, tax, insurance, oil and petrol, it will be a dreadful drain to keep up. However, anything for a quiet life! If it turns out to be a mistake we shall probably be able to get rid of it without much loss. It's a 2–3 seater coupé Belsize-Bradshaw – a very sweet little engine, though not fast. Of course it's handy for luggage and all that, and no doubt I shall learn to be fond of it in time, though I always dislike cars, which seem to me the most infernal draught-traps ever designed by mad engineers. I don't mind the wind in my face – after all, faces are built for that sort of thing – but since some poisonous man invented wind-screens, one gets it all in the middle of the back, which is unnatural. However, I suppose I've got to settle down to middle-age and a car – I'm hanging on to the solo, though!

Poor Uncle Cecil! I suppose one has to pay for a gay life, though it really would be much more comfortable to be killed off like Achilles[1] at the end of it. People who are separated never *do* send the right money along. I know lots of them, and they *never* do! It simply shows that women ought always to be financially independent, and then they could go away and live by themselves without all this degrading allowancing. I can't see why anybody should ever have to keep another person – except children, of course, that is perfectly proper up to a point – but not wives, particularly when not living with their husbands, because, after all, what is one paying them for in that case? And similarly, of course, rich wives should never part with the control of their money. That kind of thing doesn't suit modern conditions. . . .

The leopard looks very well now he is made up. Miss Quick grooms him lovingly each day and spreads his tail out with reverent hands. Yes, of course, Bloomsbury is packed with hotels of every sort and description. Let us know when you are coming and we will get you a room. . . .

After all this fuss about higher wickets and wider wickets and time-limits for batsmen and pity the poor bowler, the Ashes have been reclaimed on a bowler's wicket in just 4 days! What bosh it all is. Too much newspaper talk and too much bother about averages – that's what's the matter with cricket. – I was so cross that we didn't go to the Oval on Saturday. There was all that talk about all-night queues – and then 15,000 vacant places!

I am now in a fair way to become a Brooklands habituée. Motor racing is a little disappointing at first – the track is so huge that one simply does not realise the speed. The motor-cycles seem much faster than the cars, for some reason.

Best love from us both
    D.

[1] According to a late tradition, Achilles fell in love with Polyxena and was killed by her brother Paris.

To Her Parents   24 Great James St
23 September 1926   W.C.1

Dearest people . . .

Mac and I enjoyed having you up here enormously and we hope you will come again and stay several days. I am sure Mac likes having such a nice mother to look after – he does do the looking-after business rather pleasingly, don't you think?[1] I always feel it would be so dreadful to have married a man who was helpless with waiters or tried to argue taxi-men out of their tips, like Colin Hutchinson![2] It's so awkward standing by and trying to look as if one didn't belong! . . .

[1] Mac had met her parents at the station and had cooked the dinner.
[2] Her cousin Gwen's husband.

To Ivy Shrimpton   24 Great James St
7 October 1926   W.C.1

Dearest Ivy –

I've been in such a beast of a rush with work the last few days,
I've hardly had time even to go to the Bank – and no time to write
a line!

By the way, I couldn't help grinning after your cheery remark about
not now being so likely to break my neck! On the way home we
barged full-tilt and head-on into another bloke, or he into us or both,
smashed the car, bruised ourselves and only by extreme good luck
were not abolished off the face of the earth! Mac said it was the other
man's fault – personally I think it was because he will drive so fiercely
at night – however, I don't say so and the police accepted our version
of the matter!! Anyway, don't make any more of these unfortunate
prophecies – next time we might get the happy despatch! – I didn't
mention it at home, by the way, so please don't! . . . I don't *like* cars!

To Her Mother   24 Great James St
19 October 1926   W.C.1

Dearest Mother –

I am very sorry not to have written before, but the fact is, I have
been having (what I haven't had for years and *years*!) a nasty chill
on the liver, which turned me a beautiful bright yellow all over,
exactly like a canary!! The local medico came to look at it, but was
not much impressed. He just said I was to stay at home and live on
fish, which I have been doing, and am now almost normal in colour
again and my inside has calmed down. Mac is a splendid person to
have about when one is ill, looking after one in the most noble and
devoted way and cooking everything most beautifully, though he has
been having a very horrid cold himself poor dear. I felt quite a fraud
just lying there and being looked after, because I wasn't really feeling
particularly bad most of the time, but of course one can't go about
coloured all over like an advertisement for mustard. I really was a
sight when stripped, I do assure you, just like a Chinee! – Anyway,
I'm much better now, thanks to Mac, who is the sort of person that
the poor call 'a good husband'! This is why we haven't arranged to
see Aunt G, though we had meant to do so, but it is no good seeing
people when one is bilious and bright yellow with 'catarrhal
jaundice'!!! . . .

To Her Mother   24 Great James St
14 December 1926   W.C.1

Dearest Mother –

I am glad that article entertained you – also it is very nice of you to write all these kind things about my hair, but I really can't help laughing over your enthusiasm for my 'new style of hair-dressing'. Because

1) The photograph in question is 3 years old;
2) The 'hair' is not hair but a college cap;
3) I should indeed be an ass to go back to long hair at the very moment when a kind fashion has been brought in which puts short, scrappy hair on an equality with long hair, enables me to comb my hair back so that it looks thicker on top, displays my really fine points, viz: a beautifully shaped head and neat ears, and brings foreheads into fashion for the first time in a century!

Not on your life! – I enclose a very clever flashlight photograph taken by Mac on Sunday for press purposes, which shows me as a very handsome woman, for the first time in my life – and be damned to it! . . .

Please thank Dad very much for his cheque, and tell him I am shocked to the marrow to find him – a nice, elderly country parson, whose heart should be all charity and good-will, instantly jumping to the most scandalous explanation of the Christie business![1] Oh, dear me! What hot-beds of suspicion and scandal-mongering these quiet little villages are! . . .

Mac sends best love. He is working at high pressure trying to get my stuff into the papers, and is a perfectly magnificent press agent!

With lots of love to all
    Your (still shingled)
        Dorothy . . .

[1] Agatha Christie had mysteriously disappeared and was found eventually in a hotel in Harrogate, having, it was said, lost her memory.

To Ivy Shrimpton   24 Great James St
4 March 1927   W.C.1

Dearest Ivy –

I had been to the bank and brought away the notes all ready to send you, when Mac suddenly borrowed them from me for an urgent payment that had to be made, and as I don't want to keep you waiting

over the week-end, I'm afraid it will have to be a cheque again. I
hope it isn't too inconvenient. . . .

As for horrors – certainly we do seem to be capping each other's
efforts in a curious way – nothing you can produce can possibly equal
the dreadful death of Mac's poor friend, Parry Thomas,[1] who had his
head torn right off while trying to beat the record in his racing car
yesterday on Pendine Sands.[2] No doubt you have read all about it in
the papers. Poor soul! He was an awfully decent fellow, I believe. I
saw him, but never talked to him – a nice, friendly, unassuming
creature, and one of the greatest racing motorists that ever lived. He
is a sacrifice, I suppose, to science and the making of roads safe for
motorists. We know now that chains must be made stronger or provided with suitable safeguards, but it seems a biggish price to pay.
Horrid though the accident sounds, it was really very merciful, for
he can never have known what hit him, and it is far better to be killed
at once like that, and not pinned under a burning car in agony and
perhaps hauled out, still alive and dreadfully mutilated.

Of course, it upset Mac very much, but happily he had to get to
work at once and write up the story for his paper, and that sort of
worked it off a bit. He is at work on an article now, and keeps on
having loud conversations on the telephone with newspaper editors
and people, so that if my letter is a little incoherent, you must put it
down to the interruptions.

On account of the extreme voracity, agility and fecundity of the
mice, we have had to get a new kitten. It is very small and hasn't
caught any mice as yet, but no doubt it will before long. Our charlady,
of course, with the mistaken kindness of a Mrs Spiller, promptly
started to overfeed it, and it had to be given castor-oil. All right now
and very lively again, but I do wish people would have some sense
and not regard the stomachs of animals and children as convenient
refuse-dumps!

I am charmed to hear that John Anthony has developed a liking
for priests – I couldn't have stood it if it had been an evangelical
minister. However, if he shows any signs of being religious, I wash
my hands of him. You may remember that I've got a friend[3] who
wants to adopt him if he turns out a crook or a burglar, and I don't
want to spoil his chances. . . .

By the way, I'm trying to get an allowance for J.A. from the Income-
tax people. I've had to give them your name and address of course.
I don't suppose they'll make any bothering inquiries, but if they do,
would you be good enough to answer any questions – say I send you
the payments and so on? . . .

[1] J. G. P. Thomas, prominent in motor-racing in the 1920s.
[2] In Wales, near Tenby.

³ It is not known who the friend was. It seems that at least one friend of D.L.S. knew that she had a child.

To Her Mother   Hotel Meurice
20 March 1927   Boulogne-sur-Mer

Dearest Mother –

We rushed violently over here yesterday afternoon at about half an hour's notice. Mac is investigating the Daniels case¹ and I am fooling about, hoping that an opportunity may present itself to ask leading questions! Anyway, it was a very jolly trip over – simply glorious weather, sunshine and the cafés open till 2 in the morning. We rolled into bed about 2.30 and feel all the better for it, in spite of an intensive course of mixed drinks during the evening. Mac seems to have pals in every corner in Boulogne – taxi-drivers, pub-keepers, interpreters, ex-detectives etc. – and of course, what with the *affaire Daniels* and the Terrington case,² the place is swarming with English journalists. It seems a very good way of getting one's jaunts at somebody else's expense – in this case, *John Bull*'s – the paper, I mean – not the tax-payer. This sort of life suits Mac; he was over here for a story (alone) on Weds. and Thurs. and now we have rushed over and I go back on the 7 o'clock boat. We both feel thoroughly jogged up and pleased. . . .

¹ An English nurse named Daniels had been found dead in a field near Boulogne with a hypodermic syringe by her side. *Unnatural Death* was published by Ernest Benn on 16 September 1927 but D.L.S. was at work on it by October 1925. It contains an allusion to the Daniels case, added at a late stage. It was her custom, when she had finished a novel, to sprinkle it with topical allusions, culled from the file of the *Daily Mail*. (See her letter to Eustace Barton dated 9 February 1930.)
² Lord Terrington was arrested in Boulogne on bankruptcy charges. The case was rendered sensational by the fact that he was accompanied by a woman who was not his wife and that he collapsed and died of a heart attack soon after his arrest.

To Ivy Shrimpton   24 Great James St
4 April 1927   W.C.1

Dearest Ivy –

We had such a shock on Saturday afternoon – we have hardly got over it yet! Our char had just taken her departure and we were sitting peacefully by the fireside, when Mac suddenly said, 'Where's the kitten?' – 'In the kitchen' says I. 'No, he isn't' says Mac, going to see. We searched the three rooms of the flat high and low – opened all the cupboards, lay down and looked under the bed, called – no go. So we thought he must have slipped out when the door was opened. We searched the bathroom, the stairs, the back-yard and the other flats. At last we made up our minds that the poor little beggar must somehow have managed to get out of the street-door and, terrified by the noise of the traffic, have bolted away and got hopelessly lost. Nevertheless, I sought him at the greengrocer's, the milk-shop, the pub and in all the surrounding streets. I found one stray tom-cat, but he wasn't ours. At length we resigned ourselves, and sat mourning his loss, and starting every now and then when we fancied we heard the patter of little feet. (Pause for sob-stuff here.)

All this happened at about 2 in the afternoon. At 10.30 Mac went to bed and I stayed up to finish a book. Presently I heard an astonished voice say 'What the devil are you doing here?' and Mac called out, 'Why, the cat's here!'

Now, at dinner time I had, in desperation, promised a large candle to St Anthony if he would restore the cat, but I hadn't expected so prompt a response. 'Where is he?' I said. 'Under the mattress,' said Mac. 'Under the what?' said I, rushing in.

He was. Right under a heavy hair mattress, between that and the box-spring bed with the blankets tucked tightly in all round, to say nothing of Mac's 13 stone or so planted firmly on the top. He had been made up in the bed for 10 hours in a state – one would suppose – of complete suffocation! He seemed none the worse, except that he was very hungry.[1] Manifestly a miracle, and I must now see about that candle, for S. Anthony[2] is a keen man of business and does not care to be trifled with.

Otherwise nothing much has happened. We were over in Boulogne a fortnight ago on this Nurse Daniels mystery. It was glorious weather and we enjoyed the outing – at the newspaper's expense! I think we shall have to devise some way of going to live abroad. What with the income-tax and D.O.R.A.[3] and the licensing hours,[4] England is no country for free men! . . .

---

[1] D.L.S. later used this incident in a short story broadcast over the radio in 1954. Lord Peter Wimsey relates that when he was a small boy his kitten was lost and he called on Sherlock Holmes in Baker Street to ask him to solve the mystery. The great man suggested he should look under the mattress.

[2] St Anthony of Padua is credited with the ability to find things that are mislaid. His name-day is 13 June, the birthday of D.L.S.

[3] Defence of the Realm Act, introduced during World War I, which imposed restrictions on the consumption of alcohol. The Act is mentioned in *Have His Carcase* (chapter 21).

[4] Hours during which it was lawful to sell alcohol.

To Ivy Shrimpton   24 Great James St
3 May 1927   W.C.1

Dearest Ivy –

Herewith doings[1] and some horses for J.A. – I suppose, with the usual perversity of children, he now prefers goats or motor-cars. However!

I'm rather hard at work over my new book,[2] so there isn't much to write about. You will be sorry to hear that there are no pretty girls in it – I find them a nuisance in detective stories; they get in the way of the plot. It is a disagreeable book and no one will like it – still, such as it is, I must get on with it.

We had a very jolly Easter holiday at Maldon.[3] We found a splendid inn, where the cooking satisfied Mac, and I managed to get a good deal of writing done. We are going back there for our summer fortnight.

I saw Aunt G. a little time ago – as usual, she was very keen on running other people's business for them and had retired Dad and Mother on a pension and set them up in a private hotel or boarding-house in a seaside resort before I could say 'knife'. I pointed out that Mother would want to cut the throats of all the other inhabitants of the hotel and that Dad would be bored to death by them – to which she replied that one could easily live in a hotel without speaking to anybody. In that case, why go to a hotel? – But she seemed so pleased with the arrangement that I contented myself with an interior certainty that nobody would pay the slightest attention to her advice! Portrait of inhabitants (residents) of small hotels in 'resorts' – going to dinner – such nice people – Mother would be sure to like them!

In the meantime that infernal car has had to be taken to pieces for about the sixth time. Mac is fed up and wants to sell it and get a better one, but I have told him that we cannot possibly afford it, and such as it is, must put up with it till our debts are paid off! (Income-tax arrears, that is) – so that's that!

Hope all are well – Best love from us both.
Dorothy

¹ Slang for money.
² *Unnatural Death.*
³ In Essex, the county in which she and Mac were soon to settle.

To Ivy Shrimpton   24 Great James St
13 May 1927   W.C.1

Dearest Ivy –

How very tiresome of John Anthony! – just as you are so busy too. Mac laughed and said, 'Well, he's beginning early.' From what I've seen of J.A. I should say he was fated to break a good many bones before he had finished. The collar-bone is a good thing to begin on, though, as you say, being young he doesn't give it a chance to mend. I expect they'll have to strap him up eventually – they usually do. I believe that one never breaks the same collar-bone twice – or very sel-dom, as it is much thickened and strengthened by breaking – it is a badly-designed bone, much too slender to take the hard wear given to it by adventurous humans. I shouldn't worry much if I were you, though of course it must add a lot to your work, for which I am very sorry. I enclose cheque for £3 to carry on with. Say when you want more. I'm glad the kid has pluck, anyhow – maternal affection is by no means my strong point, I must say, but if there must be children, it is preferable that they should have some guts. Poor kid. Never mind – a collar-bone or two is a trifling matter, really – not like measles or small-pox or men-ingitis or encephalitis lethargica or any of those things. . . .

Hope your new infant is going on nicely and is not upset by the hurly-burly over J.A. – Give Isobel my love and say I'm sure she's being a splendid help looking after John. . . .

To Ivy Shrimpton   The Ship Hotel
5 June 1927   Market Hill
                                                     Maldon
                                                     Essex

Dearest Ivy –

How are you and all your troubles? Nearly over, I hope. Glad to get your card and learn that J.A. had more or less ceased from troubling.

We have been in a great scramble the last few days getting off for our holiday. Eventually we came down yesterday in two sections – 1) Myself, in light skirmishing trim, on motor-bike with two packed saddle-bags and a coat tied on with string – 2) Mac, in car, with about 10 packages, including golf clubs, a camera, a bag of knitting and an uncooked ham! Mac had been cursing the 'damn bike' the day before – however, having looked at the luggage, he remarked that it was just as well I had got the bike, as there certainly would not have been room for me in the car.

I am sending the usual money. If more is needed this month for doctor's bills, let me know. How awkward about Isobel's people.[1] Hope to see you before long – if I can get down.

> Best love
>   D.

[1] They had ceased to send money for Isobel's keep.

Ernest Benn, founder of Benn's Sixpenny Library (the predecessor of Penguin Books, which were originally sold for sixpence a volume), published three novels by D.L.S.: Unnatural Death *(1927),* The Unpleasantness at the Bellona Club *(1928) and* The Documents in the Case *(1930). He also published, in 1929, her translation of the mediaeval French poem by the Anglo-Norman poet Thomas, which she entitled* Tristan in Brittany. *D.L.S. was dissatisfied with Benn's promotion of authors and when her contract with him had been fulfilled she changed to Gollancz, who published the rest of her novels and all her short stories.*

Victor Gollancz (1893–1967) was a contemporary of D.L.S. at Oxford, but they did not know each other at that time. In 1920 he was managing director of the Book Department with Benn Brothers. In 1927 he set up his own publishing firm, with Stanley Morrison as typographer. D.L.S. was impressed by him and told him she wished him to act as her publisher when her contract with Benn ran out. In the meantime he suggested that she should select and edit a series of short stories by other authors and accepted a volume of her own. She undertook the task of editing with immense enthusiasm and eventually three volumes were brought out, entitled Great Short Stories of Detection, Mystery and Horror *(1928, 1931 and 1934). Her introduction to the first, tracing the origin and development of detective fiction, has become a classic.*

Victor Gollancz founded the Left Book Club in 1936 and in 1945 started the Save Europe Now movement to relieve starvation in Germany. He was knighted in 1965. It was said of him that he would never bring out a book that put

*forward ideas which challenged his own convictions. The charge of anti-Semitism
has frequently been brought against D.L.S. but neither Ernest Benn nor Victor
Gollancz (both of whom were Jewish) saw reason to complain of it in her
writings.*

TO VICTOR GOLLANCZ   24 Great James St
29 October 1927   W.C.1

My dear Mr Gollancz –

Having first assured myself that it was *not* your offices which the
crane fell through last night (which might have seemed an ill omen,
had it occurred), I proceed to enclose a copy of Benn's reply to mine.
I gather he rather means to have his bond. I suppose I shall have to
go and see him, and I shall take the opportunity of pointing out that
whereas I know what you can do with a book, it will be very much
up to him to show what he can do on his own!

If he does insist on having his two books, there is only one offer
which I can possibly make to you, and you will probably greet it with
shrieks and snorts of derision. I shan't mind one bit if you do, because
I know it is not at all attractive. But if you really think that my
undistinguished name is of the slightest value to your first list, there
are – I hesitate to mention them – the Lord Peter short stories. I
know that short stories are disliked at the libraries and by the majority
of the public – moreover, I don't think they are by any means among
my happiest efforts, – and I think they're a poor sort of thing to start
on, but they're all I've got to offer if Benn takes the novels. There
are nine of them at present, five of which were published in *Pearson's
Magazine* and one in *The Twenty Story Mag.*, while two were considered
'too gruesome' and another turned down by everybody for reasons
unspecified. I could, by exercising a little energy, make them up to
a dozen or so, or whatever number was necessary. – It doesn't sound
encouraging, I'm afraid! But if you feel the slightest desire for them,
you can have them like a shot on any sort of terms you think may
enable you to get rid of them without losing money. I'd be absolutely
content with anything you thought they were worth – short, of course,
of sale outright or anything obviously criminal! But please say straight
away if you think they'd only be a nuisance to you! I won't send them
along, anyhow till I've been through them and tidied them up a bit,
and put back the bits the magazines cut out, and removed the worst
blemishes. But I am quite prepared for your saying you wouldn't
touch short stories with a barge-pole.

Of course, I haven't lost all hope of rescuing the novels, but I don't
actually want a violent row with Benn, because it never pays to make

enemies of people, does it? You never know how things may come back on you – and of course, legally the man has his rights, and if he says he paid money for a thing and I'm now trying to take the thing away, I suppose he has a claim to what he has paid for. I can't do more than ask him to be a sportsman, and perhaps, as far as feelings go, he *is* a pachyderm!

Very sincerely yours
    Dorothy L. Sayers

To Her Father   24 Great James St
24 November 1927   W.C.1

Dearest Dad . . .

Aunt G. is a marvellous woman! She wasn't at the wedding[1] – yet she gathers all the juicy episodes from somebody, and sends them to you in time for them to return to me within five days, in spite of a Sunday intervening! She should have attached herself to Fleet Street – she would have made a marvellous reporter.

Mac got out of going (man-like, having committed me to going) on various specious pretexts, so I had to go alone. A beast of a day, and the usual farce! A long wait in the church, with everybody twisting their necks to see what had become of the wedding-party, and a consistently irreligious atmosphere, as always. The youngest brides-maid went to Malden, and, as you say, did not turn up till the end of the ceremony. However, we had one thrill, when the bride's mother, having come forward to give the bride away, fell full length with a crash on the floor of the chancel! We all thought she was overcome with emotion, and visualised headlines: 'Touching Incident at Fashionable Wedding' – 'Bride's Mother Carried out in a Fit' – but it turned out that she had merely tripped over something, and rose, dusting herself and putting her hat straight, in the arms of the bride-groom's father, who had rushed forward with chivalrous promptness to her assistance. This rather distracted public attention from the vows; however, we noted that no difficulty was made over the word 'obey', though in the earlier part of the service we had the bowdlerised version, substituting for those who have not the gift of continency an inharmonious and ill-constructed phrase about the regulation of the natural instincts; I do not know why the efforts of modern liturgists should sound so much like a journalese report of a scientific lecture.

After the ceremony, and in view of the fact that the church was a drizzling and inconvenient mile from the railway station, I very strategically got out before anyone else, and introduced myself to

Uncle Cecil, who looked, I thought, remarkably well, and who said, tactlessly, that he would never have known me, I had got so fat in the face. I asked, pathetically, whether it was possible to find any method of conveyance to the station, with the anticipated result that he at once and most efficiently got hold of a bright young solicitor, with the top hat and the spats and the buttonhole and everything, to drive me back to town. This passed off excellently – a halt being made on the way to have a row with a man who obstructed our progress at a corner – the solicitor getting out to argue with the man and take his number, while his sister explained plaintively that 'there was always a scene like this whenever one went out with Charles'. Accordingly, we arrived in good spirits at the reception. There, oddly enough, I met a girl who was a pupil of mine at Hull. She reintroduced herself, and I said I remembered her perfectly. So I did – she distinguished herself while I was there, by being taken up for shop-lifting at Woolworth's, though I believe the charge was never substantiated. However, I did not allude to this interesting episode.

There was the usual appalling scrum of people who none of them knew each other in rooms too small to accommodate them. The bride, as usual, looked self-possessed – long veil and all the doings; the bridegroom, also as usual, looked quite wild and unable to recognise anybody. We then scrambled to look at the presents – which you can list for yourselves – the usual silver dishes, conventional candle-sticks and glass-ware. I found our wine-funnel, with somebody else's card attached to it, and having put right this regrettable error, started to search for your gift, but was swept away by a stream of people. I observed with malicious joy that some member of the Hutchinson family had positively presented the young couple with the poems of Dante Gabriel Rossetti in padded green covers – a useful and appropriate gift to start life on! I forgot to mention that the leading parson at the service (the Dean of Canterbury?) had, so to speak, had the young couple up before him at the altar steps, while he told them what a beautiful thing it was for them to go out and present the benighted natives of East Africa with the edifying example of an English Christian home. So embarrassing for them, poor things! – No doubt the poems of Rossetti would be a great help in this direction, as typifying devotion to culture and all that sort of thing!

Having viewed the presents, we made a rush for the food, but my particular section of the assembly got rather crowded out. However, we stood at the door, hungrily, rather like a collection of Lazaruses at the house of Dives, till a resourceful young naval officer in epaulettes plunged into the kitchen, and produced for each of us an inch or so of wedding cake and half a glass of champagne. And I cannot imagine anything less satisfying to the stomach after staggering out to Morden and having no lunch! – At this point, Uncle Cecil emerged from the press and carried me off to talk to old Mrs Hutchinson, who made the remark that none of Gerald's relations were there at all, except his father and myself; so I suppose my presence gave some satisfaction to somebody. We then stood round and bored each other, waiting for the bride to come down, Mrs Hutchinson observing anxiously from time to time that she had a train to catch; while the naval gentleman went off with some boon companions to prepare a massed attack of rice and confetti. After much delay, the bride came down in a little orange silk frock and close hat with a feather, to say that she had got to say the good-byes herself, as Gerald had lost his hat, and the best man had gone to look for it. So we made more conversation – during which I noticed that a dim idea seemed to be forming in people's minds that weddings were rather tiresome than otherwise – and finally Gerald appeared, more distraught than ever, *with* his hat, – and the bridal pair were driven away with confused noise and garments rolled in rice. After which, I discovered our hostess and bade her good-bye and took farewell of Uncle Cecil and Mrs Garth, and bolted for the nearest tea-shop, where I hastily filled myself up with tea and crumpets and felt better!

The general verdict, in fact, was that it was a very pretty wedding and went off very well. But I couldn't help feeling that Mac's method and mine, of only asking about four people and giving them some decent food to eat, had a good deal to be said in its favour. Still, I can say, like Nelson, 'Thank God, I have done my duty!'

Uncle Cecil was very nice to me, and looked after me in the kindest way, which was very good of him, considering that he must have had a tremendous lot of things to think about.

So much for the wedding.

Thank you very much for what you say about a Christmas present. May we think it over and let you know in a day or two? – I believe the book[2] is doing pretty well.

> With best love to everybody
> Ever yours devotedly
> Dorothy

[1] The wedding of her cousin Gerald Sayers and Molly Garth.
[2] *Unnatural Death*.

To VICTOR GOLLANCZ   24 Great James St
25 November 1927   W.C.1

Dear Mr Gollancz,

Yes, rather, of course, like a shot! It's most frightfully good of you to suggest it and I should love to do it.[1] Indeed, I have always yearned after some book of the sort. When can we talk it over? – The only thing is that of course I have only my evenings and week-ends to work in at present, so I should have to be allowed enough time to work at it. (Damn this beastly office!) But if I wasn't too dreadfully hurried, there is no job I should like better. I think it should be kept as far as possible along the lines of mystery and detection and not too much sheer horrors and ghost-grues, because the latter has been done once or twice, whereas, so far as I know, the detective field has scarcely been touched. It ought to be hugely successful – I'm awfully thrilled!

Also, many thanks for what you say about my short stories. I will start as soon as I can to lick them into presentable shape. I am seeing Benn on Tuesday, so we shall know then about the novels. If he is adamant, then I'll push the 'Bellona Club'[2] story ahead for him and the shorts for you – and if his publicity and yours should burst on the world side by side it will no doubt be to everybody's advantage and the admiration of a dazzled world! . . .

Oh! about the finance of this proposed book – I'm sure we shall agree all right about that. I don't imagine I should quarrel with any arrangement you might suggest – but you can always argue it out with Mac, who is a Scotsman, you know!

Panting with anticipation (not of the fee, I don't mean, but of this exciting job),

> Very sincerely yours
> Dorothy L. Sayers

[1] Victor Gollancz had asked her if she would like to edit an anthology of short stories of detection, mystery and horror.
[2] *The Unpleasantness at the Bellona Club*, first published 6 July 1928.

To Victor Gollancz   24 Great James St
28 November 1927   W.C.1

Dear Mr Gollancz,
SHORT STORIES
It's very difficult to get a name for these which isn't awfully dull, or which isn't exactly like the title of fifty thousand other volumes of detective stories. The series was originally called, simply:
LORD PETER WIMSEY: UNPROFESSIONAL SLEUTH
> (Which *Pearson's Magazine*, urged by some obscure motive of delicacy or etymological accuracy, altered to 'Unprofessional Detective'!)

We might say alternatively:
LORD PETER ON THE SCENT
LORD PETER ON THE TRAIL
LORD PETER INVESTIGATES
LORD PETER TAKES A HAND
or, in a livelier vein:
LORD PETER SMELLS A RAT
LORD PETER VIEWS THE BODY[1]
    (only some of them have no bodies, owing to the editor of *Pearson's*
        not liking bodies very much)
or, further:
LORD PETER WIMSEY'S CASES (CLIENTS, TRIUMPHS,
    HOBBY)
or, in the Chestertonian manner:
THE INQUISITIVENESS OF LORD PETER WIMSEY
I'm not in love with any of them, but the name rather ties one down.
    The stories at present in existence are:

1.) The Fascinating Problem of UNCLE MELEAGER'S WILL.
2.) The Abominable History of THE MAN WITH COPPER
    FINGERS.
3.) The Learned Adventure of THE DRAGON'S HEAD.
4.) The Entertaining Episode of THE ARTICLE IN QUESTION.
5.) The Bibulous Business of A MATTER OF TASTE.
6.) The Unprincipled Affair of THE PRACTICAL JOKER.
7.) The Vindictive Errand of THE FOOTSTEPS THAT RAN.[2]
8.) The Fantastic Horror of THE CAT IN THE BAG.
    and in addition a pleasant little detective tale which is not a Lord
    Peter adventure, called,
9.) THE INSPIRATION OF MR BUDD.
    (This is the only story which has been published in America.)

These nine stories make up, roughly, 53,000 words. So that I shall
have to write about five more stories to bring the volume to 80,000
words.

OMNIBUS VOLUME

Twenty volumes of *Strand Magazine* have now arrived, and we are
having to build a new set of bookshelves. In a day or two I hope to
be able to put forward a more detailed list of suggested stories and
some suggestions for arrangement. I don't know quite whether to
keep the detective yarns and horror scopes separate or mix them up,
whether to arrange the authors chronologically or alphabetically or
what. How soon shall you be getting your first announcement out? . . .

[1] The title eventually chosen. The volume was first published 12 November 1928.
[2] Later changed to 'The Vindictive Story of the Footsteps that Ran'.

To Victor Gollancz   24 Great James St
6 December 1927   W.C.1

Dear Mr Gollancz –

I hope you aren't thinking that I am being slack, because I am really working quite hard. At present I am buried up to my eyes in old *Strands*, reading through and selecting, and I have thought of a number of other tales etc. which I had forgotten at the first selection. But it all takes time, and there is so little left when office hours are over.

Benn's book[1] is in its ninth chapter, and I am really hoping to have that pretty well off my hands by the end of my Christmas holiday, after which I shall turn to and do the remainder of your short stories for 'Lord Peter', if I can find plots! After that, I shall be able to tackle the omnibus volume with full powers, and by that time I ought to have pretty well done the preliminary selection.

If, meanwhile, you would like me to come round and see you about exact title, arrangement etc., I am at your service any evening.

    Yours very sincerely
      Dorothy L. Sayers

[1] *The Unpleasantness at the Bellona Club.*

To Ivy Shrimpton   24 Great James St
18 December 1927   W.C.1

Dearest Ivy –

Here – with all good wishes and so forth – is the money for the month with a little bit added in. I thought probably a small cheque would be the most useful form of present as you are moving. I'm so glad you have found a cottage[1] at last. I think it sounds rather jolly – with, as you say, the possible exception of the water-tap. (I hope it is not frozen up at this moment!) As regards moving, the very cheapest way is as a rule to get the local greengrocer or other trades-man to do it some afternoon when his van is not being used for other purposes – however, you probably know far more about moving than I do! If the cottage is 200 years old it is probably solidly built and on the warm side – none of your single-thickness-of-brick-blown-together-in-the-night outfits.

It will be a joy to you to be free from interference and to have *more room*. It has a little worried me, your being so cramped for space at Cowley. Of course it would be rather fun if it were haunted – only it might be bad for the children.

I have had a parcel sent off from Selfridge's containing a box of bricks for John and a toy typewriter for general family use! It is supposed to be fairly solid and durable, and with patience one can type a letter on it quite satisfactorily. I thought it might be of assistance and entertainment in the educational way. I have sent them to Cowley, as I gather from your letter that you are there till after Christmas. I am also sending a few oddments along to-day. The tea-set is Mac's special present and the fairy-tale book is mine – the little chocs and the cheap jewellery (!) for stockings – 6d at Woolworth's! – but children like them.

All good wishes and all possible success in the new venture. Heaven knows when we shall get to see you! I am getting rid of that ghastly car. . . .

---

[1] The cottage was in Westcott Barton, a village near Oxford, approached via the Banbury Road. It was originally named Cocksparrow Hall. Ivy renamed it The Sidelings.

To Victor Gollancz   24 Great James St
30 January 1928   W.C.1

Dear Mr Gollancz –

Herewith rough list of Section 1. I am still on the track of one or two admirable tales which elude me – the gentleman who eliminated people by plunging them in a tank full of liquid air, for instance. I shall probably find him in the British Museum on Saturday.

I have also a list of about 40 authors for section 2, and, in addition, a number of horrors marked down in old magazines, which I haven't yet classified. I shall be getting on to these this evening, I hope, but I am being bothered with a kind of tonsilitis, which is making work awfully difficult.

Do you think we had better leave foreign writers out altogether? If we put in one, we ought to put in all, and there's no end to it! The English-speaking field is rich enough. We might have foreign ones in a future volume.

I haven't got a great number of unknown gems. When you come to look into it, the best stories, as a rule, seem to be written by the best writers. It is curious to find how often a tale that stood out and impressed my youthful mind turned out, when investigated, to have a famous name attached to it. Either my untrained taste was surprisingly good, or else there really is a 'great gulf fixed', and success is actually the reward for merit.

I'm still struggling with the preface – can't get it quite right, but it's shaping.

I have also thought of the plot of another 'Lord Peter' short story

– making four out of the five needed to complete the volume. At present the tales will be:

The Tragical Comedy of the Automatic Call-Box[1]
The Undignified Melodrama of the Bone of Contention
The Bathetic[2] Tragedy of the Scandalous Changeling
The Uproarious Farce of the Stolen Stomach[3]

When I'm decently fit, these won't take long to write. With apologies for being such a crock –

    Yours very sincerely
      Dorothy L. Sayers

[1] This was never completed but exists in an unfinished state in MS in the Marion E. Wade Center, Wheaton College, Illinois.
[2] From the handwriting, this word could be either 'bathetic' or 'pathetic'. Nothing is known of the story.
[3] Later changed to 'The Piscatorial Farce of the Stolen Stomach'.

To Ivy Shrimpton   24 Great James St
No date, but ? May 1928   W.C.1

Dearest Ivy,

I have been living in rather a rush these few days. We go for our holiday at the end of the month, and there seem to be thousands of things to clear up before we start.

Anyway, herewith the doings. I have made it a trifle more this month, just for fun!

How are you all? We are all right, but needing that holiday badly. London is rather tending to get on our nerves. No doubt we shall come all right again in the fresh air. To-day the place is like a hot-house.

I'm glad J.A. seems to be growing up intelligent, but he seems to have a shocking habit of contradicting. However, I seem to remember having done much the same sort of thing myself. It wears off, in the course of thirty years or so!

Bless you, my dear! It's a tremendous comfort to have you there behind me. I'll pay it back to you some day – if I can – and so far as such things are repayable.

    Ever your loving
      Dorothy

To Her Mother   24 Great James St
27 March 1928   W.C.1

Dearest Mother,

Just a line to say how sorry I am to think that dear old Uncle Percy[1] is no longer in this world – though I expect it's much jollier where he is now – not so confusing and uncertain. Although I didn't keep up with him lately[2] as much as I ought to have done, I always felt he was a dear thing, and I'm glad I did at least remember to send the books along and that he enjoyed them. What a curious, lonely life he led, didn't he – what did he do exactly? I never quite knew. I always pictured him sitting in his shirt sleeves beside that little house in a clearing that we had the photograph of. Mac asked how old he was, and I couldn't quite remember. He was older than you, wasn't he?

I am so glad he has left a bit to Ivy; it will be a great help to her. She seems much happier, doesn't she, now she has that little cottage of her own. She is a solitary-minded person, too – like most of our lot, I think. It is very sweet of Uncle P. to have thought of me, also.[3] . . .

[1] Her mother's brother, Percival Leigh, who had recently died in Australia.
[2] Her letters from school show that she wrote to him regularly at Christmas.
[3] He bequeathed D.L.S. £500.

To Eustace Barton   24 Great James St
4 April 1928   W.C.1

Dear Dr Barton,

Please excuse my delay in answering your very kind letter of March 30th. Nothing would give me greater pleasure than to see you when you are in town on the 11th. Unfortunately, as both my husband and myself are out at work all day, we have no free time for callers except in the evening. As perhaps this would be rather inconvenient, would it be possible for us to meet for lunch? I should very much enjoy having a talk with you and discussing your most interesting detective story work.

I selected 'A Handful of Ashes' for inclusion[1] partly because it is an excellent story, and also, partly because I had always supposed that Mr Austin Freeman[2] was the first to use this idea of discovering how a person died through examination of his ashes after cremation. I was most thrilled to find, on studying the back numbers of the Strand, that you had anticipated him by some years; not that I would suggest plagiarism or anything of that kind on Mr Freeman's part, I do not mean that for a moment, but I feel strongly that sufficient notice has never been taken of the extremely ingenious and delightful

medico-legal plots which you and Mrs Meade[3] evolved at so comparatively early a date.

By the way, can you tell me whether 'The Sanctuary Club' was
published in book form, and if so, by whom? This information would
help me considerably in getting the necessary permission (if it *is* necessary) from the publishers.

With many thanks for the kind interest you express, and hoping
very much to see you when you are in town,

I remain,
Yours very truly,
Dorothy L. Sayers

[1] In the anthology she was editing for Gollancz. It was not ultimately included because
the publishers, Ward Lock, would not give permission.
[2] R. Austin Freeman (1862–1943).
[3] Mrs L. T. Meade (1854–1914), who initiated the medical mystery story with her *Stories
from the Diary of a Doctor*, published in 1893, which she continued in *The Sorceress of the
Strand*, published in 1902. In this volume she collaborated with Dr Robert Eustace Barton
(1868–1943), whose pseudonym was Robert Eustace.

TO HER MOTHER   24 Great James St
10 April 1928   W.C.1

Dearest Mater –

I believe Mac is writing to you, in accordance with a 'faithful
promise'. As, however, I am growing old and sceptical, I am writing
too.

We did so enjoy our week-end, and are feeling ever so much better
for it. It was so jolly seeing you all and we both thought you all
looking wonderfully well, especially considering what a damnable
winter it has been.

We saw the great Turner[1] on the way back, also poor dear old
Blankets who is getting very old, poor old thing, but looks very healthy
and happy – rather like an aged white pet rabbit. He was charmed
to see us and recognised me immediately. I then looked in at Bryant's[2]
– old B. just the same, and his shop looking wonderfully nice and
quite up-to-date, with nice, pretty materials and frocks, etc., and all
his girls in a charming dull-blue uniform. He says the big stores
have not affected him much, as he builds his success on studying his
customers' personal requirements, which *they* can't do. I congratu-
lated him on this. Miss Ely and Miss James then appeared – absolutely unchanged from 30 years ago, or so it seemed to me! – standing
side by side and giggling like schoolgirls at being specially asked for
and remembered. So we exchanged some little pleasantries about the
new fashions, and then old Bryant pranced down to the door with me,

most attentive, and saying he had read *Unnatural Death*. Everybody particularly wanted to be remembered to you and Aunt Mabel.

We had an excellent run home, arriving just about 6 o'clock when our insurance ran out! In fact, I think we had about 5 minutes without cover, but fortunately nothing untoward happened.

We haven't yet seen Tidman's cellars, by the way, as he was called out unexpectedly, but we got the wine, which was the chief thing. I hope it will be as good as the Dow '04.

> With very best love and gratitude for a splendid holiday,
>   Your loving Dorothy.

I was forgetting the most important thing – to thank you for the 'fireside chair'. I should like one very much, and it's sweet of you. I'll wait for that also, though, till I see how our colour-scheme upstairs[3] will work out. At present I incline to a basis of golden-brown, with a touch of rich blue. . . .

[1] A chemist of St Ives, an amateur entertainer. (See also letter dated 23 February 1908.)
[2] The draper's firm of John Bryant and Son, founded in 1887. In the 1890s it developed into a men's tailors and general outfitters.
[3] They were about to add the upstairs flat to their premises.

To Eustace Barton   24 Great James St
7 May 1928   W.C.1

Dear Dr Barton . . .

I am so glad you like Lord Peter. I certainly don't intend to kill him off yet, but I think it would be better to invent a new detective for any tales we do together. For one thing, people would associate his name with mine and be inclined to hand me out more than my half-share of credit for the story, which wouldn't be just. Also, it would simplify matters to have somebody with more scientific surroundings, don't you think? Lord Peter isn't supposed to know a lot about chemistry and that sort of thing, and it would mean inventing a doctor or somebody to help him out. Also, I'm looking forward to getting a rest from him, because his everlasting breeziness does become a bit of a tax at times! The job is to invent a scientific character of a new type. There have been so many of them – thin, keen ones; short, sphinx-like ones; handsome, impressive ones; queer, shabby ones; secretive, mysterious ones; aged, experienced ones; and even sturdy, commonplace ones – it's very hard to think of any sort that hasn't been done. The one kind we *won't* have is one that is blind, or humpbacked, or hasn't any legs or has to explain himself laboriously in the deaf-and-dumb alphabet! Things like that always seem to me so tedious and disagreeable, and they don't really add one bit to the interest of the character. We'll talk about it when we meet. Perhaps one of us will have thought of something by then.

I do envy you this grand weather in your peaceful corner! However, we shall be off to Scotland at the end of the month. I've got to get this wretched anthology finished up by then. . . .

To Eustace Barton   24 Great James St
15 May 1928   W.C.1

Dear Dr Barton

I did so much enjoy our meeting and chat on Saturday afternoon. I have been thinking over the mushroom story, and the more I think of it – the more I think of it! In fact, I propose to turn my attention to that as soon as I have polished off a number of short stories I have on hand, and which have got to be finished by the end of June.

In this story, as you say, it is obvious that there must be a powerful love interest, and I am going to turn my mind to making this part of the book as modern and powerful as possible. The day of the two nice young people, whose chaste affection is rewarded on the final page, has rather gone by, and reviewers are apt to say, sneeringly, that detective stories are better without any sentimental intrigues. Since, in this case, we *must* have the love to help the plot along, we must do our best to make it as credible and convincing as up-to-date standards require. I am, therefore, bending my mind to the creation of a credible, convincing and up-to-date pair of lovers, and will communicate with you further upon this touching subject as soon as I get a good idea about them. . . .

Towards the end of May Dr Barton wrote: 'We can introduce some very deep and interesting questions into the mushroom story – the subtle difference between what is produced by life and that artificially produced by man. The molecular asymmetry of Organic Products marks the difference between the chemistry of dead matter and the chemistry of living matter, and this touches on the most fundamental problems of the phenomena of life itself.'

D.L.S. asked him to explain further and he sent her the following statement:

A Theory of the Origin of Life on the Planet
It is necessary for the existence of Life that there should be an asymmetry of molecular structure. Whence rose that asymmetry? As the planet cooled from its

gaseous form, purely inorganic compounds were formed, composed of molecules symmetrical in their structure, that is, molecules that had not been formed directly or indirectly from any living tissues. And as such they would have been found to be optically inactive and incapable of rotating the plane of Polarised Light. It is known that light is circularly polarised by the light of the Sun from the surface of the sea and it is probable that when this occurred, when the vapour of the atmosphere condensed, and formed the first seas, an asymmetric agent became present on the face of the globe and by decomposing one antipode rather than another, gave rise to the first asymmetric molecule from which all living tissues arose and following the course of evolution continued to the present day. It is known that Life originated in the sea, and even we mammals retain in our Branchial Clefts the vestigial structures of fishes. May we not then look to the action of sunlight on the first oceans as the agent, through circularly polarised light, that produced the first asymmetric molecule, the starting point of Life on the Planet?

To Eustace Barton   24 Great James St
29 June 1928   W.C.1

Dear Dr Barton,

Please forgive my long delay in replying to your most interesting letters concerning Polarised Light and the Asymmetry of Organic Products. (This sounds magnificent – rather like the title of one of those lectures which thrilled earnest-minded young ladies in the 'seventies. By the way, in one of his books, poor dear Wilkie Collins makes great fun of a good lady's rapture over a discourse on: 'The conversion of radiant energy into audible sound'. How swiftly has science revenged itself upon his memory, by making the loud-speaker a vulgar commonplace!) – I think we have got hold of a really fine theme for a story here, and I am most eager to get on to it. I am still rather full up with work, and you mustn't think that my slowness in getting going is due to lack of keenness. The religious-scientific aspect of the thing will require careful handling, but ought, I think, to be very interesting to people, if we can succeed in making it clear to them. Have you seen all the radiant bosh people have been talking in the *Daily News* about 'Where are the Dead?' The biologists and chemists are a trifle less silly than the clergymen and sentimentalists; but both are equally incapable of ridding themselves of the idea of space and time. Consequently they all talk at cross-purposes, and the world is greatly edified! We don't seem to have advanced very far beyond the mediaeval philosophers who argued about how many archangels could dance on the point of a needle! Anyway, this theory of yours sounds good. I rather like 'an asymmetric agent became present on the face of the globe' as a modern substitute for 'the Spirit of God moved upon the face of the waters', though it seems a little lacking in literary charm (our scientists and religious argufyers might get a bit of fun out of this!) By the way, what inspired those old birds who wrote the Bible and the other early accounts to guess that life *did* start from the waters? That always beats me. It was all far too far away and long ago for them to have had a racial memory of it, and it's not the kind of thing that's obvious on the face of it. And yet they got extraordinarily near the correct order of things: light first – and then water – and then earth – and then vegetable life – and then fish – and then birds – and then cattle – and then man – anybody would think they had been given elementary scientific instruction in a board-school! Perhaps the 'creeping things' have got a trifle out of place, but even so, what an amazing guess! However, I am wandering! – Anyhow, the muscarine story is going to be a first-class yarn.

Meanwhile, we have been having a grand holiday in Scotland, and have come back greatly refreshed. I have been very busy the last week or so gathering together odds and ends of information about Wilkie Collins (I daresay you saw my letters in the papers).[1] He is almost as obscure a subject as polarised light, because all his family was illegitimate and therefore undiscoverable, and nearly all the people who knew him are dead. However, patience will doubtless do the trick in the end. I shall presently call on you for lots of help in tackling the medical problems in Collins' books. One of them, by the way, *Poor Miss Finch*, turns on the case of a young man afflicted with fits, who in order to cure them is obliged to take nitrate of silver, which turns him blue all over. I happened to mention this odd tale when writing home, and was delighted to receive a letter from my mother (who is a very lively and entertaining old lady) saying that when she was a girl there was a mysterious young man living near them 'who used to nearly always have a blue tint all over his face, but it was much worse sometimes than others, and was supposed to be caused by too much mercury or some drug of that kind, that was put into the medicine he had to take for his heart, or was it fits? He was always of great interest to the young ones, for what with his blue face and his living in rather an isolated home with a smart young woman that he didn't ought to have lived with, and his dashing about in a high dog-cart with this same young woman, and his sudden appearances and disappearances, he seemed to us mysterious, not to say romantic, and gave us much food for thought. He disappeared suddenly one day from everyone's ken and was never seen or heard of more, and the mystery about him was never cleared up. I remember that he greatly scandalised our little pharisaical world once or twice by appearing at church with his young woman.' I give my mother's words, because they seem to me to give such a perfect little cameo of life in the 'seventies or 80s. But what I was going to say was, I suppose, judging from this, that this nitrate of silver treatment was fairly common at that time. It's not used now, is it? And was it really any good? I see that Bruce's *Materia Medica* for 1889 says cautiously that 'some authorities believe that it (Ag NO₃) affects the nervous tissues and recommend it in epilepsy, chorea, and locomotor ataxy.' It also says the discolouration is 'a dusky black-brown,' (but if my mother says it was blue, then it *was* blue!) The epilepsy in Collins' book is supposed to have come in consequence of a violent blow on the head. Would silver treatment, if efficacious at all, be equally efficacious in a case with this particular history? Collins usually tried to be very careful about his medical facts, but he tripped up from time to time. I think he is a bit shaky about the blindness of another character in the book, which is attributed to 'cataracts', acquired at the age of 12 months, and temporarily cured by 'cutting' at the age of 23 without any necessity for spectacles. I thought the operation for cataract involved the removal of the crystalline lens – or am I quite wrong about this? And does one get cataract at 12 months? –

Well, I simply must not keep on bothering you with questions, but there is no other medical man I know who is interested in this sort of thing; and if I write on Collins I simply am obliged to deal with his medical plots.

Oh! and there's a most involved question I've got to ask you some day for a book of my own – about *arsenic*-eating.[2] What a lot of questions there are in the world!

How are you getting on? I hope you are very fit and well, and that the poor dear lunatics are being as good and happy as they know how to be. One of our typists,[3] who had been getting sillier and sillier for a year or two (symptoms including a mania for kippers and for gazing into shop-windows, a foolish pre-occupation with sex, inability to take any decision, and inordinate vanity – all supposed to be attributed to suppressed desires and the change of life) has been spending about 6 months in one of those homes where they psycho-analyse you. After a rapturous period of talking about her own complexes, talking to other softies about their complexes, lazing about and undergoing no discipline, she has emerged the poorer by about £80, very fat, sillier than ever, and so nerveless that she 'couldn't face' coming back to her job and has had to chuck it. They *said* she was discharged cured! She herself thinks she's no better. Don't you think all this psychoanalysing business ought to be kept for rich people who can afford to pay for the pleasure of chattering about themselves? I think it's a damned shame to work it off on typists who only get £3 a week!

Yours with many apologies for drivelling at such inordinate length, and with kindest regards,
Dorothy L. Sayers

[1] She planned to write his biography but completed only 5 chapters (edited by E. R. Gregory, 1977).
[2] *Strong Poison.*
[3] Cf. Miss Agatha Milsom in *The Documents in the Case.*

To Eustace Barton
24 July 1928

24 Great James St
W.C.1

My dear Dr Barton,

Thank you ever so much for your two delightful and interesting letters, which I ought to have answered earlier. I have been very busy, however – what with the office, and Wilkie Collins, and some short stories that had to be finished, – and the heat! Theoretically, I think sunshine is wonderful – it fills you chock full of vitamins (anti-rachitic factor A; only of course rickets is not the menace to me that it was about 35 years ago!) and tanning the skin to a beautiful brown (but unhappily I turn lobster-red) and combating the diseases of darkness, such as tuberculosis (a trouble with which I am not, so far, menaced) – but I do wish, personally, that it did not make me so ill-tempered, or come so hard on the feet, when one is rather large and heavy and has to walk on pavements! It must be rather jolly in your big grounds at St Andrews – only I hope it doesn't exasperate the tempers of your patients, poor things.

I am frightfully thrilled by your last, and longing to hear how you have tracked down the 'molecule'. I didn't know the discovery scene was going to be weird and pictorial – it makes it much more exciting. I thought perhaps it would have to be a dry little scientific lecture, which wouldn't be half so much fun. We must meet and have a good talk about it, and you will have to explain it all to me in words of one syllable, because I haven't the faintest idea how you polarise light, or what it looks like when it is polarised – while my mind is very vague about the appearance (if any) of molecules. I know that they are made up of atoms (or is it the other way round?) and that eventually you come down to electrons revolving round one another like solar systems. What fun it would be if all the solar systems in the universe were only atoms in a PERFECTLY ENORMOUS animal, by the way! And similarly, if all the little electrons were solar systems of worlds in which incredibly minute people had infinitesimal love-affairs and wrote preposterously unimportant detective stories! Why not? I like particularly to think of the enormous animal – it seems to reduce such matters as income-tax returns to their correct proportions . . . I am wandering . . . it must be the heat!

I think this fungus-story must be the next thing I tackle – the next novel, I mean. I have about three more short stories to get off my chest and then I shall be ready to turn my attention to the invention of the scientist and the (mush.) (I don't seem to be getting on very well with this word!) *mushroom*-gatherer (got it!) and his love-affairs! It ought, with all these threads of interest, to make a jolly story. Just for the moment I am keeping off it, for fear of being led away by its seductions to neglect the short stories etc. which I am supposed to be engaged on.

Meanwhile, I am still a little worried by Wilkie Collins and his silver nitrate. He must have got this blue idea from somebody – it's not a thing one could invent – and he certainly says 'dusky', which might fit in with what you say about the patient eventually going 'negro' colour. As a rule Wilkie Collins took care to get some sort of authority for his medical statements. Dr F. Carr Beard was the medical man who attended him, and Beard's son says that Wilkie was always pumping the Doctor for medical details for his books. I expect the right way would be to look up the medical journals and publications of the period and see if there are any accounts there of the use of silver nitrate for epilepsy, with its effects and supposed cures. Obviously people did think at that time that it was some good, and that being so, there should be records of experiment. I don't suppose anybody now thinks it's an atom of use, but if they thought it was at that time, it would be quite legitimate for Wilkie to make use of the idea – just as, nowadays, for instance, somebody might make a book turn on the lead cure for cancer. It's wonderful what a lot of things turn up for investigation the moment one begins to write a book about anything at all. I have just done the story[1] I mentioned to you about an ingenious electric safe that was made to open only to the voice of its master, and am now tackling a quite different kind of tale[2] – about a portrait painter, who got so fed up with the nasty vulgar face of a man he had to paint that he murdered him and slashed his detestable face all over, so that of course the police jumped to the idea that it was the work of the Mafia or something of that kind!

The idea of the Lost Atlantis is fascinating and may very well be true. But it must, surely, have been much more limited than our own civilisation, geographically speaking. It is hard to conceive of a convulsion that would destroy all four quarters of the globe at once. Yet a civilisation [as] scientifically advanced as our own would, one would think, have been as far-travelled. There are traces of ancient cities all over the world, of course – yet one would expect, somehow, a more definite continuity of scientific tradition from a world-wide civilisation.

I must now put my official mind to a series of exhortations to eat the wonderful yeast-vitamin food, Marmite, and usher in a Golden Age of Health and Happiness. Bah!

Very sincerely yours
    Dorothy L. Sayers

[1] 'The Adventurous Exploit of the Cave of Ali Baba', first published in *Lord Peter Views the Body* (Gollancz, 12 November 1928).
[2] 'The Unsolved Puzzle of the Man with No Face' (ibid.).

To Victor Gollancz   24 Great James St
11 August 1928   W.C.1

Dear Mr Gollancz,

Nobody could sympathise with your anxiety more heartily than myself. The situation is this: Of the five stories I had to write to complete the book, two are written, two are half-written, and one (in which a gentleman is electrocuted in his wash-basin)[1] remains to be tackled. This sounds comparatively hopeful. But:

We are moving house. (No change of address, by the way; we are adding more rooms to our flat)

The Carpets are up.

The Floor is up.

The Gas-fitters are removing and altering gas-fittings,

The Electricians are fitting electrical fittings,

The Plumbers are replacing sink in scullery and affixing splasher to wall as specified,

The White-washers are washing ceilings as per estimate,

The Painters are giving two coats of Paint, as per estimate,

The Floor-varnishers are waiting till the Electricians have put the floor-boards down again to Varnish the floor with two coats superior Varnish as per estimate,

The Carpet-cleaners are collecting two Carpets for thorough cleaning and shampooing as per my instructions by telephone,

Wallis of Holborn are delivering one Carpet with underlay, one crate crockery, glass and furnishings and a bulky Parcel marked 'Do Not Crush', which, on investigation, turns out to contain two Coal-scuttles,

Barkers are delivering one Fireside Chair (gift of my mother) and material for Curtains,

My Charwoman's niece is making and delivering the Curtains,

Gamages are delivering two Alabaster hanging bowls for Electric
    light,
Foots' are delivering easy chair complete with writing-desk and
    fittings,
The Cat is investigating the mysterious cavities between the joists
    of the flooring, with a view to getting nailed down under the
    floor, if possible,
My husband is giving his celebrated impersonation of the Mayor
    and Corporation of Ypres surveying the ruins of the Cloth-hall,
I am trying to look (on the other hand) like Dido building Carthage,
    and hoping (as I daresay she did) that the hammering will soon
    be over.
Life is very wonderful.
We are doing our best.
I will send a further bulletin when the dust has subsided.

Yours (still deeply sympathetic)
    Dorothy L. Sayers

¹ This story is not known to exist.

To Her Parents   24 Great James St
15 August 1928   W.C.1

Dearest people . . .
    I have bought myself at TREMENDOUS AND SELF-
INDULGENT EXTRAVAGANCE a wonderful trick chair, with a
back which reclines at all kinds of angles on pressure of a button, an
extension to put one's feet up on at a greater or less incline, and a
wonderful assortment of polished tables, book-rests and things
attached to it which adjust themselves in all manner of positions. The
idea is that when I come home tired in the legs after a day at the
office, I should be able to sit in it with my feet comfortably up and
write stories about Lord Peter. Up to the present, the insinuating
ease with which it converts itself into a couch has (strange to say)
induced more sleep than energy in its owner; but I am writing this
in it – the back being, for the moment, severely upright – and hope
presently to overcome the temptation it offers to laziness. . . .

To Eustace Barton   24 Great James St
3 September 1928   W.C.1

My dear Dr Barton . . .
    The scene in the laboratory will be very good.¹ I think we might

let the Great Scientist do a check experiment with genuine fungus poison first, so that the other bloke might exactly appreciate the difference between the two; it would add to the drama if, in the *first* instance, the observer could stand at the eye-piece and see the darkness change to light as the fungus-solution is put in the polariscope. It would prolong and work up the excitement a little and give the reader a feeling that he had seen the experiment worked for himself. Then the Scientist could solemnly repeat the experiment with the artificially prepared solution, and the contrast would be striking. . . .

Somewhere in the book, we will introduce the theological discussions at an earlier point, and work them into the story. And we will have in, somewhere, one of those boring matter-of-fact people who don't see any practical value in the splitting of atoms – or straws – and thinks people would be much better employed doing something energetic and useful – like advertising soap or making money or shooting things! Also, perhaps, a literary person, who thinks it so dull and unpoetical to try and fathom the mysteries of nature. (I can do this type of idiot rather well; I know several of him.) He will, of course, be somehow deeply concerned in the fathoming of this particular mystery, and will have to be shown what a silly little person he is!

The big job now will be to introduce complications into the plot. As the whole thing is supposed, at first, to be an accident, we can't avail ourselves of the wrongfully-accused person or anything like that. We shall have to work it up powerfully on the emotional side. This is rather a new line for me,[2] but it will be very interesting to have a go at it. And we shall have somehow to work the scientific-theological interest solidly into the plot (I don't quite see how at the moment, but I expect it will come), so that it will come in naturally in its proper place, and not appear to have been suddenly pushed in to elucidate the mystery.[3] I am longing to have a go at this story. I have now finished my set of short stories for Gollancz, so there is now only the Old French poem[4] to compete with our novel, and that ought not to take long.

We must consider the question of the title. I think *The Death Cap* would make an extremely good title in itself. It suggests murder and mystery, and to the person who isn't a mushroom expert it has a flavour of courts of law and the 'black cap'.[5] Indeed, the only objection I see to it is that there is already a book of murder-tales entitled *The Black Cap*, which might possibly cause confusion, but I don't think it matters much, as this book was published about a year ago, and will be forgotten by the time our novel appears.

When the time comes, I am going to work up quite an interesting little item of news out of the collaboration of Robert Eustace and Dorothy L. Sayers and push it round to the press. Remind people of

L. T. Meade and your triumphs of the 'nineties. You will, of course, be a mysterious figure, shrouded in professional secrecy – (unless, of course, you like to emerge from your hiding-place). I don't see why your long record of detective honours should be forgotten, just because Ward Lock don't reprint things. Unless, also of course, you dislike publicity; but if you remain veiled in a pseudonym it won't personally worry you, and I think the connection with L. T. Meade will interest people – it might even affect and touch them, if prettily handled. And – which is the great point – it will all help to sell the book! . . .

[1] Cf. The scene in *The Documents in the Case*, No. 52, 'Statement of John Munting'.
[2] D.L.S. had forgotten, or was disregarding, the powerful emotional element in *Clouds of Witness*.
[3] This is why she made John Munting write the kind of book he does (i.e. the biography of a Victorian author interested in science and theology).
[4] *Tristan in Brittany*.
[5] Worn formerly by a judge on pronouncing sentence of death.

To Ivy Shrimpton   24 Great James St
6 September 1928   W.C. 1

Dearest Ivy –

Lordy, lordy! What a month we have been having! We have stuck our feet to newly-varnished floors, and painted ourselves white on newly-painted panelling, and tripped over newly-laid-down carpets that retain mysterious folds and wrinkles, and blackened ourselves with dust from dim, unexplored cupboards, and eaten meals, standing, off the tops of bookshelves, and had the fire-places ripped out, and the sinks pulled to pieces, and the boards taken up and the fittings pulled down, and hung up pictures on walls made apparently of cream cheese, so that the nail goes rattling down inside the wall and the hammer after it and the workmen after the hammer, – and tried to push obstinate tables through narrow doorways, and match up materials whose colours have no parallel in heaven or earth – and the BILLS! – oh, golly!

But you know all about this – too well!

At present we are nearly fixed. We are only waiting for this, that and the other, to be quite settled and comfortable. (Mem: the Bills are only waiting for this, that and the other to be settled too!) At any rate we shan't be so near divorcing each other on account of aggravated propinquity as we were before – and that's a great comfort. Before we got these extra rooms, we really were so awfully on top of one another that we were ready to shriek! Now we can have our meals and do our work in decent comfort, and entertain our friends separately, if we like, without disorganising everything.

Meanwhile, I can produce £4.10.0,[1] and I wish it was more – and it shall be, the very minute I can manage it. But Mac being still more or less working half-time, I have to carry, for the moment, more than my share of the household expenses. However, I understand that the books are doing fairly well, and this will, with any luck, mean more money as time goes on.

We envy you having your country cottage this grand weather – especially as, the week-end being the only time I have to get in any private work, we have to stick in town. We are able to get up on the roof now, but it's rather grimy and smoky. It pleases the cat very much, though.

I hope John is behaving himself. Mac is getting quite interested in him. I haven't been shoving the kid at him, so to speak – I don't think small children appeal much to men (nor, indeed, to me). But I expect he will turn out to be quite fun in a little time.

Best love to you all
D.

[1] Four pounds and ten shillings.

To Eustace Barton
10 September 1928

24 Great James St
W.C.1

Dear Dr Barton –

Splendid! – (Meaning, things in general).

I will now devote my attention to the details of the crime, and make suitable arrangements for the Villain to poison the mushrooms without

a) poisoning himself

b) being obviously unwilling to share the poisoned dish

c) being suspected of popping a genuine 'death-cap' into the dish. If possible the trap shall poop off while the villain is away in Town, or something. By the way, I shall want to know:

1. What muscarine (artificial) solution looks like (whether clear or coloured, cloudy or transparent)

2. What is the fatal dose

3. What it smells and tastes like (like mushrooms?) in case I want to poison the dish, or the salt, or something other than the actual plants, as I rather want the villain to be out of the way when these are gathered and brought home.

Llanfairfechan[1] must be lovely now. I motor-cycled round that part a few years ago, so I know what it's like. One of my friends said it

was almost worth while to be one of your patients, to live at Bryn-y-
Kenadd – but I don't think!

    Yrs
       D. L. Sayers

[1] In North Wales, Conwy Bay.

*On 20 September 1928, D.L.S.'s father, the Rev. Henry Sayers, died of pneu-
monia. A message was sent by telephone from the post office in Christchurch
(there being no telephone at the rectory) and D.L.S. obtained leave of absence
from Benson's and went at once to Christchurch. Mac did not accompany her
but went later to help Mrs Sayers.*

To Ivy Shrimpton   Christchurch Rectory
24 September 1928   Wisbech
                                Cambs.

Dearest Ivy,
    This is just a hasty line in the middle of all the fuss and hurry, to
say three things.
    1. Do not worry about the difference Dad's death will make to you
from a money point of view. Mac and I will make it up – and also I
hope next year I shall be able to make the other sum definitely bigger.
We can manage this all right – our finances are getting straight as
Mac's debts are paid off and our earnings increase.
    2. We have had a letter from the Australian trustees to say that
Uncle Percy has left you £300. They say, however, that, whereas
Uncle P. described you in his will as 'Ivy Shrimpton', your birth-
certificate calls you 'Ivy May Shrimpton'. I take it this is their typist's
error for 'Ivy Amy Shrimpton'. In any case, you will have to go to a
lawyer, I expect, and swear an affidavit that you are the same person
who is mentioned in the will – or possibly somebody may have to go
and identify you! In any case, it is a trifling formality, and the money
will then be at your disposal. I am writing to the London agents who
have the money, to ask them exactly what evidence of identity they
require.
    3. While seeing Dad's lawyer about other things, I have given him
instructions to draw up a will for me. In this I am leaving everything
to Mac, and Mac will look after J.A. as though he were his own son.
To cover the case of Mac and myself being killed simultaneously in
an accident, I am directing that, in that event, any money I have
shall go to you. I am now writing to you to say that I want you, if

you will, to use this money for my son, John Anthony Sayers, and to consider that you hold it in trust for him, to feed, clothe, lodge and educate him as far as it will go. Keep this letter, which constitutes, I believe, what is known as a 'Secret Trust'. It is only a temporary arrangement, to cover all contingencies, in case of Mac and myself both being killed off before he can carry out his intention of formally adopting J.A.

I shall probably be here till the end of this week, but I will let you know, and shall, of course, in any case be writing to you in a day or two.

Mother thanks you very much for your very nice letter. She knows that you were very fond of dear old Dad and will sympathise, having been through so much of the same thing yourself. He died very suddenly and peacefully and mercifully, so that one can only be very thankful that there was no lingering illness.

With much love
    Yours ever
        Dorothy

To Ivy Shrimpton   24 Great James St
18 October 1928   W.C.1

Dearest Ivy . . .
It is awfully good of you to bother about a house for Mother, but we've got one!!!! Brilliant and intensive campaign on the part of Mac and me![1] We've bought a pretty old Georgian house in Witham, Essex. I'm putting in part of Uncle Percy's legacy, and Mother is advancing the rest. It was real luck hitting on it so promptly – it's ever so pretty with a garden and courtyard and four good upstairs rooms, attic, bathroom with geyser, W.C., etc., two 'reception' and offices – lots of outhouses and a greenhouse and we got it for £850! I thought it would be £1500 at least! . . .

[1] It was Mac who actually found the house.

To Eustace Barton   24 Great James St
19 November 1928   W.C.1

Dear Dr Barton –
You must think I have succumbed to mushroom poisoning or something! But I am really still alive – only busy!
I am getting *The Death Cap* clearer in my mind now. I have decided, I think, how to administer the poison and preserve the alibi intact.

Also, I am introducing a valuable witness to the death, who will be able to support the said alibi.

I have also been considering the love-affair. I don't want to make the villain *too* villainous – nor yet must the victim be a villain. I think I shall (with your approval) make the victim a harmless sort of bore, conceited and self-centred and always twaddling about his cookery and so on, and have him married to a sort of Edith Thompson woman,[1] who eggs the villain on to get rid of the husband. That will allow plenty of human nature and furious frustration and all that kind of thing.

Then I'm rather keen to try the experiment of writing the book in a series of first-person narratives, *à la* Wilkie Collins. It will be a new line to try, but I think I could manage it. My idea is that somebody – some friend of the victim's, I suppose – gets his suspicions roused, and sets out to collect statements and evidence, finishing up with the scientific experiment. Then, having put all the papers in order,[2] he bundles the whole lot off to the Public Prosecutor or the police, urging them to take it up. This gets over the difficulty which always confronts one in reading a Wilkie Collins book, namely, why, when all is settled and finished, anybody should have taken the trouble to collect and publish an account of the thing at all. It also gets over the tiresome business of an ending – whether one is to have the murderer tried, or make him confess, or allow him to commit suicide, or what! I shall just leave the Prosecutor, after reading all the evidence, seated with the papers before him, and wondering how this amazing story, with its subtle scientific explanation, is to be presented to twelve good and lawful persons of limited intelligence. As a matter of fact, I can just *see* that case coming into court – and learned counsel for the defence saying sarcastically: 'My learned friend has endeavoured to make a very subtle distinction – I am afraid it was rather too subtle for my poor intelligence to follow – about polarised and unpolarised light. We have heard a good deal lately about "splitting the atom" – perhaps I shall not be going too far when I suggest that my learned friend is splitting straws.' (Laughter in court)! . . .

[1] See Filson Young, Notable British Trial Series, *Trial of Frederick Bywaters and Edith Thompson* (Hodge, 1923).
[2] This is the origin of the eventual title, *The Documents in the Case*.

To Eustace Barton   24 Great James St
23 November 1928   W.C.1

Dear Dr Barton

Many thanks for your letter. I am so sorry I forgot to clear up the point about your share in 'The Face in the Dark'.[1] My father died just about the time when the fees were being sent out, and everything had to be done hurriedly, from a distance and with a pre-occupied mind. . . .

I must get the book you mention about Inversion – not that I am personally much affected by the subject, but because one is so often asked questions, and it is well to be able to give a reasonable and scientific answer.[2] People's minds get so confused on these subjects, and they *will* suppose that if one stands up for these unfortunate people, one is advocating all kinds of debauchery! As a matter of fact, inverts make me creep, but that is no reason why one shouldn't face the facts. Lunatics and imbeciles make me creep too, if it comes to that. Besides, the normal person often makes the invert creep; I had a friend[3] who was rather that way – a very fine person of powerful intellect – but she won't see, speak or write to me now I'm married, because marriage revolts her. So there you are. The trouble is that these poor wretches have to fall in love with normals, and that is bad for the normals. If only the male women and the female men could pair off together, nobody would care what they did to each other, because they would be part of the 'sanctities of married life'. Well, well!

Yours very sincerely
Dorothy L. Sayers . . .

---

[1] By L. T. Meade and Robert Eustace, included in *Great Short Stories of Detection, Mystery and Horror* (Gollancz, 1928), pp. 380–95.
[2] D.L.S. had asked about homosexuality in a previous letter.
[3] Possibly Muriel Jaeger.

To Ivy Shrimpton   24 Great James St
10 December 1928   W.C.1

Dearest Ivy –
Late again! I'm so sorry.

I've been damnably busy this last month, and things will be pretty hectic right on to Christmas. Yesterday I went down to Witham to see how the decorators were getting on with the house. It looks very nice, I think – but of course, when Mother went down with Mac the week before last to choose the papers etc., she couldn't seem to see anything but gloom and difficulties, and that depressed poor old Mac (who is suffering badly from nerves) till he almost had a break-down. I wish to goodness I didn't come of such a worrying family. Of course, Dad's sudden death was a shock to Mother, and I don't suppose she would really feel pleased with *anything* at the moment – still, it's rather discouraging, when one has performed almost a miracle in getting a house at all at such short notice to have *nothing* but defects commented on!!! However! – the move takes place next week, and when they are all settled down I expect it will be all right.

Very many thanks for your letters and photos. J.A. looks quite a credit to us! I must really try to feel thrilled about him – but I don't believe I ever should about *any* child under whatever circumstances! It's funny, but I don't think 'family ties' have ever meant anything at all to me. I only like people as individuals, apart from who they are. Indeed, I actively dislike nearly all my Sayers relations, or at most, tepidly tolerate them. I like the Leighs – and of course, my dear, I'm damned fond of you – but because you are you – not because you happen to be a cousin. Same with J.A. He seems to be turning out a good sort of kid, and I'm disposed to like him – but for no other reason. However, I dare say it will work out O.K. in the end.

Lord! how I hated all those Sayerses who turned up for the funeral – noisy, selfish, tiresome, stupid – all spongers and soakers – poor old Dad was the only decent one of the bunch.

Mother's beginning to realise that now, poor dear. He bored her to death for nearly 40 years, and she always grumbled that he was no companion for her – and now she misses him dreadfully. That's life, I suppose. But I must be rather abnormal about these things, because I never feel any *differently* about people just because they are dead. I wish I'd been kinder and not so impatient and so on; but I feel just exactly the same amount, and the same kind of affection for them as I did when they were alive. It's like that boy Guy Cooke, who used to do lessons with me. I always disliked him, and when he was killed in the War I didn't feel I liked him any better. Why should I? – Same with the old Guv'nor. I was always awfully fond of him, though we had very little to say to one another, and I can't feel that he is in any way changed by having died. He seems just the same to me, except that he isn't there, and that makes rather a sad blank. – Oh, well. . . .

Best love. Forgive this rather maundering letter. Mac sends his love.

Your ever affectionate
Dorothy

To Charis Frankenburg   24 Great James St
5 March 1929   London
                                                   W.C.1

Dear Charis,

When I got your card I said to Mac 'I think I must go to the Gaudy this year.' 'Certainly,' said he. 'Why not.' So I started to write for rooms. I put out a piece of paper – and then went away and did something else. I have been doing something else for weeks!

Damned slack of me!

It's not really slackness, as a matter of fact. It's one of those deep inner repugnances that the pyscho-analysts are always talking about. I don't *really* want to go.

The odd thing is that I always had this extraordinary dislike for going back. At Oxford, I attributed my hatred of remembering school days to the fact that I loathed the school[1] – but the truth is now come in on me that I thoroughly dislike *all* retrospect.[2] (This is going to be very awkward, by the way, when I am 90 or so, because I can't reasonably expect to be able to live very much in the future at that age!) I should like to know the meaning of this particular mania. I think my mental 'Censor', by the way, is very powerful; if I want to forget anything I can (unless it is especially vivid and disagreeable) do so with a completeness which entirely prevents the possibility of resurrecting it. I can abolish names and places and even states of mind beyond all recall.[3] I could not reconstruct a past state of things – supposing, for example, I wanted to do so in a novel – so as to carry conviction to anybody.[4] – The most flattering explanation of the phenomenon is that I have a violent kind of forward-looking vitality. Another – a more likely one, I am afraid – is that any present vanity despises and dislikes my former self. I think this is probably correct, because it hangs together with my general dislike of children and everything immature and unfinished. I don't think I have ever met anybody else with this extraordinary and undiscriminating impatience of the past. I like places and people for what they are now – not for what they were. I mean, I like for instance, to see you and D. Rowe, because you are both people whose company is in itself delightful – but, my God! a collegeful of people with whom I have no other bond than that we once were all there together! – it makes me feel like a resurrection-man! Have we got to sing that fool of a song about *Donec rursus impleat*,[5] for instance? And be greeted with hearty charity by kindly people whose faces we never want to see again and who ask us if we remember things? Are we expected to suppose that youth was the season made for joy? (A bloody lie, if ever there was one.) And answer imbecile questions about what we have been doing all these years? And feel sentimental? Because nothing is so tedious as sentiment. And feel ourselves young again? No bloomin' fear. Being young wasn't good enough. Besides, it's so silly.

All this being so, I suppose we must nevertheless try to resist these inhibitions. So I have written for a room – with the sneaking hope that I shan't get it, and so shall be able to say – 'There, I can't go – there's no room!' But the probability is that I *shall* get it and shall come and be offensive to a lot of bores, and everybody will say that I am just as intolerable as I was fifteen years ago – and with every justification! I *am*!!

By the way, many thanks for your suggestion with regard to the woman doctor etc. Dr Wright[6] was very nice, and fixed me up quite satisfactorily. So that's that.

Don't let my previous remarks put you off looking us up when you're in Town! They don't apply to anybody who is so to speak part of the living present. It's only this rather forced hilarity over the defunct past that gives me inhibitions. – I'm sorry I didn't take steps last time you were here, but things were being rather tumultuous at that particular moment, what with one thing and another. We have now safely lived through a number of crises – such as getting my mother's house fixed up, a financial scare, a bother about work, influenza, frozen pipes *et hoc genus omne*[7] and are beginning to sit up and take notice again. But if only there were 48 hours in the day or fewer exciting things to do in the 24! More time, O God, more time! I would live a thousand years if I could, provided I might still keep my intellects.[8]

Cheerio! I really have written for that damned room! I will sing the song. I will even sit on the floor and talk jolly. But I will not drink cocoa. There are limits. And I have developed a taste for vintage port. There is the past in its most glorious form – but who thinks of the raw alcohol when he draws the cork of the matured wine?*

Yours ever
Dorothy L. Fleming

*Merely rhetorical question because that is just what prohibitionists do – the nasty beasts!!!!

[1] Her letters written during her time at school do not bear this out.
[2] Yet three years later D.L.S. began a book of reminiscences, *My Edwardian Childhood*. In 1934 she began what she called her straight novel, *Cat o' Mary*, which draws in minute detail on her early years.
[3] She certainly forgot that she had ever set eyes on Roy Ridley in 1913 and yet he became the physical original of Lord Peter Wimsey.
[4] This is nonsense. *The Nine Tailors* is a vivid and convincing evocation of Bluntisham

and Christchurch. *Murder Must Advertise* recalls her years at S. H. Benson's and *Gaudy Night* is a deeply personal reconstruction of a past state of things.

[5] The last line of the first verse of the College song: *Omnes laetae nunc sodales / Concinentes gaudio / Uno corde conferamus / Laudem huic collegio; / Conditum quod olim iure / Nunc integritate stat / Atque permanebit orbem / Donec rursus impleat.* Let all cheerful members now / Blending voices joyfully / With one heart bestow / Praise upon this college. / Founded formerly by law / Now it stands complete / And will remain / Till its renown fills the world again. (The words *donec rursus impleat orbem* were the motto of the Somerville family.)

[6] Dr Helena Wright, a gynaecologist specialising in contraception who fitted D.L.S. with a Dutch cap.

[7] Latin: 'and all that sort of thing'.

[8] Intellectual powers, wits (archaism for intellect).

TO EUSTACE BARTON   24 Great James St
26 April 1929   W.C.1

Dear Dr Barton,

I have just had a visit from our American publisher – one, Mr Brewer of Payson and Clarke, and he is tremendously thrilled by what we[1] told him about the book. I didn't, of course, give any clue to the plot, but said that it embodied the very latest scientific ideas and so on; and I mentioned our idea about the publicity photographs of Miss Dorothy Sayers and her mysterious collaborator in the laboratory – you know, showing just the back of your head and your hands, with really fine melodramatic lighting effects. He was absolutely entranced with the idea – he said: 'Oh, that's great! That's swell.' I fancy he will give us a really good show over there and get the book wide sales in the States. I am glad of this, because I'm afraid Benn will not do anything very brilliant on this side – Benns are all thyroid-deficient, dim and wombling imbeciles, damn them!

In the meantime, I do wish we could meet and have a really good talk about the thing. I do see absolutely your point about not being able to connect the murderer directly with the poison; on the other hand, it seems such a pity to invent a (practically) ~~bump~~ (!) bomb proof secret method of poisoning, and then destroy its bombproofness by making the man put himself slap into the hands of a confederate. The murderer who takes an accomplice is always rather a second-rate technician. If only we could devise some means by which the student could *innocently* put the poison into his hands! But I am dreadfully tired of the murderer who goes to visit a chemist or a doctor and steals some poison, while the chemist's back is turned. There must, surely, be some new turn one could give to the situation.

I am not at present intending, by the way, to make any very great secret about its being a murder, or about the identity of the murderer. Because, in order to get the full effect of our polariscope story, I want

the reader to realise more or less what has been done, and wonder
how in the world the thing is to be proved. This is a little different
from the ordinary plan of the detective story, but it is much more like
what actually happens in real life. The relatives of a dead person,
and even the police, may have an absolute moral certainty that a
crime has been committed and by whom, and may yet despair of
fixing it by definite proof on the suspect. Then, when the thing seems
absolutely hopeless, and the wicked are flourishing away like green
bay-trees, comes the ray of light – the more miraculous, because we
have, so to speak, been watching it at intervals through the story –
the hand of God, science, life, truth – whatever you like to call it,
waiting from the very dawn of Creation – the light that moved on
the waters of Chaos and, somehow, formed the first asymmetric atom
on the face of the deep – ready, after millions of centuries, to catch
the murderer out. This sounds rather pompous, but we won't put it
quite so rhetorically as that.

By the way, I have thought of a fine ironic situation. I mentioned
to you that I want to base the story a little on the Thompson–
Bywaters case. The wife of the victim has been egging the lover on
to get rid of the husband – with all the usual clap-trap about their
having been made and destined by heaven for one another – you
know: 'He (the husband) has the legal right to all that you have a
right to by the laws of Love and Nature' – all that sort of thing. When
the lover goes off to stay with the unsuspecting husband in the country
shack where they do their own cooking, she is still urging him to
seize this Heaven-sent opportunity and so on. The lover, goaded into
action, does the job, arranging an alibi for himself, so that the whole
thing appears to be accident; and the wife actually believes that it
really *is* accident. She then writes to the lover, in an exalted hysterical
mood, saying that Heaven has spoken – God has declared himself on
the side of Love and Nature and all the rest of it. How wonderful
that it should be so. That, without committing what the world would
call a crime, they have gained the right to happiness! This shows that
their love is pure, and their intention innocent – and so forth and so
on. And the wretched man, with the murder on his conscience, has
to agree and rejoice and all that sort of thing, and go on being blas-
phemously jubilant – *knowing* what he has done, and in ghastly fear
that somehow it will even yet come out.[2]

I think that ought to come out rather dreadful. Of course, to
appreciate it fully, the reader must *KNOW* that it is a murder, or at
any rate must have a powerful moral certainty that it is so, though
he need not know exactly how the alibi was worked, and still less,
how the crime is ever to be brought home to the culprit. And this is
another reason why I don't want the reader to feel: 'Oh, well! I

suppose the confederate will be made to confess.' I want him to say to himself: 'Good lord! The man's going to get away with it. He *must* get away with it.' Because, of course, even if it were shown that the murderer had the motive and the muscarine and the opportunity, there could be no real proof that it was murder *unless* it could at the same time be proved that the mushrooms were definitely not the source of the poison. It would be a sort of 'not proven' verdict at best.

This will be made clear when the detective comes along. He or she (some relation of the murdered man, perhaps) will acquire the moral certainty, but despair (and the reader must despair with him) of ever bringing it to the proof. This doesn't absolutely exclude the confederate, of course, because, even if the confederate did confess, the same situation would arise – but it would make it much more plausible if we knew for a certainty that the muscarine had actually been supplied to the murderer with intent to kill; whereas, if we merely show that he had access and *might* have taken it, the possibility becomes much more shadowy and difficult of proof.

But I do want to discuss the thing in detail – follow up that muscar-ine-bottle day by day and hour by hour, and see where the point of accessibility can be placed, so that the detective, and the reader, can say: 'I know that he *might* have taken it – but *did* he take it – and how can one *prove* that he took it? After all, there is still just the bare possibility of coincidence'.

If only we can get this just exactly right, I do think the situation will be extremely powerful, and 'God's revenge against murder' very, very striking. I cannot tell you how enthusiastic I am about this plot, and how anxious I am not to spoil it by any crudity in the handling. I *do* hope you will be able to come to town next month. I go for my holiday in the middle of June, and I should like to have the whole outline of the plot dead clear in my mind by then, so that I have only to work out the details. . . .

I hope you are feeling fit again. Our doctor has worked the most amazing miracle on my husband! From a gastritis-ridden wreck, never sure whether his food is going to stay put or poison him, he has become, in three weeks, a stout, hearty, vigorous, voracious creature, without an ache or pain or a cough or a trouble of any kind, devouring five meals a day and wolfing down all kinds of things which he hasn't been able to touch for years and years. This gifted creature (the doctor, I mean) only saw his patient once, overhauled him with fer-ocious thoroughness, retired to his lair and evolved a bottle of some-thing-or-the-other and a box of pills. Since when, all has been, in the Dickensian phrase, 'gas and gaiters'! I have regained faith in the medical profession and even in bottles. I never thought any good ever came out of bottles, but apparently it does.

Meanwhile, my bald patches are being treated with mental repose and sulphate of zinc, and the path of the destroyer seems to be, so far, blocked. So all is well.

I won't go wambling on any longer – but I got rather worked up last night by this American fellow's enthusiasm, and that seems to have resulted in a rush of words to the pen. Do fix up a meeting – a long one – next time you come through town –

Yours very sincerely
    Dorothy L. Sayers

[1] Presumably D.L.S. and her agent Andrew Dakers.
[2] The power of this ironic situation, magnificently expressed here, is not fully realised in the novel.

To Eustace Barton   24 Great James St
17 May 1929   W.C.1

Dear Dr Barton,

Many thanks for your letter and notes, which will be very useful. You need not worry about the coroner's inquest. Inquests have no legal importance at all, as far as that goes, and a case can be re-opened at any time after the verdict of a coroner's jury. Thus, in the case of George Joseph Smith, who drowned his three brides in a bath, though no suspicion was aroused until the last murder, the murder for which he was actually tried was that of the first wife, Annie Mundy, who had been peacefully buried some years previously under a coroner's verdict of misadventure, the two succeeding cases being admitted as collateral evidence of design only.

The fundamental idea behind the rule of *autrefois acquit*[1] is simply that a citizen must not twice be put in peril on the same charge; but a coroner's verdict cannot put anyone in peril, since, even if he is arrested as a consequence he must still be charged and tried in the ordinary way.

In fact, the only real use of an inquest from the police point of view is the excellent opportunity it affords of trying out the strength of the evidence in the case and exploring the ground; since evidence is admissible in a coroner's court which would not be admissible on trial; e.g. hearsay and irrelevant matter of other kinds. Further, the witnesses may speak more freely, since they are not necessarily on oath.

From the novelist's point of view, coroner's inquests are a boon and a blessing, precisely on account of this laxness. One gets all the fun of a trial, without the danger of falling into so many legal traps.

Nothing is too preposterous to happen at an inquest, especially in a country town. . . .

Of the titles, I think I like best the ones about 'vital importance'. The play on words is good, and doesn't give away the plot too much. Better leave God out of it, I think – it sounds a trifle pompous, perhaps, and many people don't like having the name of God mixed up with a detective story.

I have been playing with ideas centred round Omar Khayyám –

'And the first morning of Creation wrote
What the last dawn of reckoning shall read.'[2] . . .

[1] Previously acquitted.
[2] From the *Rubáiyát*: 'With Earth's first Clay They did the Last Man knead / And there of the Last Harvest sow'd the Seed; / And the first Morning of Creation wrote / What the Last Dawn of Reckoning shall read.' (Stanza 79, Edward Fitzgerald's translation, second edition, 1868.)

On 27 July 1929 Mrs Sayers died, having survived her husband by only ten months. D.L.S. and Mac soon afterwards made the house in Witham their permanent home, which they shared with Aunt Mabel.

To Ivy Shrimpton   Sunny side[1]
5 August 1929   Witham
                                                        Essex

Dearest Ivy,

Thank you so much for your kind letter of sympathy and offer of help. Mother's death was a great shock and blow, of course. It was caused by an internal stoppage, connected with a small rupture of the bowel, which came on suddenly and turned out badly. Poor dear, if only she had called the doctor in earlier, something might have been done about it, but she absolutely forbade them to send for the doctor or for me, and when we were sent for, it was too late. The only thing is that she was at least spared being an invalid, and for that we must try to be thankful. I don't know what she *would* have done if she had been condemned to live an idle life in a chair or a bed – so perhaps it was a merciful thing in some ways. It seems hard to realise that she has gone – it seems as though she were still about the place which she had grown to be so fond of.

It is very very good of you to offer to come here, but as a matter of fact, we shall be living here ourselves the greater part of the time – that is, week-ends up till the end of the year, when I leave Benson's, and after that, more or less permanently. Evelyn,[2] the servant, is most

good and faithful, and is staying with us; she knows exactly how to
look after Aunt Mabel, and has promised never to leave her. Fortunately, my American publishers had just completed an agreement
with me which makes it possible for me to give up the office work,
so that it is very convenient for us to make this arrangement. The
house is so close to town that we can easily get backwards and for-
wards, and we shall keep a room or two on at Great James St as a
pied à terre.

You will, of course, come here presently – and it will be John's
some day – but just at the moment, I don't think Aunt Mabel would
very well be able to stand children about the house, though she is
bearing up wonderfully and carries her great age well. All the same,
it is most good of you to have suggested coming, and, if I had been
unable to leave town myself, there is nobody I would have trusted to
look after her as well as you.

I enclose £5 – I think I shall be able to make it always £5 now, till
I am able to make it more. I will also take over the payment of
Mother's little gift to you, which was paid quarterly, I think?

I shall be going over the things in the house in the next few weeks.
She wished everybody to have something to remember her by. What
sort of thing would you like best? Books? or Silver? or China? or what?
Let me know what would best speak to you of her.

> With much love
> Your ever affectionate
> Dorothy

[1] The name of the house, usually spelled Sunnyside, which had been bought for Mrs
Sayers. The address was 24 Newland Street. When D.L.S. and Mac went to live there
D.L.S. bought the house next door and converted the two residences into one.
[2] Evelyn Compline (later Mrs Bedford), who had been in service as a girl at the rectory
in Christchurch.

To Eustace Barton   24 Great James St
20 November 1929   W.C.1

Dear Dr Barton,

Thank you so much for your letter. The new idea for a story sounds
very exciting, and I should love to hear about it. There are difficulties
connected with a 'private arrangement' for collaboration which would
require careful discussion. If the present book turns out satisfactory,
and if I find myself well ahead of my contract in the next two years,
we might be able to do a book outside the contract altogether. But
perhaps we had better wait a bit till we see how this one turns out.
At present I am being rather dissatisfied with my work on it. I keep

on seeing how I could have done things better and having to re-write great chunks. I think this is due partly to the change in style between this and my other books, partly to over-anxiety – wanting to justify a new departure and not let my collaborator down – and largely to the generally unsettled feeling I have just at present, what with the various domestic upsets you wot[1] of and with the knowledge that I shall be leaving my permanent job at the end of the year. You are being wonderfully good and patient with me. I really do hope to have something very soon for you to look at. The story is turning out rather grim and sordid, and I am finding it hard to get a light touch into it. The miserable domestic situation of the Harrisons, the mental aberrations of the lady-housekeeper and the temperamental introspections of the poet combine to produce an atmosphere of tense depression which, though extremely suitable to the plot is not exhilarating, either for author or reader!

By the way, when Leader (the medical student) is showing the people over the labs, are there any other synthetic preparations of a similar sort he could mention, whether poisons or otherwise? It seems so very marked and obvious that he should happen to pick out for them just the one rather obscure poison that would fit the circumstances of the case. No doubt there are hundreds of others. Perhaps you could give me, say, half a dozen, to which passing reference might be made. . . .

I am putting off all the short stories till early next year, when I shall do a whole bunch of them, including 'Sermons in Stones'.[2] There is also one about an ingenious method of committing arson on a motor-car,[3] one about a black baby mysteriously appearing in a white family (atavistic),[4] a curious story about a similar twin with reversed physical construction[5] – heart on the right side and so on – and a nasty little horror, which I think I mentioned to you, about thyroid glands![6] A cheerful bunch!

Well, I must really see about getting down to this bit that needs re-writing!

With best wishes,
Yours very sincerely
Dorothy L. Sayers

[1] Know (facetious archaism).
[2] Nothing is known of this story.
[3] Possibly 'In the Teeth of the Evidence', first published in the collection of the same title in 1933.
[4] Nothing is known of this story.
[5] 'The Image in the Mirror', first published in *Hangman's Holiday*, 1 May 1933.
[6] 'The Incredible Elopement of Lord Peter Wimsey', first published in *Hangman's Holiday*, 1 May 1933.

1930–1936

Celebrated Author and Private Person

These are the years of Dorothy L. Sayers' greatest achievements in detective fiction. Her release from her job with S. H. Benson's meant that she could devote all her creative energy to her writing. By the end of 1936 Lord Peter Wimsey was known to readers all over the world and had made his first appearance upon the stage. Professional success brought her enjoyment and fulfilment but her private and domestic life was beset with problems.

Witham: 1930–1936 (Age: 37–43)

To Her Son
8 January 1930

24 Newland Street
Witham
Essex

Dear John,

Thank-you very much for your letter. I am glad you and Isobel like the farm. I hope all the animals arrived safely, and that the dogs and cats did not fight on the way. We have a really clever cat here, called Adelbert, who will run after balls of paper and bring them back to you to throw, just like a dog. He met a strange cat in the yard last night, and there was a fight. You should have heard the noise – such a yowling! But I am sorry to say Adelbert got the worst of it and ran away.

I was going to send you a birthday present, but I had so much to do at Christmas time that I couldn't get up to London to buy one. It was careless of you to arrange your birthday[1] so near Christmas, wasn't it? Never mind, when I go up to London again, I will send you an un-birthday present, which Humpty-Dumpty said was a much nicer thing. Do you know the book about Alice and Humpty-Dumpty? If not, perhaps you would like to have it.

> With love from
> Cousin Dorothy

[1] His birthday was 3 January. He was now six years old.

To Eustace Barton   24 Newland Street
11 January 1930   Witham
                                     Essex

Dear Dr Barton,

You will, I am sure, sympathise when you hear that our worthy friend Harrison[1] passed away this evening in excruciating agony. A particularly horrible circumstance is that the unfortunate gentleman was all alone when he met his death, in a remote cottage near the little village of Manaton, where he was accustomed to spend his annual holiday. The deceased was very fond of cooking and eating various species of fungi, and it is thought that he must have accidentally consumed a poisonous variety. The inquest will be held tomorrow. Mr Harrison, who was an electrical engineer, leaves a wife and a son to lament his loss. Mrs Harrison is naturally prostrated.

As you will see, I also have retired into the country, and, after a Christmas of bad colds and domestic upheaval generally, am forging ahead. . . .

> With best regards from my husband and myself
> Yours very sincerely
> Dorothy L. Sayers

[1] The victim in *The Documents in the Case*.

To Eustace Barton   24 Newland Street
21 January 1930   Witham
                                     Essex

Dear Dr Barton,

Just a line to say we are getting along nicely. The stepson is suspecting the murder and is about to purchase a bunch of compromising letters from a blackmailing charwoman! The novelist is having a dreadful time, torn between his natural good feeling and the fact that he was at the same public school as the murderer. The wife is a dreadful person. The murderer (who has my sympathy) has just discovered this and his feelings of misery and remorse are dreadful, but nobody knows this yet but me. He would feel worse if he knew that it was all going to be discovered – or possibly he might feel relieved – but that, no one will never know. It is all too, too dreadful.

I see the difficulty about the whereabouts of the muscarine specimen, but I expect we shall find a way round it. In any case, we had better not make it too clear that we mean University College,[1] because I have made one character make libellous remarks about the ease with which outsiders could stroll in and help themselves to poisons. We can call it something else, and build the laboratories to suit ourselves. I don't see, either, why we shouldn't use our imaginations about the inside of the Home Office labs – or I might be able to get some information about this. . . .

Yours, with my mind full of fungi,
        Dorothy L. Sayers

[1] University College Hospital in Gower Street, London W.C.1.

To Eustace Barton   24 Great James St
9 February 1930   W.C.1

Dear Dr Barton,
    Yesterday morning at 3 ack emma[1] I wrote the last words of this here tarnation[2] book and, drawing a squiggly line under them, drank a large glass of Bovril-and-milk and staggered away to bed!

To-day I took courage to review the first part of it, in which I found much to displease me, but I think it will hold together tolerably. To-morrow I shall spend the day at the British Museum, putting in passing allusions to current events, with the help of a file of the *Daily Mail*, so as to blend verisimilitude to an otherwise bald and unconvincing narrative. My tame typist, who has polished up her machine and bought a new ribbon for the occasion, will then take the job in hand and the result will be sent down to you to vet and alter where required.

One or two things will have to be seen to. I have made the investigator pay a visit to the medical student in the labs. during term. If the description I have attempted is incorrect for this, you will be able to tell me how to alter it, or, if necessary, we can change the dates all through so as to put the visit in the Easter Vac. This would make the inquiry take place rather a long time after the death, but that wouldn't matter.

I have introduced certain modifications into your sketch of the closing scene – the polariscope scene, I mean, chiefly with a view to cutting up the dialogue and avoiding a lecturing tone. And I have made the Home Office analyst not know that the muscarine is suspected of being synthetic. Consequently he gets a nasty shock. This is fun, I think. The device by which I have induced him to make the experiment is fairly simple – and I hope it will pass muster. The unfortunate poet has a rotten time – he has a nasty feeling that he is behaving rather badly to the murderer, who is a friend of his. Naturally by the cussedness of things, the discovery falls to his share and not to that of the real investigator, the dead man's son, who wouldn't care two hoots about the murderer's feelings. The woman will get off, I'm afraid. The murderer was too chivalrous to let her know what he was doing. Curse her!

I have described the muscarine as being a whitish salt as per your notes. Dixon Mann describes it as a syrupy liquid, but no doubt it can exist in a crystallised form, and it would be much simpler for Latham to steal in that form.

I couldn't get much fun into the inquest, because, owing to the form of the book, I found it natural to present it in the form of a newspaper report, but I think you will enjoy the jury's rider.[3]

I shall be in town till Friday morning, after which I return to Witham; but any day you like to come up for the photograph I can arrange to come up and meet you. Witherington's, the press photographers, would be the best people to do it, as they understand dramatic lighting and all that sort of thing, but of course they won't have any suitable chemical apparatus. Do you know where we could borrow a few of those wiggly glass things that make such a formidable impression on the lay mind? . . . My husband[4] will come and see they do it properly.

> Yours very sincerely
> Dorothy L. Sayers

[1] a.m. (formerly signallers' usage).
[2] Slang, variant of 'darnation'.
[3] See Document No. 48.
[4] Mac was an expert photographer.

To EUSTACE BARTON   24 Newland Street
21 March 1930   Witham
                                            Essex

Dear Dr Barton,

I am sending the book, but in my heart I know I have made a failure of it. Really and truly I was feeling so nervous and run-down last year, what with funerals and other worries, that I ought not to have been writing at all. It has produced a mingled atmosphere of dullness and gloom which will, I fear, be fatal to the book. As it was, the earlier half was so bad, that I had to re-write great chunks of it, and it is still bad. And during the second re-type, my typist was laid up for a week with

VIOLENT POISONING!

I'm afraid there is a jinx of some bad sort giving his attention to the book.

Please make any alterations straight on to the MS. I have 4 copies of it. I wish I could have done better with the brilliant plot.

Yours very depressed
    Dorothy L. Sayers

To Eustace Barton   24 Great James St
7 April 1930   W.C.1

Dear Dr Barton,

As I wired you yesterday, I have fixed an appointment with the photographers – Witherington of Frith St, Soho, – for 10 a.m. on Thursday, and they have undertaken to provide all the scientific apparatus themselves. They are well-known advertising and theatrical photographers and quite seem to understand what is required.

We shall be delighted to dine with you Wednesday evening – thank-you so much. It is just possible Mac may get hung up with a job, but he thinks he will be able to get along all right.

Yes, indeed – I should be delighted if you would give an eye to the proofs. I am a bad proof-reader of my own stuff, and am apt to overlook things.

By the way – I am sorry I had to make Harrison a water-colour man – it looks rather rude to you, but Latham simply *had* to work in oils, because of the Academy masterpiece. What fun being able to sell your sketches so readily! I like selling things outside my own job. I am trying to sell some translations of Schumann's songs,[1] by way of a change from poison!

Arsenic going strong.[2] I feel so steeped in arsenic that I am getting twinges of peripheral neuritis in my legs!!

Yours very sincerely
    Dorothy L. Sayers

[1] Nothing is known of these translations.
[2] She was nearing the end of *Strong Poison*.

To Ivy Shrimpton   24 Great James St
15 April 1930   W.C.1

Dearest Ivy –

If J.A. is going to turn out mathematical, it's the best thing he could do for himself. This is a mathematical era.

As regards being baptised, the parson can't eat him if he does discover it[1] though he may make himself a tedious nuisance. Personally, I am all against making sacraments into conveniences, but if you feel very strongly about it, do as you like. Being baptised without one's will is certainly not so harmful as being confirmed against one's will, which is what happened to me, and gave me a resentment against religion in general which lasted a long time.[2] My people (weakly) thought it would 'be better' to have it 'done' at school – and it was the worst possible school for the purpose, being Low Church and sentimental – and I (still more weakly) gave in because I didn't want to be conspicuous and fight it out. Afterwards, when I became High Church, I wished I hadn't done it, because then I could have undertaken it properly, without fury and resentment, and without having the dreariest associations connected with the Communion Service. What sort of bloke is the parson? Is he Catholic-minded or Evangelical? or merely 'Established'? If he is a High Churchman with a sound theology, well and good; but the cultivation of religious emotion without philosophic basis is thoroughly pernicious – in my opinion. I shouldn't worry too much. This is no longer a Christian country. The chances are that the boy will not want to be a Christian; if he does, it will be because he believes it, which is the only good reason. The Early Church, living, as we do, surrounded by a heathen population, did not baptise infants, and I dare say she was right.

To turn to other matters. All is well at home, and Aunt Mabel seems to have taken a fresh lease of life. Her great pleasure is listening to the gramophone! I am working hard at books – though what is the good of trying to make money when the Government immediately snatches it away from one I do not know. If it were not that somebody must look after Aunt M., we could cut the cable and go and live abroad, with half the expense and a greatly reduced taxation, but we are tied by the leg and there it is. One can but do one's best. . . .

We are hoping to go up to Scotland soon, where we can be quiet and get some work done. Mac is very busy painting in addition to his ordinary work. He really ought to have been an artist. He seems to enjoy painting more than anything and is really good at it.

I am sending off an Easter Egg to-day.

With best love
    Yours always
        Dorothy

[1] i.e. that he was illegitimate.

[2] Compare her letters from school at the time of her confirmation. There is no evidence in letters which have come to hand of a resentment against religion. At Oxford she attended church services regularly.

To Victor Gollancz   24 Newland Street
28 April 1930   Witham
                                            Essex

Dear Mr Gollancz,
                    STRONG POISON[1]

    Yours sincerely
        Dorothy L. Sayers

[1] Victor Gollancz had written to enquire when he might expect to receive her next novel. This letter was sent by return of post, accompanying the typescript of *Strong Poison*, which was published in September 1930.

To Arnold Bennett[1]   24 Newlands Street
15 May 1930   Witham
                                            Essex

Dear Sir,
    Having read your article in tonight's *Evening Standard*, I should like, as one of the very numerous detective-story writers who do *not* happen to be published by Messrs. Collins, to thank you for drawing attention to the fact that the so-called 'Crime Club' is, in fact, run in the interests of a single publisher. So far as I know, no other critic has had (is it the acumen, the honesty or the courage?) to do so, and it is therefore all the more gratifying that it should have been done by yourself whose influence, if I may say so without impertinence, is so powerful and so wide-spread.
    While I have the greatest sympathy with every kind of advertising enterprise, I do feel that there has been in this particular case rather more camouflage than is altogether creditable, and I hope and think I should say the same even if I were myself eligible for 'Crime Club' laurels. Your article will do much to remove the misapprehension that undoubtedly exists, and for that I should like to express my appreciation.

    Yours faithfully
        Dorothy L. Sayers

[1] Arnold Bennett (1867–1931), novelist, playwright and journalist, wrote 'Books and Persons', a series of articles for the *Evening Standard*, from 1926 until his death.

To Eustace Barton   24 Great James St
3 September 1930   W.C.1

Dear Dr Barton,

Just a line in great haste on my way back to Scotland, from which we were called home to bury an aged aunt.[1] . . .

I enclose a little bit of trouble for you from the wife of a learned gentleman who says the synthetic muscarine is all wrong![2] I have written to thank her, and have said that muscarine is in your department and that you will be happy to take up the cudgels about it. I had to put it all on to you, because I couldn't remember the name of the authority you sent me, and had left my notes at Witham! I shall be interested to hear how the battle progresses.

Our address next week will be 14A. High St, Kirkcudbright as before, till about the end of the month.

    Yours very sincerely
        Dorothy L. Sayers

I have of course, not mentioned your real name to Mrs Coulson.

[1] Aunt Mabel Leigh, who died on 16 August.
[2] The objection raised was that organic muscarine, not being a protein, was not optically active. D.L.S. took the matter calmly and delivered a breezy talk about it on the radio, entitled 'Trials and Sorrows of a Mystery Writer' (*The Listener*, vol. VII, 6 January 1932, p. 26). See, however, her letter to Eustace Barton dated 3 October 1932.

To Victor Gollancz   14a High St
20 September 1930   Kirkcudbright

Dear Mr Gollancz,

I am working away at Chapter XIV[1] and hope to be done some time next month. The nuisance is that I can't hit on a good title. As you know, I wanted to call it *The Six Suspects*, but somebody has picked that. I might call it:

SIX UNLIKELY PERSONS
   or
THE BODY IN THE BURN   Dull
   or
THE MURDER AT THE MINNOCH

THE MISSING OBJECT
   or   See remarks
THERE'S ONE THING MISSING   overleaf

or I may think of something really good or suitable as I go on.

I've thought of one little stunt to add spice to the business. When the body is found, Lord Peter and the police catalogue all the contents of the pockets etc. etc., and Lord Peter says to Sergeant Dalziel:

'There's something missing. Look everywhere for it. If we can't find it, it means Murder.'

The Sergeant not unnaturally asks what he is to look for, and Wimsey tells him, but actually the Sergeant and the reader, if he had understood enough about the dead man's occupation in life, ought to have been able to supply for himself the name of the missing object from the list of things which *were* there.

Now, what I propose to do is to leave out altogether the paragraph in which Wimsey describes the missing object and the reasons why he knows it is missing, and substitute a blank page, in which the reader is invited to use his wits.

As the story goes on, six suspects appear, against whom the evidence (as regards motive, means, opportunity etc.) is practically equal. About the penultimate chapter, various members of the police give their opinions – one saying he thinks A is the murderer, another plumping for B, the third for C, and so on. Wimsey says 'You are all very plausible, but it was B, and as a matter of fact I *know* this' – his reason being that he has discovered which of them has the missing object. The reader also will know which of them has it, provided, of course, that he has previously made up his mind what the missing object is. Wimsey then reconstructs the crime, ingeniously destroying the most convincing alibi of the whole six, and the murderer is arrested and confesses.

The missing paragraph can be printed, if desired, in a sealed page at the end of the book, or it may merely be supplied by Wimsey in conversation in the final chapter.

Do you like this idea?

By the way, a very odd coincidence has occurred. This book, in which all the places are real and which turns on actual distances and real railway time-tables, is laid in exactly the same part of the country as Freeman Wills Crofts'[2] new book, which also turns on real distances and time-tables! We only discovered this the other day, in the course of correspondence which started about something else. The two plots are, of course, entirely different, and it really doesn't matter a pin. Only there's just one point. The unspeakable Collins (as you will see if you look at Crofts' book, *Sir John McGill's Last Journey* – have furnished him with the most mean, miserable, potty, small, undecipherable and useless map, scrim-shanking, feeble and unworthy to the last degree. Possibly he drew it himself, but in that case they ought to have taken it away from him and given him some-

thing better. I look to you, as a publisher of repute, to allow me a
large, handsome, clear, well-executed, generous and convincing map,
covering both end-papers (as this prevents tearing and facilitates reference), with a proper scale of miles and everything handsome about
it, and no pettifogging talk about the expense of large blocks or the
cheapness of having one's map made by the office-boy. Whatever
happens, we must go about ten better than the intolerable Collins!

    Yours very sincerely
        Dorothy L. Sayers

[1] Of *The Five Red Herrings.*
[2] 1879–1957.

To Muriel St Clare Byrne   14a High Street
30 October 1930   Kirkcudbright

Dear Muriel,
    I am so sorry! Having received your letter, I instantly lost it, and
with it your address![1] . . .
    We have been up here practically the whole summer, and I have
just nearly finished a new Lord Peter, full of Scotch scenery and real
railway time-tables. I'm glad you liked the last two books.[2] I am
getting a bit weary of Lord Peter, but I suppose he must be kept
going, as he still seems to pay pretty well. But, as you may have
noticed, he is growing older and more staid. There are times when I
wish him the victim of one of his own plots! We hope to be back in
England any day now – in fact, we are only waiting for a decent day
on which to start a 400 mile drive. Whatever happens, I must be in
town on the 12th and 13th November, so perhaps we shall be able
to fix up a meeting then.
    With ever so many apologies for this tardy reply,

    Yours ever,
        Dorothy L. Fleming.

[1] From this it appears that D.L.S. and Muriel St Clare Byrne had not been in touch for
some time.
[2] *The Documents in the Case* and *Strong Poison.*

To Eustace Barton   24 Newlands St
7 November 1930   Witham
                                           Essex

Dear Dr Barton,
    I have received a staggerer! A Harley-Street physician has written

to ask my advice about synthetic gland-extracts!! I have replied, disclaiming any personal knowledge of these things, and saying that I am forwarding his letter to you, who will doubtless be able to give him a line on the stuff, if it is procurable. I have not mentioned your name, but just said that you were a highly-qualified person and in touch with experts in bio-chemistry. I do hope you will be able to put him on to what he wants – what a scoop it would be! First time in history that a detective-story[1] has been of any serious use to anybody!

Have you had any results from your man who was researching about optically active fungus-extracts? I don't want to do anything about the matter till I know exactly how the land lies. If the worst comes to worst, we could make it not a fungus at all but hemlock (it was hemlock you mentioned, wasn't it?), which he might be supposed to have mistaken for some other plant, but it would be better if we could say that there really was a fungus which fulfilled the conditions.

We are home at last from Scotland and settling down to a busy winter in Essex and London. By the way, do you know of anybody who could give me exact information about haemophilia,[2] particularly as to the behaviour of haemophilic blood when copiously shed (as by throat-cutting)? Would it, when separated from the living body, clot like an ordinary person's blood on exposure to air? Or would it, as I imagine, take longer to do so than the ordinary kind? And I also want details about its inheritance. I believe it is a Mendelian sex-linked characteristic, is it not?

Yours very sincerely
Dorothy L. Sayers

Please preserve Dr MacDonald's letter – it must be unique of its kind!!

D.L.S.

[1] The reference is to *The Unpleasantness at the Bellona Club*.
[2] She needed this information for her novel *Have His Carcase*.

To Victor Gollancz   24 Newland Street
22 January 1931   Witham
                                      Essex

Dear Mr Gollancz
Many thanks for your letter. I am glad you like the book.[1] I quite appreciate the point you make about the decline of the 'pure puzzle'

story – in fact, I mentioned it when I was talking to you – but I wanted to try my hand at just one of that kind. I am always afraid of getting into a rut, and like each book to have a slightly different idea behind it. I have also been annoyed (stupidly enough) by a lot of reviewers[2] who observed the identity of the murderer was obvious from the start (as indeed it is also in *Unnatural Death* and *The Documents in the Case*). Personally, I feel that it is only when the identity of the murderer *is* obvious that the reader can really concentrate on the question (much the most interesting) *How* did he do it? But if people really *want* to play 'spot the murderer', I don't mind obliging them – for once! They have also grumbled that Lord Peter a) falls in love b) talks too discursively – here is a book in which nobody falls in love (unless you count Campbell) and in which practically every sentence is necessary to the plot (except a remark or two on Scottish scenery and language). Much good may it do 'em!

Anyway, I will return to a less rigidly intellectual formula in
HAVE-HIS-CARCASE
which will turn on an alibi and a point of medicine, but will, I trust, contain a certain amount of human interest and a more or less obvious murderer. But I haven't made up the plot yet. . . .

[1] *The Five Red Herrings*, published 26 February 1931.
[2] Of *Strong Poison*.

To Ivy Shrimpton   24 Great James St
15 February 1931   W.C.1

Dearest Ivy –

So sorry I haven't answered before – I've been rather bothered. As regards the Savings Bank account, I really don't know. When Mac and I got married the understanding was that we should formally adopt J.A., but it's been put off by one thing and another. I can't quite explain. He always says he is going to do it and wants to do it, but naturally I can't push it on to him. He says he doesn't see any objection to the name Fleming being used (Sayers of course is the only one to which he has any sort of right) – in fact Mac himself suggested that it should be Fleming. But I'm damned if I really know. I wish it could be settled one way or another, but it doesn't really lie with me. Of course, it would be perfectly possible for you to open the account in your own name and transfer it to J. later at any moment. That would really be best if you could do it without J.'s feeling hurt. Just at this particular moment I can't speak very decisively. I can't go into all the whys just now, but I'll explain some day.

I enclose cheque. Aunt Mabel's estate will be wound up at any moment now and then I will advise you when to expect the things.

Yours all rather worried but with much love
D

Please thank J.A. for his letter – He writes a very good one.

To Ivy Shrimpton   24 Newland Street
17 March 1931   Witham
                                    Essex

Dearest Ivy,
Dear oh dear! What a beastly nuisance for you. I do hope the wretched disease[1] doesn't run through the house and that you, at least, will escape it. These troubles are not pleasant for grown-ups – fortunately they have more chance of escaping. Of course John must go to the hospital – it is never right, I think, to nurse infectious diseases at home, for the sake of everybody else in the place. Besides, in hospitals the patient has a much better chance in case of any complication or emergency arising, since everything is on the spot. Never, never would I be ill at home if I could possibly go and be ill in a place appointed for the purpose! I expect he will [be] wary a bit at first over being taken to a strange place, but he will get over it. The great thing is that you should give yourself and the other children the best possible chance of escaping infection. If you yourself should be stricken, let us know – I expect we shall be able to fix up something for the infants. Anyway, don't worry – children will get these things, but the chances are that the grown-ups escape. I am sending a bit extra on the month's money, which includes Aunt Mabel's quarter,[2] as you may need extra cash to carry through with.

Best love and keep your pecker up
Dorothy

[1] Scarlet fever.
[2] Aunt Mabel Leigh had made Ivy a quarterly allowance of two pounds and ten shillings during her life, which D.L.S. kept up.

To Ivy Shrimpton   24 Newland Street
14 April 1931   Witham
                                    Essex

Dearest Ivy –
I was about to write to you when your second letter came this morning with more reassuring news. Of course scarlet fever usually

does affect the ears temporarily – the only danger is that it may do so permanently, and if there is any sight of lasting trouble of that kind we shall have to get a specialist. I don't think it at all probable that the brain would be damaged unless it were indirectly through the ear-trouble. But there is no reason why, with proper care, such as he is getting, any permanent trouble should result at all. The thing that might end by affecting the intelligence is adenoids, if they really are serious. It will be best to have him properly examined a bit later on for that part of the business. Of course, I was always a tonsilly subject – had 'em removed, though whether that was beneficial I don't know. Adenoids were not tackled in my case and apparently my brain has remained pretty active in spite of them. So far, J.A. does not seem to be short on brains, though, if there is the slightest chance of his becoming Lord Chancellor or anything alarming of that kind, a little 'retarding and pruning' of the intelligence (to use the rose-growers' phrase) might not be amiss. Don't worry too much. Thousands of children do have scarlet fever and survive apparently unimpaired. It is odd that he should have picked it up, but these things get into the air and you can't possibly avoid them. It is miraculous that you and the other infants should (touch wood!) have so far escaped. I imagine it is largely due, not merely to your own will-power, which I have always known to be phenomenal, but also to the very sensible modern habit of removing infectious cases at once to hospitals, instead of cheerfully letting the disease 'run through the family', as happened in the Bad Old Days.

Don't be worried about expenses – just let me know what your visits etc. cost you and I will send a cheque along. Also, of course, for any extras that may be needed at the hospital. I am so sorry you should have had all this bother. I wish I could come along and see you, but I am bunged up with engagements in Town and various bothers connected with books and publishers which need me and which *Mean Money*!

No, I don't think Cowley would be a very suitable place for convalescence. Put Mrs Spiller off politely until J.A. is out of hospital and I will try and arrange for you to take the family to the sea or something. It ought not to cost a devil of a lot at this time of the year – say end of May – and that would give you a complete answer, without rudeness, to the invitation. . . .

Aunt G., poor old soul, can't live many months now. I saw her the other day. The disease has advanced upon the lungs, and as it is very painful, one couldn't wish her to hang on long. I think she would like to get letters, BUT I think I should say very clearly that you don't expect or wish her to bother about answering them – the exertion is really too great for her. . . .

To Ivy Shrimpton   24 Newland Street
18 May 1931   Witham
                                                   Essex

Dearest Ivy –

This is all very tiresome for you – but by now you will have already
got my letter saying that the tonsils etc. will undoubtedly have to be
tackled some day. Certainly, the sooner the better, if they are in a
really bad state. I don't know whether it's wise to undertake the
little operation immediately after the scarlet fever – I should think it
depended entirely on what the hospital doctor and / or Dr Hodges
may think. I should not, in any case, have it done at home – the
business, though not serious, is usually 'bluggy' and tiresome to look
after for a short time. The best way, if Dr Hodges isn't at home,
would be to go by what the doctor at the hospital says. I should just
find out, through the Matron or direct when they think it ought to
be done and send J. along and have it done. I can make no other
suggestion – nor could I if I were upon the spot. I could only tell
them to do the thing properly and send the bill in when it was due.
After all, the things have obviously got to come out, and the only
question is, how soon? As soon as he can stand it and while he still
remembers with pleasure his friends at the hospital, if you ask me.

Talk of your place being damp – I'd like to know what place isn't
at the moment. Of all the foul, beastly, swimming, sopping, soul-
destroying, moppy, sloppy winters, this has been the worst. We are
slug-ridden, water-logged, rheumatic, neuritic, catarrhal, irritable
and fed-up. At the moment, however, the glass, thank the Lord, is
rising!

    Love to John,
        Yours ever gratefully
        Dorothy

To Ivy Shrimpton   24 Newland Street
19 May 1931   Witham
                                                   Essex

Dearest Ivy,

This is all very complicated – I can't get away just at the moment,
and if I did, I gather I shouldn't see the all-important Dr Hodges.
Anyway, I know far less about children than anybody living.

If you are not satisfied with the doctors, tell them to get a specialist.

In any case, I don't think you ought to be bothered with this
business at home. If you do, you must get in a proper nurse. If it is

really so urgent that they can't wait for J. to become free of infection, they could probably find some kind of nursing home that would take the risk – but a nurse you must have. I will not have your being worn out and bothered with the nursing. The great thing is to make these people understand that it is not a question of money. As regards whether the two ops. should be done together or separately, that is entirely a question for the doctors. If they don't agree, get another opinion.

But before getting the wind up, I should see Dr Hodges. If necessary, I will write to him, but do make it clear that he is not to be bound by considerations of expense –

In great haste,

Yours ever
D.

To Ivy Shrimpton   24 Newland Street
3 June 1931   Witham
                                         Essex

Dearest Ivy,

Many thanks for your letters. I'm glad you managed to get J. down to the Acland (where they once had the honour of removing my appendix) – I am sure it is infinitely better than having an operation in the house. I don't believe in operations under ordinary domestic conditions. I expect he would be feeling pretty dismal when you first saw him, but that is only the anaesthetic. Foul stuff. I gather he is doing 'as well as can be expected', poor little wretch.[1]

Aunt G., they say, is not likely to last more than 6 weeks or so now – but (of course) she may go on till the Autumn. It all depends on whether the growth keeps on at its present rate of progress or whether it gets hung up for any reason. I go over and see her when I can and so does Mac, to whom she has taken a great fancy. I ran into Auntie Annie last time I was there – the least attractive of all the Sayerses, I think. I don't like the Sayerses much, you know. Dad was much the best of them – he was a dear, but the rest – no! except Aunt G., who was always a woman of great charm.

I am struggling with another book[2] – horribly complicated! But it must be done, under contract, so there's nothing for it but to wire in and work it out.

I am sending £1 extra to cover the infernal taxi (as you say, they would choose the most inconvenient day!) Anything else I will settle up when the bills come along –

    Best love
        D.

[1] D.L.S. had telephoned the Acland to enquire.
[2] *Have His Carcase*, first published 11 April 1932.

To Ivy Shrimpton   24 Newland Street
12 June 1931   Witham
                                                 Essex

Dearest Ivy,

    Many thanks for your letter. I enclose cheque to cover the Acland Home account. I have made this payable to you, since I understand that you have so far conducted the matter without giving my name – which is rather well known in Oxford.

    I hope you will now have no more health worries about J.A. You must be sick of it. I don't mind saying that I am a little weary, of late years, of illness and death-beds! I feel it would be nice to have a year go by without anybody's being operated on or buried – just as a change! However, I suppose these things have to be. Mac hasn't been very well lately, either – nothing serious, but these upsets depress him. I want to get him away to Scotland again, which always does him good; but the weather has been too foul to make any move. Earthquakes are quite amusing, but they play Old Harry with the barometer. It (the earthquake) woke us both. Mac woke first and heard the whole thing, but I didn't wake till the lurch came and all the crockery started dancing. He said it was an earthquake, but I didn't really believe it. I thought it was lorries or heavy artillery going past on the road. But he has met earthquakes before and recognised it.

    I am now struggling with Chapter II of my gentleman with the cut throat.[1] He will not come right, curse him! (Attributable to the earthquake again, no doubt – bad weather for working in.) Freda's idea of a convent sounds hopeful,[2] but *do see that the dear nuns aren't too holy to keep a decent table!* . . .

[1] *Have His Carcase.*
[2] An idea for a holiday.

To Donald Tovey[1]   24 Great James Street
29 December 1931   W.C.1

Dear Professor Tovey,

    I must hasten to thank you very much indeed for your delightful gift,

and for the very kind letter which so flatters me by its proof of an inti-
mate knowledge of Lord Peter Wimsey and all his works. Lord P. is very
well, thank you, though much worried at the moment by the problem of
a young gentleman found (by Harriet) lying on a lonely beach with his
throat cut. He has not yet burst into Bach – that will be for his moment
of triumph. I'm afraid he can't have made much of a job of *Et iterum*,[2]
for his voice is really too light for it – that is why he keeps it for the bath,
where the resonance is so helpful. (Is that what the Psalmist meant by
'Deep calleth unto deep at the noise of thy water-pipes'?[3]) But it is a
lovely passage to roar, with that paralysing hiatus at 'judicare' and the
lovely 'whop' at the last syllable of 'mortuos'! For myself, I only know
Bach through having sung and played a lot of the big stuff in my Bach-
Choir-and-Orchestra days – but I suspect that Lord Peter knows all
about it, and will be able to give your 'editorial detective work' the really
intelligent appreciation which it merits.

With again very much gratitude for your kind thought and kind
expression, and with all good wishes for 1932. . . .

[1] Professor (later Sir) Donald Tovey (1875–1940), renowned musicologist and composer.
[2] See *Whose Body?*, chapter 5: 'A distant voice singing the *et iterum venturus est* [and He
shall come again] from Bach's Mass in B minor proclaimed that for the owner of the flat
cleanliness and godliness met at least once a day . . .'
[3] Psalm 42, 7: 'Deep calleth unto deep at the noise of thy waterspouts:' (Authorised
Version). D.L.S. quotes this as an epigraph to IV, The Second Part of *The Nine Tailors*.

TO HER SON   24 Newland Street
19 January 1932   Witham
                                              Essex

Dear John,
    Many thanks for your nice letter. I am glad you liked your presents.
Yes – the Encyclopaedia is for Auntie because she says you ask so
many questions that she will have to be taken away to Dottyville
Asylum with straws in her hair if this kind of thing goes on. So, as I
am sure you would not like this to happen:–

I have sent the Encyclopaedia so that you can all look up the answers for yourselves.

I think I can clear up the difficulty about bricks. In the old days there was only one letter for 'I' and 'J' and nowadays in mailing lists of things, people sometimes keep to this old-fashioned way of doing things – I don't quite know why. . . . The old people only had one letter for U and V too, so that you hadn't quite such a long alphabet to learn in those days, because they hadn't a W either. When they wanted a W they had to make two Vs side by side, and that is why it's called 'double-U' though it looks like a 'double-V', because, U and V being the same letter, they could choose whichever name sounded best. But the French call it 'double-V'. The alphabet came from the Romans, who pronounced V as we pronounce W, and then it went to the Germans, who pronounce W like V – so it's all rather complicated, isn't it?

Yours affectionately
     Dorothy L. Fleming

To Ivy Shrimpton   24 Newland Street
19 January 1932   Witham
                                        Essex

Dearest Ivy . . .
     I enjoyed John's letter – I fear he is a bit of a prig – but so was I at his age. I am mildly informing him that he does not own the earth – or the Encyclopaedia! I'm glad the presents were favourably received.

We have been very busy this month – everything being rather complicated by attacks of 'flu. Mac and I have only had it mildly, but our maid got rather a nasty turn of it – of course choosing the four days when I was up in London doing a broadcast, so that Mac had to doctor her and do his own cooking, poor lamb!

I must get on with my work – all behind hand, curse it! I wish the days did not grow shorter as one grows older. In a spasm of middle-agedness the other day, I started to write memoirs of my childhood[1] – but I find I don't remember much about it, really!

Best love
     Dorothy

[1] *My Edwardian Childhood*, an unfinished work existing only in manuscript.

To Ivy Shrimpton   24 Newland Street
17 February 1932   Witham
                                             Essex

Dearest Ivy

Oh dear! So rushed as I have been this month! At last I have got
my book[1] off to the publisher – just in time to be free to tackle Aunt
Maud's visit. I don't know why one extra person in the house should
make such a to-do but it does! It throws Evelyn completely out of
her stride, and sets her to informing me (dreaded phrase) that she
has 'only one pair of hands'. What she really wants is a more methodi-
cal head poor girl – but that is past praying for.

Interruption – arrival of man to see about repairing furniture. If
ever I sit down to write a letter, people simply pour in. I am momently
expecting the plumber and decorator in the matter of a party-fence
and a turncock! . . .

I have for the moment abandoned my 'Memoirs', as I shall have
to get on with a new book – which is to be all about a big church in
the Fens, and a grave which is suddenly found to have an extra body
in it!![2] . . .

[1] *Have His Carcase*, published 11 April 1932. Between now and the following April, D.L.S.
fell ill and was unable to correct her proofs. See her letter to Donald Tovey dated 18
January 1934. It is not known what the illness was.
[2] Thinking back to her childhood in Bluntisham inspired her to write her masterpiece,
The Nine Tailors.

To Ivy Shrimpton   24 Newland Street
18 June 1932   Witham
                                             Essex

Dearest Ivy,

I was just about to write to you when your letter came, with your
kind good wishes and the sausage-drama. The unexpected grisliness
of your imagination struck me completely dumb for five days! However, now that I am slightly recovered, I will pull myself together to
say thank-you.

I'm afraid no editor would dare to print 'Maid in Durance', because
there are limits to the horrors they venture to subject readers to, and
cannibalism is one of them. Despite the motor-cyclist's comforting
assurance that he doesn't think the boys are in the sausages, there is
still the horrid feeling that they might be! The only place where, for
some reason, cannibalism is welcomed and applauded is the Elephant
and Castle Theatre, where *Sweeney Todd the Demon Barber of Fleet St*
(who, you remember, worked his customers up into mutton pies)

had a considerable success some years ago. But magazine editors are queasy-stomached folks. Why! they even objected to a tale of mine in which a blood-stained skewer (human-blood-stained, I mean) was concealed by being thrust into a roast chicken – even though nobody ate the chicken![1] However, personally I welcome every kind of frightfulness, and am delighted with your robust appetite for blood.

However, this is all a bit frivolous. It is certainly an original story. Where, I think, you want a little more care is in dealing with that very difficult point where the grotesquely-horrible slips over the edge into burlesque. Sometimes, just as I think you are going to freeze my blood, I'm brought up against a sentence that sounds like parody. For instance, the sentence 'what odd joints they had at home lately!' strikes just the right note of uneasy apprehension; the next sentence but one 'Poor boys, perhaps they were in these very sausages', is somehow just wrong. Besides, it's not needed – the reader can guess that bit. Did I ever send you the Second Series of *Great Short Stories of Detection, Mystery and Horror*?[2] There is a beastly little story in that, called 'Cut-Throat Farm',[3] which is a masterpiece in the art of telling a tale – much the same tale in the essentials – without ever making a definite statement about anything. By the way, I should shorten the motor-cyclist's explanations – we don't really need to be told how he came to interfere, we can take that as read. When you've made your chief point, wind the thing up as quickly as possible is a good rule. I suppose he has to turn out to be the long-lost nephew, but let him disclose himself with as little delay as possible and drop the curtain on him briskly.[4]

It's all very well for me to deliver this lecture. I'm a shockingly poor hand at short stories myself and usually tumble into precisely the faults I have been picking out in your story!

To return to your letter. Re Snakes. Probably it was only a ring-snake, but you never know. If it was very long and handsome, with an olive-green back and a patch of yellow behind the head and a lovely black-and-pale-gleam underneath, it was as innocent as mutton. But if it was shorter, and had a black diamond pattern down the back, it was an adder, and not very nice to know. We saw a whole lot of adders in Scotland last year. They like basking in the sun, but the ring-snake likes cool grass near streams and is a great swimmer, though the adder can swim too if it wants to. On the whole they are best avoided when in doubt.

Mac hasn't been up to much lately, but I think he's better now. He sends love. By the way, returning to Snakes. Tell J.A. never to pick a snake up by the tail – if he must pick up snakes, let him catch 'em just *behind the head* so they can't BITE! I remember catching

a ring-snake in a butterfly net at Bluntisham – I fancy you were with me at the time. For some reason, the grown-ups did not take kindly to the creature. I can't think why, can you? It was a nice snake. I think Chapman slew it!

    Cheerio!
        Dorothy

[1] 'The Vindictive Story of the Footsteps that Ran', first published in *Lord Peter Views the Body*, 12 November 1928.
[2] Published by Gollancz, 13 July 1931.
[3] By J. D. Beresford, pp. 555–9 (from *Nineteen Impressions*, Sidgwick and Jackson, 1918).
[4] It is not known whether Ivy Shrimpton's story was ever published.

To VICTOR GOLLANCZ   14A High Street
14 September 1932   Kirkcudbright

Dear Mr Gollancz,
    Mr Higham[1] has passed on to me your letter about the *Five Red Herrings*. I'm afraid that when I wrote to him I rather picturesquely exaggerated my distress of mind! I wasn't actually so heart-broken, and in the case of any other book I shouldn't have bothered at all.[2] It is just that the *Herrings* are in a peculiar position up here, enjoying a sort of mild and regular seasonal sale, and it seemed tiresome that it should have chosen to peter out just at that moment. You see, what happens is this: Even at this distance of time, people arrive at hotels in Gatehouse and Kirkcudbright and say they've come to spend their holidays there because they read a book called *The 5 Red Herrings*. Whereupon the proprietor says: 'Och aye? Weel, the authoress is just stayin in Gallowa' the noo – maybe ye'd like tae be meetin' her.' So presently I am displayed as one of the local amenities, and the visitor says: 'Now, I've just bought a copy of your book – I wonder if you would write your name in it for me.' Which I do, if the book is available, and everyone is happy. But it's a bore if they come bleating to say that they can't get the book, and when the booksellers sob on my shoulders. Anyway, it's very decent of you to bother to reprint, and I'm glad the new lot is out as I am just arranging a little window display next week in the leading stationer's for a few fellow-D.C.[3] members and myself, and the *Herrings* will be wanted.
    The new book[4] is nearly done. I hate it because it isn't the one I wanted to write, but I had to shove it in because I couldn't get the

technical dope on *The Nine Tailors* in time. Still, you never know what the public will fancy, do you? It will tell people a little about the technical side of advertising which most people are inquisitive about, and it deals with the dope-traffic, which is fashionable at the moment, but I don't feel that this part is very convincing, as I can't say I 'know dope'. Not one of my best efforts. *The Nine Tailors* will be a labour of love – and probably a flop!!

Yours very sincerely
Dorothy L. Sayers

¹ David Higham, literary agent, then member of the firm of Curtis Brown.
² *The Five Red Herrings*, first published in March 1931, went into its fifth impression in September 1932.
³ Detection Club.
⁴ *Murder Must Advertise*, first published 6 February 1933.

To Eustace Barton   24 Great James St
3 October 1932   W.C.1

Dear Dr Barton,
I have just received the attached from Dr Ainsworth Mitchell, the editor of *The Analyst* and author of *The English Witness*, who is the leading Home Office authority on the chemical detection of forged documents and so on. You will see Dr Hewitt's[1] reference to our muscarine book on p. 594 – a great act of courtesy, I think, from one of the leading organic chemists in the country. It looks as though, after all, we were not quite so wrong as we thought we were! In any case, muscarine seems to be a vexed question even among scientists of the most terrific repute, and with names like Kögl, Duisberg and Erxleben (oh, gosh!) – so that we may be excused for any slight confusion.

Will you let me have the paper back when you have finished with it. It isn't the sort of literature I should select for bedside reading (!) but I should like to keep it as a trophy.[2] . . .

My husband is busily making pastel pictures and getting out a colossal book on Cookery![3] (not the cooking of Amanita Rubescens,[4] though!) . . .

¹ John Theodore Hewitt, F.R.S. (d. 1954).
² Dr Barton replied on 17 October: 'I have now got a copy of the *Analyst* and have re-read carefully . . . Dr Hewitt's review, and his most courteous reference to our book, and I gather that although the *structure* of muscarine is still in dispute among these learned gentlemen, there is no doubt about its optical activity, and that is the whole point so far as we are concerned. It is very comforting after all the agonies and the criticisms we had.'
³ *Gourmet's Book of Food and Drink* (Bodley Head, 1933), under the pseudonym of Hendy.
⁴ The Latin name of 'warty cap'.

To Ivy Shrimpton   24 Newland Street
19 November 1932   Witham
                                         Essex

Dearest Ivy –

Later than ever this time! This has been a busy month and no
mistake. But my beastly book[1] is in the publisher's hands, thank the
Lord! Also a nice, bright, Christmas murder dealing with refined
persons in high society has been written for the *Radio Times*.[2] Also, a
new book begun. Also an incredible quantity of Club business dealt
with. I have now only two lectures and a speech to write, and deliver,
and then we may be able to breathe.

I will try to procure a book about Robin Hood. I see this morning
that some ethnological and archaeological (and probably also patho-
logical) ass has come forward to prove that Robin Hood is really an
Egyptian god, Ra-Binadd, or something, with a temple at Whipsnade
(where the Zoo is). King Arthur ditto. I don't believe it. I don't, in
any case, believe the story of Robin Hood is found anywhere earlier
than the Middle Ages. I thought all that sun-god myth stuff had gone
out of fashion – I will see that whatever book I do get has no bosh
about Ra-Binadd in it! I will also inquire about Nesbit books.[3]

Everything here is much as usual, including Mac's unaccountable
tummy, which makes housekeeping one long problem. I forget if I
told you that the wrongly-named Peter presented us some time ago
with 4 kittens. Two were removed to other spheres:

but the other two are still
with us. One of these (called
'Squeaker' because he
squeaks if you pick him up)
is going to a new family to-
morrow; the remaining one
will live with us. We call him
'Thomas Yownie' after the
boy in John Buchan's story
'Huntingtower'[4], because
nothing ever upsets him. He has a grey striped back and a white front
underneath a white face – that is, when he remembers to wash it. He
is very ugly, but very intelligent.

Best love
      Dorothy

---

[1] *Murder Must Advertise*.
[2] 'The Queen's Square', also published in *Hangman's Holiday*, Gollancz, 1 May 1933.
[3] Edith Nesbit (1858–1924), writer of children's books, of which the best known are *The*

Story of the Treasure Seekers (1899), concerned with the Bastable children, *The Phoenix and the Carpet* (1904), and *The Railway Children* (1906).

[4] John Buchan (1875–1940). *Huntingtower* was published in 1922. Tammas Yownie is alluded to in *Gaudy Night*, chapter 17.

To Harold W. Bell[1]   24 Newland Street
4 February 1933   Witham
                                 Essex

Dear Mr Bell,

Just a line to thank you for your too-generous letter. I was really feeling rather uneasy about the R.H.L.,[2] and, indeed, have been kicking myself violently with hob-nailed boots for my original stupidity in overlooking the matter of Bank Holiday. If you really think my rather strained explanation will stand, I am more than content, though I do wish it hadn't involved quite so much acrobatic wrestling with the text. On the matter of the shop-window I am, however, adamant, picture or no picture. What amount of authority would you be inclined, in general, to attribute to the pictures? They cannot, surely, be put on a level with the text. We must suppose the portraits of S.H. and Dr W.[3] to be substantially correct, together with the costumes, since the artist would be as familiar with them as with those of any other prominent public character – thus, in a story about Winston Churchill, we should expect his face and his hats to be in character. But we need not, perhaps, suppose that a personal visit was paid to every place mentioned in the text. Probably Reginald Musgrave, for example, would have objected to throwing open his house and grounds to a magazine artist; he seems to have been a stiffish customer, and probably disliked the publicity given to him very much. By the way, have you tackled at all the objection to 'The Musgrave Ritual' which was raised by somebody, viz. that the two trees from which the elevations were taken seem to have suffered neither growth nor decay in 200-odd years? I am ignorant about trees, but should welcome an authoritative pronouncement – say by the Ministry of Agriculture or the School of Forestry – on this point. It seems to me that the trees must have been full-grown in 1687 (or whatever the date was), and I should not expect them to have added much to their stature; perhaps they would rather tend to decline in height and vigour – or it may be that a tree, once fully grown, is stationary in height, increasing only in girth till decay sets in; but the point has been raised and ought, I feel, to be settled one way or another. (The oak was still 'a magnificent specimen' in 1878 and the elm, though struck by lightning, was apparently in good health up to this accident.)

I am extremely glad to hear that you are satisfied about Blakeney's

1888 theory.[4] It left me completely bewildered, owing to its method of presentation, which seemed to assume casually so many things that were either not proved, or proved on some other page without cross-reference.

I did not see Ronnie Knox's article in the *New Statesman*,[5] but I am in no way surprised to hear that he made a bad break. He made quite a number in the *Essays in Satire*,[6] the most blatant being, of course, the passage in which he scornfully demands how one could trim a Johann Faber pencil so that the letters NN only remained on the stump. They were, of course, not on the stump at all, but on the chip, and it is so stated: a man who could so tamper with the facts would do anything.

Very well; I will preserve an open mind on the question of the marriages, though I cannot quite see why Holmes should have suffered two marriages in silence and then denounced the third as 'the only selfish action, etc.' Either the circumstances were exceptional, or Holmes was getting very crotchety.[7] The 'Gloria Scott' is hopeless, but if Holmes was taken in by it, it must have been because he classed English history, together with Galilean astronomy, as useless lumber. May I safely deduce from it that, whatever he read at college, it was not Modern History?

Holmes as a Cat-Lover is a fascinating theme. I recollect that he had a cat-like love of personal cleanliness, but cannot otherwise put my finger on any reference to cats. On the other hand, dogs are fairly numerous. There was Mrs Hudson's dog in *The Study in Scarlet* – Holmes referred to it as 'this wretched dog' – but that was under stress of pardonable emotion. Previously he had called it 'that poor little devil of a terrier' – an expression which, though colloquial, is not destitute of sympathy. It was, however, Watson who carried it up in his arms. Can it, by the way, have been the presence of this poor little dog which accounts for the otherwise inexplicable disappearance of Watson's bulldog? Holmes made no objection to the bulldog in the original agreement (though his only other recorded encounter with a bulldog had been a painful one). Was it perhaps that Mrs Hudson's terrier was afraid of the bull-pup, and that Watson parted with his own dog rather than distress his landlady? In *The Sign of Four*, Holmes speaks highly (p. 192) of the dog Toby. Here again, Watson is dispatched to find the animal, but Holmes's attitude towards it (p. 198) is that of a man friendly to, though not perhaps intimately familiar with dogs. (It is rare to find a real dog-lover addressing a dog as 'Doggy'.) Nevertheless, Holmes's strong sense of justice is shown (p. 205) when he refuses (even in a moment of bitter disappointment) to blame the dog for acting 'according to his lights', and on this occasion he himself lifts Toby from the tar-barrel, regardless of the tar-stains which he might have picked up in the process. 'Poor Toby', he says indulgently, 'is not to blame.' He himself suggests that they should 'keep Toby' in the house overnight (p. 210) but it is Watson who feeds the dog at breakfast-time, apparently on ham-and-eggs (pp. 211, 213). In *The Missing Three-Quarter*, Holmes speaks pleasantly and familiarly to Pompey, and takes him on the lead himself; he also shows himself familiar with the dog's liking for aniseed. In *The Hound of the Baskervilles*, neither man displays the smallest sympathy with the hound (which also, when you come to think of it, 'acted according to its lights'); Watson speaks of its 'dreadful head' and 'cruel eyes' and seems to have been jolted quite out of his usual dog-mania. Possibly, however, when writing this story, Watson was affected in retrospect by the thought of Dr Mortimer's spaniel, with which he had enjoyed playing in the train (p. 328) and concerning whose loss he had 'given Mortimer such consolation as he might'. On the discovery of the spaniel's remains, Holmes is sympathetic but not expansive; Watson seems to have been struck dumb with terror.

I cannot think of any more dogs at the moment; but I suggest that Holmes tolerated and even liked dogs, though without fanaticism; and I certainly think that the detached independence of the cat would have suited his character better. Watson's own affection for him was – if you like – dog-like in the best sense, that of fidelity, but it did not show itself in noisy demonstrations or in self-abasement – if it had, Holmes would probably have been disgusted. If Holmes kept a cat at Baker St., it is odd that he should not have mentioned it *à propos* of the bull-pup; unless we are to suppose (which is possible) that he did keep one and that the cat was one too many for the bull-pup, so that Watson had to withdraw his terrorised pet. In that case Watson, as you say, suppressed all reference to the cat, not liking to admit that his dog could not stand up to its claws!

I shall of course be most happy to collaborate in any proposed volume on S.H.,[8] provided that it does not have to be rushed out in a hurry, since this is really only a hobby of mine and I couldn't lay everything else aside for it. I am not very happy about the hand-writing; I have no great facility in consistent forgery! I do, however, feel clear that Watson used a decayed J pen!

I really quite agree with you about the typing, and only put that bit in *ex abundantia cautelae*,[9] in case anyone should suggest a typist. It is far more likely that Watson's handwriting went direct to the printer, and that he didn't bother to correct his proofs. Probably his copy always reached the office at the last moment (he was a dilatory man) and when the proofs arrived (marked URGENT – MESSENGER WAITS) he was usually out with Holmes, or trundling off on the rounds he should have completed earlier, so that the Editor, getting no reply, had to print from the uncorrected proofs and hope for the best. If so, we may allow a margin for unintelligent corrections made by the printer's reader, who, struck by some discrepancy, might easily make some hasty alteration to bring it into shape, thereby introducing an entirely new series of errors. I know that, in the case of Old French texts, we were always attributing this kind of thing to 'the scribe'; besides, my own publisher's reader does exactly the same thing, writing '?Lupin' in the margin, when I refer to Poe's 'Dupin', of whom he has never heard and, in America, calmly putting 'a pint of bitters' for 'a pint of bitter' according to his own will and fancy.

Please never apologise for writing a long letter. For one thing, your letters give me great delight, and for another – if you apologise for length, what must I do? I never seem to send you less than a young volume.

The inquiry into S.H.'s college career[10] proceeds slowly; at the moment much hangs on the question of compulsory chapel, which I don't know much about, since my college, being undenominational, had no such thing. I feel sure that Holmes would not voluntarily have attended unnecessary chapels and I think it is only early chapel that is compulsory, but I must be certain of this. If the chapel was morning chapel, the University was almost certainly Cambridge.

> Yours very sincerely,
> Dorothy L. Sayers

[1] An American scholar, of Boston, author of *Sherlock Holmes and Dr Watson: The Chronology of their Adventures* (edition limited to 500 copies). D.L.S. said of it: 'I have read with intense interest this most scholarly and comprehensive study . . . the only work on the subject which makes any pretence to completeness . . .' (See also letter dated 12 March 1933.)

[2] 'The Red-Headed League.' D.L.S.' article 'The Dates in "The Red-Headed League"' was first published in *The Colophon, A Book-Collector's Quarterly*, part 17, no. 10, June 1934. It was later republished under 'Studies in Sherlock Holmes' in *Unpopular Opinions* (Gollancz, 1946, pp. 168–76). In this she uses H. W. Bell's work as a basis.

[3] Sherlock Holmes and Dr Watson.

[4] T. S. Blakeney, *Sherlock Holmes: fact or fiction?* (1932).

[5] 'The Mathematics of Mrs Watson', the *New Statesman*, 12 September 1932.

[6] Published by Sheed and Ward, 1928.

[7] See D.L.S.' article 'Dr Watson, Widower', published in *Unpopular Opinions*, pp. 152–67.

[8] See note to letter dated 12 March 1933.

[9] Latin: 'out of abundance of caution'.

[10] See note to letter dated 12 March 1933.

TO MISS DOROTHY HORSMAN[1]
No date, but previous to 6 February 1933

Dear Miss Horsman,
      Herewith corrected proof of *Murder Must Advertise*. I really don't

think it's libellous anywhere, but you might have a look in the P.O. Directory to make sure that there isn't a Dr Garfield in Harley Street! (It would be awkward if there was, especially if he is a specialist in nervous diseases.) If there is, we will call him something else.

Tell your reader that I have already had two experienced cricketers on that cricket chapter, and that any errors can be put down to them![2] But I have reduced the scores of Barrow and Pinchley, so as to allow a little more room for extras, in the first innings. I hope this will make him happier. As far as I can now make it out the first innings score stands thus:–

Barrow	b.	27	
Garrett	b.	6	
Hankin	lbw	4	
Ingleby	c.	0	
Tallboy	played on	7	
Pinchley	c.	16	AND BE BLOWED TO IT!
Miller	run out	12	
Beeseley	c.	3	
Haagedorn	b.	0	
Wedderburn	not out	1	
Bredon	not out	14	
		90	
Extras		9	
		99	

Yours sincerely
Dorothy L. Sayers

[1] In charge of production at Gollancz.
[2] For an analysis of the cricket match, see Andrew Lewis, 'An Almost Perfect Match: Dorothy L. Sayers on Cricket', in SEVEN: *An Anglo-American Review*, Volume X, 1993, pp. 127–37. The reader was probably Jon Evans.

To HAROLD BELL   24 Newland Street
12 March 1933   Witham
                                                      Essex

Dear Mr Bell,
    I have two letters from you to acknowledge. As the former of them required consideration, and as I was in London and rather busy when it arrived, I put off answering until my return here.

To take the second first: I am so glad you enjoyed *Murder Must Advertise*. The plot is rather hasty and conventional, because I wrote the book against time and rather against the grain; but the advertising part is sound enough. I was nine years in an advertising agency, so I ought to know the ground! As regards the dates – I'm afraid I usually mix these up on purpose, to prevent people like you from attributing the events narrated to any particular year! (Thus, in *Have His Carcase*, the times of High Tide at Whatever-it-is were those of Bristol in 1931, with a constant of 1h.20m. added or subtracted, I forget which now, but the days should be self-consistent, so that it was wrong of me to make May 25 a Monday. But no doubt the imaginary year was an imaginary leap-year, calculated by the calendar of Nephelocorcygia![1]

I will resurrect the Dowager Duchess one day soon, but, as you say, one finds it better to give the characters a rest from time to time – especially when they have well-marked tricks of speech, which are apt to become tedious and stereotyped. Pray thank your Mother for her very kind message, and say I am delighted to know that the book amused her. It is a great compliment to have one's work liked by the older generation, because I think that, on the whole, they have a higher standard of comparison. Of course, I don't know how old your Mother is, but she is probably old enough to find a certain thin querulousness in the post-war author rather irritating. Not that this applies so much to detective stories, except that I find modern writers falling into two schools: 1) the Desiccated: all finger-prints and time-tables, with no characterisation; 2) the Psycho-analytical, whose characters are all perversions and complexes. Both are liable to lose the human interest, but it is rather a job to strike a golden mean between them.

Enough! Let us return to Sherlock. You raise several points:–

The Illustrations: Must we not give them just a little documentary importance? They are, for instance, the only authority (correct me if I am wrong) for the bowler-hattedness of Watson and for S.H.'s deerstalker and Inverness cloak. But (as I said before) we can always assume that S.H. and W., being public characters, were faithfully represented by the artist, who then worked up the backgrounds according to his own taste and fancy, assisted by W.'s notes. Where the artist conflicts with the text, or with our legitimate deductions from the text, that is *his* fault. Artists are often careless in these matters, and it is very improbable that Watson had any opportunity of correcting errors, since (as I know too well from experience) the wretched author seldom sees the illustrations till they confront him, with all their enormities, in the published page! In the R-H. L.[2] the artist simply drew a pawnbroker's shop as he thought it ought to be, and didn't bother either to study the text or visit the actual shop. But we must have the bowler hat!

Since writing to you, I came across a bit about the *height of trees* in W. H. Hudson's[3] *Hampshire Days* which confirms my own impression. He says (p. 199): 'Trees, like men, have their middle period, when their increase slowly lessens until it ceases altogether; their long stationary period, and their long decline: each of these periods may, in the case of the yew, extend to centuries; and we know that behind them all there may have been centuries of slow growth.' He does not specifically mention oaks, but these, also, are slow-growing trees; elms I don't know about. But if we suppose the original measurements to have been taken about the period when the trees were reaching their maximum stature, and the second measurement when they had almost imperceptibly begun to decay, we shall not, perhaps be allowing too much for the 'long stationary period'.

I do still feel sceptical about *Watson's marriages*, I admit – particularly about Marriage No. 2, the evidence for which appears to me to be very slight. Still, I keep an open mind! In any case, a possible difference of opinion on this delicate matter will not, I hope, interfere with the harmony of our relations!

Cats: I suspect you of having a passion for cats. We have three cats: Adelbert, Thomas and Peter. The last-named (called after Lord Peter) shocked us by having kittens last year, of whom Thomas is one. Thomas is ugly, but a genius in his way. We had one called Wilkie (after Wilkie Collins) but he was a little potty. He died, deeply regretted, of some trouble in his throat. I feel sure, now you have pointed it out, that Sherlock was a cat-man.

Sherlock Holmes Books: Yes; Roberts,[4] certainly. I don't know Behrens' work, but it sounds good, MacCarthy[5] and Milne[6] are both good names: Milne especially would help sales. Vernon Rendall's[7] work I have heard about, but somehow missed seeing. Knox[8] – yes, he is dreadfully slipshod, but I think his name is a good one. The public enjoy his wit: for instance, my husband, who cares nothing for scholarly exactitude, and won't even trouble to read your or my fiddling researches into dates and places, will chuckle over the Holmes essay in *Essays in Satire*[9] again and again, just because of its effervescent humour. Is there no subject you could offer to Knox which could exploit his brilliance without requiring him to be accurate? Could he not, for example, examine the religious and philosophic opinions of Sherlock Holmes? That is a sphere in which accuracy, and even honesty, are neither expected nor required. Blakeney has made a feeble effort at it, but he has not the equipment. I think Knox might do it excellently, if you could bring him up to scratch. He is a difficult man to get work out of, and he likes some prospect of pecuniary reward, but I think he could be got to do it, and I am sure he would help to sell the book on this side. He is a member of my club and I know him slightly, so that if you decided to include him I might help to shove him along. Blakeney is a difficulty – he is so terribly incoherent, and I shouldn't think his name would cut much ice. I should think he might very well be left out.

Vincent Starrett:[10] Don't know him, but I like his idea of writing up untold tales immensely. I should certainly like to try my hand at one. There are many intriguing titles. I wouldn't tackle any Forgery Cases or the Nonpareil Club Scandal, not being strong on club-life or forgery, but I might manage the Cumberwell Poisoning Case, the Curse of Vamberry the Wine-Merchant, Wilson the Notorious Canary-Trainer, the Ferrers Documents or something like that. The French Will Case would demand a knowledge of French law, which is difficult. Would Knox, I wonder, be able or willing to undertake the Vatican Cameos, The Two Coptic Patriarchs or the Death of Cardinal Tosca? Two detective writers with quite a pretty turn for parody are Helen Simpson[11] and Gladys Mitchell,[12] especially the former – and they would, I think, both be keen (This is really a job rather for story-writers than for Holmes experts.) Then there is E. C. Bentley[13] – even more difficult than Knox to bring up to the collar, but a Holmes-lover and a scholar as well as a real writer. I could get him, I think. Milward Kennedy[14] is a man of great charm, energy and affability and writes good English – I don't know whether he could imitate the Holmes style, but he has wit and humour – he is a 'possible', I think. I know several others who would eagerly try, but who would not, perhaps, be quite able to catch the authentic note. It is a delicate matter. Anthony Berkeley,[15] for instance, is too rough a parodist. F. W. Crofts[16] too pedestrian, and dear old John Rhode,[17] though a perfect elephant for work, not enough of an artist. (Please keep these libellous opinions confidential!!! they are all friends of mine!)[18] By the way, in your list of the unrecorded cases I note that you do not include the remarkable affair of 'The Politician, the Lighthouse and the Trained Cormorant'. Or was it not, technically, a 'case', and if not, why not? I suppose 'ante 1927' is all we can say about it – was it a spy story, do you suppose? Or does it belong in the category of 'social and official scandals of the late Victorian era'? I should be glad to have your opinion.

H-W Dictionary: Excellent! It is curious, certainly, how the S-H stories are haunted by certain names. The Higher Critic of the old school would probably use that fact to prove that all these people were myths or variants one of the other, like Mary of Bethany and

Mary of Magdala – but, after all, in my own fifth form at school there were five Dorothys including myself and four Marjories – Christian names go by fashion. And even strange combinations of Christian and surname turn up oddly side by side. There are two Winston Churchills and two D. Wyndham-Lewises. Within the same three years at my own college there were: Miss Scott, Miss Scott-Scott, and Miss Scott-Stokes; Miss Brown, Miss Bryan and Miss Bryan-Brown. (These last three were all up in the same year, and all pronounced, by persons with cockney accents, indistinguishably 'Miss Brahn', causing endless confusion.) We need not necessarily look for any myth or complex in Watson's records.

At this point I bring forward a shy suggestion about Watson's second name.[19] It is certainly odd that his wife should on one occasion have called him 'James'. Very likely this merely represents a printer's error due to Watson's handwriting. But there is another possibility. To begin with, I do not feel obliged to accept Roberts' suggestion of 'John Henry' after Newman – (I think it was Roberts). There seems to be very little support for it, and certain arguments have, I fancy, been advanced against it, though I forget where. No; I venture, very tentatively, to suggest that the second name was 'Hamish'. This is, of course, a Scotch name, and Watson was certainly very English, but that is nothing against it. The average Anglo-Saxon's brutal insensitiveness to Celtic national feeling is notorious, and nothing more exasperates the Scot than the English habit of annexing names which he (the Scot) holds sacred to his own soil. Donalds and Douglases, Ians and Andrews abound in English suburbs, for no other reason than that the parents thought the names pretty or uncommon or romantic – and so, of course, do Brians and Patricks and other Irish names. If Watson's mother had, by a flight of fancy, christened her boy 'Hamish' it is quite possible that his wife may have used this name, playfully re-Englishing it as 'James'. What is more usual than for a wife to have a special name for her husband, and what is more likely than that Watson, accustomed to hearing her use it, should thoughtlessly incorporate it into his story, without stopping to reflect that it might have an odd appearance to the reader, who would know nothing of the history behind it? As a nearly parallel case, I am acquainted with a girl whose 'christened name' is (I believe) Elsie. All her family call her so with the exception of her father, who usually addresses her as 'Eliza'. But indeed, if you come to think of it, there is no reason at all why Watson should not have had a partly-Scotch mother. (That need not affect his essential Englishry; I am very English, but my father was at least half Irish with a bit of Scotch mixed in somewhere – most English are mongrels, and the more mongrelly the more English, in a sense.)[20] In that case, we might perhaps trace to the Scottish strain in him that 'vein of pawky humour' which, on one occasion at least, took Holmes a little aback (*Valley of Fear*, p. 460).

But I grow tedious – forgive me! I *will* stop. There must be limits to garrulity.

Yours very sincerely
       Dorothy L. Sayers

I have mentioned my husband – but 'Miss Sayers' is correct in literary correspondence and all works of reference. My married name is Fleming.

[1] A town in the clouds built by the cuckoos, cloud-cuckoo land (Aristophanes, *The Birds*).
[2] 'The Red-Headed League'.
[3] William Henry Hudson (1841–1922), writer on nature.
[4] S. C. Roberts (1887–1956), Master of Pembroke College, Cambridge, Secretary of the Syndics of the Cambridge University Press and authority on Sherlock Holmes.
[5] Sir (Charles Otto) Desmond MacCarthy (1877–1952), critic and eminent Holmesian scholar.
[6] A. A. Milne (1882–1956), creator of Christopher Robin; also author of a detective novel, *The Red House Mystery* (1922).
[7] Vernon Horace Rendall (1869–1960), author of *The London Nights of Belsize* (1917).
[8] Monsignor Ronald Knox (1888–1957), essayist, theologian and detective-novelist.
[9] 'Studies in the Literature of Sherlock Holmes' in *Essays in Satire* by Ronald A. Knox, pp. 145–75 (Sheed and Ward, 1928).
[10] (Charles) Vincent (Emerson) Starrett (1886–1974).
[11] Novelist, playwright and historian (1897–1940). She was a member of the Sherlock Holmes Society and of the Detection Club.
[12] Detective novelist (1901–83).
[13] (1875–1936), author of *Trent's Last Case* (1913).
[14] Milward Rodon Kennedy Burge (1894–1968).
[15] Detective novelist (1893–1971).
[16] Detective novelist (1879–1957).
[17] Pseudonym of Major C. J. C. Street, detective-novelist (1884–1965).
[18] *Baker Street Studies*, edited by H.W.Bell, was published by Constable in 1934. It contained essays by Dorothy L. Sayers, Helen Simpson, Vernon Rendall, Vincent Starrett, Ronald A. Knox, A. G. Macdonell, S. C. Roberts and H. W. Bell. The article by D.L.S., the first in the book (pp. 1–34), is entitled 'Holmes' College Career'. It was republished in *Unpopular Opinions*.
[19] Cf. 'Dr Watson's Christian Name', first published in *Queen Mary's Book for India*, (Harrap, 1943, pp. 78–82), later included in *Unpopular Opinions* (Gollancz, 1946).
[20] Cf. the conversation between Lord Peter Wimsey and Harriet Vane in *Gaudy Night*, chapter 4.

To Ivy Shrimpton   24 Great James St
21 June 1933   W.C.1

Dearest Ivy,

I have been tremendously hard at work this last week, or I'd have written sooner. I've taken on some reviewing work[1] in addition to my

other jobs, which has meant reading two novels a day or thereabouts
– rather strenuous. However, I've got well ahead with the thing now
and it won't be so bad in future. But I haven't had time to tackle
your little story yet – I want to give it proper attention.

We shall have to see about sending J.A. to school soon, as he is
getting so big! Give him whatever message he prefers – a little time
ago 'love' was taboo, so pray make it my 'compliments' or 'greetings'
or whatever is most fancied. And many thanks to you all for kind
birthday greetings.

Mac – as I think I told you – is having a long series of sessions
with a doctor, who is doing a little 'mampipulation' (wasn't that the
word?) on his inside. He is improving a lot under treatment, but still
has a good deal left to be done. This is keeping us in London, so I
don't know when, if ever, we shall be able to get away.

We have succeeded in placing all our kittens in good situations;
but hope Peter will be moderate and not present us with a fresh lot
too soon, or the unemployment crisis will extend to felines. The eldest
boy has gone to be a butcher:

+ two of the girls are put out on a farm :-

the two girl to the butcher's own farm : —

+ the remaining boy has taken up residence with the parish nurse :-

+ I'm sure I hope they will all behave themselves!

I must now stop and write a particularly horrid tale about a wicked
dentist![2] . . .

[1] For *The Sunday Times*. See Ralph E. Hone, 'Dorothy L. Sayers: Critic of Detective Fiction',
SEVEN: *An Anglo-American Literary Review*, Volume 6, 1985, pp. 45–69.

To Ivy Shrimpton   24 Newland Street
18 August 1933   Witham
                                      Essex

Dearest Ivy –

Oh dear! What a trouble and to-do we have been in the last month!
We have had to sack the servants – as though we hadn't already had
bother enough with the woman being so ill – and all over a pound
of bacon!!

Anyway, I have the satisfaction of saying that I never did like that
man! No, I did NOT like him. Mac said he thought the fellow was
all right and that I was too much down on him. But I knew he was
incorrigibly lazy and a liar. And *if* that is any satisfaction, I have it!
But I really think he is a bit dotty as well.

It all began when the cook, Mrs Purfield, had gone for her holiday.
Rather fortunately, I had gone up to Town for a couple of days and
Mac was left to carry on by himself with the man Purfield and with
Mrs Sutton, who came in to help in Mrs P's absence. So Mac then
realised (what I had always known) that Purfield never did any work
if he could help it. Also, when Purfield had disappeared into the
servants' bungalow for 4 hours one afternoon, Mac went in search of
him and found him saying his prayers. This was, of course, suspicious
in itself, and disposed Mac to expect the worst. On my return, Mac
expressed his belief that Purfield was falling into religious mania. He
(Purfield) seemed to be taking no interest in his work, but explained
this by saying he had taken a Seidlitz powder – though why a Seidlitz
powder should involve saying his prayers in the middle of the afternoon was never made clear to anybody.

Very good. The next day I said to Mac: 'What would you like for
dinner?' He replied, 'Kidneys and bacon.' I went to Mrs Sutton and
asked 'Is there any bacon in the house?' 'Oh yes,' said she, 'plenty.
A pound was ordered on Wednesday and I put it in the cellar.' Cellar
and larder were investigated, but there was no bacon. Thus this Act
of the Drama opened.

Myself (to Mrs Sutton): You had better ask Purfield what he has
     done with it.
Mrs S. (to Purfield in the Bungalow): Where is the bacon?
Purfield: The bacon was tainted and I gave it back to the grocer's
     boy.
Mrs S.: Well, you'd better come and tell Mrs Fleming about that.

Myself: Purfield, where is the bacon?

Purfield: The bacon was unfit for human consumption, and I sent it back to the grocer.

Myself: What? – And have they not sent another pound in its place?

Purfield (in a confused manner): I said there was no great hurry and I would call for it this evening.

Myself (severely): It is not your business to call for it, but theirs to deliver it.

Purfield: Shall I go and fetch it now?

Myself (loudly and very emphatically): NO! I will go myself. When did you return the first lot?

Purfield: I gave it straight back to the boy when he delivered it.

Myself: Which day?

Purfield: I think it was yesterday.

Myself: But to-day is Friday, and the bacon was delivered on Wednesday and Mrs Sutton says she took it from the boy and put it in the cellar, so how could you have given it back to the boy straight away?

Purfield (looking up at the sky and round at the landscape and every where but at me): The bacon was tainted and it would not have been sanitary to eat it and I have sometimes had to bury things that had become tainted and –

Myself (bewildered): Did you bury the bacon?

Purfield: No, I gave it back to the boy.

The next scene took place at the grocer's. The grocer denied having received the bacon back and the boy denied taking it. After two other minor scenes in which a) I told Mac all about it and b) Mrs Sutton 'hoped we should not think *she* had anything to do with it', we arrive at the grand scene of the Confrontation of Witnesses, when the Boy (arriving with a fresh supply of bacon) was brought up before Mac in company with Purfield.

Mac: Purfield, you say you sent this bacon back because it was unfit for human consumption?

Purfield: Yes.

Mac: Is this the boy to whom you gave it?

Purfield (raising his eyes to Heaven and lifting his hand in a theatrical manner while addressing the Boy): I don't want to get you into trouble. You may have an aged Mother depending on you –

Mac: CUT THAT OUT! Did you give the bacon to this boy?

Purfield: Yes – I sent it back, because –

Mac (to the Boy): Did Mr Purfield give you back that pound of bacon?

Boy (goggling very much – a gooseberry-eyed boy with glasses):
  No, Sir.
Mac: Did Mr Purfield take in the groceries that morning?
Boy: No, Sir. Mrs Sutton took them in.
Mac: Did you see Mr Purfield at all on that occasion?
Boy: No, Sir.
Purfield: Well, I may not have seen the boy. I may have put the
  bacon back into the basket in the kitchen and it may have fallen
  out on the way back.
Mac (to Boy, who is goggling now so perilously that his eyes seem
  about to fall out on the carpet) – Cut along, Sonnie – you are
  all right.
(To Purfield) You are a —y liar!
Purfield: My conscience is clear.
Mac: You're sacked. Get out of the house immediately!

This was the gist of it. In the end it turned out that the man had
sent the bacon away to his wife (who instantly told the truth about
it) – and the silly thing was that if only the fool had asked permission
to send it, he could have had it and welcome. I don't think he exactly
meant to steal it. I think he just sent it off, – perhaps meaning to pay
for it later – and got nervous about saying so, plunged into a silly
story, and couldn't extricate himself. But the whole thing (which of
course took much longer than I've written it) suggested something in
a detective story, and I couldn't help thinking that of all people to
pick on to deceive with a ridiculous tale which wouldn't hold water
for two minutes, we were about the worst choice the man could possibly have made!

So then we had a week or so of glum discomfort, when the wife
returned in tears, and we decided we couldn't do anything about it,
and they had to pack up and push off all in a hurry – and after
that, about three weeks of putting in advertisements and answering
applications from the most amazingly virtuous and industrious
couples – all with something a little wrong with them, of course – till
at last we have settled on a rather youthful pair who take up residence
next week, and have faithfully promised not to have babies – but,
blast them! I expect they will.

So, in all the uproar, everything has gone by the board, and as for
writing letters or doing any work, I might as well have been sitting
in the middle of Piccadilly Circus! . . .

To Ivy Shrimpton   24 Great James Street
11 November 1933   W.C.1

Dearest Ivy

So sorry; life has been full of all sorts of bother – financial, domestic
and otherwise.[1] But I shall be passing through Oxford about Nov.
25th and will look you up then, as I've got a bit of business[2] to discuss
with you –

Yours with love
    D.

[1] Matters between D.L.S. and her husband had reached crisis point and she was considering leaving him. Her handwriting in this and the following letter is uncontrolled, as always
occurred when she was under emotional stress.
[2] The business was the adoption of John Anthony.

To Ivy Shrimpton   London
23 November 1933

Dearest Ivy

I can't come on Saturday, as I have a committee meeting and
dinner engagement in Oxford. I will be along some time on Sunday
– probably shortly after lunch. I shan't be able to stay long, as I shall
be motoring through with a friend,[1] but our little bit of business won't
take a moment.

I have been ordered off for a three-weeks' complete holiday,[2] and
shall be pushing round the country with the friend –

Love
    D.L.S.

[1] Muriel St Clare Byrne.
[2] Overwork and matrimonial stress had brought on nervous exhaustion.

To Victor Gollancz   24 Newland Street
31 December 1933   Witham
                                                    Essex

Dear Mr Gollancz,

Thank you so much for your letter with Mr Williams'[1] lyrical
appreciation of *The Nine Tailors*. I only hope he isn't pulling my leg
– it sounds too good to be true! . . .

I'm so glad you feel really better for your holiday. I have an idea that this is going to be a year of great activity in the book world. I must get on with that straight novel of mine![2]

    Yours very sincerely
        Dorothy L. Sayers

[1] Charles Williams (1886–1945), to whom Gollancz had sent a copy of *The Nine Tailors*, which was published in January 1934. Charles Williams had written: 'Your Dorothy Sayers . . . ! Present her some time with my profoundest compliments. It's a marvellous book; it is high imagination – and the incomprehensible splendours of the preludes to each part make a pattern round and through it like the visible laws and the silver waters themselves . . The end is unsurpassable . . .'
[2] Announced by Gollancz as forthcoming and entitled *Cat o' Mary*, it was never completed.

To Donald Tovey   24 Newland Street
18 January 1934   Witham
                                         Essex

Dear Professor Tovey,
    Many thanks for your kind and sympathetic letter. Let me clear up the two musical points first.
    1) You are alas! about the 500th and oneth person who has pointed out the slip about the *Moonlight*. In one of those vague moments I wrote it down in error for *Pastoral*,[1] and, being very unwell at the time, was unable to correct my own proofs. I'm very sorry.
    2) I didn't quite follow the bit about Haydn and the Beethoven C. Minor, because I can't possibly have intended any allusion to Beethoven, and shouldn't recognise the work if I heard it, I expect. But I've sung *The Creation* many times. I don't remember what Munting said about it, but I expect it was something about the tremendous effect of 'Let there be light – and there was LIGHT' after the rhythmic drumming notes of the 'moved upon the face of the waters' accompaniment,[2] which in its simpler way moves me nearly as much as the rather similar effect in the B minor *Crucifixus*. If it wasn't that, I don't know what it was.
    You are one of the very few people with intelligent sympathy for Lord Peter and his Harriet. Most of them beg me not to let him marry 'that horrid girl'. They don't understand the violent conflict underlying her obstinacy – I am glad you do. There's stuff in Harriet, but it isn't the conventional heroine stuff, you see. My only reason for holding her up is that the situation between her and Lord P. is psychologically so difficult that it really needs a whole book to examine and resolve. *The Nine Tailors*, by the way, goes back a few years to an almost pre-Harriet period. But I will tackle the problem one of these days, and in the howl of execration that will go up when I marry

Lord Peter off, I shall hope to hear your voice uplifted in defence of
his happiness and of Harriet!

With many thanks for your kind appreciation

Yours sincerely
Dorothy L. Sayers

[1] In *Have His Carcase*, chapter 20, Constable Ormond attends a concert at the Winter
Gardens. In the first edition the text ran: '... the *Eroica* had been substituted at the last
minute for the *Moonlight*, owing to some difficulty about mislaid band-parts'. Since the
Moonlight is a piano sonata, no band-parts would have been involved. In a later edition
this was changed to *Pastoral*.
[2] See *The Documents in the Case*, No. 52, 'Statement by John Munting'.

To Ivy Shrimpton   24 Newland Street
21 August 1934   Witham
                                                     Essex

Dearest Ivy

A queer and upsetting thing has happened. I have only just found
– unopened – under a pile of books in the bedroom, a letter you wrote
on the 5th of June about going away for a holiday. Now, I was in
Town on the 6th June, and the letters were taken up to Mac, who
must have completely forgotten to send them on or to tell me about
them. The fact is that Mac is getting so queer and unreliable that it
is not safe to trust him to do anything at all, and if he is told that he
has forgotten anything, he goes into such a frightful fit of rage that
one gets really alarmed. The doctors say that he *is* getting definitely
queer – but there doesn't seem to be much that one can do about it.
I have now told the servants to post any letters that come while I am
away directly on to me, but even that is not very certain because, if
Mac should happen to get hold of them first, they may still get mislaid.
So if at any time you should send me anything requiring *immediate*
answer and the answer doesn't come, will you write again and ask if
I've had it. This isn't the first time that things have gone astray, but
it is the first time that I have definitely been able to prove that Mac's
forgetfulness is at fault. I am terribly sorry about it – naturally if I
had received the letter I should have written at once. It is all very
worrying, but only part of the major worry which is caused by this
mental trouble of Mac's, which is due to some kind of germ or disease
or shock or something – probably a result of the War. Doctors don't
seem able to do much about it, and it makes everything very difficult,
and explains a lot of what you must have thought slackness and
queerness on my own part. It also makes the financial position very
awkward, as he can't earn any money, and what with his illness and

the difficulty of managing his odd fits of temper and so on, it isn't easy for me to get any work done regularly and properly.

Don't refer to this too openly when you reply, in case he should see your letter. I'm enclosing £10 now for you to get some kind of holiday if you can manage it at this late date and to cover the little bills for teeth. This is all I can manage at the moment.

Please think that I'm doing my best, and be sure that if I'd ever had your letter I wouldn't have just let things go. I can't explain on paper quite how difficult things are. There seems no remedy for them but patience.

I'm so awfully sorry
Dorothy

To Helen Simpson[1]   24 Newland Street
20 December 1934   Witham
         Essex

My dear Helen,
Being unhappily persuaded that your poor, wronged daughter had her pencils stolen by her unnatural parents, I am trying again! THIS IS HER BOOK-TOKEN, for her to exchange with her own hands for *Three Little Kittens* or *Deadwood Dick* or whatever she fancies – and don't you and Browne[2] go and use it to purchase *The Sexual Neuroses Associated with Lycanthropy in Central Europe* (with plates) or *Goop on the Umbilical Chord* (annotated, with an appendix on the Use of Squirts), or *Mangelwurzel on the Oesophagus*, or anything like that! Curse you!

It would look much better if I had competently remembered the child's name.[3] These lapses account for my unpopularity with parents.

Wishing you all the best

Yours ever
Dorothy L. Sayers

[1] See Note 11 to letter to Harold Bell, dated 12 March 1933. The novel *Busman's Honeymoon* is dedicated to her (as well as to M. St Clare Byrne and Marjorie Barber).
[2] Denis Browne, a surgeon, husband of Helen Simpson.
[3] Her name was Clemence.

During the period when D.L.S. was at work on Gaudy Night, *a sweep was sent for to clear the chimneys at 24 Newland Street. He wore a number of pullovers, which he peeled off, one after the other, as he warmed to his task.*

D.L.S. was much amused by him and shortly afterwards, visiting her friends Muriel St Clare Byrne and Marjorie Barber in London, she described him, saying how much she would like to put him in a play. 'Why don't you?' asked Muriel. This was the origin of their collaboration on the play Busman's Honeymoon, *in which the Witham chimney sweep is immortalised as Tom Puffett and Lord Peter Wimsey and Harriet Vane appear on the stage. It was a turning-point in the writing career of D.L.S.*

To Muriel St Clare Byrne   24 Great James St
14 February 1935   W.C.1

Dear Muriel,

The day has been marked by a strange pair of portents.

On setting out to do some business this morning, I met a *chimney-sweep* in full panoply. This I took to be a good omen.

Returning home just now, I beheld from my window a man carrying on his shoulders a *complete set of sweep's rods and brushes, brand-new* – a sight I had never seen in my life before, and which must be comparatively rare.

I hasten to communicate to you this extraordinary coincidence, which cannot, surely, be without significance.

My solicitor confirms that the money-lender would lend the money to the old man on his note of hand, when satisfied that he had a house and a business, without demanding the deposit of securities. So that makes us sound on the financial side.

I am anxious that before we go too far, some experiment should be made with the murder-machine. A pendulum of 3¼ ft. swings once every second, whatever the distance covered and whatever the weight. A pendulum of 6 ft. will, of course, take longer; but the speed of the *movement* will be naturally determined by the size of the arc covered by the swing. As it will have to fall through 90° before hitting the object, the speed and weight should combine to give a nasty knock; but we shall have to see about the *timing*. If the pendulum is too long, it might give the man too much warning between the shout of 'Look out' and the fall of the weight. It ought to be tried out for the optimum measure of effectiveness. I am no expert in mechanics and am probably expressing myself badly, but you will see what I mean.

Yours ever
        Dorothy L. Sayers

To Muriel St Clare Byrne   24 Newland Street
16 February 1935   Witham
                                           Essex

Dear Muriel,

I have had a shot at roughing out the dialogue for Act 1, to get
the shape of it. At present it's only about 4000 words, if that; but I
think most of the essentials are there, to be padded out with extra
dialogue and business.

The time-scheme will want to be made clearer. I have left out,
now, the idea that the Wimseys arrived too soon, as a needless complication. The idea is now:

> Noakes received Wimsey's draft Wednesday morning and wrote
> on the same day, sending the deeds etc. and saying he would have
> the cottage ready that day week. He at once prepared to skip.
>
> He could make no move till he got rid of Crutchley that evening.
> He promised him he would give him his money on the Wednesday,
> mentioning that he had sold the house, but not saying anything
> about the Wimseys' arrival.
>
> He was murdered that night.

More details of this can come out in the next act. If you don't think
it will work like this, we can go back to the original idea.

Note: Crutchley. I think it is important that before he arrives Miss
Twitterton should call out to him that they *can't find* Noakes. He will
come expecting that the body is in the sitting-room. To find people
there will be a shock for him, and he had better get this over *before*
he actually comes on, and receive the assurance that nothing has yet
been discovered. Otherwise his calm behaviour will be unnatural.

He must be wondering what has really happened. The trap has been
sprung – but where is the body? He had better not appear too much
and when he does must insist that he expected to find Noakes there.

I thought it better to reserve his alibi in detail till Act 2.

The chain. Note that this comes down the chimney and is finished with
while Crutchley is off the stage. Otherwise he might take alarm and
try to get rid of it. I haven't made enough of Miss Twitterton, but
she can be filled in a bit more. Also Harriet's sentimental stuff about
the old house.

We shall also want more dialogue when people go out to fetch
things – the gun, etc.

Final page

It may look unnatural that the policeman should be wandering by
just at the right moment; but he helps to make a curtain and we can

lay stress in Act 4 on his opportune appearance and make it look suspicious.

I don't think Peter and Harriet must say too much in Act I about the upset to their honeymoon when the corpse is discovered. It looks heartless. They can do their 'Calamity Cottage' stuff in Act II.

MacBride should give a few more financial details. He represents the solicitors for the money lenders. Perhaps the story of the loan should come in here.

But you will best be able to see *which* points want strengthening and where the incidental merriment ought to be put in. This is the merest skeleton.

It seems perhaps best to say MURDER firmly in Act I. Everybody will know that it *is* murder. We can make Miss Twitterton's behaviour more suspicious if required.

And put in some more about the only other key to the cottage? Let me know what you think and put in anything you feel to be necessary. Perhaps your Secretary could get out a rough typescript of the act as amended.

Your partner in guilt
Dorothy L. Sayers

When several people are all on together, I find it difficult to keep them all talking! I've put in the essential bits – we must find lines and business for the others.

To Muriel St Clare Byrne   Bodleian Library
6 March 1935   Oxford

Dear Muriel –

Just to say – 1) that Aristotle[1] was a huge success! – Great fun – . . .

But – my dear, my heart is BROKEN! I have seen the *perfect* Peter Wimsey. Height, voice, charm, smile, manner, outline of features, *everything* – and he is – THE CHAPLAIN OF BALLIOL!![2] *What* is the use of anything?

In the meantime I have completed the love scene, except for the infernal quotation, which won't come right. It is too, too shy-making for words, and kept on falling into blank verse in the most unfortunate manner. I expect it will have to be scrapped. I will ring you up to-morrow in town. I am absolutely *shattered* by this Balliol business. Such waste – why couldn't he have been an actor?

Two lines of blank verse ejected from the love-scene – did I invent them, or have I remembered them?

We have come
To that still centre where the spinning world
Sleeps on its axis, – to the heart of rest.[3]

If I did invent them, they are rather good! . . .

[1] 'Aristotle on Detective Fiction', an address given first at Oxford on 5 March 1935 and
to the English Association on 21 June 1935. Published first in *English: The Magazine of the
English Association*, vol. 1, no. 1, 1936, pp. 23–35 and later in *Unpopular Opinions* (Gollancz,
30 September 1946).
[2] Maurice Roy Ridley. D.L.S. first saw him in 1913, when he read his Newdigate Prize
poem in the Sheldonian Theatre, Oxford, on the occasion of the Encaenia. She described
the event in the letter to her friend Catherine Godfrey, dated 29 July 1913, and said she
had fallen in love with him. In later years she completely forgot this first 'sighting' but
his appearance had contributed in her subconscious to that of Lord Peter Wimsey. (See
Barbara Reynolds, op. cit., pp. 55–7.)
[3] These are lines from the octave of the sonnet which Harriet Vane composes in *Gaudy
Night*, chapter 11. D.L.S. had forgotten that she had written them. By the time of this
letter she was already working on chapter 17.

To Peter Haddon[1]
March 1935

PRIVATE AND CONFIDENTIAL
Dear Mr Haddon,

An extremely unpleasant situation has arisen in connection with the
film, *The Silent Passenger*. You were perfectly right about Mr Mason; his
script is extremely bad. I was obliged to let the Phoenix people know,
by Curtis Brown,[2] on Friday, that under no circumstances would I
allow them to use either my name or Lord Peter Wimsey's in connection with the script as it stood. They have made a complete hash of
all the detective part, turned Wimsey into a kind of Gaiety[3]-Bar
lounger, and produced a story and dialogue which contrive to be at
the same time excessively vulgar and excessively dull.

The Phoenix people seem to imagine that you will not play Wimsey
as a straight high-comedy part on the 'great gentleman' lines that I
have tried to lay down for him. They have reduced your part to a
matter of some very dull clowning in uncommonly dubious taste,
much of which leads to nothing and is only put in to raise an easy
laugh. They have made no real attempt to make Wimsey dominate
either the actors or the plot; and I can see your being gradually
shouldered out and cut down, and being treated much as you were
in Broadcasting House. They appear to think you will be satisfied
with this, provided they give you this clowning.

Now, this is not at all the impression I got from your conversation with me. You said then that you wanted drama and character; and I am prepared to revise the script for you in order to get the character and dialogue right, and to strengthen and enliven the action. I can undertake to provide the real Wimsey that his own public know and will want to see. Since they have apparently read all my books without understanding a word of them (as far as Peter is concerned) I have drafted a sketch of Wimsey's character *as it has been laid down in eleven books, and as he is known and genuinely beloved by thousands of people.* If Wimsey is to be played at all he must be played on these lines. This *you* will understand, and if you will assist me in making them understand and accept it I am prepared (though this is *not* part of my contract) to revise the script for you on these lines. If they refuse this offer I can do nothing more. My last word to them is, that neither my name nor the character of Lord Peter Wimsey can be used in connection with this story, unless the script is revised in accordance with the suggestions that I have made. The film people have put themselves in the wrong by getting the script passed by the renters before the dialogue was submitted to me, since it was agreed before witnesses that I should have a free hand with the dialogue and the character, with right of veto.

I do not wish to make any suggestions that will involve major alterations in any of the sets; and as they do not propose to start work until April 8th my offer to get the work of revision done within ten days is a perfectly reasonable one.

Yours very sincerely,
D.L.S.

[1] The actor (1898–1962), who was considering playing the part of Lord Peter Wimsey in the film *The Silent Passenger*. He later withdrew. The screen play was by Basil Mason, based on D.L.S.' original, unpublished story commissioned by Phoenix Films.
[2] The literary agent.
[3] The Gaiety was a theatre in London.

To Muriel St Clare Byrne   24 Newland Street
30 March 1935   Witham
                                            Essex

Dear Muriel,
As regards Kirk and Sellon – I think what has really happened is this:–

During the past 24 hours, Kirk has been thinking matters over in his slow way, and he has decided to tax Sellon with the discrepancy in his story. Sellon has protested that he only spoke the truth. Kirk has said: 'Very well – I am going up to the house this morning to see

Lord Peter about something or other, or to see if anything, any clue
– e.g. blunt instrument turns up during the move, or for some such
reason. You can come with me – and I will *show* you where the
difficulty is.' That is why they come first to the window. I don't see
how that situation is to be made clear in the dialogue, but that is
what was in my mind.

I think it exceedingly likely that Kirk would think very carefully
before letting Sellon know exactly what the case is against him – but
his natural good heart would probably lead him to make the decision
to do so.

I feel that this is somehow better than if Peter – in the middle of
constructing a case, – were to send for Sellon – still more for Kirk,
who might be at Broxford. But I do feel, thinking it over, that I have
made Peter take this unexpected confirmation of his case too coolly.
It ought to stagger him more.

I think that in this scene my mind has been so closely set upon the
construction of the thing – the making it *water-tight* – that I have probably missed some of the necessary emotion. This, as you know, is the
prime difficulty of detective denouements. I have also been worried
by keeping the balance between the comedy note – which *must* be
kept going – and the tragic note – which is bound to creep in if a real
murderer is going to be really detected and hanged. The least tip the
wrong way, and the thing will become either heartless or really grim.
I think Miss Twitterton's attitude is fairly well worked out, in outline.
She has got to be released from the Crutchley-complex and the inferi-
ority-complex, if she is not to be left as a tragic figure. Hence the
insistence upon the importance and grandeur of the funeral. For
country people, a funeral simply DOES make all the difference. It
comforts and sustains them in a way you or I would find preposterous.
I remember a woman, who had lost a son in the War, and who said
to my Mother, at the end of a memorial service which Dad had held
for all the fallen, in a packed church: 'It's almost worth while to lose
a son, to have such a beautiful service held over him.' That is a fact.
But I can well believe that with my mind fixed on establishing the
when, how and where of the crime, I may have failed to get these
things over. Please don't mind altering anything at all that seems to
you weak or inadequate. I trust your judgement quite implicitly.

 Best love
  D.

To Muriel St Clare Byrne   24 Newland Street
1 April 1935   Witham
                                       Essex

My dear Muriel,

I have glanced through Act I again, and find myself rather vague in my mind about it. I think it best to send it along with my very rough notes and additions scribbled as they stand.

One or two points are really important:

1. The note-case – This needs perhaps a bit of emphasis, as it is to figure so prominently in Act II.
2. Crutchley – I am not satisfied with his attitude to the disappearance of Mr Noakes, nor with his relations to Miss Twitterton. Yet I seem to be so close to the thing that I scarcely know how to deal with it.

   One thing – I think (this is my fault entirely) that in the first two acts we have made him too rough in his speech and not sufficiently plausible in his manner. I think now that Miss Twitterton has contrived to endue him with a sort of veneer of 'superiorness' – he will always, naturally, tend to drop this under stress of emotion – e.g. over the £40 and the discovery in Act II about the money on the body – but I think I should have given him a smoother manner to start with. He is always, I think, a rather sulky-looking fellow, but with that kind of sulky good looks that is attractive to women. We *must* explain why Miss T[witterton] was fond of him and the vicar thought well of him. Only in Act III do we see the real brute peasant.

By the way, with what curious and (to me) unconscious symmetry we have builded to make, not only one, but *all* the masks come off, one after the other, in Act III sc. 1 – Bunter, Crutchley, Miss Twitterton and finally, Harriet and Peter, by whose central sincerity all the rest are, as it were, put to the proof! I don't want to exaggerate about it all – it is mere comedy – but I have a feeling that, since it worked out naturally so, it is, in its small way, right. Probably you saw this side of it before I did – I was simply thinking of making a dramatic contrast in the two love scenes, and put the Bunter bit in for sheer fun – but the thing seems to have made its own symbolism as it went along, which appears to me to be the right way about.

I must really get on now with the blasted book.[1] Peter must be got safely engaged!

    Best of luck to all of us
        D.L.S.

[1] i.e. *Gaudy Night*.

To Muriel St Clare Byrne   24 Newland Street
24 June 1935   Witham
     Essex

Dear Muriel . . .

I think I have got over most of the technical snags in *Gaudy Night* now, but the writing is being horribly difficult. Peter and Harriet are the world's most awkward pair of lovers – both so touchy and afraid to commit themselves to anything but hints and allusions! I feel sure that at some point after their engagement (not necessarily in the book, though) the following piece of dialogue occurred:

Harriet: I thought there was so much I had to say to you. But now there seems to be no need to say anything.
Peter: No; we have passed that point . . . I have been talking for twenty years to conceal my thoughts. With you, thank God, I can at least be silent. (They are eloquently silent)

But in the meantime, they are still talking! . . .

To Ivy Shrimpton   24 Newland Street
16 July 1935   Witham
     Essex

Dearest Ivy,

I have been putting in hand arrangements for J.A. – which accounts for my delay in writing. I think it is time he went to a tutor and so to school. Properly speaking, I suppose, he ought to have gone earlier; but I have not much opinion of schools for the very young, and I don't think he will have missed much by enjoying a certain amount of freedom up till now. He will, no doubt, need a certain amount of coaching before he is plunged into school routine; so I am looking out, through my lawyers, for one of those excellent clergymen who undertake this kind of job. He appears to be intelligent (J.A., I mean, not the clergyman) and in my opinion he will do as well with a little intensive coaching for, say a year, as he would have done if he had been hammered into prep school routine from early childhood. I may be wrong – but from what I have seen of the 'all-school' product, the common effect is to stamp out all personality (which you, on the other hand, have fostered) and produce a stereotyped product. On the other hand, at about the age of 13, school *will* be absolutely necessary.

I have put things off a little, because I didn't want to take him away from you while he was the only one you had; but now, I think, it can perhaps be done without too much hardship on either side. He has got on very well and I am terribly grateful to you for your care of him. Both you and he will feel the parting very much, I'm sure – but of course, these things have to happen. I am letting the lawyers handle the preliminaries so far as possible (in the circumstances it is better, as, for reasons I have mentioned before, I find it difficult to discuss these matters with Mac) but I shall try and make sure that the clergyman will be a suitable sort of person. If you will break it to John that this kind of thing is to be the next step, then, as soon as I hear from the lawyers, I will let you know how things go on. I should imagine that September or October will be the best time for him to start, and will see that he is then suitably equipped and dealt with. . . .

Let me know what you think of the clergyman idea. It seems to me the best way. I shall try and find one where there are two or three, or more, other pupils so that J.A. may get a bit of companionship with other boys before plunging into school conditions. This ought to give him an opportunity to adjust himself more easily. He will come back to you for holidays, if that suits you. Here, owing to the curious domestic conditions which you know about, I can't do anything. . . .

> With best love,
> Yours affectionately
> Dorothy L. Fleming[1]

[1] This is the only known time she signs her name in this form to Ivy Shrimpton. It may be because she has been writing letters to her lawyers about her son. The handwriting of the signature is hurried and uncontrolled.

To Ivy Shrimpton 24 Newland Street
4 September 1935 Witham
Essex

Dearest Ivy –

Well, here we are! After examining the credentials of various worthy clerics, we have pitched upon this one. My lawyer has seen him and thinks he seems a decent bloke; but if we don't like him we can throw him away and get another.

Term starts on, I think it is, the 21st. I enclose the list of requirements and a cheque for £30. If Oxford won't provide the necessary, then probably one of the big London stores like Gamages or Harrods would be best. If you need more money, let me know.

J.A. had better take the name of Fleming as per schedule. I hope he'll find the place all right – but if he doesn't like it, of course he needn't stay there. Mr H.[1] will be taking a party of boys down with him from town on the 21st, and it will be best, I think, if J. meets him and goes down with them.

I don't seem to know what I'm writing. I have been working on the last part of my new book[2] this last week or so till I'm blind and stupid. Very involved and tedious and I'm horribly late with it. . . .

Tell me if you think this place at Combe Florey[3] (can't spell!) looks nice. It seemed much the best of the lot we got in. I hope they are decent sort of people. They seem so. If it's a nice school I should think J. would soon find his footing, though he'll probably feel a bit queer at first.

Best love – let me know how the money pans out. I don't know much about these things. Don't stint anything, but just let me know.

    D.L.S.

[1] Mr Hyland, the headmaster.
[2] *Gaudy Night.*
[3] In Somerset.

To Muriel St Clare Byrne   24 Newland Street
8 September 1935   Witham
                                   Essex

Dear Muriel,

Gaudy Night being now finished (*Gaude, Gaudy, Domini in laude!*)[1] I am able to answer your letter; which I didn't actually get till last night, since, as I told you, Aunt Maud and I went up to Town for a couple of nights to celebrate Peter's engagement with a binge and two theatres. (The second theatre was the Open-Air *Love's Labour's Lost*, wherein we were greatly contented, being favoured with glorious sunshine, a warm air, good seats, an outburst of blossom in the rosery, a good performance, and all things in a concatenation accordingly. And why anybody should ever say that *Love's Labour's Lost* is a bad play, the Lord He knoweth; for to my mind it is one of the most *réussi*[2] things of its kind ever made. Phyllis Neilson-Terry[3] is too beefy, I think, for the Princess – it is all pure fairy-tale; and some of the loveliest lines in the lyrical-witty mode ever written).

I had a feeling that you weren't liking *Gaudy Night* particularly, which was bad luck for you – I mean, bad luck having to write a letter about it; because it is maddening to have to write and tell people one doesn't like things.

I may say that I had anticipated beforehand practically all the objections you [made], and had undertaken the thing with my eyes open; and that was why I told you it probably would not be popular. But when you say that the average reader 'doesn't want the real

Oxford', are you suggesting that the real Oxford must not be written about, or that it should be falsified to suit the average reader's ideas? If the former: you may be right, from the practical and financial point of view – but that consideration has, I suppose, never yet deterred anybody who genuinely wanted to write about anything! But if the latter, then you would be asking the writer to commit that ultimate and unforgiveable sin whose unforgiveableness is the whole theme of the book – the sin against intellectual integrity. To make a deliberate falsification for personal gain is the last, worst depth to which either scholar or artist can descend in work or life: which, as it happens, is what *Gaudy Night* is about. Here, of course, the theme of the plot is also the theme of the book; and, indeed, the whole theme of the Peter –Harriet complication as well: I mean, that no relation can ever be sound that is not founded in faith to the fact. So that, unless the heart and mind are brought into this true relation, they must be kept apart or produce nothing but discord.

The first three chapters move slowly, I admit; but the book is a very long one, and it seemed necessary to set the heart-mind problem against a wide background. As for 'autobiography', it is, of course, autobiographical to precisely the same extent as parts of *The Nine Tailors, Murder Must Advertise, The Bellona Club* and *The Five Red Herrings*, in the sense that it deals with a background which I personally know; the whole book is personal (though not autobiographical) in the sense that it presents a consistent philosophy of conduct for which I am prepared to assume personal responsibility. What reviewers like E. C. Large may think of it I do not know, and certainly cannot think of caring. I mean, one can scarcely be frightened off writing what one wants to write for fear an obscure reviewer should patronise one on that account. As the greater part of the book was on paper before Mr Large loomed so large on the horizon, I shall take the liberty of not modifying it for him.

I think it quite certain that people will say again, as they have said before, that they can't see what Peter sees in Harriet. (This is frequently said about people in real life, if it comes to that.) But to save argument, Peter has obliged, this time, by telling the world what he sees. At least, he has told *her*, which comes to the same thing. All through the book (except for two very short moments) he is never seen through any eyes but hers, and she is, in this sense, the focal point of the book. To take another well-worn metaphor, he is the catalyst which, itself unchanged, changes everything that comes in contact with it. I mean that the opposition of heart and mind, and the opposition of private and public loyalty are an extension and external reflection of the conflict in Harriet's consciousness of her intellectual and passional (bad word, but let it pass) relationship with him. His answer to that is: see that the mind is honest, first; the rest may follow or not as God wills.

You may say, certainly, that a detective story is not the proper medium for all this; but *Gaudy Night* is not really a detective story at all, but a novel with a mild detective interest of an almost entirely psychological kind. But the plot, so far as it goes, is part of the theme. I mean that the fundamental treason to the mind which wrecks a man's career and makes the basis of the plot is the same fundamental treason which might easily have wrecked the Peter–Harriet combination if they had not, each in turn, refused to allow it. And that this is the one fundamental treason which the scholar's mind must not allow is the bond uniting all the Oxford people in the last resort. I'm sounding rather cross and pompous about all this, but I don't mean to be: I find it easier to put the case in a novel than to make a commentary on it. The one thing that seems to me quite impossible is to take into consideration the kind of book that one is expected to write; surely one can only write the book that is there to be written.

No – I couldn't clutter the book with Miss Climpson and a lot more female characters; but her organisation had to be mentioned, as Peter makes use of it, off-stage, to save time in his investigations.

Aunt Maud has come to take a very sympathetic interest in Harriet. Having discovered that Peter has a 'past' as well as she, she (Aunt Maud) is disposed to think she (Harriet) may be good enough for him after all; and has followed the breaking-down of Harriet's inhibitions with great – sympathy is again the only word I can find for it. Anyhow, she thinks the development of this situation is quite sound, which on the whole I believe it is. But it developed so many subsidiary complications as it went along that I began to feel that nothing but the parenthetical style of a Henry James could cope with it. I hope, however, that I have avoided that indifferently well!

I hope I am not sounding irritable and offended. It is always an awkward business 'defending one's thesis' on paper. The only thing that really worries me is that you should worry so much about what the average reader or reviewer may think. It is a nuisance that my typist should have been afflicted with a spasm of extra work just after the first three chapters, as this inflicted the 'instalment system' on you at the worst possible point. By the way, the editress of the *Woman's Journal* – having read the first 13 chapters (the pre-Peter part) committed herself to the statement that it was 'entrancing' (!!!!!) and is making tentative gestures towards it. This is all very profitable, but will help to hang things up. I gather that, if they do it, they will want to make very long instalments, so as to publish it in not more than three portions. This will mean a lot of cutting; but it seems the magazines have now taken a fancy (caught in America) for publishing books in huge chunks. This does *not* please the publishers; a furious storm is raging; Nancy Pearn and I are sitting back and saying nothing – except that I have said I *must* supervise the illustrations! Otherwise we shall have some dirty work among the caps and gowns! But perhaps the serialisation will fall through, and I emerge poorer in purse though richer in honour.

My typist (blast her!) has now gone on holiday, so the last three chapters may arrive rather slowly. I'm sorry about this. The said typist, by the way (if she is any sample of the average reader) said she liked the first three chapters, explaining that 'you could *see* that college'. Possibly the average reader may like to 'see that college'. One never knows.

Well, anyhow, many thanks for writing what you thought so frankly. If I seem to be being obstinate about it, it is just that I couldn't write the book any other way. It came like that . . .

Best love and many thanks
    Dorothy L. Sayers

[1] Rejoice, in praise of the Lord!, the canting motto on the bell given by the Gaudy family in *The Nine Tailors*.
[2] Well-executed, successful.
[3] 1892–1977. In 1935 she was forty-three.

To Ivy Shrimpton   24 Newland Street
9 September 1935   Witham
                                               Essex

Dearest Ivy

I only got your letter yesterday, as I had to go away for a day. Adopted son will be best.

If Elliston's are not right or too expensive and troublesome, you can get practically all you can need for school outfits by mail-order on approval from the big stores in Town. I saw an advertisement of Swan and Edgar's to-day – but I think they practically all supply them.

If there is any extra money left please stick to it, as you deserve a little extra compensation for all this bother. I'm so glad you think the school looks nice. I liked the look of it.

My book is now, thank goodness! practically finished – ages late, and not altogether satisfactorily, but there! It just *wouldn't* come right.

Aunt Maud is going up to London for a treatment for rheumatism. Mac is better in some ways, but I think his queerness is getting rather worse, if anything. It is all very worrying, but I don't think one can do much. Some days he is all right and others all wrong.

Best love
D.

To Ivy Shrimpton   24 Newland Street
15 September 1935   Witham
                                                     Essex

Dearest Ivy,
    Many thanks for your letter – I am sure you have done excellently. If anything further is needed, or the things are not exactly what the other boys are wearing, we shall know during the first term. Cricket pads will not be needed till next summer; and all games equipment of that kind will probably be obtainable through the School and is best left to them.
    'Mr Fleming' will probably be better than 'Major' – as a matter of fact, I don't believe Mac is really entitled to call himself 'Major' at all now but only 'Captain' – but better leave it at 'Mr'. Better warn J.A. to leave 'Dorothy L. Sayers' out of it. 'Mrs Fleming' is unknown, but 'Sayers' will be the signal for autograph-hunting and nuisance. Explain to him that professional writers want their business and private affairs kept separate – which is true enough, God knows! I spend my time in Witham choking off the bores who want to call on Mrs Fleming for the sake of seeing Miss Sayers, confound them! 'Dear Mother' will be all right – but don't let the poor kid bother himself writing to me more than once a month or so. It is to you that he will want to write – and as for myself, I swear that, with the exception of the absolute necessary minimum of business correspondence, I can scarcely pull myself together to get pen to paper! I have just struggled through the confounded book – about 150,000 words, and hate the sight of pen and paper! And there are three infernal great hulking jobs waiting to be done! Which is why I write letters so seldom, and always with the most passionate hatred of the job.[1]
    By the way, the sort of things he will want to have at school are things like a good stout penknife, a reliable watch and a fountain-pen – these things lend importance. Not cheap ones – the knife should be bought at a good ironmonger's, not a stationer's, and will cost about seven shillings and sixpence – the watch had better be stout – say a fifteen-shilling Ingersole or something like that; and the pen a good make (Swan, Waterman, Onoto etc.) and will cost anything from fifteen shillings to seventeen shillings and sixpence; the very cheap

one's aren't much good. I think you have still a little money in hand
– if you want more, let me know. I should be glad if you could
take him up to Town; the station of departure will, I suppose, be
Paddington, which will save the trouble of crossing. I enclose £5 for
fares – though probably the master will take all the boys' tickets and
charge them in the bill. As soon as I hear from the lawyers I will let
you know exact time and place of meeting.

My servants are away on holiday, Aunt Maud is suffering from
some kind of internal attack and Mac at the moment is also under
the weather! I should like, for a change, to have a healthy set of
people to look after!

    With best love and many thanks
      Yours affectionately
      Dorothy

[1] A characteristic overstatement, dictated by the mood of the moment. D.L.S. derived
great pleasure and creative stimulus from writing letters.

To Victor Gollancz   24 Newland Street
26 September 1935   Witham
                               Essex

Dear Mr Gollancz,
    Thank you so much for your wire. I am tremendously relieved and
glad that you like *Gaudy Night.* Quite apart from the great respect I
have for your judgement, I know what a difference it will make to
you if you feel you can push out this rather peculiar book with genuine
conviction in your own mind about it. I know quite well what a job
I have given you with this overgrown monster which is neither flesh
nor fowl nor altogether good 'red herring', and now that you have
read it you will realise why I was rather worried about it. It is the
only book I've written which embodies any kind of a 'moral' and I
do feel rather passionately about this business of the integrity of the
mind – but I realise that to make a 'detective story' the vehicle for
that kind of thing is (as Miss de Vine says of the Peter—Harriet
marriage) 'reckless to the point of insanity'. But there it is – it's the
book I wanted to write and I've written it – and it is now my privilege
to leave you with the baby! Whether you advertise it as a love-story,
or as educational propaganda, or as a lunatic freak, I leave to you.
It may be highly unpopular, but, though I wouldn't claim that it was
in itself a work of great literary importance, it is important to me,
and I only hope it won't be a ghastly flop.
    To come to practical considerations. I don't think there is any
chance of serialisation in America. As you know, we are doing all we

can and Nancy Pearn[1] has just written a personal note to Harcourt Brace saying that *if* they think it hopeless from the serial point of view, we hope they will very kindly say so *as soon as possible*. I don't think we can possibly do any more about this than we are doing, and I am quite sure Pearn Pollinger are taking the matter *most* seriously.

I think you will probably feel that a plan of the college is desirable. I am getting my tame architect[2] to get out a simplified version of the enormous and elaborate plan from which I worked when writing, and will let you have this in good time to make your blocks. Do you think that a list of *Dramatis Personae* is required, so that people who get confused among all the dons and students can look it up for reference? Or will this just increase the formidableness of the thing and put them off? I can easily prepare one if it is wanted.[3]

Again, very many thanks for your kind thought in wiring, and for your patience with me during the prolonged and difficult gestation of this odd offspring of my fancy –

Yours very sincerely and gratefully
    Dorothy L. Sayers

---

[1] Her agent, of the firm of Pearn, Pollinger and Higham.
[2] J. W. Redhead (*c.* 1876–1941), an amateur architect, who drew the church of Fenchurch St Paul for *The Nine Tailors* and Bredon Hall for *Papers Relating to the Family of Wimsey*. He was an inhabitant of Witham, where he designed 5 and 5a Newland St.
[3] Neither plan nor list of characters was published. It is not known if they exist in manuscript.

TO HER SON   24 Newland Street
14 October 1935   Witham
                                        Essex

Dear John,
Thank you very much for your letter. I am glad you like school and don't get 'ragged' too much, and also to hear from Cousin Ivy[1] that you are taking a good place in class. I expect, as you settle down, you will get on very well with the other boys and make some nice friends. You must let me know if there is anything you need in the way of books and clothes and so on which we haven't thought of. I am enclosing a little note for you to give to Mr Hyland about your pocket-money.

I would have answered your letter before, but I had to go up to London and was very busy for a few days. I think the house must be

very delightful with its little flight of stairs and odd corners. Old
houses are much more fun to live in than new ones.

  With love
  Your affectionate mother[2]
      D. L. Fleming

[1] Ivy Shrimpton was in fact his first cousin once removed.
[2] From now on John was told to regard himself as her adopted son.

To Ivy Shrimpton   24 Newland Street
15 October 1935   Witham
                                              Essex

Dearest Ivy,
  Many thanks for your two letters. I am very glad John seems to
be settling down and doing so well. I was afraid he might feel a bit
strange at first – but I know you always said he was a philosopher.
I have written to Mr Hyland asking him to allow John whatever is
the suitable sum for him to have as pocket-money. The great thing
is that he should have about the same as the other boys, so as neither
to be put to shame by superior wealth nor to be made snobbish by
plutocratic display! Please don't bother to send all the receipts – I
feel confident that you have laid the money out with your usual wis-
dom. And if there is any over, please stick to it.
  I am sure you must miss him and Isobel very much – it was nice
for you to have her with you for a bit.
  That John should be doing so well reflects very great credit indeed
on your love and care for him. Believe me that I am grateful to you
from my heart.

  With best love,
  Most affectionately yours
      Dorothy

To Helen Simpson   24 Newland St.
15 November 1935   Witham, Essex

Dear Helen,
  By way of contrast with Mr Francis Iles,[1] I send you copy of a
portion of a letter from the nephew of Gerard Manley Hopkins.[2] The
beginning was quite amusing – about how he was himself Peter's
contemporary at Balliol, and had met him at Robert Bridges' house.
Then he went all serious, and produced this, which appears to be

quite sincere, though hyperbolical. At least, I don't *think* he is drunk or pulling my leg.

Forgive egotism:

> Mr. Iles
> Should be debagged in the middle
> of St. Giles
> For calling Peter Wimsey
> Flimsy

(an epithet which only members of 'Pop'[3] are allowed to use of 'the great Flim').

This is me on my beautiful new type-writer – much better than the old one.

Have you seen the lovely group of you and me drinking beer together at the Club? It came out in the *Weekly Illustrated*, whatever that is. I am trying to get some copies of it from the photographers – it is the best one of myself I've ever had done – and your expression of eager enjoyment is the thirstiest thing I have seen for a long time!

Best love,
     Dorothy L. S.

[1] Pseudonym of Anthony Berkeley [Cox], used for his newspaper criticism of crime fiction.

[2] Gerard Hopkins had written:

'I don't want to gush, neither do I send you empty compliments, but I cannot rest until I have told somebody (preferably yourself) how deeply I have been moved and shaken by *Gaudy Night*. The mere Oxfordry of it is enough, of course, to win me, because nothing in life has ever lessened for me the loveliness and magic of that place. We all, at some time of our lives, want to write – and many of us do write – Oxford novels. . . . Failure is almost universal, but I place *G.N.* with *Zuleika Dobson* (though in a different mode) as being outstanding in its power to create and make beautiful the real place and the atmosphere that haunts it. . . . *Gaudy Night* frightens me and enchants me. It has, I think that quality which none but great works have, of starting as one thing and suddenly becoming another – of setting out as particular and individual, and ending as universal. I feel that perhaps we shall have no more of Peter, but even this I can face now, because I know that he is out of your hands. Whatever becomes of him is of his nature and of the nature of the universe.' . . . In her reply dated 13 November 1935, D.L.S. had said: 'Oxford did mean something beautiful and valuable to me, beyond the "dreaming spires" kind of beauty, and it offends me to the soul when disgruntled young men and women write about it as though it was nothing but a futile kind of opium vision on the one hand or a nest of perversions and repressions on the other.'

[3] An Eton society.

To Donald Tovey   24 Newland Street
22 November 1935   Witham
                                                   Essex

Dear Professor Tovey,

Very many thanks, from me for your kind letter and from Peter
and Harriet for your delightful wedding-present.

I am terribly glad you liked the book[1] – although the development
didn't, as it turned out, fall in with your suggestions. I find that
characters have a way of taking hold of the situation and working it
out for themselves, regardless. But Peter owes you an eternal debt for
having always been kind to his Harriet. He is the kind of person who,
while not saying much, is, I know, sensitive about people's attitude
to his wife, and appreciative of those who appreciate her. He is at
present having a difficult time with his sister-in-law, the reigning
duchess, who has as pretty a turn for offensiveness as any woman I
know.

I will, when the time comes for it, suggest to my publisher a Peter
–Harriet Omnibus, which would make rather a jolly book, and enable
me to clear up a few discrepancies of dates and data which have crept
in. But he, the publisher, will certainly not allow me to tamper with
the Cave of Ali Baba, for which he cherishes a great affection. However, I find I was wrong about the date of this; it must have taken
place a few years earlier – shortly after the Duke's trial; a period
when Peter was probably only too anxious to escape abroad and hide
from notoriety. It was at this time that he was living with the lady
who – But I haven't worked out that story yet; only I know that it
had peculiar and melancholy consequences. I don't mean that it
created any trouble between Peter and his wife; only that the lady
came to a sad end, and that Peter had to pay his debt to her under
painful circumstances. I don't know why I put all this in the past;
it hasn't happened yet, any more than the distressing business
about Saint-George, which will leave Peter heir to those damned
strawberry leaves, or that dreadful domestic drama which I shall
probably have to chronicle before long, under the title of *Thrones,
Dominations*.

You will see from this that Peter has no intention of retiring
altogether from public life; though I fancy he will do rather less purely
police work in future, and deal more in human drama among his own
circle of acquaintance.

I do absolutely agree with you about the magnificent achievement
of *The Moonstone*:[2] I have often thought that Rachel Verinder was
one of the most remarkable characters in fiction – a virtuous young
Victorian gentlewoman, who is yet high-spirited and interesting. The

thing is so well done that people simply don't notice what a remarkable *tour de force* it is. Except really remarkable people, like you and me!

Harriet is rather inclined, I think, to encourage Peter to do a little writing of some kind. I can see him engaged, rather slowly and fastidiously and elaborately, on something to do with history or music or poetry – perversely occupied with a period that nobody is particularly interested in, and turning leisurely phrases by lamplight in the library. They are moving into an eighteenth-century house in Audley Square or thereabouts, with a library and a music room, where they may study the art of conjugal counterpoint to their hearts' content.

Forgive me for writing all this twaddle*.

I hope your rising temperature wasn't the prelude to anything serious, and that whatever it was has now departed from you.

> With very many thanks,
> Yours very sincerely,
>   Dorothy L. Sayers

* Among my long-suffering friends this is known as 'Peterising'.

1 *Gaudy Night*, which had just been published on 4 November 1935.
2 Novel by Wilkie Collins, published 1868.

To Her Son   24 Newland Street
17 December 1935   Witham
                                     Essex

Dear John,

Mr Hyland has written to ask whether you are to go back to Oxford through London (the way you went to school) or cross-country by Swindon. If you come by Swindon, it will mean travelling by yourself and changing at Swindon. I don't know whether you will feel you can manage this – the guard would look after you and find a porter to put you into the right train – in which case, of course, you must remember to give them a tip – threepence to the porter would be correct and a shilling to the guard, if Mr Hyland has not tipped him already.

If you come by London, you will have to book again at Paddington and find the right platform, and, as this is rather complicated I have said to Mr Hyland that I will try and arrange for somebody to meet you, if you go this way, and see you into the right train for Oxford. Will you consult with Mr Hyland and find out what he thinks will be the best thing for you to do.

I am sending you £5, some of which is to be used for your journey money, and the rest is a Christmas present – I should think you would have about £3 left over for yourself when all the fares are paid, or perhaps rather more if you take the direct route through Swindon. I thought perhaps you would rather have the fun of laying the money out for yourself than have a present chosen for you; but I should consult carefully with your Aunt Ivy before you decide what to buy.

I have asked Mr Hyland to let Auntie know in good time what train you will go by, so that she can meet you at Oxford. Remember that at any point on the journey, if you are not quite sure about anything the railway people will be glad to help you if you ask them. The great thing is to see that your luggage isn't left behind anywhere and that you and it get into the right train. You will only have to ask the porter.

I hope you have had a good term and will enjoy the Christmas holiday.

> With love
> Your affectionate Mother
>   D. L. Fleming

To Muriel St Clare Byrne   24 Newland Street
18 December 1935   Witham
                                           Essex

Dear Muriel . . .

Have been struggling with the Dowager[1] – great difficulty in fitting in Uncle Pandarus's[2] point of view. I shall have to leave out the incident of the omnibus-ride, because it will take up too much room – and too much time. As it is, I can only get them to Talboys by 9 o'clock by allowing considerable speed, both between Oxford and London (Dowager's house) and London and Talboys – i.e., they will have to *average* twenty which in crowded roads is pretty good considering that on the second journey they have the PORT in the car! It would be simpler if they went straight across-country from Oxford to Talboys – but that would mean having the reception in College, and I don't want to have to get up the College atmosphere again. If I put the wedding much earlier than 2 o'clock, it would make it very awkward for the guests to get there in time. Perhaps I could make it 1.30 – unusual, but not impossible. The ceremony fortunately takes less than half an hour (without hymns and parson's palaver) so that's all I need allow. Must decide where Talboys is. If I put it on the

West side of London, where scenery etc. is suitable, it would make it so absurd to go from Oxford to London and back again in same direction. South (Surrey, Kent, etc.) too overgrown altogether. This leaves North (also rather built up) and East – rather too near Denver – but perhaps Suffolk? All very awkward.

I realise that the *technical* difficulty of the book version will be to keep the cactus out of the centre of the picture. In a *play* it's all right never to ask the question 'Suppose the cactus wasn't there when Sellon looked in?' because you can cut off one act and begin another on a new note. But in a book, it's going to look obvious. Also, in a *book*, it's going to be stupid of Peter not to suggest that there may have been a murder-machine which was cleared away by Twitterton or someone during the week. Must think of a way round these difficulties – there will probably have to be some much closer alibi-work for everybody, proving that nobody *could* have entered the house during those 7 days. . . .

> Best love and hope you aren't too exhausted,
>   Dorothy

[1] D.L.S. was now writing the novel, *Busman's Honeymoon*.
[2] Paul Austin Delagardie, brother of the Dowager Duchess.

On 5 February 1936 David Higham wrote to D.L.S. to ask if the epitaph in verse beginning 'Here lies the body of Samuel Snell' in The Nine Tailors *was her own composition. He had received a request to quote from it in a memorial to a bellringer. D.L.S. replied as follows:*

To David Higham   24 Newland Street
7 February 1936   Witham
                                     Essex

Dear Mr Higham,

The verse in question is mine. I am glad you feel the doubt about it because I thought myself that I had imitated the 18th-century Tombstone Style pretty well, and I am glad if somebody has mistaken it for the real thing.[1]

I can, of course, have no objection to its being used for a memorial to a bellringer, and should not want a fee, but under the circumstances do you think some acknowledgment ought to be made? Otherwise, if people suppose it to be genuine it may go the rounds and get into places like collections of epitaphs and so forth where it is not entitled to be. . . .

[1] The verse is as follows:

> Here lies the Body of SAMUEL SNELL
> That for fifty Years pulled the Tenor Bell.
> Through changes of this Mortal Race
> He Laid his Blows and Kept his Place
> Till Death that changes all did Come
> To Hunt him Down and Call him Home.
> His Wheel is broke his Rope is Slackt
> His Clapper Mute his Metal Crackt,
> Yet when the great Call summons him from Ground
> He shall be Raised up Tuneable and Sound.

(*The Nine Tailors*, III, The First Part.)

TO NANCY PEARN[1]   [24 Newland Street[2]
28 February 1936   Witham
                                                Essex]

Dear Bun,

Thank you very much for your letter. Of course you know the answer already.

I will not enter into any agreement for the filming of any book of mine unless I am assured before hand that I shall have:– (a) Full control of, and final veto upon the shooting script and continuity. (b) Full control of, and final veto upon the casting of the featured roles. (c) Final veto upon every foot of film before it leaves the studio.

In any case I would not look at ten thousand dollars.

In the meantime, please thank the enclosed lady kindly and say I fear I cannot go to Leicester.

    Yours affectionately,
      [D.L.S.]

[1] D.L.S.'s agent, of Pearn, Pollinger and Higham, Ltd, founded in 1935, now David Higham Associates.
[2] Square brackets enclosing both address and signature indicate that the letter is reproduced from a carbon copy of the original, typed by a secretary.

TO HER SON   24 Newland Street
10 March 1936   Witham
                                                Essex

Dear John,

I had just started to write you a long letter when I heard about Mr Hyland's sudden death. This rather took me aback, so I have had to start all over again. It is an upsetting kind of thing to have happened, in any case, and if you had grown really fond of Mr

Hyland, you must be finding it all rather sad. I am so sorry about it. Death is just one of those things that one has to face and reckon with in this world. I hope it isn't worrying you too much. Of course, everything to do with funerals and so on is always gloomy and depressing and I expect this will be rather a doleful week for you all.

Mr Hyland's son tells me that the school is to carry on as usual till the end of this term and that he will let me know later what arrangements are being made for the future. If he decides that it is to go on as before under another headmaster, I expect you will like to stay among the friends you have made. It is always a pity to make a break, unless it is absolutely necessary, as it is unsettling to work and so on to keep on making a fresh start. Naturally, I don't know at all what Mr Hyland may have in mind; I am only suggesting what I think would probably be the best thing to do in case he makes some arrangement of the kind I have mentioned. Whatever happens, we shall do our best to see that you land on your feet all right!

I was very glad to hear you had been doing so well with your work and getting on so fast. Auntie Ivy tells me you were asking about riding lessons, and I had written to Mr Hyland to ask what this would involve in the way of expense, etc.; but just at present, of course, his son will have a good many other things to think about and, as it is getting late in the term, we shall have to wait and see how things turn out before settling any questions of that sort. I hope you are all free from coughs and colds now and getting through the various disgusting kinds of weather we've been having as comfortably as possible.

We are getting along pretty well, except that your father has sprained his wrist, which is a great nuisance for him and prevents him from doing any writing or painting. I have been awfully busy lately with work and dull things like committee-meetings – that is why I didn't write earlier.

I must now write a line to Mr Hyland,[1] so I'll say good-bye for the present and keep cheery.

Your loving mother
D. L. Fleming

[1] The deceased headmaster's son.

To Her Son   24 Newland Street
16 March 1936   Witham
                                    Essex

Dear John,
Many thanks for your letter. I have written to Mr Lindsey for a few

more details about Mr Webb's school,[1] and if it all seems satisfactory I
dare say we shall be able to arrange for you to go with him, since
you feel this would make you happy. Of course, I can't absolutely
promise until I have heard from him, but you may be sure I shall do
my best about it, so keep cheery.

    Your affectionate mother
       D. L. Fleming

Only a hurried note, because I am just running off to catch a train.

[1] In Bideford, Devon.

To Dr R. W. Chapman[1]   24 Newlands Street
24 March 1936   Witham
                                          Essex

Dear Dr Chapman,
    Many thanks for your letter. I don't think I made myself quite
clear about the authors' names.
    What I mean is that, whatever one may call them in private, any
public and formal reference should give the name as it stands on the
title page, because this name is part of the author's 'publicity'. This,
of course, applies alike to men and women. For instance, the college
friend whom I in private refer to as 'Muriel Byrne' would, if I were
writing a review of her work or announcing her to speak at a public
dinner, always be: 'M. St Clare Byrne'.
Similarly:
    E. C. Bentley – not 'Edmund Clerihew', or 'Edmund C.', still less
'Jack', though that is how I personally address him.
    Freeman Wills Crofts – not 'Freeman Crofts' – though I think I
might, in a *private* communication, put 'F. W.' on the envelope to
save space.
    C. Daly King – not 'C. D. King' or any other variation.
    G. D. H. Cole – not 'G.' or 'G. D.' or his Christian names, whatever
they are.
    To the use of the surname alone there can be no possible objection
– it is a proof that one has arrived. I might suitably refer in an article
to 'Byrne on Elizabethan Life' (alluding to Miss M. St Clare Byrne's
book on that subject), and my own publisher very properly announces
the publication of 'Sayers' *Gaudy Night*.' And, of course, 'Miss Byrne'
or 'Mr Bentley' is always courteous and sufficient, provided the identity is already established.
    The form 'Dorothy L. Sayers' is, as you yourself point out in Galley
12, more commonly used for women than for men, and has, for

women, I think, nothing particularly American about it – 'Charlotte M. Yonge' and 'Ethel M. Dell' are firmly established. My personal objection to 'Dorothy Sayers' is that it invites the pronunciation of 'Sayers' as an ugly spondee; my old headmistress always pronounced it so, and gave me a distaste for the form that I cannot get over. I cannot object to it in private; but in public I think it is not too much to ask reviewers etc. to take the trouble to discover how I prefer to be called – it is printed large enough for them to see! . . .

[1] Robert William Chapman, Secretary to the Delegates of the Oxford University Press.

In February 1936, Mr C. W. Scott-Giles (1893–1982), an authority on heraldry and one of Her Majesty's Officers of Arms with the title Fitzalan Pursuivant of Arms Extraordinary, wrote to D.L.S. to say that in his opinion the arms of the Wimsey family (sable, three mice courant argent, with a domestic cat as crest and two Saracens as supporters) had the appearance of antiquity. Should not an opportunity be found to explain that the arms were in fact ancestral and only by chance reflected Lord Peter's interest in criminology? D.L.S. replied in similar vein and a correspondence developed in which the family history of the Wimseys was 'discovered'. These letters formed the basis of The Wimsey Family *by C. W. Scott-Giles (Gollancz, 1977). He was also to provide the diagrams for D.L.S.'s translation of Dante.*

To C. W. Scott-Giles   24 Newland Street
18 February 1936   Witham
                                         Essex

Dear Sir,

The original arms of Wimsey are held to have been, sable, three plates. Tradition asserts that the Baron Fulk de Wimsey (or Guimsey) encouraged King Richard I to persevere in the siege of Acre, quoting to him the analogy of the patience of a cat at a mousehole; and that, after the fall of the city, the plates were changed to silver mice in recognition of the Baron's good advice, the crest being assumed at the same time. It seems more likely, however, that the incident occurred during one of the later crusades,[1] and was transferred to the earlier date by the antiquarian enthusiasm of the family chronicler. The plates and the mice occur interchangeably on tombstones and elsewhere during the 13th century. The tomb of Gerald, Earl of Denver (temp. Richard II) shows the effigy of a cat supporting the feet of the deceased, and by the time of the Wars of the Roses, the animal is well established as the family crest, as is shown by the popular saying:

When the Catt sits on the Bear's shoulder
Craft doth make treason bolder

(in allusion to the notorious third duke, who was involved in the political intrigues of the King-maker)[2].

The supporters appear first in a roll of arms of the time of Elizabeth; and the canting motto (which exists in two forms)[3] is apparently due to the fanciful invention of 17th-century heralds.

Yours faithfully,
Dorothy L. Sayers

[1] It was eventually identified as the crusade of 1270–72, led by Prince Edward, later King Edward I. (See C. W. Scott-Giles, *The Wimsey Family*, op. cit., p. 31.)

[2] Richard Neville, Earl of Warwick, known as 'the Kingmaker' (1428–71). Scott-Giles identifies 'the third duke' as the sixth Earl of Denver, who 'while whispering in Warwick's ear . . . was receptive to whispers in his own, and he knew when the moment had come to jump off the Bear's shoulder. He joined Edward IV in the campaign which ended in Warwick's defeat and death [in 1471].' (See *The Wimsey Family*, ed. cit., pp. 42–3.)

[3] 'I Hold by my Whimsy' and 'As my Whimsy takes me'.

To C. W. Scott-Giles   24 Newland Street
26 February 1936   Witham
                                        Essex

Dear Sir,

I am much obliged by your letter, and shall look forward to receiving further details of the interesting de Guimsey stall-plate formerly at Windsor. The suggested connexion with the Waunceys (or Vanceys) appears very probable; and I believe there is also a family of Ganzey or Gansie who claim to be descended from the same stock – but to tell you the truth, I have not yet gone very deeply into the matter.

I like extremely your suggestion about the origin of the 'Three Blind Mice'.[1] It fits in charmingly with all I know of the Wimsey family, who were at no time above seeking political and territorial advantage from Royal condescension. They contrived to collar an extraordinary amount of confiscated Church property by taking the correct constitutional view of Henry VIII's divorce, and to hold on to it with singular tenacity during the troublesome reigns of Edward VI and Mary I, turning up (again on the right side) at the accession of Elizabeth full of loyal acknowledgments of favours to come. That 'husbandly' lady was, however, a match for the Duke of the period, for you may remember her classic rebuke to him – or, on second thoughts, you may not, since it is recorded in a hitherto inedited volume of Harington's Memoirs.[2] The duke was a very prolific nobleman, and the number of patents, monopolies and so forth distributed among his numerous family was considered scandalous even for those days. Eventually, however, he went too far, 'for', says Harington,

> . . . my lord of Denver at many times urgently requiring of her (the Queen) divers places about her household for the gentlemen of his kin, and in especial for his sister, my lady Bredon, to be made mistress of the Spicery, Her Grace flew into a great passion, saying 'Our household? Our household? God's death, my lord Duke, we must look to our housekeeping, for with the mice in the barn and the cat in the pantry we are like to be eaten out of house and home'. Whereat my lord, knowing the Queen's stomach and having no mind to provoke her to further choler, withdrew himself from the Court on the excuse of a sudden distemper.

(All the same, he thought it politic to present the Queen, on her next birthday, with a manor in Warwickshire and a handsome new dress of cloth of gold embroidered with great pearls, all of which made a nasty hole in the Wimsey revenues.)

But I will not trouble you further for the time being. A little more solemn playing of the game, and the Wimsey family history will indeed be ready for publication.

With many thanks for your kind interest,
Yours very truly,
    Dorothy L. Sayers

[1] Scott-Giles had suggested that the rhyme, 'Three Blind Mice', who 'all ran after the Farmer's wife' was a lampoon dating from the reign of George III ('Farmer George') and referred to the then Duke of Denver's pursuit of Queen Charlotte hoping to obtain a place in her household for members of his family. (See *The Wimsey Family*, op. cit., pp. 16–17.)
[2] Sir John Harington (?1560–1612), courtier and wit, godson of Queen Elizabeth, is said to have been the inventor of the water closet. He was the first translator of Ariosto's *Orlando Furioso*.

To C. W. Scott-Giles   24 Newland Street
28 February 1936   Witham
                                                    Essex

Dear Mr Scott-Giles,

My most grateful thanks to your wife and yourself for the noble shield of arms received this morning. Whatever fault you may be disposed to find with the 15th-century mantling and accessories, the escutcheon itself, with its handsome disposition of the charges to fill the field, is undoubtedly characteristic of the best period of heraldic design. I am particularly delighted with the fine, spirited treatment of the mice courant, emblematically expressing the nimbleness of these little household creatures, and the hilarity with which they skip behind the wainscotting and dance among the cheese and candle-ends. In the less conventionalised handling of the crest, the artist has nevertheless not lost to view the essential attributes of the domestic cat: her patience, her vigilance, her cunning and the natural ferocity underlying the meekness of her demeanour (she being, until a very recent period, still recognised in Law as *ferox naturae*[1]).

With regard to the Cat's markings, I believe that she always appears in the Wimsey arms as a Cyprian,[2] or tabby, or as the Scots say, a stripit cat; at any rate, she is so represented in a rather florid piece of Flemish glass in the Chantry in Duke's Denver parish church; as well as in a curious and elaborate miniature prefixed to a late 14th-century missal still preserved at Bredon Hall. This depicts the Earl of Denver, dressed in an extremely rich houppelande lined with miniver, an enormous chaperon and shoes of unconscionable length, presenting his countess (also very fashionably attired) and his three sons to Our Blessed Lady in the Stable at Bethlehem, under the admiring gaze of St Joseph, St Thomas of Canterbury and a couple of Archangels. In the margin, the white mice and the tabby cat pursue one another through the intricacies of some conventional foliage. The presence of St Thomas in the composition suggests that the miniature may commemorate a pilgrimage to his shrine at Canterbury.

I shall await with eagerness any further results of your researches into the family history, and shall also take pains to communicate to you some of the more heroic exploits of the Wimseys as I may come upon them in the course of my reading. As with most wealthy families, their annals seem to record a sadly high proportion of political intrigues, ill-tempered law-suits and dubious adventures of fortune-hunting – so disappointing is the evidence of historical documents as compared with the fancies of historical novels!

> With again many thanks,
> Yours very truly,
> Dorothy L. Sayers

[1] Latin: wild by nature.
[2] D.L.S.'s short story, 'The Cyprian Cat', included in *In the Teeth of the Evidence* (Gollancz, 1939), was first published in *My Best Thriller: An Anthology of Stories Chosen by Their Own Authors* (Faber and Faber, 1933).

To C. W. Scott-Giles   24 Newland Street
25 March 1936   Witham
                                        Essex

Dear Mr Scott-Giles,

As I said in my letter yesterday, your theory about the origin of the Cheshire Cat[1] is in my opinion absolutely brilliant, and in view of the illuminating quotation from the French chronicler, may, I think, be taken as definitive.

The story of the murrain of mice,[2] on the other hand, can, as you say, scarcely be taken literally, though doubtless there was a popular tradition to that effect, of which traces are preserved in the 'Alice' saga.[3] Peter, being the other day at Denver, had a word about it with the family genealogist – a mild old gentleman, a distant relation and impoverished pensioner of the Wimseys,[4] who potters harmlessly round the library at the Hall, tolerated by the duke and duchess, teased mercilessly by Saint-George and delighted to have an occasional chat with Peter, who is the only member of the family to treat him with any sort of deference. According to him, the unsavoury epithets applied to the 'comte d'Enfer' are a matter of historical fact, and he, with some modest hesitation, has put forward a theory of his own, viz: that the churchman's curse ('The mice on whom you have preyed shall turn and plague you') may have been symbolically fulfilled, though possibly not in the sense that the monk foresaw. Not to put too fine a point upon it, the Earl, having in his career of rapine *chassé dans de sales trous*,[5] returned home suffering from various unpleasant maladies, and (here, says Peter, Cousin Matthew paused and took snuff in a deprecating manner) died shortly after of the pox. (At this, Peter burst out laughing, clapped Cousin Matthew on the shoulder and exhorted him to cheer up, since, after all, it was a very long time ago and the disease had had time to wear itself out.)

It is a curious fact that, throughout the history of the family, there have always been two Wimsey types, cropping up with extraordinary persistency. The commoner type is that of the present Duke and his father – bluff, courageous, physically powerful, honest enough, but rather stupid and entirely unimaginative, hearty eaters and swearers, *grands coureurs de filles*,[6] and, if cruel, yet without malice or ingenuity. The other, occurring only sporadically and usually as the result of 'breeding out' into a foreign strain, is physically slighter, subtler, more intellectual and sensitive, with enormous nervous vitality, and with lusts no less powerful but more dangerously controlled to the furtherance of a long-sighted policy. To this type have belonged the wily statesmen and churchmen who have from time to time adorned the family tree; some of them have been notorious traitors, but here and there they have produced poets and saints. The first Duke Peter, the friend of the King-maker, was of this type – (the one of whom it was said, 'When the cat sits on the bear's shoulder'), and so was the duke of Edward's time, who did so well for himself in the matter of Church property. But so, too, was the saintly Dr Gervase Wimsey, Canon of St Paul's, who embraced the new religion and perished in the Marian persecutions; and that delicate and fastidious gentleman, scholar and poet, Lord Roger Wimsey, who was Sidney's friend and died, too young, of a 'wasting fever'; and the gentle eighteenth-century naturalist, Lord Paul, who lived in retirement in Dorset, writing innocent, and to this day valuable, notes on such subjects as the habits of the burying-beetle and the melodic elements in the song of the missel-thrush (he was one of the musical ones); and that strange eccentric, Mortimer Wimsey, who, in the rationalistic eighteen-hundreds, conceived himself to be one of the fish netted by St Peter the Apostle, and lived many years alone in a hut on the sea-coast of Norfolk, wholly mute and eating nothing but shrimps and seaweed; until, one morning, when the sun was rising over the North Sea, he beheld Christ walking on the waters and swam out to meet him (as witness the narrative of the three peasant children who observed him), crying out in a melodious voice as he swam, 'Thou shalt open my lips, O Lord! the tongue of the dumb shall sing!'; whereby, many days afterwards, the Lowestoft trawlers brought up his body, along with a great draft of herrings ('so that their nets brake'); and they buried him at the sea's edge, with the fisherman's net for his sole shroud; but the churchyard in no long time being undermined by the tides (as is common in those parts) the sea had him in the end, till St Peter shall draw him home again at the Day of Judgment.

The women, too, fall into these two main types, the majority being energetic, amiable, faithful and fertile, and good practical house-keepers, busying themselves with their domestic affairs. But every so often they produce a portent, such as the infamous red-haired Marguerite la Saure, surnamed also le Succube, who was burned as a witch (temp. Henry VI) after seven husbands and innumerable lovers had perished of her insatiable appetite; or that dreadful old woman, Lady Stavesacre, who was an incurable litigious pest and boxed the ears of Bacon the Lord Chancellor when he gave judgment against her; or the Catholic nun, Mother Mary of the Immaculate Conception, who, in 1632, sailed from France with a cargo of nuns and lepers to found a hospital colony in an island in the South Seas; or Mistress Lucasta Brand, who, being condemned for high treason under Charles II, spoke such terrible and searching words to the Lord Chief Justice Jeffreys that even he was abashed at the sight of his own wicked heart thus stripped bare before him and being choked with rage and terror fell down in a fit and had to be assisted from the court.

There have been, of course, intermediate types of all sorts; but these two recur continually. The physical characteristics, too, are very persistent; Peter's hands 'go back in the family portraits for three hundred years',[7] and the fair colouring and beaked nose go back further still, though in him they are exaggerated almost to the point of caricature. In fact, if he had bred in instead of (by good sense and fortune) breeding out into yeoman stock, one might be rather alarmed about the results for his descendants; in Saint-George, in spite of the steadying influence of the Delagardie blood, there is already a touch of instability, his father having married his own cousin.

To return, however, to the points you raise; I am uncertain about *Le Chat Infidèle*.[8] How late should we be likely to encounter an inn-sign in French? The treacherous Duke Peter of the Wars of the Roses had the greatest reputation for infidelity, if that date is possible. By the way, Peter once, I think, referred to this gentleman as the third Duke. This would mean that there had been two other dukes beginning after the 'comte d'Enfer' (i.e. between Agincourt and the Wars of the Roses) – unless the Agincourt earl was made a duke by Henry V. Perhaps the first two perished rather quickly in the troublous reign of Henry VI – or Peter may have been wrong; he is not always accurate when telling the tale for his own purposes. At any rate, the present duke is the sixteenth, which, averaging them out at 30 years to a generation, takes us back to the middle of the fifteenth century.

I am so much encouraged by your researches, and so keenly stimulated by them to make further researches of my own, that I really hope to be able, in due time, to prepare a brief History of the Wimsey Family – perhaps for private circulation, or publication in a limited edition.[9] My friend Miss Helen Simpson, who is learned in the Hanoverian period (and who can write quite shatteringly good *pastiche* of almost any period) has promised to assist with inquiries into the later Wimseys; while Miss M. St Clare Byrne (who has been collaborating with me in a 'Lord Peter' play which may or may not reach the footlights) will no doubt be able to shed fresh illumination on the innumerable Wimseys who over-ran the court of Queen Elizabeth, as also on the able bunch of early Tudor Wimseys already alluded to.

In the meantime I remain,
yours very appreciatively,
Dorothy L. Sayers

[1] Scott-Giles had suggested that Gerald, 2nd Earl of Denver was called by the French the Earl of Hell (le comte d'Enfer – a play on his name) by reason of his ferocity. He served at Agincourt with Henry V. 'A French chronicler wrote that he moused like a hunting cat:

> ... le comte d'Enfer
> Sourisoit comme un chat chasseur ...

words which have come down through the centuries, though by the omission of one letter from *sourisoit* [s] and by the distortion of *chasseur* they have become the otherwise inexplicable phrase, "grinned like a Cheshire cat".' (See *The Wimsey Family*, ed. cit., p. 39.)
[2] It was further part of Scott-Giles' fictional reconstruction that the same Earl was cursed

by a priest who was about to be hanged by his command. This came to pass in the form
of a plague of mice which crawled over his body. (See op. cit., pp. 39–41.)
[3] D.L.S. was thinking of the White Knight in Lewis Carroll's *Through the Looking-Glass*,
who carried a mouse-trap on his horse's back. If mice did come, he said, 'I don't choose
to have them running all about.'
[4] He appears in the novel *Busman's Honeymoon*, 'Epithalamion II'.
[5] Hunted in dirty holes.
[6] Great runners after women.
[7] Quoted from *Gaudy Night*, chapter 14.
[8] Scott-Giles thought this might be the origin of the phrase (often found as an inn-sign)
'the cat and the fiddle'. Mrs Scott-Giles later suggested that the origin might be 'the Cat
and Infidel', referring to the Wimsey crest and the Saracen supporters. D.L.S. thought
this interpretation more likely.
[9] D.L.S. achieved this only in part. *Papers Relating to the Family of Wimsey* was printed
privately 'For the Family' by Humphrey Milford in an edition of *c.* 500 copies in December
1936. C. W. Scott-Giles, Helen Simpson and M. St Clare Byrne helped with the preparation of this pamphlet.

To HELEN SIMPSON   24 Newland Street
25 March 1936   Witham
                                                    Essex

My dear Helen,

This is simply marvellous! I wish to God I could write this stuff
as you can. I am afraid I cannot at the moment throw light on
this distressing piece of family history,[1] which seems to me entirely
characteristic of the family temper, and might very well occur, *mutatis
mutandis*,[2] between the present duke and his son – so far I mean, as
concerns their general behaviour (as you know, the connubial misfortunes by which the present viscount is doomed to be overtaken are
of a different sort).[3] Did you gather at all from Bubb Dodington[4] what
the circumstances were which caused the marriage to be so much
delayed? Do you, I mean, suppose that the young lady was inferior
in rank and fortune to the gentleman, or that there were some other
circumstances (as lack of genuine affection on the gentleman's part),
which caused him to delay so long before making an honest woman
of her? The matter is of some importance since it affects the question
of the other descendants, if any, of this young couple. If, for example,
the marriage was undertaken against the bridegroom's inclination,
and only in consequence of the lady's importunity or the threats of
her relations, we may well suppose that it was followed by a separation
a mensa et thoro,[5] and that there were no further offspring of the union.
The succession in that case would pass to another branch. If, on the
other hand, it was as we say a marriage for love with a social inferior,
we might expect a numerous progeny accompanied by such results
of outbreeding as I have previously indicated as being likely to arise.

I should be deeply interested and exceedingly grateful if your further researches into Georgian memoirs can produce any further illumination on the subject.

To pass to another subject: I went last night to the local cinema[6] and saw an American gangster film in which, from beginning to end, there was only one episode which afforded me the smallest entertainment; I think it will interest you and Browne also. The chief gangster, who seemed to be suffering from some sort of disease or injury (though we[7] arrived too late to discover exactly what), after being hurriedly bundled into a motor car from one place to the other, and doing a great deal of vigorous telephoning in bed, and giving orders to six members of the gang to do something or the other which we never discovered, became extremely ill, so that an excessively drunken doctor who arrived from a great distance in a motor car in the middle of a thunder storm, pronounced that he would die unless he had blood transfusion. The doctor, though drunk, seems to have had a few dim notions that the operation was a ticklish one, for he observed to the gangster's sister, that unless the blood was the right kind it would not work. The girl then sensibly asked, 'couldn't we make some tests?', to which the doctor replied, 'No, we can't very well do that', and stripping off his coat told the girl to get the things out of his bag and proceed. In the next 'shot' they had collared the donor (who, incidentally, was the young policeman engaged in tracking down the gangster) and, for some reason which I cannot determine, had undressed him and put him to bed. They then connected the two patients with about ten feet of rubber tubing like a pipe-line, and went ahead. Presumably they struck it lucky (which was more than they deserved) for shortly after, the gangster, who had never seemed to be very ill, was dashing about in full health and vigour and was able to take a vigorous part in a defence of his house against intensive machine-gun fire by the police! This shows how much better they order this matter in America; if you do not trouble to make any tests, there is no chance of the tests going wrong!

With love,
yours gratefully
      Dorothy L. Sayers

[1] The marriage of Lord St George to a hosier's widow in 1751.
[2] Latin: with the necessary changes.
[3] This event was never written up.
[4] Lord Melcombe (George Bubb Dodington), Baron (1691–1762), author of a diary covering the period.
[5] Latin: from board and bed.
[6] Now Witham Library, where a Dorothy L. Sayers Centre has been set up.
[7] Evidently Mac accompanied her.

To David Higham   [24 Newland Street
28 March 1936   Witham
                                         Essex]

Dear Mr Higham,

No, no! I will not alter a word of 'Blood-Sacrifice';[1] they must print it as it stands, or not at all.

I was asked to commit the perfect murder; and the whole point of the story is that the only perfect murder is one in which the murderer can neither be charged nor even suspected. If once suspicion is directed to the killer, the murder is imperfect; the only *certain* way to defeat the police is to make sure that they are never called on to deal with you.

Even if Scales had *seen* the plate turned round, it would make no difference, for nobody could possibly make him admit it in court. He has only to say, 'Certainly I never noticed any such thing', and, since on the face of it he had no motive for getting rid of Drury, but rather the contrary, the jury must take his word for it. But all these considerations are beside the point: for he would never be asked any such question. Nobody could suspect that the blood was of the wrong type, except the doctor, and he would be more likely to suppose that the clotting was due to some special incompatibility between Scales's blood and Drury's, which (time being so short) he was unable to match up directly. He would, however, not be likely to raise the point at the inquest, for any inquiry would only tend to show that he (if anybody) had been negligent. He would say: 'The patient had a main artery severed and was in a state of collapse. A blood-transfusion was tried, but it unfortunately failed to save his life, death was due to loss of blood and shock'. If he was pressed to say whether the operation was in itself successful, he might admit that it was not, adding that he had been unable to match the bloods directly. If they asked him why he had not done this, his reply would be simply: 'If I had waited to do so, the man would have died'.

There is no possible means whereby either the doctor or anybody else could begin to suspect Scales; though Scales murdered the man as surely as if he had put a knife into his heart. Of course, Scales never had the slightest doubt in his own mind that the plate had been turned round, though he might persuade himself that he doubted and even in the end bring himself to believe that he knew nothing. But in such a case, the failure to mention the *doubt* was as morally criminal as though he had actually *seen* the plate shifted.

The only person, I think, against whom any charge could be brought would be the motorist – for manslaughter. The whole ironic beauty of the story is that the motorist (guilty of nothing but consideration for a cat) would get the heaviest blame; the doctor (guilty of a little negligence in not keeping the specimens on two separate plates) would be commended for having done his best in a crisis; while Scales (who had killed his friend with deliberate murderous intent) would be sympathised with and exalted into a head-line hero for his 'Sacrifice' on Drury's behalf.

It might be well to refer Mr Cornish to Mr Denis Browne and Helen Simpson (whom he knows) for confirmation of what I have said about the doctor. The doctor would not, and could not, say anything whatever to throw any sort of suspicion on Scales.

All that Mr Cornish can do, I think, is to admit there are murders which are not crimes in the legal sense. Scales could not be charged with negligence; he could not be charged with anything; for he could not under any circumstances be suspected. This *is* the perfect murder, and the only kind of murder that can be called perfect.

If Mr Hunt does not like it, let him send the story back; we can easily place it elsewhere. But I will not alter it; for if I am challenged to produce a perfect murder, then they must be content with a murder that is perfect. The crime is a crime *de facto*, if not *de jure*,[2] for the man was killed deliberately, with full knowledge and malice aforethought, but in circumstances under which the murderer could be neither convicted, charged, nor even suspected. It is unreasonable to challenge one to produce a perfect murder and then rule it out on account of its perfection.

Psychologically, by the way, the story is one of the best bits of work I've done. Nothing will induce me to alter a word of it.

Yours very sincerely,
    [D.L.S.]

[1] The short story, 'Blood Sacrifice', was first published in *The London Daily Mail*, 23 April 1936. It was later included in *In the Teeth of the Evidence* (Gollancz, 1939). D.L.S. had consulted the surgeon Denis Browne (the husband of Helen Simpson) concerning blood transfusion, on which the story turns.
[2] Latin legal terms signifying 'in fact' and 'in law'.

To DAVID HIGHAM   [24 Newland Street
28 March 1936   Witham
                                             Essex]

Dear Mr Higham,

Since writing to you this morning I have been able to get my ideas into better shape. I think the sub-joined Post-Script to my letter bears more directly on the point that Mr Cornish has raised:–

I am not bound to establish that the murder was committed; only that, *if* it was so committed, it would be wholly undetectable.

Actually, from the *reader's* point of view, the murder is proved: that is to say, I have established the *mens rea*:[1] – the motive; the desire to kill, (clearly shown in Scales's eagerness to conceal his real feelings from the reporter); the *intent* to kill (shown by the fact that Scales would have drawn the doctor's attention to the doubt about the plate, if the sound of Drury's voice had not reawakened the murderous impulse); and the fact that death followed as a direct consequence of the infusion (as is strongly suggested by the symptoms: i.e. pain in the lumbar regions, cyanosis, congestion of the respiratory systems, etc). Murderous intent, followed by a 'vicious act' (in this case a 'vicious inaction') and attended by fatal consequences is enough, even in law, to constitute a violent presumption of murder; where the criminal is safe is in the impossibility of proving either the *mens rea* or the 'vicious act'.

By the way, I see that for no earthly reason I can ascertain, the *Mail* has taken it upon itself to alter the name of the understudy from Brand to Karl. I have instructed them to put back the name originally chosen by me. If they want to interfere in this kind of way they must ask permission, and in any case there seems no conceivable justification for it.

Yours very sincerely,
[D.L.S.]
PLEASE SEE THAT THOSE BRUTES GET MY NAME RIGHT.

[1] Latin: 'guilty mind, intention'.

To David Higham   [24 Newland Street
3 April 1936   Witham
                                         Essex]

Dear Mr Higham,

Thank you for sending me the extract from Mr Hunt's letter about 'Blood Sacrifice'. Will you tell him that when Mr Cornish's criticism appears I shall be happy to let him print the enclosed letter from Lord Peter Wimsey, to whose judgement Mr Cornish appears to be willing to submit the case. Cornish, as a matter of fact, has run off upon a side-track and failed to see the obvious way in which, if Scales were fool enough to make a confession, confirmation might be found of his guilt. Please tell Mr Hunt, however, on no account to let Mr Cornish see this letter beforehand as he might then wish to alter his observations!

I am afraid Mr Hunt may have thought me fussy about the name 'Brand'. The whole point is that to alter the name upsets the balance of the sentence, and so spoils its rhythm. As he has got it now, it will be quite all right.

Yours very sincerely,
     [D.L.S.]

FROM LORD PETER WIMSEY   [110a Piccadilly
                                           W.1]

Dear Sir,
    Since my name has been dragged into the discussion about the death of Garrick Drury, I am happy to offer my opinion, such as it is.
    First of all, let me say plainly that I do not think it would be possible to convict John Scales of murder, provided he kept quiet about it. The doctor would be unlikely, in his own interests, to suggest at the inquest that the death was the result of the transfusion, but would probably attribute it to loss of blood and shock. Even if it were suggested that the plate had been moved, it could not be proved that Scales had noticed it. He would only have to say, 'I saw nothing of it' and the jury would believe him, since Drury's death was so obviously to his own disadvantage.
    If Scales were to make a confession, it would be a very different matter. I think it is the last thing he would do, since, at the end of the story, he is shown busily persuading himself that he noticed nothing wrong, and in the end will probably come to believe it. But if he did confess, then obviously the first step would be to ask him to allow his blood to be tested again. If it proved to belong to Group 2, then there would be a definite confirmation of his story. The doctor would probably remember that the patient's blood was of Group 3, since this is the rarest of all the groups in this country. We should thus have the immediate cause of death established for a certainty, and, in view of Scales's admission of a motive and a guilty intention, and his circumstantial account of the way in which he saw that the plate might have been moved and yet failed to speak, there might be a good basis on which to found a murder charge. It would be no defence to say that the man might have died in any case; if you find a man suffering from cancer, and plunge a knife in his heart, it is murder, even though he would certainly have died before long of his disease.
    Short, however, of Scales's own confession, I do not see how one could establish either the guilty intention or the vicious act which have to be established to justify a charge of murder; in fact, I do not see that it would be possible even to suspect him. I should like to

add that, in my opinion, no murder can be called a 'perfect murder' which lays the guilty person open to police suspicion. The only sure way to 'baffle' the police is to take pains that they shall not be called upon to deal with the case.

I am, etc.
PETER DEATH BREDON WIMSEY

To C. W. Scott-Giles   24 Newland Street
10 April 1936   Witham
                                              Essex

Dear Mr Scott-Giles,

Having now found leisure to go more carefully through your paper in detail, I beg to present the first results of my researches. I turned first to the period for which you particularly desire further information, viz: the 14th century, and it occurred to me at once that there ought to be something in Froissart.[1] The attached episode at once rewarded me. It is contained in a fragmentary manuscript in the private collection of the Earl of Severn and Thames, who was good enough to allow me access to it. It belongs to Froissart's account of the siege of Rennes (1357), though, oddly enough, it is not included in any of the three manuscripts (already edited) which contain this account, nor even in the MS. of the Château du Verger, which belonged to the du Guesclin family (B. N.[2] 6474). It can scarcely have been omitted on account of the family's susceptibilities, since it shows the Constable in a very favourable light. One can only put down the omission to pure inadvertence on the part of the scribe. In our MS., it occurs immediately after the episode of Jehan Bolleton and the partridges, to which it forms a kind of parallel. No doubt this business of riding beneath the walls of the city to challenge the garrison to private fights became a kind of fashion, and served to vary the monotony of the nine months of the siege.

The manuscript is, I think, earlier than that of the Château du Verger, since it preserves far more of the original dialectal traits, and in this more closely resembles B.N. 6477 / 9, though it is not consistent throughout. Its grammatical peculiarities can, no doubt, safely be put down to the carelessness of the scribe.

It is clear that the Gerald de Guimsey concerned is the fifth Baron, the one who wedded the heiress of Bredon. He is represented as being 50 years old in 1357, and must therefore have been born c. 1307. This gives us a slightly more exact date for the birth of his father Ralph, who can scarcely have been born later than 1290, and who may perhaps be put a year or two earlier. The episode throws no very great light on the family history, beyond proving that Gerald served in France under the Duke of Lancaster, and was 'a good man of his hands'. It shows him, I think, as a man of blunt speech, and a rough sort of native wit – a very 'normal' Wimsey.

I hope you will find the passage of interest. You will notice that it definitely refers to the Wimsey cat as a '*chat du foyer*' or 'domestic' cat. I do not know whether Froissart means that Wimsey actually paraded before the walls of Rennes in full jousting panoply, tilting heaulme, crest and all – it would be inconvenient for fighting on foot. Probably he only means to say that this *was* the device of the Wimseys, and that the fact was known to the 'oultrecuydant'[3] young captain and to the other members of the garrison. Presumably the captain was not of sufficiently good birth to fight the baron himself, which makes his insulting behaviour all the more shocking; du Guesclin seems to have felt this keenly – but then, du Guesclin's courtesy and chivalry were proverbial.

Finally, and by way of disarming criticism, it is twenty years since I wrote any Old French,[4] so I offer this contribution to the game 'with all faults'!

Please go on playing!

Yours very sincerely,
Dorothy L. Sayers

[The passage 'discovered' in Froissart's Chronicle was translated by C. W. Scott-Giles as follows:]
And there too was my Lord Giraut de Guimsey, who was reputed to be the proudest of all the barons of England, and was very doughty and valiant in arms though he was already fifty years old. And he bore a shield of sable with three white mice, and on his helm a couchant cat of the kind called '*cat du fouier*' [i.e. hearth-side or domestic cat] which was his device. Now, there came a day during the siege when Messire de Guimsey came riding before the gate of the city, armed at all points and bearing himself very haughtily. Above the gate there was a young captain of the Constable's company, who was a very presumptuous man. And it so happened that this captain picked out the Baron as he rode by, and from the height of the wall threw down on him the stinking body of a dead cat, saying, 'Hi, old cat! Go and mouse by the hearth, for this is no place for you!' Then said Messire du Guesclin, who heard him, 'when the cat's away the mice will play! [*La ou caz n'est li souris se revele*] Upon my word, it is unbecoming a knight to insult a lord of such high lineage and so renowned for prowess!' Then cried Messire de Guimsey, 'To your holes, you mice! For if you dare to come out and fight with me, you

will find that the old cat has claws to tear you with!' 'Alas!' said the Constable. 'For a mean remark we shall all be shamed.' Then Messire du Guesclin offered to fight against my Lord de Guimsey, who was delighted at this. Then the Constable came down from the walls and, getting into a small boat, crossed the moat. And Messire de Guimsey alighted from his horse and set himself on foot. And for a long time the Baron de Guimsey and the Constable of France fought hand to hand, and gave such a great display of their skill in arms that all marvelled at it. Then Messire de Guimsey was sorely wounded in the right arm, and Messire du Guesclin in the shoulder. And at nightfall, when neither had the advantage of the other, they saluted one another most courteously. Then said the Constable, 'Now I see well that no man can contrive to correct an old cat, for the cats of England are lions for valour!' And Messire de Guimsey replied, '*A bon cat, bon rat!*'[5] Then each withdrew to his own following. And this was held to be a notable passage of arms.

[1] Jean Froissart (*c.* 1337–1405), French chronicler and poet, author of an Arthurian verse romance, *Meliador*. His *Chroniques* cover events in Western Europe from 1325–1400.
[2] The Bibliothèque Nationale in Paris.
[3] Overweening.
[4] Strictly speaking, French of the fourteenth century is not 'Old French' (with a capital O), a term used by linguistic historians for the earlier, inflected language, in which, for example the *Chanson de Roland* was written and of which the earliest MS. dates from the twelfth century.
[5] To every good cat a good rat.

To C. W. Scott-Giles   24 Newland Street
15 April 1936   Witham
                                                Essex

Dear Mr Scott-Giles,
   Words fail me to express my gratitude for the magnificent effigy which reached me safely this morning. It is extremely beautiful – and indeed its only drawback is that it disturbs me from my proper work, by encouraging me to wander off into vague dreams of mediaeval fancy, altogether delighful and unprofitable. I am glad the Wimseys chose a black-and-silver coat: it is less gaudy and striking than a riot of colour, but has a fine, sober impressiveness, especially when thus cunningly relieved by the spots of red and gold on the belt and weapons. I like to imagine it brooding like a thundercloud upon the fringe of some gathering of angry barons, or bursting through the mêlée of tournament to roll the blues and scarlet in the dust! I rather hope this is our friend of the Du Guesclin episode, laid so peacefully to rest with his cat at his feet, after his long war service. He lived (if Froissart's date of 1307 is right for his birth and yours of 1370 right

for his death) to the age of 63 – a very respectable age for a fighting man in those tough times. In default of evidence to the contrary, shall we say that this was he?[1] Unless, with a seal, an effigy and an anecdote, he is already over-represented?

Where, I wonder, is the effigy? We shall have to go more closely into the question of family residences. I rather imagine that nothing remains of the original Denver Castle of mediaeval times. The present place in Norfolk, Bredon Hall, is, I think, a large, rambling place, chiefly Palladian, with some Tudor remains and additions of all kinds in various tastes (largely bad) up to the time of the 15th Duke. Its contents (which Miss Simpson and myself are awaiting an opportunity to examine at leisure) constitute a perfect junk-shop of the old and beautiful and the modern and awful. The present Dowager (a woman of taste) was always trying to get rid of the accumulation of Victorian atrocities, while her husband (fox-hunting and violent-tempered) was constantly adjuring her to 'let the place alone'. The present Duchess has no taste at all. (It was she, by the way, who insisted recently on establishing a new guest's bathroom exactly in the place where 'Uncle Roger', a Jacobean Wimsey, is accustomed to 'walk' of an evening; this is highly disconcerting for female guests, who are not pleased to see a gentleman walk suddenly out of the hot-towel cupboard when they are in no state either to receive him or to retreat into the passage. But the Duchess Helen does not see ghosts and refuses to believe that other people do.)[2] The present Duke prefers to spend his time in a large room called, on the *lucus a non lucendo*[3] principle, his 'study', whose walls proliferate the heads of horned animals, remarkable fish in glass cases, and trophies of native weapons, picked up by some wandering Wimsey or other in the last century; while the floor is horrid with tiger-skins, over whose heads people trip in the dark. Peter says these things set his teeth on edge; this bewilders the Duke, who asks, What's wrong with the room? *He* can't see anything wrong with it. The Library is Peter's despair. It contains quite a lot of fine old books, uncatalogued and untended, together with piles of rubbish of all kinds, on all of which he itches to lay his fingers – but it means a lot of work and the Duchess dislikes him so much that he has never been able to face making a prolonged stay at the Hall and getting down to it himself. He has, however, succeeded in getting the family to offer a home to old Cousin Matthew, who roots slowly about the piles of books and papers like a short-sighted mole, making endless genealogical and historical notes with a maddening lack of system on pieces of paper which he loses the moment he sets them down. There is also a little room upstairs, containing several chests full of family letters and goodness knows what, from which, by leisurely burrowing, Cousin Matthew from time to time extracts something interesting, only to lose it again among his own litter in the Library. One never knows what it will be – a farrier's bill or a rent-roll, or a marriage settlement, or a recipe for the ague, or a long-dishonoured note of hand; once it was somebody's George and Garter – and one of these days he may put his hand upon King John's gold circlet or the first earl's patent of nobility. (The Library is haunted by 'Old Gregory', who usually appears in a flowered bed-gown and a night-cap; while 'Lady Susan' in a pink sacque confines her walks to the East Wing and the Upper Terrace.[4]

But to return to the tombs: I think there is probably a Wimsey Chantry of the late 14th century attached to the parish Church of St John-ad-Portam-Latinam at Duke's Denver (this, by the way, must not be confused with the village of Denver near Downham Market; the Earl took his title from the village, but built his castle at another place in the same county, so that the village of *Duke's* Denver takes its name from the dukedom, and not vice-versa – thus keeping up the time-honoured tradition that everything to do with the English nobility shall be made as confusing as possible for foreigners and other persons not in the know).

There is also some sort of family place somewhere in the Shires,[5] and, I dare say, other bits of property as well. The present duke's income is derived, I fancy, not from the Norfolk property, which in these days of agricultural depression must be more of a liability than an asset, but from some property or other on the coast, on which there exists a thriving seaside resort or two. Peter, by the way, is a landowner in his own right, having been left an odd piece of land somewhere on the outskirts of London. This, which before the War was of trifling importance, has recently become immensely valuable for building. In fact, finding about ten years ago that it was falling into the hands of the speculative builder, he suddenly developed a conscience about it and took the thing into his own hands, so that he is now the landlord as well as the ground-landlord of practically the whole of his own Estate. This is profitable, and also a good thing for the inhabitants, since he insists on a reasonable standard of efficiency and comeliness in such buildings as are put up on his property. His pubs are the object of his especial consideration, and the publicans have to mind their p's and q's, since the landlord has a way of dropping in from time to time to sample the beer or throw a dart with the customers. As for his passage-of-arms with the Peculiar People,[6] who wanted to erect a chapel of exceptionally hideous construction just opposite a particularly nice little block of experimental model houses put up by his own architect – that has become local history.

But I am straying away again! . . .

In conclusion, thank you very much for what you say of Peter. It will be pleasant to him to meet in Limbo, not only with Mr Pickwick, whom he has long desired to know, but with his own Cheshire Cat and the incomparable Duchess. And if he were permitted to share a cup of ghostly sack with Sir John Falstaff he would ask for no better Elysium. . . .

[1] He was so identified in C. W. Scott-Giles' book. (See illustration facing p. 37.)
[2] Cf. the novel, *Busman's Honeymoon*, 'Epithalamion II', where the relevant passage is almost identical, except that 'Uncle Roger' becomes a captain of the guard.
[3] Latin: light the brighter for being inconspicuous.
[4] Cf. *Busman's Honeymoon*, 'Epithalamion II'.
[5] A geographical term, loosely applied to the Midlands (e.g. Warwickshire, Leicestershire, Nottinghamshire).
[6] A religious sect without preachers, creeds or church organisation.

To Helen Simpson   24 Newland Street
15 April 1936   Witham
                                     Essex

Dear Helen,

Here at last is the ghastly great tome I have produced about Wallace![1] I am afraid I have kept on straying away into argument so as rather to disturb the chronology of the events; but I hope the outlines of the story are still intelligible. The case is pretty well-known, and I have tried to concentrate rather upon the opportunities it offers for speculation, than upon the dramatic presentation of the actual facts. Do go through it, and if there is anything that seems to you redundant or badly argued, don't hesitate to cut out or alter it. I really am terribly apologetic to you and the Club for my long delay in getting this together. John Rhode and Anthony Berkeley were very fierce with me at the last meeting when you were not there to protect me!

In the meantime Mr Scott-Giles has been overwhelming me with favours; the Seal of Gerald the fifth Baron and a magnificent coloured Effigy from the tomb of the fourteenth century, which we take to be either the fifth or the sixth Baron. In writing to him I have suggested that he and his wife (who appears to be an enthusiastic Wimsey historian) should some day meet you and me for lunch when we are all in Town. . . .

[1] 'The Murder of Julia Wallace' in *The Anatomy of Murder: Famous crimes critically considered by members of the Detection Club* (John Lane, Bodley Head, 1936). Other contributors were: Helen Simpson, John Rhode, Margaret Cole, E. R. Punshon, Francis Iles, Freeman Wills Crofts.

To E. C. Bentley   24 Newland Street
17 April 1936   Witham
                                          Essex

Dear Jack,

I meant to have written earlier to thank you for *Trent's Own Case*[1] and tell you how much I enjoyed it; but I was frightfully busy finishing up some urgent stuff and didn't want to write in a hurry.

It is completely delightful. I do wish to Heaven you had given us more of these books, instead of letting twenty years flow between the banks of Trent![2] With you to help us, we should have not taken half so long to get the detective novel recognised as literature. Because, of course, that is the first thing and the last thing one feels: that yours are BOOKS, full of humanity and the Humanities, touching life on all sides instead of being directed along one narrow line to an infinitesimal point, like so much of our stuff.

I won't waste time saying that the plot is sound and the detection satisfying, because one knew that that would be so – (though I particularly liked the bit about taking the evening dress for granted, which of course one would, seeing a top hat and a muffler). To tell you the truth, I didn't worry too much about guessing the thing, because I was just savouring the way the story was told and submitting to the spell of beautiful writing, in a lobster-eating fashion that no critic ought to indulge in. That is a magnificent description of the Impasse de la Chimère (what a grand name!) and the Hôtel du Petit Univers and the Pavillon de l'Ecstase – where, by the way, do you get that spelling? 'Exstase' seems to be the only form recognised by the Academy[3] – but that doesn't matter. Trent himself, I rejoice to see, hasn't altered a scrap, and reappears with all his old humour and charm, and with vigour unimpaired by his long rest on the shelf. He is, you know, the only modern detective of fiction I really ever want to meet (except, possibly, Father Brown,[4] and even he might be a trifle too much on the religious tack, taken in large quantities). I am always ashamed to admit how much my poor Peter owes to Trent, besides his habit of quotation.

I'm afraid these remarks of mine are not in the least what publishers want for jackets, especially as many of the things I most want to say are of the sort that look silly in blurbs – as, for instance, that when all is said and done, nothing about a book is so unmistakable and so irreplaceable as the stamp of the cultured mind. I don't care what the story is about or what may be the momentary craze for books that appear to have been hammered out by the village blacksmith in a state of intoxication; the minute you get the easy touch of the real craftsman with centuries of civilisation behind him, you get literature. Poor dear Berkeley and Crofts and Rhode work so hard with their big machine-looms and make an intricate pattern; and then you come along, and all your figures get cheerfully up and walk out of the tapestry and talk and eat and move about in three dimensions, as if it was the simplest matter in the world. It's not, of course; but you have the enormous advantage over them of knowing, in the fullest sense of the words, how to read and write.

I don't know whether, out of this exceedingly ill-expressed letter, you and Michael Sadleir[5] will be able to gather anything you can use. Perhaps you can collect a few expressions into a neat phrase or so to which I can put my name – though I think it's really a sort of impertinence in *me* to approve *you* for public exhibition, and about as becoming as for Jones minor to observe patronisingly that Sir Isaac Newton was a pretty good astronomer!

I mustn't wind up without telling you what very great pleasure your book has given to my Aunt.[6] I forget whether you have met her, but she is a woman of great ability and with immense appreciation of beautiful writing. She was charmed beyond measure and lamented bitterly when she got to the end, because there was no more of it to read. I am to thank you from her for giving her so much enjoyment.

I do hope Trent has a big success. . . .

[1] Published in 1936, in collaboration with H. Warner Allen.
[2] E. C. Bentley's first detective novel, *Trent's Last Case*, was published in 1913.
[3] L'Académie Française, the arbiter of the French language.
[4] G. K. Chesterton's detective.
[5] Author and publisher (1888–1957).
[6] Aunt Maud Leigh, who was once a guest at the Detection Club.

To Sir Donald Tovey   24 Newland Street
18 April 1936   Witham
                                  Essex

Dear Sir Donald,

Thank you so much for your letter; I am very glad you enjoyed Uncle Paul's bit of biography. I think, myself, it is rather fun, and I am hoping to bring Uncle Paul on the stage in person some time or the other. I am sorry about the cave of Ali Baba, but you must not rob Peter of his bravura passages!

I doubt whether the story of the Attenbury emeralds is of sufficient importance to make a book, and it would be difficult to go back at this date to the early Peter. I think it more likely that this part of his psychology will tend, more and more, to emerge in 'flash-backs' as his wife gets to know more about him. What I have got in mind, is the complete history of all Peter's earlier women, leading up to their reappearance from time to time in his detective present. We shall then know what happened to Barbara, to the Viennese singer and also to that unknown lady who was his partner during the Ali Baba period; and may also have some information about those 'trustworthy hands' in which Uncle Paul established him in Paris.

I am also, with the assistance of several friends, engaged on historical research into the Wimsey family from the middle ages onwards (for private publication only), so you will see that I am pretty busy.

With many thanks,
yours sincerely,
Dorothy L. Sayers

To Maurice Browne[1]   24 Newland Street
4 May 1936   Witham
                                                             Essex

Dear Mr Browne,

Miss Byrne has passed on your Aristotelian *marmouset*[2] for me to tackle.

To take the last part first: though the *explicit statement* of the HOW theme is an afterthought, the *theme itself* is implicit in the structure of the play; since, materially speaking, that structure consists in the successive removal of all adventitious impedimenta, so as to expose the bones of the HOW – viz: the cabinet, the pot, the clock and the chain. That is why, by the agency of Messrs. MacBride and Solomons, the stage is literally cleared in the last scene of almost everything except those objects. As a matter of history, that was the idea with which we started when we began to write.

As regards Peter: it would be entirely out of his character and method to be 'unwaveringly on the trail' throughout. (Few modern detectives are, except the abominable Philo Vance[3] who, as we all know, 'needs a kick in the pants'.) What nearly always happens to Peter is to collect all kinds of facts, usually in a mood of hopeless bewilderment, until, quite suddenly, the essential facts of the HOW arrange themselves to form a synthesis (by which time, of course, they usually include the WHY as well). This happens in the very first book, *Whose Body?* (the passage known to his friends as the 'SCISSORS' Motif), where the discovery of the WHO surprises and shocks nobody more than himself. In *Unnatural Death* he gets exactly the same kind of enlightenment at the moment when he connects the use of the hypodermic syringe with the air-lock in the petrol-feed in the stranger's motor-cycle. In *Gaudy Night*, he is certainly on the right track from the start – but only because Harriet has collected all the HOW-facts and presented them to him on a plate; and here he really is careful to point out that she would and must have seen the thing for herself, if she had concentrated on those facts and not been misled by an entirely fallacious notion of the WHY. But he is just as liable to be led astray as other people – as in *The Nine Tailors*, where the whole structure he has built up on the idea of the jewel-robbery motive is knocked on the head by the discovery of the emeralds in the church – at which point 'Lord Peter is Called Wrong'.

(By the way, if you are interested in theories of detection, the notorious real-life case of William Herbert Wallace provides an extraordinarily interesting commentary. There was an incredibly elaborate HOW-structure, in the best detective-story style, which, as it happened, might have fitted *either* Wallace himself *or* some other person who wanted to inculpate him. No motive could be shown for anybody. The jury, feeling that the only person who could be thought to have a motive for murdering a wife was the husband, convicted Wallace, in face of the judge's summing up; the Court of Appeal reversed the judgment, on the ground that the HOW was not proved against him. The whole trouble was that there was no Key-incident in the HOW – i.e. nothing that could have been done *by Wallace and no one else*. The case is a classic, as showing that, though WHY may add valuable weight to a HOW structure complete in itself, it is valueless in cases where the HOW cannot be established without it.)

But of course, to the *audience* the problem must be presented as a WHO-problem, in the hope that they will gallop off on the trail of the motive; this being the essential ψευδῆ λεγειν ὡs δεῖ.[4] In every case, Peter is unwilling to proceed along the line of motive: what worries him about Sellon is not the blackmail or the quarrel, but the apparent difficulty over the clock; the reason why he is so reluctant to tell Kirk what Miss Twitterton said when the body was discovered is that he knows the ghastly danger of stressing motive, and what makes the increased motive in Act III so overpowering against her is her possession of the keys and lack of an alibi; what keeps him off Crutchley is far less the apparent lack of motive than the cast-iron alibi for the essential times. It is an interesting fact, by the way, that people to whom the play has been read usually pick Miss Twitterton as the criminal a) because of the motive and b) because she kills chickens – admirable example of the ineradicable human tendency to plump for motive and character rather than method.

My own reason for preferring the play in its new form is that the academic discussion takes the place of some rather tedious fooling among the what-nots, which we put in, rather against our own inclinations, as a sop to the popular conception of the tom-fool Peter.

Forgive this long exposition. You too have engaged in the schoolmastering trade, like Miss Byrne and myself – that is my excuse! . . .

¹ Maurice Browne (1881–1955), actor-manager and dramatist.
² French: grotesque figure, conundrum.
³ Created by S. S. Van Dine (Willard Huntington Wright), 1888–1939.
⁴ 'Speaking falsely in the appropriate manner' (Aristotle, *Poetics*). D.L.S. quoted this phrase in her lecture 'Aristotle on Detective Fiction'. She there interprets it as 'framing lies in the right way'. She gives the phrase to Lord Peter Wimsey to use in the course of his conversation with the Warden of Shrewsbury (*Gaudy Night*, chapter 17).

To DAVID HIGHAM   24 Newland Street
19 May 1935   Witham
                                        Essex

Dear Mr Higham,

In reply to your letter, pray inform the German publishers (1) that they may make abbreviations, but must not alter anything. I mean by this that, though they are certain to cut out one or two slightly acid references to Mr Hitler's policy, they must not alter these references into any expression of agreement with it. (2) The word 'Aryan' has no biological significance whatever, but only a linguistic one. You may, however, inform them that on my father's side I am descended from a line of English squires who, in the early seventeenth century, settled in Ireland, and there married sometimes with the Irish, and sometimes with the Scotch. My family on the mother's side owned land in the Isle of Wight and Hampshire from the time of Queen Elizabeth. On both sides they bore coat armour for three centuries. If this is any contribution to the problem, the information is at their service. . . .

To NANCY PEARN   [24 Newland Street
29 May 1936   Witham
                                       Essex]

Dear Bun,

First of all will you please kill off the Bolton Women Citizens for me, I cannot go so far? Secondly, since you seem to feel strongly about the National Society for Women's Service I will think it over: but I have a foolish complex against allying myself publicly with anything labelled feminist. You will say that this is kicking down the ladder I climbed up by; and so it is. All the same, I feel that at this time of the day one can probably do more by taking the feminist position for granted. I mean that the more clamour we make about 'the women's point of view', the more we rub it into people that the women's point of view is different, and frankly I do not think it is – at least in my job. The line I always want to take is, that there is the 'point of view' of the reasonably enlightened human brain, and that this is the aspect of the matter which I am best fitted to uphold.

In addition to all this there is the fact that I have been speaking at this and that during the last few months, and I do want to cut these engagements down as far as possible. However, I will let it simmer for a little while.

Thirdly, about 'Striding Folly'; is it really worth having one's stuff cut about like this for 15 guineas? Frankly I do not think it is. Would you be willing to stand behind your author if she firmly said 'No'?"[1]

Yours ever,
    [D.L.S.]

[1] 'Striding Folly', first printed in *The Strand Magazine* (vol. 89, no. 43, July 1935), was reprinted 'slightly abridged by permission of the author' in the *Sunday Graphic and Sunday News* (no. 1107, 21 June 1936, pp. 22–34). Reprinted, New English Library, 1972.

To HELEN SIMPSON   [24 Newland Street
4 June 1936   Witham
                                           Essex]

Dear Helen,
    Here are the further letter and plan from Mr Ridley and also Dr Mitchell's rather naive communication.

With regard to the Detection Club Dinner, we really ought I suppose, to have a Committee Meeting in time to send out notices about three weeks before the Dinner, especially as it is to be a Guest Night. I do not want to attend Committee Meetings, but it is my duty and I will.

Yours ever,
    [D.L.S.]

P.S.
    Yesterday I saw the architect[1] who has so obligingly undertaken to make a few preliminary studies for a sketch of Bredon Hall. I suggested to him that our pamphlet[2] might probably be produced demy size; I think this would be much better than octavo, because it would allow any illustrations to be of a better size. If you see any objections to this, let me know before he gets started on anything.

[1] J. W. Redhead. See also footnote 2 to letter to Victor Gollancz dated 26 September 1935.
[2] *Papers Relating to the Family of Wimsey.*

To Her Son   24 Newland Street
7 June 1936   Witham
                                                    Essex

Dear John,

Many thanks for your letter and letter-card. I am very glad you like Bideford so much. You sound as though you were having a very good time, with the sea and one thing and another. Your headmaster says you're getting very big and brown. I only hope you are getting a spot more sunshine there than we are here. We had hail yesterday, thunder the day before and plain rain to-day! Your father is all tied up with rheumatism, I'm sorry to say.

I think a good, reliable bicycle, new, should cost about £4, but next time I am in London I will make inquiries and see. Of course, it is possible to get quite a useful one second-hand, and that might be the wiser plan, since you may very well grow out of it rather quickly.

How do you like the boys at North Bank? Did many of your friends go with you from Combe Florey to Mr Lindsey's house? And I hope the new Head, now you have made his acquaintance, suits your ideas of what a Head should be better than Mr Hyland Junior. In any case I don't think you would have cared for Derbyshire as much as Devon – it is as cold, bleak and stony a county as one could wish to find – very bracing, no doubt, but (I should think) uncommonly disagreeable in the winter.

Are all your new clothes and things all right for you? Let me know if there is anything you need.

With best love
Your affectionate Mother
    D. L. Fleming

To Her Son   24 Newland Street
15 June 1936   Witham
                                                    Essex

Dear John,

Yes, certainly you can go camping with Mr Lindsey – I hope you will have a very good time and that the weather will stop drizzling for you.

I am very glad you are getting along well with your work. Auntie Ivy tells me you are having a good shot at keeping top of your form against heavy odds. That's fine. I hope you enjoy playing cricket – it's a first-class game.

With love
Your affectionate Mother
        D.L.F.

To Mrs G. K. Chesterton   [24 Newland Street
15 June 1936   Witham
                                           Essex]

Dear Mrs Chesterton,
    This is just a line to tell you what you know already, that I am most deeply sorry for your husband's death, which comes as a very personal loss to me, quite apart from the loss to the Detection Club.
    I think, in some ways, G.K.'s books have become more a part of my mental make-up than those of any writer you could name. I remember vividly the extraordinary excitement of reading *The Napoleon of Notting Hill* at a very impressionable age; and I owe him a debt of gratitude of a kind which it is foolish to try and express in words.[1]
    You will, of course, shortly receive a letter to express the feelings of the Detection Club at the loss of its President; but I should like to say, on my own behalf, how important I feel your husband's work to have been in showing us how to dignify a kind of literature which had fallen on very bad ways by restoring to it that touch with the greater realities which it had almost entirely lost.
    As you know, Mr Chesterton was always extraordinarily kind to me, and although we did not meet often, it is a great grief to me to know that our Club meetings will be deprived of his great personality and genial friendliness.

    Believe me, with deepest sympathy,
    yours very sincerely
        [D.L.S.]

[1] D.L.S. read *Orthodoxy* while at school (see letters of third week in February 1909 and April 1913). She read *What's Wrong with the World* while at Oxford (see letter dated 2 March 1913) and asks for a quotation from *The Napoleon of Notting Hill* (letter dated 19 January 1913). See also her description of G.K.C. in letter dated 17–18 May 1914.

To Her Son   London
20 June 1936

Dear John,
　I hope you have had a good week-end and enjoyed your camp. I have been in London, where it was (and is) terrifically hot. Last night I got caught in a big thunderstorm which drenched down as I was coming out of the theatre with some friends.
　I had great fun on Thursday morning – just came round the corner in time to see the flood in Theobald's Road – a lovely sight, with stones and bricks being washed down the street and the water like a young river. It poured in cataracts down the steps of a Men's Lavatory at the corner of the street – so that presently a courageous man had to take off his boots and [socks] and rush down to the rescue of a painfully embarrassed gentleman who had got marooned down there, and was assisted back to daylight amid loud and hearty cheers from the crowd. The bobbies looked rather comic, trying to maintain their dignity with water gurgling over their constabulary boots and wetting them nearly to the knees as they paddled about.
　I am having a box of grub sent down to you – I hope it will get there all right. I thought camping might have sent you back with an appetite.

　　Your loving Mother
　　　D.L.F.

I go back to Witham to-day.

To Helen Simpson   24 Newland Street
2 July 1936   Witham
                                                                  Essex

Dear Helen,
　So far as I can see, the thematic structure of *Thrones, Dominations*[1] – is going to work out something like the enclosed.[2] I have drawn it out very prettily, because I like fooling about with different coloured inks. PH (the green line) stands for the Peter–Harriet combination. M (red line) and V (purple line) being respectively the murderer and the victim, for whom I must try and find names. The scheme looks nice and neat; and is very nearly symmetrical except for the little bulge of PH emotional development, which leads to the solution. I find this scheme so satisfactory that it hardly seems worth while writing the book, does it? . . .

P.S.
I have just found a grand motto for the book from *Paradise Lost*:

Thrones and imperial Powers, off-spring of heav'n,
Ethereal Vertues; or these Titles now
Must we renounce, and changing stile be call'd
Princes of Hell?[3]

This seems to give the whole theme of the book in a nutshell.

[1] An unfinished novel, existing only in MS.
[2] The plan of the novel is in private hands. PH stands for Peter / Harriet; M stands for Murderer; V stands for Victim.
[3] The words of Beelzebub, Book 2, lines 310–13. The title of the novel is taken from the words of God, Book 5, lines 600–2: 'Hear all ye Angels, Progenie of Light, / Thrones, Dominations, Princedoms, Vertues, Powers, / Hear my Decree, which unrevok't shall stand.'

To Nancy Pearn   [24 Newland Street
4 July 1936   Witham
                        Essex]

Dear Bun,
Many thanks for your letter. I agree with you that it might be quite fun to go to Holland, and we will see whether it can be arranged. I imagine that the phrase £6.os.od., per lecture, probably only means £6.os.od., for one lecture. It might, however, be possible to arrange for a second lecture on the same visit so as to make the expedition better worth while. If so many people in Holland study the English language, there might possibly be some school or college in Haarlem which would be willing to pay for an address. This is only a suggestion and may not be possible; on the other hand, I do get rather tired of making long journeys with only a small fee at the end of each.
I am coming up to Town for a few days on Tuesday, and should like to come in and see you to talk about *Busman's Honeymoon*, and one thing and the other, should you be free about 11 o'clock on Wednesday morning the 8th.
In the meantime, I have received an invitation to speak at Edinburgh: this time with no fee and nearly as long a journey. Do you think it is worth it? Edinburgh is a University and also a very fine town; but it takes a devil of a lot of time and energy to get there.
I again return Mr, Mrs, or Miss C. O. de Winkel-Tadema's letter so that you may communicate with him or her. If I did speak there, I should think it had better be on the development of the detective

novel in England; which is the only subject I am really qualified to speak on.

Yours ever,
    [D.L.S.]

To Ivy Shrimpton   24 Newland Street
23 July 1936   Witham
                                                  Essex

Dearest Ivy,

I understand that Mr Kellow-Webb has written to you about John's train. I think it might be as well that Isobel should meet him.

I cannot understand the situation at North Bank – the letters from Mr K-W and Mr Lindsey contradict one another flatly, and John's own letters are highly mysterious. I think it is best that he should leave, and have given notice.

I have in view for him a good school at Broadstairs, which has been personally recommended to me by my solicitors. I shall try to go and see it. It is extremely expensive; fortunately, this year I shall be a good deal better off than I was last year.

Forgive all this bother and nuisance. I really do not know what these men are driving at – perhaps John may be able to tell you something more coherent when he gets back. His letters have to me a curious air of being inspired or dictated by Mr Lindsey or somebody – and I am convinced that a *complete* change is indicated.

Best love
    D.

I enclose cheque for journey expenses, etc.

To C. W. Scott-Giles   24 Newland Street
5 August 1936   Witham
                                                  Essex

Dear Mr Scott-Giles,

Thank you so much for your letter, which crossed with mine, and for the magnificent coat of arms. The Saracens seem to me to be all that 17th-century Saracens should be. I am inclined to think that since the drawing will have to be very much reduced to appear on the title page of the pamphlet,[1] it might be better if it could be executed in a rather bolder and more woodcut style; otherwise I am afraid a good deal of the very beautiful detail may fill up, particularly as we are not printing on a calendered paper. . . .

The pamphlet is being printed for us by The Oxford University Press, of Amen House, Warwick Square, E.C.4. I wonder whether it would be possible for you to get into direct communication with Mr Charles Williams[2] there, as he would be able to tell you better than I should what degree of detail the block would stand. It is so long since I have been in direct contact with the making of line blocks that I feel a little uncertain about the possibilities; but I should be very much distressed if your beautiful design were not done justice to by the printers. I think I shall have to put in a note somewhere about the two different versions of the motto;[3] I believe you are quite right in feeling that 'I hold by my whimsy' is the earlier of the two – actually it *was* the earlier invented of the two! . . .

[1] i.e. *Papers Relating to the Family of Wimsey.* The title page bears the reproduction of the coat of arms. The frontispiece is a reproduction of a study in charcoal crayon of Thomas, 10th Duke of Denver. This was drawn by Mrs Scott-Giles. On p. 11 of the pamphlet it is stated: '[It] was found in a cupboard in an attic at Bredon Hall . . . [and] bears a striking similarity in features, lighting and pose to the portrait by Thomas Hudson which hangs in the Gallery at Bredon Hall; sufficient, indeed, to justify the opinion that it is the original study on which the painting was based.'

[2] The author, concerning whom D.L.S. wrote to Scott-Giles on 12 August 1936: 'I am glad you saw Mr Williams; he is a very sympathetic character and a devoted Wimsey fan.' (See letter to Victor Gollancz, 31 December 1933, and note.)

[3] She did not do so.

To Nancy Pearn   [24 Newland Street
5 August 1936   Witham
                                            Essex]

Dear Bun,

Many thanks for your letter. It has come, perhaps at a rather unfortunate time, when I am feeling a little fagged out and am, moreover, coping with the arrival of a new domestic staff; but I must say that as things are, the prospect of preparing eight lectures of one and a half hours each on so limited a subject and delivering them in ten days in a country of which I do not know the language, and all for a fee of £48 minus travelling expense, does rather appall me. The perpetual travelling by train and living in and out of one's suitcases does tend to be exhausting, quite apart from all the preliminary nuisances of passports and so on. I should not mind nearly so much in France, or even Germany, where I could cope with porters and taximen in their own lingo. It would have to be in February or March which are two beastly months, since I must be in London in the second week in April, and have had a notion of going away with some friends towards the middle or end of that month. Do you honestly think that kind of thing is worth the fag? In a general way I am all for seeing new places, but not under these fatiguing conditions. I am getting old.[1]

Yours ever,
    [D.L.S.]

[1] She was forty-three.

To DAVID HIGHAM   [24 Newland Street
26 August 1936   Witham
                                         Essex]

Dear Mr Higham,
    Thank you so much for your letter of the 24th August which relieves me, as I am sure you know, of a great deal of anxiety. I am naturally extremely grateful to Harcourt Brace for the exceedingly kind and generous attitude they have taken up in the matter of the film rights: in fact their attitude has been extraordinarily kind all along, and I can only hope that the sales of *Gaudy Night* have, to some extent, justified the very great consideration they have shown to me during the long and very difficult period when I was getting myself established. I do feel strongly that it is rather essential to the reputation of the books themselves that any film treatment of Lord Peter should be subject, as far as possible, to the author's control; needless to say, however, we should always give the most careful and sympathetic consideration to any offer from any American company who seemed disposed to work along the right lines, and I should be willing to go to a great deal of personal trouble to help any such company to get the thing right. I hope you will convey to Messrs. Harcourt Brace my very best thanks for everything they have done, and my assurance that I will do my best not to be so tiresome in future.
    With many thanks also to yourself for conducting this delicate negotiation to such a successful close.

Yours very sincerely,
    [D.L.S.]

To DAVID HIGHAM   [24 Newland Street
5 October 1936   Witham
                                         Essex]

Dear Mr Higham,
    I have just had your letter; I think I cannot have made myself clear

about this question of the relation between the book and the Play.[1] What I thought I had said was this: that it must be made quite clear that the story was originally written as a Play, and that the novel was to that extent 'the book of the Play'. I have rung up Mr Victor Gollancz who says that this was also what he understood from me, but what I have told him is, that I have written a dedication to the book in which it is made quite clear that the Play comes first, and that in view of this he need not make any announcement on the wrapper. He in return has promised to hold up all his preliminary announcements (with the exception of the general reference to 'the new Lord Peter story') only for the production of the Play. He is quite willing to do this as I have pointed out to him that it is extremely important from the management's point of view that people should not suppose the Play to be 'the novel with all the best bits left out' which is the sort of thing critics and audiences always say if they imagine that the Play has been taken from the book. I have suggested that it would be quite a good thing if Mr Gollancz were to get into direct touch with Mr Roger Maxwell as regards the preliminary announcements on both sides, so that they should not unwittingly tread upon one another's toes.

So far as I am concerned the arrangement about the Play publication is quite satisfactory; I will let Gollancz have the script of this as soon as the necessary alterations have been made in rehearsal.

Will you remind Nancy that Gollancz is champing for a copy of the novel to set up and that she had better let him have hers if my copy is not yet returned from the producer.[2] I think you may now destroy your Ms. of *Gaudy Night*.[3]

Yours very sincerely,
    [D.L.S.]

[1] *Busman's Honeymoon*. Both the play and the novel were published in February 1937.
[2] The novel was completed by this date.
[3] What a disaster! [Ed.]

The following letter marks the beginning of a new direction in the career of Dorothy L. Sayers. From 1928 onwards, the Dean of Canterbury, George Bell (later Bishop of Chichester) had encouraged the performance of drama in the cathedral, something that had not been permitted since the days of Oliver Cromwell. Of the plays enacted there the best known is T. S. Eliot's Murder in the Cathedral, *first presented in 1935. This was followed by Charles Williams's* Thomas Cranmer. *Miss Margaret Babington, the Festival Organiser, then approached D.L.S.: would she consider writing the next play for Canterbury?*

This, at the time, was an unexpected move and surprised D.L.S. herself. Very few people at that time knew that she had written a play. Busman's Honeymoon *was not even in rehearsal and was, in any event, a secular comedy. She had not then written or spoken on religious themes and nothing was known of her views on Christian drama. Margaret Babington said that she wrote at the suggestion of Charles Williams. He was an admirer of* The Nine Tailors *and many years previously he had read and expressed approval of her brief dramatic poem 'The Mocking of Christ' (included in* Catholic Tales and Christian Songs). *It is possible that Maurice Browne, who had read and tried to find backing for* Busman's Honeymoon, *also put in a word. Whatever the explanation, D.L.S. allowed herself to be persuaded. It proved a momentous decision.*

To Margaret Babington   [24 Newland Street
7 October 1936   Witham
                                                       Essex]

Dear Miss Babington,
    Thank you very much for your letter. I hardly know what to say about this invitation to write you a play for Canterbury. Naturally I am much honoured at being asked, and should like very much to try my hand at it; but as you will realise, it is rather out of my usual line and there is also the very serious question of whether I could possibly find the time to devote to it. I shall be in London on Wednesday next, the 14th, and should be happy to see you then. Should you mind, however, if I asked you to come to my flat at 24, Great James Street, Bloomsbury, W.C.1. as I shall be up there on business connected with my forthcoming Play and shall want, if possible, to be within reach of my telephone? I suggest that about 12 o'clock in the morning would suit me best if that is convenient to you.

    Yours very truly,
        [D.L.S.]

To L. C. Kempson[1]   [24 Newland Street
10 October 1936   Witham
                                                       Essex]

Dear Kempie,
    Ever so many thanks for your letters. The Play is actually cast at last – that is to say as regards the principals – all the people being quite different from the ones we first thought of! Nicholas Hannen turned the Play down, ostensibly because he did not like it, actually, as we know from underground sources, because he was hoping for

something much better, so after a terrible period of suspense and agitation during which the most impossible names were suggested, we have got Dennis Arundell,[2] who gave us a lovely performance at a preliminary reading (in spite, poor thing, of a heavy cold, a heavy overcoat and a heavy muffler which gave him no help in playing passionate love scenes!) and we really think he will give an excellent interpretation of Peter both as regards appearance and personality. He has what so many of these modern young men completely lack, the really finished style.

Margaretta Scott was tied up in film contracts and could not join the cast; we [are] having Veronica Turleigh[3] who is, perhaps, a better name and will give the part, I think, great distinction. For Bunter we are having dear old Norman V. Norman who also has the manner, and though seventy-one is amazingly spry; he will have to be, poor old man, since he has to spend all the time carrying things about and climbing step-ladders. However, Beatrice Wilson, who is his wife, says she thinks she can produce him all right. I believe Christine Silver[4] is playing Miss Twitterton and Nellie Bowman Mrs Ruddle; both, Muriel thinks, good choices. The rest of the cast is still rather undecided, but we have got a beautiful lumbering young elephant to do the pathetic police constable.[5]

I will let you have all further news as it comes along.

With best love from Muriel and me,
Ever yours,
    [D.L.S.]

[1] Fellow of Somerville College, on whom Miss Martin in *Gaudy Night* was based.
[2] (1898–1988).
[3] (1903–71). She also played Helena in *The Emperor Constantine*.
[4] (1883–1960).
[5] Alastair Macintyre.

To Margaret Babington   24 Great James St
18 October 1936   W.C.1

Dear Miss Babington,

Thank you so much for sending me the literature about Canterbury;[1] I have not yet had time to study it, but shall hope in the course of this rather agitated week to look through it and see whether there is anything in it which to my mind suggests a play. I will also, if I am still alive, try to give you some sort of decision about whether I can do the job or not. I am so sorry to be as vague as this, but I know you quite understand what the position is.

Believe me, however, that if I see any prospect of being able to do it I should like, above all things, to have a shot at it. . . .

¹ Margaret Babington had sent a copy of the Latin chronicle by the monk Gervase, which told the story of the burning and rebuilding of the choir in 1174, as well as her own book, *The Romance of Canterbury Cathedral.*

To C. F. JOHNSTON   [24 Newland Street
25 October 1936   Witham
                                            Essex]

Dear Sir,
    Thank you so much for your very kind invitation to the dedication to your new Ring at Croydon Parish Church; I should like very much to come and to be present at the tea. I am so glad that my book has been so kindly received by Bellringers and Bellfounders.¹ I am afraid I have to confess that I really know nothing of Bellringing and have never, as a matter of fact, even seen a peal rung!
    Apologising for any errors I may have committed in my book, and looking forward very much to meeting some of the practitioners of the art,

        yours very truly,
            [D.L.S.]

¹ She was elected an honorary member of the Ladies Guild of Change Ringers in 1937.

To HER SON   24 Great James St
28 October 1936   W.C.1

Dear John,
    Do forgive me for not having answered your letters before. We are plunged into rehearsals for my play which is being produced in Birmingham in 10 days' time (Nov. 9th) and are more terrifically busy than you can imagine. Every day we go into the theatre at 11, and work furiously till past 1 o'clock – then snatch hasty food some-where, and bolt back at 2, and then on again till 5. And after that, either one has to go and consult with the producer about alterations in the play, or rush off with the stage designer to see about furniture and 'properties', or go to a tailor or dress-maker to give an opinion about the costumes, or interview the Press, or tell the management how to write the advertisements – and if one isn't doing that, one is taking agitated actors and actresses out to dinner and telling them how marvellous they are, and what a wonderful performance they are going to give, and generally soothing their shattered nerves and

encouraging them, poor dears! So at the end of the day, one tumbles exhausted into bed, thinking of new things to do to the play, and absolutely incapable of writing two coherent words about anything to anybody. However, we've got a grand cast, and it's going to be a splendid show, I hope. I expect it will be on in Town during the Christmas holidays, and you and Aunt Ivy will be able to come and see it. It is tremendous fun doing it – rather like playing a grand dressing-up game with grown-up people; only every so often, of course, one stops and thinks, 'Gosh! this is *serious*; and if it's a flop, these poor people won't get any salaries, and how guilty one will feel for having let them down.' But we hope it's going to be a success.

In between-times, I've had to go rushing round the country delivering lectures, with my mind anywhere but on the job – so you see, life is being pretty strenuous.

I'm glad you like the school.[1] I thought it all looked awfully nice when I went down – though of course it was all sort of shut up for the holidays, and the front of the house was all over scaffolding and workmen and building alterations. You're doing jolly well to be fourth in the school – it looks as though you were putting in a lot of good work. Are the other boys nice? And the masters? I liked Capt. and Mrs Card very much, though of course I only saw them for a short time.

I simply wasn't able to even *think* of getting away for half-term; we were just in the throes of starting work at the theatre. Another term I really will try. And when you come up to see the play we must meet and do something jolly. Do you do any theatricals or anything at school?

I think I forgot to say anything to Mr Tendall about dancing for you, one way or the other. If you feel it would be a good thing, you can learn, of course; though I don't know that it's really very important until one is a bit older. Let me know if there's anything else you would like to learn or do. How goes the music exam?

I must stop now, and get going on some wretched proofsheets, which have been waiting goodness knows how long, till I can get time to correct them.

With love and all the best
Your affectionate mother
    D.L.F.

[1] He was then at a preparatory school in Broadstairs, Kent.

To Her Son   24 Great James St
8 November 1936   W.C.1

Dear John,
 Yes, certainly you may go out with your friend for half-term. I am
so sorry I can't come myself, but you see how things are.
 Just off to Birmingham for our First Night.

 With love
    Mother

To Margaret Babington   [24 Newland Street
14 November 1936   Witham
                                             Essex]

Dear Miss Babington,
 Thank you so much for your kind wire of good wishes, it was so
good of you to think of us. We had a very successful first night and
a splendid Press, and all that worries us now is this question of finding
a London theatre.
 I have not, as you may imagine, had very much time to think about
the Canterbury play, but I should like very much to do it and am
going really to try and get down to it as soon as all the excitement is
over. I have an idea for the general scheme of the play which I think
may work out quite well. I fear, however, that mine will be but a
simple and unimpressive kind of play compared with the fine verses
and elaborate mysticism of Eliot and Charles Williams. However I
will do my best and try and send you shortly a suggested outline of
the thing, and perhaps a few specimen passages so that you may see
what you think of the idea. In the meantime, I am hunting up information about the rule and order of St. Benedict in order to get the
local ecclesiastical colour really right.

 With again many thanks,
 Yours sincerely
    [D.L.S.]

To David Higham   [24 Newland Street
27 November 1936   Witham
                                             Essex]

Dear Mr Higham,
 I do not think I answered your letter about the French translation
of *Whose Body?*; by all means go ahead with it. Certainly they can

soften the thrusts against the Jews if they like and if there are any.
My own opinion is that the only people who were presented in a
favourable light were the Jews!

Yours very sincerely,
        [D.L.S.]

To Margaret Babington   [24 Newland Street
27 November 1936   Witham
                                         Essex]

Dear Miss Babington
    Thank you so much for your letter. Of course I am quite ready to
accept the same financial arrangements that you have made in the
case of your other and much more distinguished authors. As regards
the producer, I am inclined to favour Harcourt Williams[1] rather than
Bridges Adams; I do not know either man personally, but I feel, and
a number of my theatrical friends agree, that Williams's style of work
is rather better suited to the production of the scenic effects which
are necessary in a Play of our kind than that of Bridges Adams, who
rather tends to encourage underplaying. I know what extraordinarily
good work Harcourt Williams did at the Vic when he was producing
John Gielgud there, and should be inclined to trust him to do what
we want. As regards the costumes, I find that the story of the building
of the Choir, which seems to me to afford admirable material for a
play, is going to land us with rather a sombre company of black
monks! I shall do what I can to get in as many brightly coloured
laymen and women as possible, and am rather proposing to let myself
go over a kind of explanatory chorus consisting of the Recording
Angel and the three Archangels! If we can get these really effectively
costumed in the manner of the early primitives, with something of
the wing effects used by Tyrone Guthrie in *Tobias*,[2] they ought to lend
a good deal of splendour to the scene. . . .

[1] Harcourt Williams (1880–1957), actor and director. He also directed D.L.S.'s second
religious drama, *The Devil to Pay*, in which he played the part of Faustus.
[2] *Tobias and the Angel*, by James Bridie (O. H. Mavor), 1888–1951. Tyrone Guthrie (1900–
71) directed it at the Westminster Theatre, where it opened in March 1932.

To Nancy Pearn   [24 Newland Street
29 November 1936   Witham
                                        Essex]

Dear Bun,
    Many thanks for your letter; I am glad to hear there is interest in

the Play over in America. Just here, as you may have heard from Mrs Allen,[1] we are going through rather a trying time, being not altogether satisfied with the production as it stands, and hope to get it tightened up in time for London, if we ever get so far! In the meantime I am handing you a bunch of stuff to get rid of for me. I think I really must turn down all these antiquarian book-sellers and Bacon societies and so forth; I simply cannot do as much speaking next year as I did last. As regards the Waggoners, I had a telephone conversation with Mr McCullough in which I asked if I might leave it open, but I really think I shall have to turn it down; it probably coincides with the last phases of our struggle over the Play, and Mr Broadley's letter seems to suggest an evening so exhaustingly bright and strenuous that I really do not think I can cope with it, so please turn them down kindly on the score of the Play. Nor do I wish to be Vice-President of the Poetry Review. Still less do I feel myself qualified to speak about housing; let the shoemaker stick to his last. As for Hodder and Stoughton, would you ask Mr Higham to tell them that nothing would induce me to put a finger into the *Edwin Drood*[2] pie. This beastly book has been completed by at least a dozen people, and every attempt is more wearisome than the last. It is an infallible recipe for boredom; so please, dear Bun, take these incubi away from me, and believe me, most gratefully,

Yours,
    [D.L.S.]

[1] Dorothy Allen, who handled dramatic rights.
[2] The unfinished novel by Charles Dickens.

To Laurence Irving[1]   [24 Newland Street
6 December 1936   Witham
                                Essex]

Dear Mr Irving
    I have had a letter from Miss Babington suggesting that you and I might meet next week to discuss the Canterbury Play. I have to acknowledge beforehand, that my ideas about it are still exceedingly vague, and that I have the gravest doubts whether I can write anything fit to be produced at Canterbury. Needless to say, however, I should be exceedingly grateful for your help and advice in the matter. Miss Babington suggests that we might meet in London either on Thursday or Friday the 10th and 11th; either of these dates would

suit me, shall we say Thursday at about five o'clock at my flat 24, Great James Street, W.C.1.?

Yours very truly
    [D.L.S.]

[1] Laurence Irving (1897–1988) designed the permanent sets in the Chapter House against which the play was produced. He was the son of H. B. Irving and the grandson of Sir Henry.

To C. F. Johnston   [24 Newland Street
13 December 1936   Witham
                                  Essex]

Dear Mr Johnston,
    I do want to thank you and your wife most cordially for the really lovely time you gave me yesterday; it is a long time since I enjoyed anything so much. I was immensely grateful for the opportunity of hearing your beautiful peal, and watching the ringers and the bells at close quarters. It was also most delightful to meet all those prominent members of the ringing world, and I must say again how very much I felt honoured by the extraordinarily kind appreciation they all expressed of *The Nine Tailors*. It was most good of you to invite me and to be so hospitable to me, and the only way I can thank you is to express again the very great pleasure it all gave me.
    I did not have the opportunity to speak again to Mr Goldsmith and tell him personally of the real thrill I got from his ingenious 'moving picture' of the change-ringing; it was most fascinating to watch in actual movement the thing I had tried so hard to understand on paper, particularly the Kent Treble Bob which occupies so large a place in my story. I got quite excited recognising the movements of the slow Hunt bell, and seeing Number 3 actually stand to make her fourth's place at the Bob! It was so good of you to promise that I should sometime come to see a bell cast. I shall greatly look forward to a visit to the foundry; when the time comes I shall be strongly tempted to cast aside every other duty in order to be present.

With again very many thanks to you all
yours very sincerely,
    [D.L.S.]

To Miss Maxwell Fraser   [24 Newland Street
13 December 1936   Witham
                                          Essex]

Dear Miss Fraser,
    Thank you so much for your letter and for the delightful bell-ringing
verses.
    I had the great pleasure yesterday of going to Croydon to attend
the dedication of their new ring of twelve, and of actually seeing peals
rung for the first time in my life. I went up to the bell-chamber where,
I am happy to say, I did not drop dead – but I certainly should not
have cared for six hours of it at close quarters!
    As regards Barrow-in-Furness, I do not know that I had any par-
ticular reason for placing Parker's childhood there, as I do not know
the town at all; I rather felt it to be the kind of industrial place which
gave Parker a background as far as possible unlike Peter's, and further
than that I can hardly find any good reason for my selection. I myself
was born at Oxford and was a scholar of Somerville, so that any
personal topographical information must attach itself to *Gaudy Night*
rather than to any other of my books; though I had, of course, a long
connection with the Fen country of *The Nine Tailors*, since my Father
had two parishes in East Anglia.

        Yours sincerely,
        [D.L.S.]

To L. C. Kempson   [24 Newland Street
20 December 1936   Witham
                                          Essex]

Dear Kempie,
    Ever so many thanks for your letter of good wishes. We had an
enthusiastic reception on our first night, and a splendid performance,
and the box office at present seems to be feeling pretty cheerful. I
hope you and your Highgate friends will enjoy it when you see it after
Christmas. I am sorry you could not get in on Boxing afternoon –
sorry, that is to say, *qua* your friend, but *qua* author, exceedingly
glad! I am sending you a few postcards wherewith to circularise your
Bromyard and other acquaintance!
    The constitutional crisis[1] seems to have passed over with remark-
able tranquillity (and jolly thankful we are that it hit us at Leeds and
not in London). All sorts of things now keep coming out; Scott T.[2]
tells us 'from a well-informed source' that it was *all quite true* about
Mrs Simpson's being hand in glove with the German Embassy and

having access to all King Edward's despatch boxes in the Nazi interest. She is also responsible for a terrific rigmarole, which I cannot quite follow, about a strange publicity campaign concerted between the late King and Lord Rothermere[3] who, it appears, was offered the crown of Hungary on some unspecified occasion, and has his statues in every Hungarian town! From Ketteringham Park in Norfolk come reports through Helen Simpson, no relation to Mrs Ernest, that King Edward was much disliked at Sandringham both for having sacked all the staff there and for running about the place with Mrs Simpson in an undignified manner in shorts! Some working man said to somebody the other day 'Well, I think we've got the pick of them now; the lot of them ain't much good, but such as they are, I think we've got the pick' (meaning George).

I heard that *Figaro* last week had a magnificent cartoon beautifully drawn, of Henry VIII depicted *à la* Holbein, straddling across the hearth rug and saying of a minute King Edward slumped dismally in an armchair: '*Mon dieu, quel amateur!*'[4] One of the American papers, I believe, also has a cartoon of Mrs Simpson and King Edward displayed upon a wall of a gallery, the picture being entitled: 'The Wallis Collection'.[5] So far as I can see, public opinion in London is, that all is, on the whole, for the best, except among the second-rate intelligentsia who prefer to be agin the Government. The Archbishop of Canterbury is generally held to have spoken out of due time. Meanwhile the manufacturers of mugs are doing a roaring trade in pottery, commemorating the coronation which never took place.

In the meantime, Kempie dear, while the Empire remains, let us wish one another a merry Christmas and a happy New Year. I am sending you Helen Simpson's and my little jest in the shape of the Wimsey papers which I hope you will enjoy in the spirit in which it was meant. It may, in any case, prove to have a trifling value as a collector's piece. . . .

[1] The abdication of Edward VIII.
[2] Miss Scott Thompson, a contemporary of D.L.S. at Somerville.
[3] Harold Sidney Harmsworth, first Viscount Rothermere (1868–1940), the newspaper proprietor, who admired Mussolini and Hitler.
[4] My God, what an amateur!
[5] A pun on the Wallace Collection, an art gallery in London.

To Ivy Shrimpton   24 Newland Street
21 December 1936   Witham
                                   Essex

Dearest Ivy,
    As you may have seen in the papers, we have at last, after incredible

exertions all round, got *Busman's Honeymoon* running in London.[1]
Goodness knows whether it will run very long, but there, at any rate,
it is. You cannot imagine the work it has been for my collaborator
and me – attending rehearsals, tearing round the provinces, circularis-
ing the public, giving parties to the cast, holding people's hands,
soothing frayed tempers and generally trying to help things along.
The result is that I simply have not had a single moment in which
to think about Christmas or anything else!! I am enclosing a cheque
for £15 – £5 for you, £3 for John, £4 for Isobel, and the rest to go to
John's journey-money and expenses.

I should like you all to come up to Town and see the Show. Will
you let me know which day which of you can manage it, and I will
send you the tickets. A matinée would be best, I expect – these are
on Tuesdays and Fridays, as well, of course, as Boxing Day. Whichever day you and John come, I will try to meet you in Town, if I can
manage it, and we could have lunch or something. (I won't promise
to come and sit through the play – I have now seen it about 157
times, and even I cannot bear the sound of my own words *any* longer!!)
I should choose a day about the first week of January; I can't get
away from home over Christmas – as it is, I have scarcely been seen
under my own roof since last September! Mac is getting very cross –
but indeed, he really isn't responsible for half he says – Still, I must
stay here for a bit.

What with one thing and another, not counting the Constitutional
Crisis, which hit us when the play was at Leeds, and not, thank
Heaven! when we were in Town – life has been a kind of wild see-saw
for the last few months. Meanwhile, Aunt Lil[2] writes, wanting to
know 'the truth about the King' – meaning, King Edward VIII!!! As
if anybody knew it! Aunt Maud and I soothe her with soft platitudes.

> With best love to you all,
> Yours ever affectionately
>   Dorothy

[1] At the Comedy Theatre.
[2] Lilian Sarah Leigh, married to Norman Logan, who lived in California.

To Basil Blackwell   [24 Newland Street
21 December 1936   Witham
                                       Essex]

Dear Basil,
    As you will have seen, we contrived to get our London theatre after
all (though by the skin of our teeth), and so did not need to avail

ourselves of your kind intervention in Oxford for which, nevertheless, I thank you very much.

Will you accept as a little Christmas gift the enclosed exercise in pastiche by Helen Simpson and myself?

As you will see, the whole edition is limited to five hundred, this being one of the hundred and fifty presentation copies, distinguished from the others by heavier paper and a wrapper in duller blue.

With kindest remembrances to Christine and the family, and the best of good wishes to you all for Christmas and the New Year.

Yours very sincerely,
    [D.L.S.]

To Laurence Irving   [24 Newland Street
28 December 1936   Witham
                                   Essex]

Dear Mr Irving,

Here is a copy of the suggested opening scene of the Canterbury play now that I have revised and shortened it. I have cut out two unnecessary monks and changed the action about a bit so as to tighten it, and it should now – allowing the usual speed of a page a minute – play roughly a quarter of an hour, including the Interlude. My idea is, to have five sections of about a quarter of an hour each, bringing the thing to an hour and a quarter, which is about the length you asked for. The Versicles and Responses could, of course, be intoned in the usual ecclesiastical way; but the Interlude, which is adapted from Ecclesiasticus, might, I think, have suitable music written for it in accordance with the suggestions you made to me.

Would it be convenient for me to run down to see you and Miss Babington at Canterbury some time during the first week of January? I have to be in Town on Saturday the 9th, and it would probably be most convenient for me to come down say on Wednesday the 6th, or Thursday the 7th, if that would suit you. By that time I shall, perhaps, have recovered sufficiently from the agitations from *Busman's Honeymoon* to be able to talk more or less coherently about archangels. You will, I know, be glad to hear that we have made a good start at the Comedy, and have so far been doing excellent business. How long it will last, of course, we do not know; but we are hoping for the best.

With all good wishes for the New Year,
Yours sincerely
    [D.L.S.]

To Ivy Shrimpton   24 Newland Street
30 December 1936   Witham
                                                    Essex

Dearest Ivy,

Right-ho! I have taken dress-circle tickets for you and John for the
matinée of Tuesday 5th, and if you let me know your train I will either
meet you at the station or fix a place to meet for lunch, according to
what time you get up. I couldn't write yesterday, because I was
waiting to hear whether I had to go to Canterbury that day, but
Canterbury has now been fixed for the Tuesday following. Would
Isobel like to bring up a friend with her on the 8th? Because, if so, I
will have a couple of tickets kept for them.

I enclose – what I should have sent earlier, but I have been in a
deuce of a rush – John's report and the report on his Music exam. –
both seem very satisfactory and promising. I see he is advised to read
up some History and that he tends to write 'journalese'! (I remember
much the same thing being said about my writing – it is a fault that
wears off with the reading of good stuff.) Anyway, there is good cause
for congratulation. . . .

To Laurence Irving   [24 Newland Street
30 December 1936   Witham
                                                    Essex]

Dear Mr Irving,

Thank you very much for your letter; I could come down on Wednesday the 13th if that is more convenient to you, and I shall be
delighted to stay the night. I am glad you like the Play so far as it
goes; I think we shall have to be a little careful about how we make
up Williams to resemble anybody, since I am rather undermining his
moral character somewhere about the middle of the play![1] However,
that is a detail. I will try and get some more sketches out before I
come down, but just at the moment I am laid up with a bad cold,
and feel rather stupid in the head.

Looking forward to meeting you again,
Ever yours sincerely
      D.L.S.

[1] Laurence Irving had suggested that Harcourt Williams should be made up to resemble
the architect Sir Edwin Landseer Lutyens (1878–1944).

To Maurice Browne   24 Newland Street
31 December 1936   Witham
     Essex

Dear Mr Browne . . .

Thank you so much for your kindly messages and good wishes. The play seems to have made some of the critics very cross indeed; oddly enough, the incalculable public seem to find the thing amusing, and persist in laughing at all the bits they have been told not to – and even in taking seriously all the bits they have been told to find pompous and preposterous.[1] It's a hard world. Goodness knows how long the G.B.P.[2] will keep it up – for the moment they seem to have decided that we are part of the Pantomime season, and are booking accordingly.

The profoundest spiritual shock was, I fancy, sustained by our leading couple, who, having dubiously resigned themselves to playing the 'quarrel scene' with a deep inner conviction that it had no conceivable relation to life, found themselves, at Leeds, plunged into the Constitutional Crisis, so that every sentence became fraught with an appalling topical significance. Even in London, Miss Byrne, prowling about the Upper Circle at the moment when Harriet says, 'What kind of life could we have if I knew you had become less than yourself by marrying me?' was gratified to catch the syllables 'Mrs Simpson!' hissed fiercely by a woman to her neighbour. So you never know your luck, and it's an ill wind that blows nobody any good. . . .

Our one regret is that you are not with us sharing the fun – not that we could possibly have a nicer management than we've got, because they have been absolutely top-hole in every possible way; but you were the first that ever believed in us and it seems a dashed shame you weren't in at the kill.[3] Still, you never know, and it may flop next week. Which is why I say, do if you can come and have lunch before the first fine careless rapture departs. . . .

Yours very sincerely,
Dorothy L. Sayers

[1] The differing attitudes of the public and press to *Busman's Honeymoon* were to be repeated when the play was revived at the Lyric, Hammersmith in 1988.
[2] Great British Public.
[3] Maurice Browne had tried to find backing for the play.

'There is good cause for congratulation', D.L.S. said in her letter to Ivy Shrimpton on 30 December 1936. There was indeed. She had written twelve novels which made her famous all over the world; her Lord Peter Wimsey comedy, Busman's Honeymoon, was a West-End success; her son was doing well at school. If she had died then, her achievement would have been accounted remarkable. Yet all her greatest works were still to come. Her first play for Canterbury Cathedral, soon to be entitled The Zeal of Thy House, was the first of a series of Christian dramas which brought her a new kind of renown. From then on she became a public figure, whose views were sought on religion, education and national affairs. She came to be regarded one of the outstanding lay theologians of her time. Her final task, undertaken in a spirit of profound evangelism, was to translate and interpret Dante.

The letters covering the last twenty years of her life show this versatile author at the height of her creative powers.

Index